Wills, Trusts, and Estates
for Paralegals

ASPEN COLLEGE SERIES

Wills, Trusts, and Estates for Paralegals

Diana L. Anderson

Wolters Kluwer

To contact Customer Service, e-mail customer.service@wolterskluwer.com, call 1-800-234-1660, fax 1-800-901-9075, or mail correspondence to:

Wolters Kluwer
Attn: Order Department
PO Box 990
Frederick, MD 21705

Printed in the United States of America.

1 2 3 4 5 6 7 8 9 0

ISBN 978-1-4548-3302-4

Library of Congress Cataloging-in-Publication Data

Anderson, Diana L., 1966- author.
   Wills, trusts, and estates for paralegals / Diana L. Anderson.
      pages cm – (Aspen college series)
   Includes index.
   ISBN 978-1-4548-3302-4
1. Wills — United States — Outlines, syllabi, etc. 2. Estate planning — United States — Outlines, syllabi, etc. 3. Trusts and trustees — United States — Outlines, syllabi, etc. I. Title.

KF753.A97 2015
346.7305–dc23

                              2014041688

About Wolters Kluwer Law & Business

Wolters Kluwer Law & Business is a leading global provider of intelligent information and digital solutions for legal and business professionals in key specialty areas, and respected educational resources for professors and law students. Wolters Kluwer Law & Business connects legal and business professionals as well as those in the education market with timely, specialized authoritative content and information-enabled solutions to support success through productivity, accuracy and mobility.

Serving customers worldwide, Wolters Kluwer Law & Business products include those under the Aspen Publishers, CCH, Kluwer Law International, Loislaw, ftwilliam.com and MediRegs family of products.

CCH products have been a trusted resource since 1913, and are highly regarded resources for legal, securities, antitrust and trade regulation, government contracting, banking, pension, payroll, employment and labor, and healthcare reimbursement and compliance professionals.

Aspen Publishers products provide essential information to attorneys, business professionals and law students. Written by preeminent authorities, the product line offers analytical and practical information in a range of specialty practice areas from securities law and intellectual property to mergers and acquisitions and pension/benefits. Aspen's trusted legal education resources provide professors and students with high-quality, up-to-date and effective resources for successful instruction and study in all areas of the law.

Kluwer Law International products provide the global business community with reliable international legal information in English. Legal practitioners, corporate counsel and business executives around the world rely on Kluwer Law journals, looseleafs, books, and electronic products for comprehensive information in many areas of international legal practice.

Loislaw is a comprehensive online legal research product providing legal content to law firm practitioners of various specializations. Loislaw provides attorneys with the ability to quickly and efficiently find the necessary legal information they need, when and where they need it, by facilitating access to primary law as well as state-specific law, records, forms and treatises.

ftwilliam.com offers employee benefits professionals the highest quality plan documents (retirement, welfare and non-qualified) and government forms (5500/PBGC, 1099 and IRS) software at highly competitive prices.

MediRegs products provide integrated health care compliance content and software solutions for professionals in healthcare, higher education and life sciences, including professionals in accounting, law and consulting.

Wolters Kluwer Law & Business, a division of Wolters Kluwer, is headquartered in New York. Wolters Kluwer is a market-leading global information services company focused on professionals.

To Thomas, my love.

Summary Table of Contents

Table of Contents

Chapter 3   **Testamentary Capacity: Undue Influence 37**

Chapter 4   **Basic Wills 55**

Chapter 12   Estate Litigation 205

Preface

This text was written with the intention of helping teach a paralegal the skills necessary to assist an elder law attorney, or an attorney who does a great deal of estate and trust work. It contains practical tips and skills, activities that will give real-life experience to a student in estate administration and trust administration, while also providing legal theory and examination of the law where necessary. It may initially appear that some of the material is too complex for a paralegal text, or goes beyond what the paralegal would be expected to do. I strongly suggest that the complex material be, at the very least, introduced to the students so that he or she may become familiar with the concepts involved. I have included a lot of background material beyond what may typically be included in such a text because it is material that my paralegal, Denise Lohnes, has learned while working with me and other attorneys in our firm. Denise always took the time to ask questions to try to understand why certain language was used, or the reason a pleading was filed. As a result, she has become an invaluable asset to our firm, and to my practice. There have been countless times that Denise's questions about a pleading, procedure, or document have caused me to take a second look at something, thereby avoiding a mistake. My own practical experience has taught me that the more that a paralegal can understand about the legal theory behind a document, the more the paralegal can anticipate problems, identify deficiencies, and help the client. I have been blessed with a great paralegal, and I wrote this book with the intent of helping others become great paralegals.

Acknowledgments

I would like to thank Elizabeth Kenny, Developmental Editor, for her patience and help throughout the process of writing this text. I would also like to thank Cynthia Mussinan for all of her behind-the-scenes assistance in endless rewrites and revisions of page after page of handwritten edits, suggestions, motivation, and more rewrites. Cynthia, I think you will find some of the "characters" in the text both interesting and familiar. Your willingness to help, and your friendship, have been priceless. Finally, I would like to thank all of the following reviewers for their time and effort in reviewing the material and providing helpful, insightful comments and suggestions that greatly improved the text:

Gregory Dalton, Genesee Community College
Hyman Darling, Bay Path College
Steven A. Dayton, Fullerton College
Robin Dec, Eastern Michigan University
Sharron Dillon, University of Hartford
Terrence Dwyer, Western Connecticut State University
Shaquan Gaither, Savannah Technical College
Timothy Gibbons, University of Akron
Stacy Hopkins, West Valley College
Brian McCully, Fresno City College
Kathryn L. Myers, Saint Mary-of-the-Woods College
Christine Simcox, Bucks County Community College
Kathy Smith, Community College of Philadelphia
Ann H. Still, Finger Lakes Community College
Janis Walter, University of Cincinnati

Introduction and History of Estate Planning

A. Introduction

This text is intended for use in teaching a paralegal the necessary skills to assist with the preparation of wills and trusts and with the administration of estates. It begins with an understanding of the history and development of estate planning laws, continues through the preparation of the documents needed to create an estate plan, and ends with how to administer an estate. Included within the text are ethical considerations that all attorneys, and paralegals, must follow. Many of the concepts are complex, and some go beyond the paralegal's responsibility. The complex concepts are introduced for general understanding only. If a paralegal has a general understanding of the concepts and language used, the paralegal will be in a better position to assist the attorney. If the underlying reason why certain documents are needed is understood, the paralegal can recognize when issues are missed or make suggestions as to ways to address the clients' needs. It is also essential to learn the vocabulary of estate planning — to know the meaning of different terms and to use the terms correctly. We will begin with a general introduction to *estate planning*.

Estate planning is a general term that begins with having a last will and testament in order to distribute possessions at death. A complete estate plan will also include a power of attorney and an advance medical directive to appoint a representative to help with financial and medical decisions if the person is unable to make those decisions. Each of these documents will be examined at length later in the text. Every adult with assets, regardless of his or her age, should have some type of estate plan. Ideally the estate plan would consist of a last will and testament, a power of attorney, and some type of medical directive. Let's start by taking a brief look at the history of a last will and testament and how the laws of estate planning developed.

> **Estate planning:** a general term to describe the plan to distribute possessions after death

B.   State Law Versus Federal Law

Many of the U.S. laws regarding estates are founded on the common laws of England. Some of the states in the western part of the United States also have elements of Spanish law in addition to English common law. There is one state that is an exception: Louisiana. Most of the law in Louisiana comes from French and Spanish law instead of English law because Louisiana was originally a colony of both France and Spain. The law in Louisiana is based on the Napoleonic Code, the laws established by Napoleon Bonaparte. The other original colonies, which are primarily located in the northeast, were colonies of England.

The law of estates is state law, not federal law. Each state is free to adopt its own set of laws, provided those laws do not conflict with the federal laws and do not address an issue that is covered by federal law. The laws that govern wills and estates are state laws, with federal laws having very little or no impact on the average estate. The U.S. Constitution and federal laws are the highest laws of the country. Article VI, Section 2, of the U.S. Constitution provides that the "Constitution, and the Laws of the United States . . . shall be the supreme Law of the Land." This means that federal law preempts state law if there is a conflict. Federal law is limited to the rights and duties set forth in the Constitution. Most of the everyday law in the United States is state law. Each state has its own laws pertaining to estates, property ownership, marriage, divorce, state taxes, and so forth, many of which change often. The only federal law that impacts estates is the federal estate tax law that applies to estates of a certain size. Federal estate tax law will be discussed at length in Chapter 6 pertaining to complex estates.

Because the laws of each state vary greatly, a will that is written in one state may or may not be valid in another state. It is necessary to have a will written in conformance with the laws of the state in which the person is ***domiciled***. *Domicile* refers to the place in which a person resides, pays taxes, has a driver's license, and so on. A person can own more than one residence, but only one of those residences will qualify as the domicile. For example, a person domiciled in California may have a vacation home in Montana. The Montana home is the person's residence, but the person is domiciled in California. The specific laws of each state as to the contents of a will, the administration of an estate, or any other aspect of estate planning can be unique to each state. It will be absolutely necessary for a paralegal to become familiar with the laws of his or her state.

Domicile: the place in which a person resides, pays taxes, has a driver's license, and so forth

There are some uniform laws adopted by several states. One such law is the Uniform Probate Code (UPC). As of this date, the entire UPC has been adopted by only 16 states: Alaska, Arizona, Colorado, Florida, Hawaii, Idaho, Maine, Michigan, Minnesota, Montana, Nebraska, New Mexico, North Dakota, South Carolina, South Dakota, and Utah. The other states have adopted some parts of the UPC but not the entire code. The index provides a list of useful links, including links to look up the estate and probate laws of each state.

C.   Creation and Distribution of Estate

When a person dies, all of the assets owned by the person create the person's *estate*. An **estate** is all of the assets and possessions of the person who died, who is also called the **decedent**. The estate can consist of any number of different types of assets, real and personal property, bank accounts, investment accounts, businesses, works of art, and so forth, and/or his or her assets. The decedent's assets can pass to others, or are distributed to others, in any combination of four different ways:

1. Last Will and Testament: If the person who has died has a last will and testament, the will directs who gets what assets.

2. Intestate: The laws of the state in which the person lived could direct how the assets must distributed because (a) the person did not have a last will and testament, (b) the person was married and lived in a state in which the assets of a married couple are community property, or (c) the will does not dispose of all of the estate assets.

3. Form of Ownership: The person's assets can be jointly owned in a manner that allows the assets to pass to the joint owner.

4. Beneficiary Designation: Certain assets such as an investment account or annuity can include language that designates who receives the asset after the owner dies.

The possible ways that assets can be distributed will be discussed in detail below.

Estate: all of the assets and possessions of the person who died, who is also called the decedent

Decedent: the person who has died

D.   Last Will and Testament

A *will*, or more formally called a **last will and testament**, is a legal document that provides for the distribution of the assets of someone who has died. The last will and testament appoints an **executor**, or personal representative, who will be in charge of the estate. A **trust** is a legal document that establishes a set of rules for the use of funds that are held for another person or group of people. An **estate plan** is the plan that is put together to manage a person's assets and care if the person becomes incapacitated or dies. An estate plan can include a will and a trust. The purpose of an estate plan is to distribute a person's assets after death.

Estate planning is a general term that describes the plan to distribute possessions after death. An estate plan begins with a last will and testament. It should also include a **power of attorney** and an **advance medical directive** that appoint representatives to help with financial and medical decisions, respectively, if the person is unable to make those decisions. Each of these documents will be examined at length later in the text. Every adult, regardless of age or the amount of money he or she has, should have at a minimum an estate plan consisting of a last will and testament, a power of attorney, and some type of advance medical directive. If the client has young

Last will and testament: a legal document that provides for the distribution of the property of someone who has died

Executor or personal representative: the person appointed by a last will and testament to be in charge of the estate

Trust: a legal document that establishes the rules for the use of funds that are held for another person or group of people

Estate plan: the documents that comprise the plan that is put together to manage a person's assets and care, if the person becomes incapacitated or dies

Power of attorney: a legal document that appoints a representative to help with financial decisions if the person is unable to make those decisions

Advance medical directive: a legal document that records a person's choices with regard to medical treatment and appoints a representative to help with medical decisions if the person is unable to make those decisions

children, the client may also need a trust to hold money for the children, a trustee to manage the trust, and a guardian to care for the children. One of the most difficult decisions for an estate-planning client is deciding who is going to serve as the trustee and guardian for minor children.

> ### *Practice Tip*
>
> Every client who makes an appointment to discuss estate planning should be told that in preparation for the meeting, the client should begin thinking about whom he or she wants to receive assets, and who is going to be in control of the estate. This is something that can be discussed with the client when the appointment is being scheduled.

There is a trend in the law to use more "user-friendly" language by eliminating most of the Latin terms that used to be used in the law. Despite this trend, much of the language in a will is still very formal and old fashioned. The idea of writing a document to govern the distribution of assets when a person dies is a very old legal concept, dating back hundreds of years. Therefore, much of the case law is also very old and uses old-fashioned language that is no longer commonly used other than in a will. This old-fashioned language can make a will difficult to read and understand, especially if it was prepared many years prior to the person's death. A last will and testament even looks old fashioned because, in many states, wills are still prepared on legal-sized paper (8 ½ by 14 inches), instead of letter-sized paper (8 ½ by 11 inches.) Even in states where legal-sized paper is no longer used for contracts and other documents, it is often still used for wills.

E.   Intestate Succession — Laws of Intestacy

Testate: when a person dies having written a will

Intestate: when a person dies without having written a will

Testator: a male who has written a will

Testatrix: a female who has written a will

Laws of intestate succession: govern how an estate is distributed if the decedent fails to make a will, or dies intestate

When a person dies having written a will, the person is said to have died **testate**. When a person dies without having written a will, the person is said to have died **intestate**. Many of the terms used in estate planning law, such as testate or intestate, sound similar because they have the same root word. The word *testate* is derived from the Latin word "testari" meaning to make a will. Any words derived from "testari" pertain to the last will and testament. For example, a **testator** is a male who has written a will; a **testatrix** is a female who has written a will. Other examples, which will be found later in this chapter and in other chapters, include *testamentary trust* and *testamentary capacity*.

It is not completely accurate to say that someone who dies without having drafted his or her own will dies without a will because the laws of each of the 50 states provide for the distribution of an intestate estate. These laws, called the **laws of intestate succession**, govern how an estate is distributed if the decedent fails to make a will. When someone dies intestate, it is as if the laws of intestate succession become the will for the decedent. Unfortunately it may not be the will that the testator would have chosen.

There are also occasions when a decedent has a will, but the terms of the will do not dispose of all of the assets in the estate. For example, a will could state, "I leave my house, all the contents of my house, and my Bank of America bank accounts to my nephew." If the person dies owning a car, a Wells Fargo investment account, and some savings bonds in addition to the assets listed in the will, the disposition of those other assets are not directed by the will. The assets that are not disposed of through the will may then pass to the heirs by way of intestate succession.

The main difference between testate estates and intestate estates is the recipient of the decedent's estate. In a testate estate, the decedent can leave the entire estate to anyone he or she chooses, with one major exception: the decedent's spouse. There are laws in 49 of the 50 states that guarantee the surviving spouse at least some portion of the spouse's estate. In Georgia, the surviving spouse can make application for support from the estate. A spouse cannot be disinherited or left nothing. The laws in the other 49 states that leave a portion of the estate to the surviving spouse are known as the **marital share, statutory share**, or **elective sharer** laws. With the exception of the spouse, a decedent does not have to leave the estate to any other family members. The decedent, if not married, can leave the entire estate to a charity, or a neighbor, or anyone the decedent wants to name as a **beneficiary**. *Beneficiary* refers to the person who is receiving the benefits (or proceeds) of an estate, retirement plan, annuity, trust, or life insurance policy. **Heirs**, also known as the **next of kin**, or **distributees**, make up a category of beneficiaries that is limited to the persons who by application of the laws of intestacy inherit the property of a person who died intestate.

The laws of intestate succession require a determination of who is related to the decedent, and by what degree. The relatives in the generation above the decedent are called **ancestors**, or **ascendants**. An example of an ancestor is a parent or grandparent. The relatives in the generation below the decedent are called **descendants**. An example of a descendant is a child or grandchild. The relatives in the same generation as the decedent are **collateral relatives** (Figure 1-1). Collateral relatives have a

Marital share, statutory share, or elective share: laws that prevent a spouse from disinheriting or leaving nothing to the surviving spouse

Beneficiary: the person who is receiving the benefits (or proceeds) of an estate, retirement plan, annuity, trust, or life insurance policy

Heirs, next of kin, or distributees: persons who, by application of the laws of intestacy, inherit the property of a person who died intestate

Ancestors or ascendants: the relatives in the generation above the decedent

Descendants: relatives in the generation below the decedent, such as the decedent's children

Collateral relatives: those who have a common ancestor to the decedent

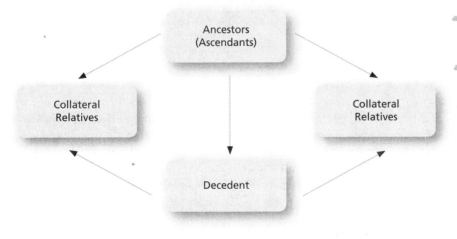

Figure 1-1. Collateral Relatives

common ancestor to the decedent. An example of a collateral relative is a cousin, a niece, or a nephew.

Each state's statutes defining who is an heir at law will be unique to that state. However, the statutes generally give a right of inheritance only to blood relatives, adopted children, adoptive parents, and the surviving spouse. None of the 50 states' intestate laws give any inheritance rights to friends or charities. Most states favor the **lineal descendants**; that is, those who have descended one from the other such as grandfather to father to son, or those who are descended all from a common ancestor. In most states, descendants are given priority over ascendants, or ancestors. For example, if a man, whose wife had predeceased him, died without a will, his children would receive a distribution from the estate before his father would receive a distribution. If the man had no children or no descendants, then the ascendants, or the man's parents or grandparents, would be entitled to a distribution.

If there are no lineal descendants or ascendants, the next set of relatives that would receive a distribution from the estate are the **collateral descendants**. Collateral descendants are cousins, nieces, nephews, brothers, sisters, and others who are not direct descendants of the decedent but have a common ancestor with the decedent. For example, two people who are cousins may have the same grandfather. If one of the cousins dies, the surviving cousin is a collateral descendent. State law usually provides that direct descendants, the children of the decedent, have first preference in the order of succession, followed by ascendants, and finally, collateral heirs.

Each generation is called a *degree* in determining the *consanguinity* or blood relationship. The blood relationship of the heirs is called the **degree of consanguinity**. The relationship is also known as the **degree of kinship**. Figure 1-2 presents a chart commonly used to help attorneys and paralegals determine the degree of consanguinity.

To understand the operation of the chart, start on the left at the rectangle labeled "person." The first degree down from the person who passed away is the person's children. The first degree up from the person who passed away is the person's parents. On the chart, this can be found by moving down one rectangle from the person, to children, or up and to the right one rectangle to parents. The children and the parents of the decedent are one degree of separation. The second degree is the grandchildren or the grandparents. Down two rectangles from the person are the grandchildren, and up and to the right two rectangles are the grandparents. This chart is very useful when trying to determine more distant degrees of kinship.

Knowing the degree of relationship is important because all of the descendants in the same degree have to be treated equally. For example, all of the first cousins of the decedent have the same rights to the decedent's estate, and the right to serve as administrator of the estate. Figuring out the degree of relationship can sometimes be difficult, especially in families that are blended. In order to determine the degree of consanguinity or kinship of more distant relatives, start with the common ancestor. For example, a client indicates that a distant cousin named Marjorie has died intestate, and the client needs help in probating the estate. The first step in determining the degree of relationship between the client and Marjorie is to determine

---

Lineal descendants: those descended one from the other or all from a common ancestor

Collateral descendants: those descended from an ancestor who is common to the decedent, but who are not direct descendants of the decedent

Degree of consanguinity or degree of kinship: the blood relationship of the heirs

Figure 1-2. Table of Consanguinity

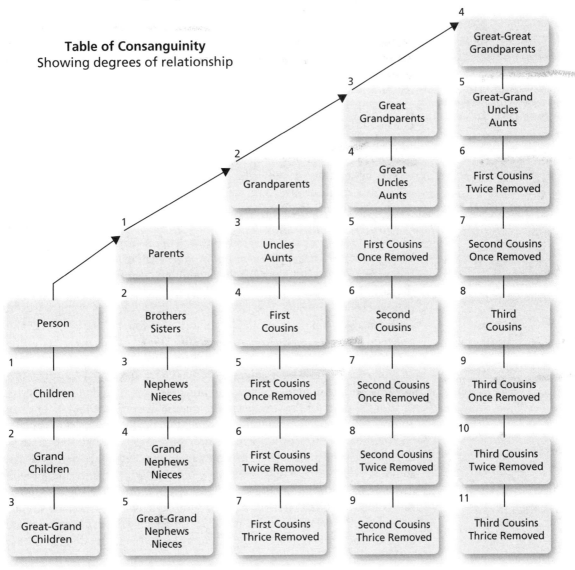

what relative Marjorie and the client had in common. After making some calls to other relatives, it is determined that the client's grandfather and Marjorie's father were brothers. Put the client in the rectangle labeled "person." Go up and to the right two rectangles to the client's grandparents. Go to the right one rectangle to the spot labeled "great uncles aunts." The client's great uncle, or her grandfather's brother, was Marjorie's father. Marjorie is one rectangle down from the "great uncles aunts" spot. Therefore, the client and Marjorie are first cousins, once removed.

F. Community Property

Community property: property owned by married couples with each spouse owning a 50 percent interest in the property

In certain states in the United States, married couples are considered to own all of the property acquired during the marriage jointly, with each spouse owning a 50 percent interest in the property. This type of property ownership is called **community property**. Community property includes income, property purchased during the marriage, and any property one spouse owned separately but put into joint names. A spouse can keep his or her interest in property that is inherited, purchased before the marriage, or kept separate by agreement between the spouses. The agreement to keep property separate after marriage is called a **prenuptial**

Prenuptial agreement: the agreement to keep property separate after marriage

agreement. Community property laws govern what happens to the property owned by a husband and wife when their marriage ends, whether that end comes as a result of divorce or death of one spouse. Because each spouse owns one-half of the marital property, each spouse has a right to dispose of his or her share of the community property in whatever way desired. When one spouse dies in a community property state, only one-half of the marital property is inheritable because the surviving spouse already owns one-half of the marital property. The spouse can give his or her half of the community property to someone other than the surviving spouse. In addition, the deceased spouse can give away any property that was kept separate.

Basis: the purchase price paid for an asset

Capital gains taxes: taxes imposed on the gain in an investment

When a surviving spouse inherits community property, the property value gets a step up. **Basis** is the purchase price paid for an asset. When the asset is sold, taxes could be imposed on the appreciation, or gain in value, that occurred from the date of purchase. **Capital gains taxes** are taxes that are imposed on the gain in an investment. For example, a house is purchased for $100,000 in 1980. At the time of the death of the first spouse, the house is worth $400,000. The appreciation is $300,000. This appreciation could potentially be subject to capital gains tax. Married couples, including same-sex couples, get a step up in basis, meaning the new basis for the asset becomes the value at the date of death. In the example above, the stepped-up basis for the house is now $400,000, the value at the date of death. If the surviving spouse sells that house at a price of $400,000, no capital gains tax is due. If the surviving spouse continues to own that asset for several more years and sells it when the value is $475,000, capital gains tax is imposed only on the difference between the sale price of $475,000 and the stepped-up basis of $400,000.

The community property states are Arizona, California, Idaho, Louisiana, Nevada, New Mexico, Texas, Washington, and Wisconsin. Community property laws apply only in those states. Community property laws do not apply in any other state and do not apply if the couple dies intestate. If a couple living in a community property state does not make an estate plan, then the intestacy laws in the state in which they live will govern the distribution of their estate. It is unclear how a same-sex married couple would be treated in a community property state that has not legally recognized same-sex marriages. As of November 2014, the Montana courts struck down the laws preventing same-sex marriages, making Montana the 35th state, as well as Washington D.C., to legally recognize same-sex marriage.

G. Forms of Ownership

Assets can pass by way of a will or, in the absence of a will, by the laws of intestacy and/or community property. Property can also be transferred to another owner outside of a will if the property is owned in a specific form of ownership. The ownership of real property can take many different forms as discussed below.

Practice Tip

When interviewing a client in preparation for an estate planning consultation, it is not enough to ask what real and personal property the client owns. It is also necessary to ask how it is owned, and to confirm the form of ownership by reviewing the deed. If the paralegal is responsible for conducting the initial interview with the client, copies of ownership documents should be requested.

When a property owner owns all of the rights associated with a piece of property, the ownership is described as **fee simple**, or **fee simple absolute**. Fee simple ownership is considered to be the highest, or most complete, form of ownership. The owner of a fee simple can sell or transfer the ownership rights, or leave those rights in his or her will to the beneficiaries. For example, a client Oliver Wood purchases a home. He will most likely own the home in fee simple, with only his name on the deed.

Fee simple or fee simple absolute: when a property owner owns all of the rights associated with a piece of property

Tenants in common is a different form of property ownership. *Tenants in common* is an ownership interest of two or more people who own separate but undivided interests in property. Each of the tenants in common has the right to sell his or her share of the property or to distribute the share by way of his or her own will. For example, if our client Oliver Wood decides to buy a property with Olivia Wood, they can own the property as tenants in common. The deed would read as follows: Oliver Wood and Olivia Wood, tenants in common. Some states require that the individual be identified as being single to avoid the inference that the tenants in common are a married couple. If the ownership rights of one tenant in common are sold or otherwise transferred to another person, the new owner becomes a tenant in common with the other previous tenants. In our example, Oliver can sell his interest to another person who then becomes tenants in common with Olivia. Upon the death of a tenant in common, the property passes to the decedent's beneficiaries instead of the surviving tenants in common. The property will pass to the beneficiaries named in the will or will be distributed following the laws of intestacy if the decedent had no will. In our example, if Oliver Wood dies, his share of the tenancy in common passes to his heirs either through the laws of intestacy or through his will.

Tenants in common: an ownership interest of two or more people who own separate but undivided interests in property

Joint tenancy is another form of ownership of real property used when two or more people own property together. Each of the joint tenants, or co-owners, has an equal, undivided interest in the property, and a **right of survivorship**, meaning that if one owner dies, that owner's interest in the property will pass to the surviving

Joint tenancy: a form of ownership of real property in which two or more people own property together

Right of survivorship: if one of the joint tenants dies, that owner's interest in the property will pass to the surviving owner or owners by operation of law

Operation of law: assets pass by the application of an ownership law, such as joint ownership, designation as POD or TOD, or a beneficiary designation

owner or owners by **operation of law**. This means that each of the surviving owners automatically acquires the deceased owner's rights. It is abbreviated as JTWROS (joint tenancy with right of survivorship). In our example, Oliver and Olivia can purchase a property as joint tenants with right of survivorship. The deed would then read Oliver Wood and Olivia Wood, JTWROS. If the joint tenants agree to sell the property, they must equally divide the proceeds of the sale regardless of the amount each contributed to the purchase of the property. An interest in a joint tenancy property does not pass by way of probate. If Oliver dies, then Olivia is the surviving joint tenant and acquires full ownership of the property.

Four unities: the four elements—time, title, interest, and possession—required to create a joint tenancy

In order to create a joint tenancy, each of the joint tenants must acquire their ownership rights with what is known as the **four unities**: (1) they must acquire the property at the same time; (2) they must have the same title to the property; (3) they must own an equal share of the property; and (4) they must have an equal right to possess the whole property, meaning that no one joint tenant is considered an owner of any particular portion of the property. These four unities are known as time, title, interest, and possession. If any of these elements is missing, the joint tenancy is ineffective, or not valid, and the joint tenancy will be treated as a tenancy in common in equal shares.

Each of the joint tenants enjoys the same rights until one of them dies. Under the right of survivorship, the death of one joint tenant automatically transfers the remainder of the property in equal parts to the survivors. When only one joint tenant is left alive, he or she receives the entire estate.

Tenants by the entirety: a special form of joint tenancy for married couples

Tenants by the entirety is a special form of joint tenancy for married couples. It can only be created by will or by deed, and it creates a right of survivorship. In our example, Oliver Wood gets married to his girlfriend Opal. They buy a house together where they will live as husband and wife. The deed will read Oliver Wood and Opal Wood (H/W) as tenants by the entirety, to acknowledge that the two parties are husband and wife.

Because tenants by the entirety is a form of property ownership that is dependent on the owners being married, if the owners get divorced, they become tenants in common, losing the right of survivorship. If one spouse passes away, the property owned as tenants by the entirety automatically passes to the surviving spouse. Holding a property as tenants by the entirety provides the added benefit of credit protection, because it protects one spouse's interest in the property from the other spouse's creditors. This type of ownership may not be available in all states. Same-sex couples may also hold title as tenants by the entirety.

POD (payable on death): a designation on an account that a specific beneficiary is to receive that account; the POD designation is used for checking accounts and savings accounts held at a bank

Joint tenancy usually refers to ownership of real property. However, bank accounts and other types of investment accounts can also be owned as joint tenants. If a bank or investment account is owned as joint tenants, there are the same rights of survivorship for each of the joint owners as there are with real property. For example, two people can own a bank account, and the account is designated as a joint account. Very often the names of the two owners will be listed with the abbreviation JTWROS.

TOD (transferable on death): a way to designate a specific beneficiary who is to receive that account; the TOD designation is used for stocks, bonds, mutual funds, or other similar investments

There are other designations on bank accounts, certificates of deposit, and other types of investment accounts that also affect the ownership rights. An account that is designated **POD**, payable on death, or **TOD**, transferable on death, is a way to

Figure 1-3. Certificate of Deposit, Payable on Death

ACCOUNT # CD04400124

❏ SAVINGS   ❏ MONEY MARKET   ☒ CERTIFICATE   ❏ HOLIDAY CLUB*

THIS CERTIFIES THAT

Oliver Wood POD
Harold Wood

holds an account in

OCEAN   BANK

In addition to the receipt of this passbook, I also acknowledge receipt of and agreement to abide by the Bank's Terms & Conditions, Fee Schedule, Account Agreement, product disclosure and other applicable documents.

DATE ISSUED: FEB 04, 2010

by_____
                                          Authorized Signature

NOT TRANSFERABLE EXEPT ON THE BOOKS OF THE DEPOSITORY INSTITUTION

designate a specific beneficiary who is to receive that account. The POD designation is used for checking accounts and savings accounts held at a bank. The TOD designation is used for stocks, bonds, mutual funds, or other similar investments. The transfer of an account that has the POD or TOD designation is triggered by the death of the owner and occurs whether or not the decedent has a will. The person designated as POD or TOD has a right to access the asset upon the presentation of the decedent's death certificate.

An example of a POD designation can be as simple as opening a certificate of deposit, or CD, at a bank and asking the the name on the account be listed with a second person as POD. If our client Oliver Wood wanted to have a CD designated as POD for his nephew Harry, the bank book would look like that presented in Figure 1-3.

A bank account with a POD designation is also referred to as a **Totten trust**. This is an informal trust that is created when the grantor puts money into a bank account and designates that upon the death of the grantor, the monies in the account pass to a named beneficiary. The name *Totten trust* comes from the *Matter of Totten*, 179 N.Y. 112 (1904), a case decided by the Court of Appeals of New York. In that case, the court ruled that even though designating an account as transferable on death did not meet the formal requirements of a trust, it was still a legal means by which property could be conveyed.

Totten trust: an informal trust that is created when the grantor puts money into a bank account and designates that upon the death of the grantor, the monies in the account pass to a named beneficiary by way of a POD designation

H.   Beneficiary Designation

The fourth way in which the assets of a decedent can pass to others is by a beneficiary designation. Certain types of assets can have a beneficiary named who will receive the remainder of the asset upon the death of the owner. The term *beneficiary* in this use

Figure 1-4. Beneficiary Designation Form

1. **Policy Owner's Full Name:** _____

2. **Birth Date:** _____/_____/_____

3. **Social Security Number:** _____

4. **Primary Beneficiary(ies) – percentage must add up to 100%**

	Beneficiary Name	Relationship	Birth Date	Amount
1.	_____	_____	_____	_____
	Address _____			
2.	_____	_____	_____	_____
	Address _____			
3.	_____	_____	_____	_____
	Address _____			

5. **Contingent Beneficiary(ies) – If primary beneficiary is not living at my death, payment is to be made to:**

	Beneficiary Name	Relationship	Birth Date	Amount
1.	_____	_____	_____	_____
	Address _____			
2.	_____	_____	_____	_____
	Address _____			
3.	_____	_____	_____	_____
	Address _____			

   Percentage must add up to 100%

6. **SIGNATURE OF OWNER** _____ Date _____

   Mailing Address: _____

   Daytime Telephone No. (_____ **)** _____

Primary beneficiary: the first person to receive the benefits of the policy

Contingent beneficiaries: beneficiaries who are eligible to receive a distribution if the first (primary) beneficiary has predeceased

refers to the person who is receiving the benefits (or proceeds) of a retirement plan, like an IRA or 401(k), an annuity, a trust, or a life insurance policy. The owner of a life insurance policy, for example, can designate his wife as the **primary beneficiary**, the first person to receive the benefits of the policy. She will receive the proceeds from the policy upon his death, and if she passes away before him, his children would be **contingent beneficiaries**.

The owner of an asset that has a beneficiary designation can change who the beneficiaries will be at any time prior to the owner's death. The beneficiary can be a single person or a group of people. A group of beneficiaries can all receive an equal share of the asset, or the owner can designate the percentage that each beneficiary is to receive.

For example, the owner of an annuity whose husband has predeceased her can indicate that her three children are all primary beneficiaries and that the remaining balance of the annuity should be split between them equally. The owner of the annuity could also decide that one child should receive 50 percent and the other two children should split the remaining 50 percent, with each receiving 25 percent of the balance. Figure 1-4 presents an example of a beneficiary designation form.

A beneficiary designation form can be completed by hand, or the information can be typed onto the form. The form must be submitted to the investment company managing the asset or the insurance company that holds the insurance policy. The owner of the asset, or the insured, can change the beneficiaries at any time, unless the asset is a retirement asset. The beneficiary of certain retirement assets must be the owner's spouse, unless the spouse consents to the designation of another beneficiary.

I. Probate and Nonprobate Assets

After the death of the testator, the will is admitted to probate. **Probate** is the process by which the validity and legality of the will are proven in a court. All of the decedent's assets and possessions make up the decedent's estate. The estate is divided into two categories: the **probate estate** and the **nonprobate estate**. The probate estate consists of all of the decedent's assets that are in the decedent's name alone. Distribution of the probate estate is done in accordance with the provisions in the will. The nonprobate estate consists of all of the decedent's assets that pass by operation of state law as in Section B above, by form of ownership as in Section C, or by beneficiary designation as in Section D. The provisions of the will do not govern the distribution of the nonprobate estate. For example, a will can direct that all of the assets pass to the surviving spouse, but if a parcel of real property is owned as JTWROS with a business partner, the property will go to the business partner, not the decedent's wife.

The decedent's will only directs the distribution of the probate estate. The will does not usually override the designation of assets that pass by operation of law,

Probate: the process by which the validity and legality of a will are proven in court

Probate estate: all of the decedent's assets that are in the decedent's name alone

Nonprobate estate: all of the decedent's assets that pass by operation of state law, by form of ownership, or by the provisions of the will

Probate	Nonprobate
House	House in names of two joint owners
Car	Life insurance policy with beneficiary named
Bank account	Bank account with POD named
Clothing, jewelry, personal items	IRA with beneficiary named
Investment account	Investment account with TOD named
	401(k) with beneficiary named

Figure 1-5. Examples of Probate and Nonprobate Assets

Account of convenience: a joint account designation done for an elderly person's convenience

unless the designation is done for convenience. For example, an elderly person can make a checking account a joint account with a grandchild to make it easier for the grandchild to help with check writing but not in order for that account to go to that relative upon death. A joint account designation that is done for the elderly person's convenience is called an **account of convenience**.

Some assets can be either probate assets or nonprobate assets, depending on how the asset is owned. For example, a piece of real property owned as JTWROS is a nonprobate asset and passes by operation of law. A piece of real property owned as tenants in common goes into the estate of the decedent. It is a probate asset, and the distribution of the property is governed by the will. There are also occasions when a nonprobate asset becomes a probate asset and is distributed according to the will. For example, a client has a life insurance policy naming his brother as the beneficiary. At the time of the client's death, the brother has predeceased, or died before the client. The client did not name a contingent or backup beneficiary on the policy. Because there is no other beneficiary named, the proceeds of that life insurance policy will become a probate asset, to be distributed in accordance with the decedent's will.

The distinction between the probate estate and nonprobate assets and how those assets are treated in the estate will be discussed further in Chapter 3.

J.   Client Intake

A paralegal may be required to conduct the initial meeting with a new client or at least to gather some preliminary information before the first meeting. The paralegal should be careful not to give legal advice during a client interview. Many attorneys and paralegals use a checklist or intake form to make sure that all of the pertinent information is obtained from the potential client. A sample of such an intake form is presented in Figure 1-6.

This type of intake form lists suggested questions that a paralegal may need to ask a client at the initial meeting. There are certain items that will not be applicable, such as naming a guardian or a trustee if the potential client is not creating a trust or does not have children. It is helpful to use this type of intake sheet so the pertinent information is not forgotten. This form can be modified as you become more familiar with the questions needed.

Practice Tip

Client intake can sometimes be very emotional or stressful for a client because it involves thoughts of dying, providing for loved ones after death, or perhaps the appointment with an attorney was prompted by the recent loss of a spouse or parent. The paralegal must be sensitive to the potential emotions of a client during the intake.

Figure 1-6. Sample Intake Form

ESTATE PLANNING INFORMATION

1. Client's full name _____

2. Spouse's Full name _____ _____

3. Address _____

    _____

    State _____ Zip _____

4. Telephone: Home _____ Business _____

5. Any existing wills _____ Where located _____

6. Children of present marriage: Name, sex, age, residence, and marital status

    _____

7. Children of prior marriage(s) or from unmarried relationship: Name, sex, age, parentage, residence, and

    marital status _____

    _____

8. Grandchildren: Name, sex, age, parentage, residence, and marital status _____

    _____

    _____

9. Stocks, bonds, and other securities: How registered (joint, survivorship, POD, trust, custodial) _____

    _____

    _____

10. Estimated gross estate: $_____

11. To spouse: _____

    _____

    _____

    Special conditions or contingencies _____

    _____

12. To children or others: Relationship and address, age if under 18 _____

    _____

    _____

    _____

13. Residuary estate _____

    _____

14. Provisions regarding gifts or bequests to minors or incompetents _____

    _____

(continued)

Figure 1-6. Continued

15. Charitable bequests _____

_____

16. Payment of inheritance, estate, death taxes _____

17. Executor(s) and alternate(s):

               To serve with □   without □   Bond □

    Name _____ Relationship _____

    Address_____

    Name of alternate _____ Relationship _____

    Address _____

18. Trustee(s) and alternate(s):

               To serve with □   without □   Bond □

    Name _____ Relationship _____

    Address _____

    Name of alternate_____ Relationship _____

    Address _____

19. Guardian(s) and alternate(s):

               To serve with □   without □   Bond □

    Name _____ Relationship _____

    Address _____

    Name of alternate _____ Relationship _____

    Address _____

    Address _____

    Date: _____ Information taken by: _____

    Type of will suggested: _____ Fee: _____

POWER OF ATTORNEY:

    Name _____ Relationship _____

    Address _____

    Name of alternate _____ Relationship _____

    Address _____

LIVING WILL:

    Name _____ Relationship _____

    Address _____

    Name of alternate _____ Relationship _____

    Address _____

There is certain information that is pertinent to blended families, or nontraditional families. Clients will be same-sex couples with biological and/or adopted children, foster families, grandparents raising grandchildren, families with special needs children or adults, families that acknowledge both biological and adoptive parents, or any combination of these elements. It will be necessary to make a careful record of the familial relationships in order to address the clients' needs.

K. Ethical Considerations

Estate planning law and the administration of estates give rise to particular ethical concerns because the attorney is often serving as a **fiduciary** or representing a *fiduciary*. A *fiduciary* is someone who is responsible for the property or assets of another person. Each state has its own set of ethics rules. The American Bar Association (ABA) adopted Model Rules of Professional Conduct, abbreviated as the Rules, or the MRPC, which were adopted as is or modified by each state. The Rules establish what is to be considered proper attorney conduct, and the scope of the lawyer's representation of the client. For example, is it a conflict of interest to represent a husband and wife in preparing an estate plan? When can a client's documents be released to another person? What if a person is not mentally capable of preparing an estate plan? The Rules provide a guideline for dealing with ethical considerations in the day-to-day practices and procedures of a law office. There are some differences in the states' use of the Rules. The paralegal must know and adhere to the specific ethical rules adopted by the state in which he or she is working. The 2010 version of the ABA Model Rules can be found in the index at the end of the text. The Rules govern things such as forming an attorney-client relationship, proper representation of the client, and the attorney's duties to the client.

A paralegal needs to be aware of the most common ethical considerations that arise in estate planning and estate administration, and what to do to ensure that the attorney remains in compliance with the Rules. At different points in the text the ethical considerations will be identified along with ways to avoid common pitfalls.

Fiduciary: someone who is responsible for the property or assets of another person

Summary

Estate planning involves preparing for the distribution of one's assets upon death. There are various ways that the assets can pass to heirs and/or beneficiaries, depending on whether the assets become probate assets, or non-probate assets. The laws of estate planning, and the documents needed, are unique to each state. The paralegal will need to be familiar with state specific laws of property ownership, intestate succession, and attorney ethics, as well as general laws pertaining to beneficiary designations.

Review Questions

1. What are three documents included in an estate plan?

2. Can a married person disinherit his or her spouse?

3. What are the laws of intestate succession?

4. Are the estate planning laws in each of the 50 states the same?

5. What should a client with young children be considering in an estate plan?

6. Complete the sentence:

   A grandmother is a(n) _____ of the decedent.

   A cousin is a(n) _____ of the decedent.

   A child is a(n) _____ of the decedent.

7. Research the laws of your state. Do you live in a community property state? Has your state adopted the Uniform Probate Code?

8. Tom and his brother Richard want to buy a piece of real property as an investment. What are the two different ways they can own the property, and what are the rights associated with each form of ownership?

9. What are the "four unities" of property ownership?

10. List three types of probate assets and three types of nonprobate assets.

11. A decedent dies with a will. The estate consists of the following assets: checking account, savings account, 401(k) with the decedent's niece as beneficiary, car, house, and life insurance policy with decedent's late husband named as beneficiary. Which assets are probate assets and which are nonprobate assets?

12. A new client, Richard, comes into the office with regard to the estate of his elderly, distant relative Helene. Richard has always referred to Helene as his aunt. Upon further investigation and questioning, it turns out that Richard's great-grandfather and Helene's father were brothers. What is the relationship between Richard and Helene?

13. Complete the sample beneficiary designation form using the following facts:

    Policy holder Jack Loper, Sr., is married to his wife Susan. They have two children, Jack Jr. and Angelina. Jack Jr. is a struggling artist who makes very little money; Angelina is a successful neurosurgeon who is very well off. Jack Sr. and Susan want to leave most of their estate, including life insurance, to Jack Jr. The couple has decided that Jack Jr. will receive 75 percent of their assets, and Angelina will receive 25 percent.

1. **Policy Owner's Full Name:** _____
2. **Birth Date:** _____/_____/_____
3. **Social Security Number:** _____
4. **Primary Beneficiary(ies) – percentage must add up to 100%**

	Beneficiary Name	Relationship	Birth Date	Amount
1.	_____	_____	_____	_____
	Address _____			
2.	_____	_____	_____	_____
	Address _____			
3.	_____	_____	_____	_____
	Address _____			

5. **Contingent Beneficiary(ies) – If primary beneficiary is not living at my death, payment is to be made to:**

	Beneficiary Name	Relationship	Birth Date	Amount
1.	_____	_____	_____	_____
	Address _____			
2.	_____	_____	_____	_____
	Address _____			
3.	_____	_____	_____	_____
	Address _____			

    Percentage must add up to 100%

6. **SIGNATURE OF OWNER** _____ Date _____

Mailing Address: _____

Daytime Telephone No. (_____ **)** _____

(a) What additional information do you need from the client?

(b) What other decisions does the client need to make?

True or False

1. T   F   JTWROS, POD, and TOD are all designations for things that pass by operation of law.

2. T   F   A bank account can be held as joint tenants.

3. T   F   The laws of intestacy governs the distribution of an estate according to the decedent's will.

4. T   F   Fee simple ownership is considered to be the highest, or most complete, form of ownership.

5. T   F   A brother and sister can own property together as tenants by the entirety.

6. T   F   The probate estate includes assets that have a beneficiary named.

Key Terms

Account of convenience
Advance medical directive
Ancestors or ascendants
Basis
Beneficiary
Capital gains taxes
Collateral descendants
Collateral relatives
Community property
Contingent beneficiaries
Decedent
Degree of consanguinity
Degree of kinship
Descendants
Domicile
Estate
Estate plan
Estate planning
Executor
Fee simple or fee simple absolute
Fiduciary
Four unities
Heirs, next of kin, or distributees
Intestate

Joint tenancy
Last will and testament
Laws of intestate succession
Lineal descendants
Marital share, statutory share, or elective share
Nonprobate estate
Operation of law
Personal representative
POD
Power of attorney
Prenuptial agreement
Primary beneficiary
Probate
Probate estate
Right of survivorship
Tenants by the entirety
Tenants in common
Testate
Testator
Testatrix
TOD
Totten trust
Trust

What Is a Last Will and Testament?

A. Introduction

What is a last will and testament? Historically, a "will" distributed **real property**, such as real estate, and a "testament" distributed **personal property**, such as bank accounts, personal possessions, or cash. A last will and testament became the document by which all of a person's possessions are distributed. Today, the general term "will" is used interchangeably with the term "last will and testament."

A will is a set of instructions that describe how the assets of the **decedent** are to be distributed. The person who has died is referred to as the *decedent*. The person writing the will is called the **testator** if the person is male, or **testatrix**, if the person is female. In states that have adopted the Uniform Probate Code, the term *testator* is used to describe persons of either sex. For ease of reference, in this chapter, we are going to use an example of a male person who is writing the will, and we are going to refer to him as the testator.

A new client comes to the office. His name is Frank Bryce. Frank is a single man in his late 30s who lives alone. He has a great job as an audio engineer that has him traveling around the United States providing audio services for meetings and conventions. Frank's brother passed away last year, without a will, and this made Frank think about his own estate. Frank has acquired some assets that he wants to be able to leave to his brother's two young sons to help with their college expenses.

In our example, Frank is the testator. He wants to write a will to distribute his assets among his beneficiaries. The term **beneficiary** generally refers to the person or persons who are receiving a distribution from an estate. Frank wants his two nephews to be the beneficiaries of his estate. The term *beneficiary* can also refer to someone who receives a distribution from a retirement plan, annuity, or life insurance policy. If Frank had life insurance, he could name his nephews as the beneficiaries of the life insurance policy. The term *heir* is another name for a beneficiary. Heirs are usually related to the decedent and are entitled by law to receive the estate of a person who dies intestate, or without a will.

Real property: real estate, such as vacant land, a home, or a commercial building; includes anything that is growing on the land, such as crops or timber

Personal property: movable items such as personal possessions, bank accounts, cars, or other items. The rights to the items are not tied to a specific location, and the items can be sold, gifted, or otherwise transferred to another person.

Decedent: a person who has died

Testator/testatrix: the person who is making the will

Beneficiary (or heir): the person who is receiving the benefits (or proceeds) of an estate, retirement plan, annuity or life insurance policy

A last will and testament for Frank will be relatively simple. Generally, a will consists of several distinct sections, each of which must be drafted in a specific way. The will must be **executed**, or signed, by the testator and the witnesses, in the specific way required by the state in which the testator lives.

Exccuted: to formally sign a legal document in front of a witness and/or notary

B. Requirements to Make a Will

There are two requirements that the testator must meet in order to be able to make a will: first, the testator must be of a certain minimum age, and second, the testator must be competent to make a will.

1. Age

Adult: someone who has reached the age of majority, usually age 18 or older, or someone who is married or emancipated, even if younger than the age of majority

The first requirement of writing a will is to determine if the testator is a competent adult. In most states, an **adult** is someone who has reached the age of majority, usually age 18 or older. In Georgia, a person only needs to be age 14 to make a will. In Louisiana, the statutes pertaining to wills do not specify a minimum age, although the minimum age to witness a will is age 16. Many states also provide for someone who is married or emancipated to be considered an adult even if younger than the age of majority in that state. Our new client Frank is in his 30s, so we are not worried about whether or not he is an adult.

2. Capacity

Competent: capacity to write a will

Capacity: ability to govern yourself and your own affairs

Testamentary capacity: knowing the nature of your bounty and the objects of your affection; what your assets are and to whom you want to give them

Bounty: the assets that one owns, either real or personal property

Frank must be **competent**, or have the **capacity** to write a will. *Capacity* generally is the ability to govern yourself and your own affairs. **Testamentary capacity**, or the capacity to write a last will and testament, is defined in old case law as knowing the "nature of your bounty and the objects of your affection." In today's language that means knowing what your assets are and to whom you want to give them. **Bounty** is the word used to describe the assets that one owns, either real or personal property. As long as Frank knows that he is creating a will and that it is intended to dispose of his assets, Frank meets the minimum requirements to be able to write a will.

There are different levels of legal capacity required for different types of legal documents. The capacity to draft a will is the lowest form of capacity needed to execute a legal document. As stated above, an adult needs to know only the assets that he or she has and to whom those assets are to be left in order to have sufficient capacity to draft a will. For example, your great-grandmother can be in the beginning stages of Alzheimer's, but if she knows that she has bank accounts at Bank of America, knows that she has an investment account at Merrill Lynch, knows the address of the home she owns, can tell the lawyer or paralegal the names of all of her children and that she wants all of her assets to go to them equally, she most likely has sufficient capacity.

In most states, a contract is one example of a legal document that requires a much higher level of capacity upon signing. The capacity needed to be able to sign a contract would be more than just knowing assets and the names of children. Your great grandmother with the early stages of Alzheimer's should not be entering into a complex contract for the sale of her portion of a business that she and your great grandfather started, because she may not be able to understand the financing, terms, and conditions. A complex contract requires a much higher level of capacity.

Because testamentary capacity is the lowest form of capacity, it is possible to lose capacity for other legal actions, such as signing a contract, but to still have testamentary capacity. For example, you might not want your great grandmother to drive a car, but she could still have sufficient testamentary capacity to write a new will. She might need assistance with various activities but still be clear minded enough to have testamentary capacity.

Every experienced elder law practitioner develops his or her own set of rules and guidelines for determining capacity. Many start by asking simple questions in the beginning of a client intake interview, such as the client's children's names and addresses, and the names of any grandchildren. Evaluating the client's ability to respond to these questions is often a matter of experience. Determining what the client knows, and does not know, can give clues as to whether or not capacity is an issue, but this is not an exacting science. For example, not remembering a date or zip code does not mean that a client lacks capacity. In contrast, if the client does not remember that her spouse has already passed away, or she answers that she has only two children when in fact she has four, capacity might be an issue.

As an example of the differences between a client who has capacity and one who potentially does not, let us look at two different clients: Ms. Bailey and Mr. Farnham. Ms. Bailey calls and asks to make an appointment with the attorney. She requests that the attorney come to her home, as she no longer drives. The paralegal takes down some basic information and relates to the attorney that the client seems very sure of herself on the phone. The appointment is scheduled for the following week. Upon arriving at the home at the designated time, Ms. Bailey greets the attorney and welcomes the attorney into her home. After a brief discussion the attorney learns that she was never married, cared for her father first and then her mother, thereafter inheriting her parents' estate. She worked as an administrative assistant to an executive at Exxon Mobil for most of her adult life. She had been very frugal with her money. She was currently receiving a good bit of income from various investments. She was able to name several of the investments, brokerage accounts, and bank accounts but thought she might be forgetting some accounts. She said she kept the statements in a file cabinet and could look up the exact accounts and the balance in each account, if necessary. She knew that she wanted to leave most of her estate to her sister's three children of whom she was very fond. She was able to tell the attorney all of the children's names and the states in which they lived, but she could not remember the street address of one nephew as he had moved recently. Ms. Bailey seems like she may have some very minor age-related memory issues but otherwise has the necessary capacity to prepare a will.

In contrast to Ms. Bailey, let us look at an interaction between an attorney and our second potential new client, Mr. Farnham. Mr. Farnham has just moved to an assisted living facility after completing a stay in rehab following a stroke. On the date of the scheduled appointment, the attorney finds Mr. Farnham in his room in his pajamas. He has clearly forgotten the appointment. After several minutes of reminding Mr. Farnham that he contacted the attorney's office regarding a new will, Mr. Farnham finally remembers. Mr. Farnham states that he has two children. He indicates his wife died some years ago, but he cannot remember when. He says he has some bank accounts and a retirement account but is unable to provide any details. He says the assisted living is "OK," but he would really prefer to go home. Midway through the meeting, there is a knock on the door and a young woman enters greeting Mr. Farnham as "Dad." She tells the attorney she is the youngest of three daughters. She also relates that her father's home was sold about six months ago when her mother died. She says her father has been living with her since then. It is possible that Mr. Farnham is having a bad day, but the preliminary assessment may be that he lacks the necessary capacity to draft a will.

If an attorney or paralegal suspect capacity may be an issue, the attorney should proceed with caution. It may also be necessary to ask the client general questions such as the date, the name of the president, or a current event in order to get a complete picture of the client's competency. If the paralegal has any questions or any reason to doubt a client's capacity, he or she should always bring those questions to the attorney for discussion.

C. Ethical Considerations: Capacity

Capacity and competency issues may be of concern with some estate-planning clients because of age-related disease or health concerns. Of course, many estate-planning clients are also young and single, or parents with young children who have no issues regarding capacity. When interviewing an elderly or ill client, the attorney will have to be concerned with the client's capacity from the date of the initial meeting through the finalization of the documents. A client may be fine at the initial meeting and then over the course of completing estate-planning documents have some type of medical emergency that causes him or her to lose capacity. Other clients may be experiencing some form of impairment at the first meeting but still seem to be clear in what documents are desired. Capacity is not measured by a diagnosis or an age. A diagnosis of Alzheimer's disease or dementia is not an automatic finding that the person lacks capacity. Similarly, age is not a defining factor. A client of a very advanced age could be perfectly competent, while a much younger client suffering from early onset Alzheimer's may have already lost capacity.

The ethical concern that arises in conjunction with capacity is the ability to form the attorney-client relationship necessary for the attorney to be able to represent the client. The Rules of Professional Conduct (known as the RPC or Rules) provide guidance for attorneys dealing with a client who is impaired. The Rules state that the attorney must, as far as is reasonably possible, maintain a normal attorney-client relationship with the client (Rule 1.14).

As discussed above, the level of capacity needed in order to be able to create a will is very low. The attorney's job is to determine if the testator has the requisite level of capacity, and to record and preserve his decisions with regard to the disposition of assets, in case the testator loses capacity at a later time. If a client has the capacity to make legal decisions, then it is the attorney's duty to ensure that the client gets to make the decisions with regard to where the client's assets will go upon death.

D.   Nonlawyer Wills

Although a will has certain formal requirements, it is not necessary to have a will prepared by an attorney. There are several online resources that can assist in drafting a will. There are pre-made templates and form wills for sale in office supply stores. However, anyone who relies on a form will, or a fill-in-the-blank type of will found on the Internet is taking the risk that the will does not distribute assets the way that was intended, or worse yet, that the will is challenged in the courts. A legal challenge to a will can cost thousands of dollars, and if the will is not properly drafted or executed in accordance with the specific laws of the state, the assets in the estate can be tied up in the courts for years. Having a "simple will" prepared by an attorney is relatively inexpensive and, although not a guarantee, can reduce the risk that the property is not distributed the way the testator wanted.

Competent adults can make their own will without using an attorney or an Internet form. A will that is written in the testatrix's own handwriting is known as a **holographic will**. The requirements to create a valid holographic will vary from state to state. Some states require that a holographic will be witnessed, and others do not. Some states do not recognize holographic wills at all. At a minimum, the holographic will has to be written in the testator's own handwriting, not typewritten, and there must be evidence that the person writing the document intended it to be used to distribute his or her property after death.

Holographic will: a will that is written in the testator's own handwriting; known as a last will and testament; a legal document that distributes both the real and personal property of someone who has died

Under extreme circumstances, a will can be oral, if the testator is close to death, and there is a witness. A **nuncupative will** is a will that is dictated to another person in the presence of a witness. Many states do not recognize nuncupative wills. Those states that do recognize nuncupative wills often require that the words spoken by the decedent be reduced to writing within a certain period of time after death.

Nuncupative will: a will that is dictated to another person in the presence of a witness

A will must be witnessed, whether the will is prepared by an attorney or is holographic, in order to prove the validity of the will. This means that the witness has to see the testator sign the will. The witnesses must understand that they are witnessing the testator affix his signature to the will and must be competent to testify in court to the fact they were witnesses, if necessary. The witnesses must also be adults, either age 18 or meet the state's requirements for the age of majority, and may not be interested parties. An **interested party** is one who stands to benefit from the will. A beneficiary of an estate should never act as a witness to the testator's signing of the will.

Interested party: one who stands to benefit from the will

E.   Ethical Considerations: Who Is the Client?

There are certain ethics issues that must be considered in creating a last will and testament for a client. To illustrate how those issues arise, let us look at an example of a typical set of facts for an estate-planning client. Mary Cattermole calls the office and asks to make an appointment for her mother Ann Norbert. Ann is 88 years old, and her husband has recently passed away. Ann needs some estate-planning advice. Some initial information is taken over the phone, and an appointment is made for Ann.

The first question that should be asked is who is the client, or more accurately, who will be the client? Is it going to be Ann? Is it Mary? Is it some other member of Ann's family? The answer to the question "Who is the client" is going to depend on the attorney's determination of whether or not Ann has capacity. We will discuss capacity at various points throughout this text. Generally, capacity is described as the ability to govern oneself and one's own affairs. The exact legal definition varies from state to state. The level of capacity also varies for different types of legal documents or legal activities. For example, in New Jersey, the level of capacity needed to be able to write a will is much lower than the capacity needed to enter into a contract. The important part of the facts as we know them so far is that Mary called the office to make an appointment for Ann. Ann did not call for herself. This may be relevant later on, so a note on the appointment calendar or file should be made that the appointment is for Ann, but that her daughter Mary called to actually make the appointment.

Additional Facts: Ann arrives at the office with her adult daughter Mary, and Mary's husband Reg, who is an accountant. The paralegal is given the task of getting some background information from the client in preparation of meeting with an attorney. During the initial meeting, Reg explains that he believes "Mom" has an estate tax issue and wants to discuss estate planning and possibly gifting to reduce her potential tax burden. He gives a brief overview of Ann's assets and outlines his concerns regarding potential estate tax. Ann listens attentively during this meeting but does not offer any input in the conversation.

What Are the Ethical Considerations?

After the additional facts have been gathered, the question of who will be the client becomes even more relevant.

- Does Ann have capacity? The attorney will have to determine whether or not Ann has sufficient capacity to form an attorney-client relationship. The attorney will have to review the capacity needed for the specific tasks that are to be undertaken and determine if Ann has capacity or not. Every attorney will develop his or her own methods to determine if a client has capacity. It may also be necessary for a doctor to document the mental status of a client. At this point in the process, it is sufficient to raise the concern that Ann might lack capacity because she is not responding to questions and is allowing her son-in-law to do all of the talking for her.

- Who is the client? If the attorney finds that Ann does have sufficient capacity, Ann will be the client. If the attorney feels Ann does not have sufficient capacity, Ann cannot be the client, and then other options such as a guardianship will have to be discussed, and Mary or another family member may become the client. Guardianship is discussed in Chapter 4.

What Should You Do?

Carefully document who called to make the appointment on the intake sheet or notes taken at the first meeting with the client. Who called to make the appointment may not seem important, but it can be a factor in determining if Mary was trying to influence Ann, or if there were questions about whether or not Ann had capacity. In Chapter 1, we discussed the use of some form of an intake sheet to record all of the information gathered from the first meeting with a new client. Make a habit of noting the source of the client call on the intake sheet for every new estate-planning client.

Get the background information as requested, paying close attention to any input from Ann, and the daughter and son-in-law's reaction to that input. Are Reg and Mary telling Ann to be quiet and let them talk, or are they encouraging Ann to participate? Do Reg and Mary have specific ideas about how they think Ann's estate should be distributed? Are there other adult children, siblings of Mary, who are not present at the meeting? The answers to these questions, although they might not seem important now, could be clues as to Ann's mental state. All of the notes regarding the first meeting with the potential client should be kept in the file. Explain to Reg and Mary, and any other family members who are attending, that the attorney will need to meet with Ann on her own at first, and that this is done for her own protection.

Additional Facts: The attorney meets with Ann by herself, after explaining to Reg and Mary that this is done for Ann's protection, as well as for the protection of Reg and Mary. The attorney should explain that Reg and Mary would be able to join Ann in a few minutes. After speaking with Ann, the attorney determines that Ann has sufficient capacity to be an estate-planning client. Ann is oriented to time and place and provides facts about her children and grandchildren. She tells the attorney she has two children, her daughter Mary, and a son Jeffrey, and that Mary and Jeffrey each have two children, for a total of four grandchildren. She tells the attorney the names and approximate ages of her grandchildren. She has discussed the potential estate tax issue with Reg and understands the concerns because her husband has left her with a sizable estate. It seems that even though Ann prefers to allow her daughter or son-in-law to answer questions, she is fully aware of the nature of her assets and understands the potential estate tax issue.

F. Assets = Real and Personal Property

A will distributes the assets of the *testator*. The term *testator* refers to the person who is making the will. After the testator dies, the will is admitted to **probate** which is the court proceeding by which the validity and legality of the will are proven. A person who dies with a will is said to have died **testate**, and a person who dies without a will is said to have died **intestate**. The will governs the administration of a testate estate. The administration of an intestate estate follows a different path. Estate administration will be examined in detail in Chapter 11.

When a person dies, his or her estate consists of all of the assets, both personal property and real property owned at the time of death. *Personal property* is made up

Probate: the process by which the validity and legality of the will is proven

Testate: a person who died with a will

Intestate: a person who died without a will

of movable items such as personal possessions, bank accounts, cars, or other items. The rights to the items are not tied to a specific location, and the items can be sold, gifted, or otherwise transferred to another person. For example, a bank account is personal property. A bank account can be liquidated, and the funds can then be moved to another bank. The bank account can be moved to where ever the owner wants it to be. Personal property, unlike real property, is movable.

Real property is real estate, such as vacant land, a home, or a commercial building. The term *real property* also includes anything that is growing on the land, such as crops or timber. Real property is the land, and the rights pertaining to the land stay with the land. The right of ownership of the land can be transferred to another owner, but ownership rights are not "movable" to another piece of land. For example, a client owns real property that consists of a timber forest in Vermont. The client can sell the right to timber from the property to another person, while still retaining ownership of the property. The person who buys the right to cut timber from the client's property cannot transfer that right to another property. The right to cut timber is associated with the specific piece of real property owned by the client.

Bequest: a distribution of personal property in a will

Devise: a distribution of real property in a will

Devisee: a person who receives the devise

Legatee: a person who receives real property through a will; also describes a beneficiary who receives personal property

A last will and testament directs the distribution of real and personal property. A distribution made in a will is called a testamentary gift. A testamentary gift can be either a devise or a bequest. Strictly speaking, a **bequest** is a distribution of personal property in a will, while a **devise** is a distribution of real property. Most states no longer distinguish those two terms and instead use them interchangeably, but there are a few states that make a distinction between the two types of gifts. The person who receives a devise is called the **devisee**. A person who receives real property through a will is also called a **legatee**, although legatee can be used to describe a beneficiary who receives personal property. The Uniform Probate Code also provides definitions for most of these terms at Section 1-201.

G. Testamentary Bequests

Specific bequest: a specific item, or amount of money, that is given to a single beneficiary

Demonstrative bequest: a gift of a certain amount of property from a specific source

General bequest: a gift of property payable from any asset in the testator's estate

Residuary bequest: the amount remaining after payment of estate expenses, taxes, and the specific, demonstrative, and general bequests, if any

There are four types of testamentary bequests: *specific, demonstrative, general,* and *residuary*. A **specific bequest** is a specific item, or amount of money, that is given to a single beneficiary. For example, a specific bequest can give $1,000 to the testator's church, or alma mater, or can state that the testator wants his diamond cufflinks to be given to his oldest grandchild. A **demonstrative bequest** is a gift of a certain amount of property from a specific source. For example, the testator can state that his house is to be sold, and his three grandchildren each receive $10,000 from the proceeds of the sale. A **general bequest** is a gift of property payable from any asset in the testator's estate. For example, the testator can state that he wants each of his three grandchildren to receive $10,000 without specifying the source of the bequest. The final type of bequest is a **residuary bequest**. Residuary bequests distribute the money and assets remaining in the *residuary estate*, which is the amount remaining after payment of estate expenses, taxes, and the specific, demonstrative, and general bequests, if any.

It is not necessary to have all of the types of bequests in a will. A will could simply have one bequest, for example, "I leave all of my estate to my spouse."

Specific bequests are written in several different ways. A specific bequest can give an exact dollar amount: *I bequest the sum of $1,000 to the American Cancer Society.* Alternatively, the specific bequest can provide for a percentage distribution from the estate: *I bequest an amount equal to 10% of my total estate to the American Cancer Society.* Specific bequests can sometimes have an unintended effect and must be used carefully. Remember, specific bequests are paid first. Each specific bequest is paid, in full, in the order in which it is presented, even if payment of the specific bequests completely depletes the estate. Consider the following examples using an estate where the testator has three children.

Estate #1

$50,000 in assets (savings, checking, investment accounts)

Home worth $250,000
Car valued at $10,000
Total estate value = $310,000

Language in will:
Specific bequests: I hereby give, devise, and bequeath the following:

1. *The sum of ten thousand dollars ($10,000) to the March of Dimes*
2. *The sum of ten thousand dollars ($10,000) to the American Cancer Society*
3. *The sum of ten thousand dollars ($10,000) to my alma mater, Adams College*

In this example, let us assume estate expenses of $10,000. Estate expenses are paid first. Next, the three specific bequests of $10,000 each will be paid. The money remaining after payment of the estate expenses and the specific bequests will then go into the residuary estate.

Total estate value = $310,000
$ 10,000 — estate expenses
$ 30,000 — specific bequests ($10,000 × 3)
$270,000 — residuary estate

In our example, after paying the estate expenses, and paying $10,000 each for the three specific bequests, there is $270,000 left in the residuary estate. Therefore, each of testator's three children receives a one-third share of $270,000, or $90,000.

But what happens if there is significantly less money in the estate? What if the testator had a lot of money and intended to be very generous in gifts to charitable organizations, but then spent most of his money before his death? Nursing home costs can run as high as $10,000 to $15,000 per month. If a testator suffered a long period of illness prior to death, or lived for years in a nursing home, the assets in the estate could be significantly less than what he had when the will was drafted. This could lead to an unintended result.

Estate #2

$25,000 in assets remaining in estate

Home was worth $250,000 — the house was sold and the proceeds used to pay for care
Car was valued at $10,000 — the car was also sold and the proceeds used for care
Total estate value = $25,000

Language in will:
Specific bequests: I hereby give, devise, and bequeath and bequest the following:

1. *The sum of ten thousand dollars ($10,000) to the Boy Scouts of America*
2. *The sum of ten thousand dollars ($10,000) to the American Cancer Society*
3. *The sum of ten thousand dollars ($10,000) to my alma mater*

In Estate #2, most of the decedent's assets were sold off and the proceeds used to pay for his care. There is very little remaining in the estate. After payment of estate expenses of $4,000 there is $21,000 remaining in the estate. The first specific bequest of $10,000 to the March of Dimes is paid; the second bequest of $10,000 is paid to the American Cancer Society; and the testator's alma mater, Adams College, receives the remaining $1,000. There is nothing left to go into the residuary estate, and nothing left to go to the residuary beneficiaries, the testator's children. At the time the will was written, the testator most likely imagined the bulk of his assets going to his children. Unfortunately, because a specific dollar amount was used to define the specific bequests, there is nothing left for the residuary beneficiaries. This result can be avoided by using a percentage of the total estate value as a means by which the bequest is defined.

A will can provide for a specific bequest stated as a percentage of the total net value of the estate. Using a percentage ensures that all beneficiaries, both specific and residuary, receive some portion of the estate, no matter how small. The language used for a percentage-type of specific bequest is the following:

I hereby devise, give, and bequeath the following:

1. *An amount equal to ten percent (10%) of my estate to the March of Dimes*
2. *An amount equal to ten percent (10%) of my estate to the American Cancer Society*
3. *An amount equal to ten percent (10%) of my estate to my alma mater, Adams College*

Going back to Estate #1, there was $310,000 in assets. Assuming the same administration expenses of $10,000, a net estate of $300,000 is left for distribution to the beneficiaries. Using the percentages included in the will, the three specific bequests are each paid 10% of the net estate, or $30,000. The total paid to the specific beneficiaries is $90,000 ($30,000 × 3 beneficiaries). Therefore, $210,000 goes into the residuary estate ($300,000 − $90,000). Each of the three residuary beneficiaries gets an equal share of the residuary estate, so each beneficiary receives $70,000 ($210,000/3 beneficiaries).

In Estate #2 there were only $25,000 of assets in the estate. Assuming estate expenses of $4,000, a net estate of only $21,000 was available for distribution.

When a specific dollar amount was used, the residuary beneficiaries received nothing. However, when a percentage is used, each residuary beneficiary receives a small distribution. Using the percentage language listed above, each specific bequest is paid 10% of the net estate, or $2,100, for a total of $6,300. ($21,000 × 10% × 3). That allows $14,700 to go into the residuary estate. ($21,000 − $6,300 = $14,700). The residuary estate of $14,700 is then divided in equal shares, with one share going to each of the three residuary beneficiaries.

Using percentages to determine the amount of the specific bequests ensures that at least some amount of money goes to each specific beneficiary, and that there will still be some portion of the estate assets available to be distributed to the residuary beneficiaries. The residuary bequest is a type of "catch-all" bequest, whereby everything left in the estate, consisting of whatever assets remain after the payment of estate expenses, and satisfaction of all of the other bequests, is gathered and divided among a group of beneficiaries. No one knows what will be in the residuary estate until after the expenses and specific bequests are made. Therefore, residuary bequests are never expressed as specific dollar amounts.

H.   Lapse of a Bequest

A **lapse of a bequest** occurs when the beneficiary dies or predeceases the testator. What happens to a lapsed bequest depends on the type of bequest. When a residuary bequest lapses, the property passes according to the **intestacy statutes** of the state in which the decedent lived. *Intestacy statutes* are laws that govern the distribution of the assets in an estate when the decedent dies intestate or without a will. These will be discussed later in this chapter. For example, our client Gary Olivane has a will that states, "*I leave all the rest and residue of my estate to my son, Milburne Olivane.*" Gary's wife June died many years ago. When Gary dies, he is in a nursing home and had been for many years. During the last years of his life, Gary suffered from senile dementia and was unaware of his surroundings, including the fact that his son Milburne died in a car crash. Because Gary's son has predeceased him, the residuary estate will pass to Gary's heirs according to the intestacy statutes in the state in which he lived. This could mean Milburne's children, if he had any, or Gary's siblings, or Gary's siblings' children.

When a specific, demonstrative, or general bequest lapses, the property goes into the residuary of the estate, unless there is a provision in the will directing where the property goes in the event of a lapse. If Gary left a specific bequest of $10,000 to his son Milburne, but left the rest of his estate to charity, the bequest to Milburne would lapse and go into Gary's testator's residuary estate. Gary could specify what would happen if he predeceased him, for example, the will could specify that the bequest would go to Milburne's children if Milburne predeceased Gary.

Most states have adopted **antilapse statutes** that will save the bequest if it has been made to a person who has predeceased the testator, and the person is included in the list of beneficiaries protected by the statute. If the predeceased beneficiary was related to the decedent and had children, the antilapse statutes provide for children of the deceased beneficiary to take the gift instead of the beneficiary himself. Following our

Lapse of a bequest: occurs when the beneficiary dies or predeceases the testator

Intestacy statutes: laws that govern the distribution of the assets in an estate when the decedent dies intestate or without a will

Antilapse statutes: state laws that will save a bequest if it has been made to a person who has predeceased the testator, and that person is included in the list of beneficiaries protected by the statute example above, the specific bequest of $10,000 to Gary's son would not lapse if Milburne had children. An antilapse statute would prevent the bequest from being added back into the residuary estate and would instead allow it to go to his children.

There is no uniform antilapse statute; each state provides a specific list of the family members that are included in the statute. The states that have adopted the Uniform Probate Code follow the antilapse statutes contained in the UPC. The UPC provides an antilapse provision at Section 2-603. For example, Massachusetts has adopted the UPC and includes an antilapse statute at Section 2-603 as follows:

> If a devisee who is a grandparent or a lineal descendant of a grandparent is dead at the time of execution of the will, fails to survive the testator, or is treated as if he predeceased the testator, the issue of the deceased devisee who survive the testator take in place of the deceased devisee and if they are all of the same degree of kinship to the devisee they take equally, but if of unequal degree than those of more remote degree take by representation. A person who would have been a devisee under a class gift if he had survived the testator is treated as a devisee for purposes of this section whether his death occurred before or after the execution of the will.

When you first read this statute your reaction will probably be, "What??" Let us break down the first part of the statute and decipher it. We already know that a devise is a distribution of real property in a will, and a person who receives the devise is called the devisee. A lineal descendant is someone who is descended one from the other or all from a common ancestor; for example, your lineal descendants are your children, grandchildren, or great-grandchildren. **Issue** is just a way of saying children, grandchildren, or great-grandchildren. This antilapse statute provides for the children, grandchildren, or great-grandchildren of the deceased person to get the bequest if the beneficiary has died. However, the only beneficiaries that are included are the grandparents or the lineal descendants of the grandparents, not more remote relatives, in-laws, or any nonrelated parties. Figure 2-1 shows an example explained in a diagram.

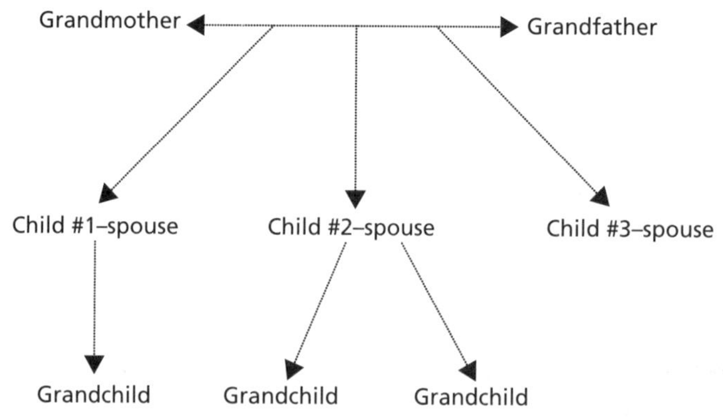

Issue: children, grandchildren, or great-grandchildren; lineal decsendants

Figure 2-1. Example: Lineal Descendants

A husband and wife have three children, and each of the three children is married. Child #1 has one child, the couple's grandchild. Child #2 has two children, also the couple's grandchildren. Child #3 has no children. If a bequest was left to Child #2 and Child #2 predeceased, the antilapse statute would apply. Child #2's issue, the two grandchildren, would take Child #2's share in equal shares. The distribution of estates can get very complicated.

If the will contains a bequest to a person not on the list, such as a friend or more distant relative, and that person predeceases the testator, the bequest will lapse. Some states limit the predeceased beneficiaries that are protected by the statute to a child or other descendent of the testator. Under those state's statutes, if the predeceased beneficiary is not a child of the testator, the gift lapses. Some states include descendants of the testator's parents, meaning the testator's brothers and sisters. Expanding the class of included beneficiaries to the testator's brothers and sisters also expands it to children of the testator's brothers and sisters, meaning the testator's nieces and nephews. Other states include all of the relatives of the testator, as long as they are blood relatives and not relatives by marriage. Only the relatives included in the list provided in the state's antilapse statute are protected if they predecease the testator. Any bequest to a predeceased beneficiary not on the list will lapse.

Here's an example to show the difference in the way different states treat beneficiaries under the antilapse statutes. Cynthia leaves a specific piece of property to her brother Edwin. At the time of her death, Edwin had already predeceased, leaving three children. In a state that includes only the children of the testator in the antilapse statute, Cynthia's bequest of property lapses and then passes by the laws of intestacy. In a state that includes the children of the testator's brothers and sisters, Cynthia's bequest of real property to her brother Edwin does not lapse and is instead distributed to his three children, Cynthia's nieces and nephew. But what happens if one of Cynthia's nieces or her nephew also predeceased, for example, if Cynthia's niece died before Cynthia? In most states, the share going to the predeceased niece would lapse and would not go to her surviving spouse, because the spouse is not a blood relative of Cynthia. The bequest would, however, go to the deceased niece's children, if she had any.

I.   Estate Expenses

A will also typically describes how estate expenses are to be paid. Estate expenses can include the cost of hiring an attorney if necessary, maintaining the decedent's assets, such as paying property taxes, utilities, homeowner's association fees of real property, funeral expenses, and costs of last medical treatment. Estate expenses can also include payment of inheritance or estate taxes. The estate expenses must be paid from estate assets, but how those expenses are allocated among which beneficiaries must be specifically designated in the will.

Summary

A last will and testament is a legal document created for a competent adult to distribute his or her estate after death. The will provides for the appointment of a personal representative, the distribution of assets, and the payment of debts and expenses, A will must be executed in accordance with specific state laws, and cannot contain provisions that are unenforceable. The paralegal needs to be aware of the ethical consideration in preparing a will, including determining the client's capacity and avoiding a conflict of interest.

Review Questions

1. What is the difference between a holographic will and a nuncupative will? Look up your state's law and determine whether your state allows for holographic and/or nuncupative wills.

2. What is testamentary capacity, how is it determined, and when does it become relevant?

3. An estate consists of $125,000 in assets. The funeral bill is $10,000; the total outstanding costs of the decedent's last illness are $1,000; and the accountant's fees are $500. There are two specific bequests of $5,000 each. What is the net estate? What is in the residuary estate?

4. A new client, Katie Miles, has an estate with a gross value of $500,000. Katie's husband has predeceased her. She has two children, Megan and Laura. She wants to leave most of her estate to her daughters but wants to leave a bequest of about $10,000 to her alma mater, Catholic University. What are two different ways the bequest to Catholic University can be drafted?

5. A former client calls and wants to make an appointment for her mother to draft a new will. Her mother is elderly and in a nursing home, and she asks that the attorney go to the nursing home to speak to mom. What are some of the ethical concerns, and how should those concerns be addressed?

True or False

1. T F   Anyone can make a will.

2. T F   A testator wants a provision in his will to give his grandson $1,000. This is an example of a residuary bequest.

3. T F   A husband can serve as a witness to his wife's will.

4. T F   A holographic will is one written in the testator's own handwriting.

5. T F   A will only distributes the testator's personal property.

Key Terms

Adult	Intestacy statutes
Antilapse statutes	Intestate
Beneficiary	Issue
Bequest	Lapse of a bequest
Bounty	Legatee
Capacity	Nuncupative will
Competent	Personal property
Decedent	Probate
Demonstrative bequest	Real property
Devise	Residuary bequest
Devisee	Specific bequest
Executed	Testamentary capacity
General bequest	Testate
Heir	Testator
Holographic will	Testatrix
Interested party	

Testamentary Capacity: Undue Influence

In this chapter, we will examine two challenges to a will that pertain specifically to the status of the testator: lack of testamentary capacity and undue influence. These two challenges often go hand in hand with both being alleged in an attempt to invalidate a will. In order to understand how to draft a complaint alleging lack of testamentary capacity and/or undue influence, it is first necessary to review and understand case law and statutory law from various states. The case law from one state to the next will be different, as each state's court has examined different sets of facts that led to different conclusions. This chapter will provide an overview of testamentary capacity and undue influence that will be illustrated by reference to case law and statutory law from different states.

A. Case Law Versus Statutory Law

As we briefly discussed in the first chapter, the "everyday" law in the United States is state law. Federal law may be the supreme law of the land, but the laws that most people deal with on a day-to-day basis constitute state law. Estate planning and administration law, for example, are state law, not federal law. Each of the 50 states develops its own laws, some of which may be unique to a particular state. There are two forms of state law: **statutory law** and **case law**. *Statutory law* is found in the state statutes that have been adopted by the legislature and codified, or arranged in a code. *Case law* is developed in the courts. It evolves with each new case that is heard. Let us look at a very simplistic example. A state adopts a law that says a will is valid only if it is handwritten and signed by the testator. That law is statutory law. Case law develops when a case comes before the court where a party is seeking a determination as to whether a will written by someone else but signed by the testator is valid. The court will look at the facts involved and make a determination whether the will, even though written by someone other than the testator, is valid. The rule regarding handwritten wills in that state is then partially statutory law — there is a statute

Statutory law: law that is found in statutes which has been adopted by the legislature and codified, or arranged in a code

Case law: law that is developed in the courts through the application of statutory law to specific facts governing handwritten wills — and partially case law — there is a case interpreting and applying the statute that indicates under certain circumstances a will written by someone else and signed by the testator will be valid. The law could potentially evolve further when another case comes before the court to determine the validity of a handwritten will, but the facts are slightly different than in the first case. The court will develop new case law by applying the holding of the previous case to the facts in the second case.

Case law can be preempted by statutory law. An example of preemption following the example above would be if the law indicating that a handwritten will signed by the testator is valid is amended to include elements of the case law so that the law now clearly stated a handwritten will is valid *only* if written by the testator *and* signed by the testator.

B.   Lack of Testamentary Capacity

There are volumes of legal cases about what constitutes adequate "testamentary capacity" and case law that has developed about determining if a testator had capacity at the time the will was signed. An inquiry into testamentary capacity can be made at two different times. First, the attorney asked to draft the will for the client may be concerned about the client's testamentary capacity at the time the will is being prepared. Second, the issue of whether or not the testator had testamentary capacity at the signing of the will can arise after the testator has died, when the will is being admitted to probate. In any attack upon the validity of a will, it is generally presumed that the will is valid, and that "the testator was of sound mind and competent when he executed the will." See, for example, *Gellert v. Livingston*, 5 N.J. 65, 71, 73 A.2d 916 (1950), *Jackson v. Patton*, 952 S.W.2d 404, 407 (Tenn.1997). The presumption that a testator had the necessary capacity can be rebutted, or overcome, by factors such as medical evidence that the testator lacked testamentary capacity on the date that the will was signed. It is important to note that allegation of lack of testamentary capacity pertains to the date on which the testator met with the attorney who prepared the will, and when the testator signed the will. Testamentary capacity is not measured as of the date the testator passes away.

1.   Definition of Lack of Capacity

Testamentary capacity: whether the testator can understand the objects of his or her affection and the nature of his or her bounty

Testamentary capacity is traditionally defined as whether the testator can understand the objects of his or her affection and the nature of his or her bounty. In other words, is the testator aware of the assets that comprise the estate, to whom he or she wants those assets to go, and how the estate-planning documents accomplish the desired distribution? See, for example, *In re Estate of Tolin*, 622 So.2d 988, 990 (Fla. 1993); *In re Will of Landsman*, 319 N.J.Super. 252, 267 (App.Div.1999); *Matter of Kumstar*, 66 N.Y.2d 691 (N.Y. 1985).

A testator is required to know that the document being prepared is a will that is intended to dispose of his property. Every state uses these basic criteria and then expands upon them as case law and statutory law in the state develops. For example, Florida Statutes, Section 732.501, require a testator be of "sound mind." California Prob. Code Ann. 6100.5 states

An individual is not mentally competent to make a will if at the time of making the will either of the following is true: (1) The individual does not have sufficient mental capacity to be able to (A) understand the nature of the testamentary act, (B) understand and recollect the nature and situation of the individual's property, or (C) remember and understand the individual's relations to living descendants, spouse, and parents, and those whose interests are affected by the will.

Tex. Prob. Code §57 also requires that the testator be "of sound mind." Texas law expands the general criteria of knowing the objects of affection and the nature of bounty:

[M]emory sufficient to collect in his mind the elements of the business to be transacted, and to hold them long enough to perceive, at least their obvious relation to each other, and to be able to form a reasonable judgment as to them. [*Prather v. McClelland*, 13 S.W. 543, 546 (Tex. 1890)]

In Mississippi, the state supreme court has held the following:

A person's testamentary capacity to execute a will depends on three factors that must all be considered from the perspective of the time the will was executed: (1) whether the testator was able to understand and appreciate the effects of his decision to execute the will; (2) whether the testator was able to understand the natural objects or persons to receive [his] bounty and their relation to [him]; and (3) whether the testator was capable of determining how he wanted to dispose of his property. [*In re Estate of Holmes*, 961 So. 2d 674, 679 (Miss. 2007)]

2. Burden of Proof

The **contestant**, or person alleging a lack of capacity, must prove lack of capacity by **clear and convincing evidence** [*In re Coffin's Estate*, 103 N.J.Super. 1 (App.Div.1968)]. *Clear and convincing evidence* is the level of **burden of proof** that a contestant must meet in order to prove an allegation of lack of testamentary capacity. The *burden of proof* generally includes the requirements that a party must meet to prove the case. There are various levels of burden of proof. In order of increasing requirements, the most common levels of the burden of proof are the following:

Preponderance of evidence — the party has to prove that the allegation is more likely to be true than not
Clear and convincing evidence — a midlevel standard requiring the party to prove that the allegations are more probable to be true than not
Beyond a reasonable doubt — the highest level of proof requiring the trier of fact has no doubt as to the guilt of the party; the standard most often used in criminal matters

In order to meet the burden of proof of clear and convincing evidence, a party alleging that the testator lacked testamentary capacity would need to produce some

Contestant: person raising the allegations in the complaint, also known as the plaintiff or petitioner

Clear and convincing evidence: a midlevel standard requiring the party to prove that the allegations are more probable to be true than not

Burden of proof: the set of requirements that a party must meet to prove the case

Preponderance of evidence: the party has to prove that the allegation is more likely to be true than not

Beyond a reasonable doubt: the highest level of proof requiring the trier of fact has no doubt as to the guilt of the party medical evidence of the testator's capacity at the time the will was executed. The evidence cannot simply be a diagnosis. For example, a person diagnosed with Alzheimer's is not automatically deemed to lack testamentary. An example of the proof necessary to support a claim of lack of testamentary capacity would be medical records indicating that a physician noted that the patient did not have capacity to give consent for a medical procedure, and that consent was obtained from the person's agent appointed through an advance directive.

To meet the burden of proof, the testimony of the treating physicians, nurses, or others providing care can be included. The proof would have to include specific reference to the testator not being oriented to time or place, not understanding the will, not remembering family members' names, or not remembering the plan for disposing assets. The testimony of the witnesses who were present at the signing will be given a lot of weight. The facts of what occurred at the signing have to be established — that is, did the witnesses question the testator, did they interact with him or her at all, was any discussion held between the parties, was the testator able to sign the will easily or was a lot of direction and assistance given.

3.   What Is and Is Not Proof of Lack of Capacity?

As was previously mentioned, a diagnosis, such as Alzheimer's, is not positive proof of lack of capacity, although it could be a factor. It is also not sufficient proof of lack of capacity to claim that the decisions that the testator made were "unfair" to the testator's beneficiaries. The fact that the testator disposed of property contrary to what others usually consider fair is not sufficient to declare his will void [*Hellams v. Ross*, 268 S.C. 284, 290, 233 S.E.2d 98, 101 (1977)]. Remember that a testator does not have to leave any property to family members other than a spouse. The testator has every right to leave his or her estate to whomever he or she desires. Bill Gates, billionaire founder of Microsoft, has pledged to leave his entire estate to charity, rather than to his children. It is doubtful anyone will claim lack of testamentary capacity upon his death.

Practice Tip

If the testator does not intend to leave the estate to his or her children, the cautious lawyer will clearly document testamentary capacity, as well as the reasons behind the testator's decision. With a very large estate, it could be wise to obtain a doctor's report as to the mental status of the testator and/or to videotape a dialogue with the testator as evidence of his or her mental status on the date the will was signed.

There are different methods of determining whether or not a client has testamentary capacity before drafting a will, and different methods of proving that the testator lacked testamentary capacity if you are challenging a will. One of the most irrefutable ways to determine that the client has testamentary capacity is to require a doctor's certification. The client could submit to an examination for the purposes of determining capacity and obtain a certification or report from his or her physician regarding testamentary capacity. However, this is done only in the most extreme cases, where the testator is certain that capacity is going to become an issue, or when there is a very large estate at stake. In most cases, it is up to the attorney to determine and document the testator's capacity or lack of capacity. The attorney's notes, and/or doctor's notes, can be used in proving capacity or lack of capacity.

A claim of lack of testamentary capacity is not supported by evidence that the testator was "eccentric," behaved strangely, or did things most people would consider "odd." In the famous case of *Lee's Heirs v. Lee's Executors*, the court examined allegations that a testator did not have capacity when the will was executed. The testator, Mason Lee, was well known for his eccentricities; he thought people were casting spells on him, lived in a house that was smaller than a shed without any furniture, slept in a hollow log, and many other examples cited in the case. He left a will devising his entire estate to the states of South Carolina and Tennessee. His heirs objected to this distribution, asking the court to throw out the will on the basis of lack of testamentary capacity. The court ultimately ruled that the will was valid, holding the right to make a will carries with it the right to disregard what the world considers a fair disposition of property [*Lee's Heirs v. Lee's Executors*, 15 S.C.L. (4 McCord) 183 (1827)]. A copy of the full case is included on the companion Web site.

A person with dementia or someone who has been diagnosed as having Alzheimer's could potentially still have the necessary capacity to sign a will. A person who appears confused may also have a "lucid moment" in which he or she is perfectly clear as to what the estate-planning documents should include. It is very common that a client will say an elderly relative is better in the morning or in the afternoon after a short nap. If the estate-planning documents are executed during a lucid moment, the circumstances of that lucid moment should be well documented. It is possible that an attorney meets with a client, the client seems fine, but then at the second meeting, the client has deteriorated, or is simply having a bad day. The point to remember is that capacity can be fluid, changing from one day to the next, and is very fact sensitive.

If the attorney prepares a great number of wills, it is likely that many different levels of capacity will be encountered. Clients may be unable to read the document due to loss of eyesight. They may be unable to sign documents due to stroke or other debilitating diseases. They may be able to understand what is communicated to them, but will have limited ability to respond or communicate. It is important to remember that none of these physical disabilities is indicative of a lack of capacity. If a client suffers from any disability, it will be necessary to document the level of capacity at the time the will is executed, including how the level of capacity was determined.

Attorneys whose practice is concentrated in elder law and estate planning will develop his or her own tools to measure capacity. It is sometimes a matter of instinct, or picking up on subtle clues, which is why recording information such as who made the appointment and how a client arrived at the office is important. It can be helpful to review information about capacity for your particular state. Capacity can be gauged using evaluation tools such as the Folstein Mini-Mental Examination (http://www.dhs.state.mn.us/main/groups/county_access/documents/pub/dhs16_159601.pdf). This evaluation is used to determine the level of cognitive impairment, if any. Physicians use it, but an attorney or paralegal can ask some of the same questions to help establish capacity.

Referring to items on the following checklist can be helpful:

Mental Ability Assessment Checklist

1. What can the client report about personal history?

    Date of birth
    Date of marriage
    Occupation
    Names of children
    Where children live

2. What can client report about current history?

    Current age
    Address
    Telephone
    Emergency contact

3. What does the client know about personal finances? Size of estate? Location of assets?

4. What can client report about current events?

    Names of president, governor, mayor
    Recent news item

5. Does client know today's date?

    Year, season, month, day, date

6. Does client know where he or she is at the moment?

    Lawyer's name
    Location of office
    City
    State

7. Can client recall an address after three minutes?

8. Can client read a sentence and repeat the content? If client cannot read small print, what size objects can be seen?

Knowing or not knowing the answers to the questions listed above should not be used as a strict determination of whether or not a client has capacity. Determining capacity is much more subtle than simply being able to answer questions on a checklist. For example, a client may have a brand new grandchild with an unusual first name. If the client cannot remember that grandchild's name, it does not mean the client does not have capacity. If, however, a client did not remember that he or she had any grandchildren, that may be a reason for concern.

C. Undue Influence

Undue influence is a legal claim challenging the validity of a last will and testament. It arises after the testator has passed away, when the will is being admitted to probate. An *undue influence* claim alleges that the will is not the testator's own decisions but is instead the product of influence exerted by another person. The undue influence occurs because the testator is in a vulnerable condition, and the person exerting the influence is in a position to influence the testator to the point of overcoming the testator's free will.

Undue influence: a legal claim challenging the validity of a last will and testament, alleging that the will is not the testator's own decisions but is instead the product of influence exerted by another person

1. Definition of Undue Influence

Undue influence has been defined in case law as "mental, moral or physical" exertion that has destroyed the "free agency of a testator" by preventing the testator "from following the dictates of his own mind and will and accepting instead the domination and influence of another" [*In re Neuman's Will*, 133 N.J.Eq. 532, 32 A.2d 826 (E. & A. 1943)]. Traditionally, undue influence is established by proof of four elements: (1) susceptibility to undue influence, (2) opportunity to influence, (3) disposition to influence, and (4) coveted result [*Lee v. Kamesar*, 81 Wis. 2d 151, 158, 259 N.W.2d 733 (1977)].

The term *undue influence* is also defined in some states' statutory law. For example, the California Civil Code Section 1575 defines undue influence as follows:

1. In the use, by one in whom a confidence is reposed by another, or who holds a real or apparent authority over him, of such confidence or authority for the purpose of obtaining an unfair advantage over him;
2. In taking an unfair advantage of another's weakness of mind; or,
3. In taking a grossly oppressive and unfair advantage of another's necessities or distress.

In the California code, the general term *undue influence* can refer to a contract case or a probate case.

2. Proving Undue Influence

The party alleging undue influence bears the burden of proving that claim. See, for example, *In re Estate of Varish*, 170 Wn. App. 594 606, 287 P.3d 610 (2012); *Goodman v. Atwood*, 78 Mass. App. Ct. 655 (2010); *In re Estate of Holmes*, 961 So. 2d 674, 680 (Miss. 2007); Frank L. White, Will Contests — *Burden of Proof as to Undue Influence: Effect of Confidential Relationship*, 44 Marq. L. Rev. 570 (1961); *Algoe v. Johnson*, 787 N.W.2d 480 (Iowa Ct. App. 2010). Remember that there is a presumption that the will is valid. The party alleging that the will is not valid, either because of lack of testamentary capacity or undue influence, bears the burden of proving that claim.

Undue influence can be much more subtle than capacity and therefore much more difficult to prove. Undue influence generally involves one person taking advantage of another because one person is in a position of power over the other. In the context of estate litigation, it can mean one person influencing another in a way that changes testamentary intent. The person subject to undue influence is usually dependent in some form on the person exerting the influence. An example of undue influence could be the following. An elderly client no longer drives and she depends on one grandson to take her to the store, the doctors, and so forth. Over the course of many years, the grandson tells his grandmother, "I'm the only one that would do this for you," or repeatedly says to her, "I hope you remember that out of all of your grandchildren, I'm the only one who drives you around." As time goes by, she becomes more and more dependent on him to bring groceries when she can no longer shop, to manage her bank accounts and pay her bills, and to help her with her prescriptions. After years of hearing that the grandson was the only one to help her, he suggests she make a new will so that she can show how grateful she is for all of the help he has given her. If she does what her grandson suggests, she has been subject to undue influence.

If the client previously had an estate plan whereby she left all of her assets to all of her grandchildren in equal shares, but now wants to change that at the suggestion of one grandchild who is in a position of power over her, it is possible that she is subject to undue influence. The grandson is in a position of power over his grandmother because she is dependent on him for transportation, food, medical assistance, and basically everything. He has changed her testamentary intent because she previously wanted her estate divided equally. This is the type of situation in which a paralegal making notes as to who called to make the appointment, and observing how the client and her grandson interact while waiting to see the attorney could prevent a case of undue influence.

3. Confidential Relationship

A threshold issue in an undue influence claim is whether or not the person who benefited from the will was in a position to influence the testator. In some jurisdictions the position is expressed as an "opportunity to influence." In other jurisdictions it is described as a "confidential relationship" between the testator and the person alleged to have exerted the influence. "A confidential relationship 'exists whenever trust and confidence is reposed by the testator in the integrity and fidelity of another'" [*Matter of Heer's Estate*, 316 N.W.2d 806, 810 (S.D.1982) (quoting *In re Estate of Hobelsberger*, 85 S.D. 282, 291, 181 N.W.2d 455, 460 (1970))]. "[A] [c]onfidential relationship is not restricted to any particular association of persons. It exists whenever there is trust and confidence, regardless of its origin" [*Hyde v. Hyde*, 78 S.D. 176, 186, 99 N.W.2d 788, 793 (1959)]. "Such a confidential relation exists between two persons when one has gained the confidence of the other and purports to act or advise with the other's interest in mind" [*Schwartzle v. Dale*, 74 S.D. 467, 471, 54 N.W.2d 361, 363 (1952); see also, *Kase v. French*, 325 N.W.2d 678 (S.D. 1982)]. A confidential relationship exists where one person is in a position to exercise dominant influence over the other because of the latter's dependency on the former due to weakness of mind or body, or due to trust; the law considers such a relationship to be fiduciary in character [*Madden v. Rhodes*, 626 So.2d 608, 617 (Miss. 1993)].

After the party alleging undue influence has proven the existence of a confidential relationship, and other elements of undue influence, the burden of proof will switch to the party defending against the claim. The switch in which party bears the burden of proof is often based on a showing of **suspicious circumstances**. Suspicious circumstances include (1) participation by the donee in the procurement of a gift; (2) lack of independent and disinterested advice to the donor; (3) secrecy and haste in the transfer or gift; (4) change in the donor's attitude toward others; (5) change in the donor's plan of disposing of property; (6) an unjust and unnatural gift; and (7) the donor's susceptibility to influence [*In re Reddaway's Estate*, 214 Or. 410, 329 P2.d 886 (1958); *Van Marter v. Van Marter*, 130 Or. App. 500, 504, 882 P.2d 134 (1994)].

Other suspicious circumstances giving rise to undue influence include (1) secrecy concerning the will's or conveyance's existence; (2) the grantor's advanced age; (3) the lack of independent advice in preparing the conveyance; (4) the grantor's illiteracy or blindness; (5) the unjust or unnatural nature of the conveyance; (6) the grantor being in an emotionally distraught state; (7) discrepancies between the conveyance and the testator's expressed intentions; and (8) fraud or duress directed toward the grantor.

Suspicious circumstances: factors that switch which party bears the burden of proof in a case alleging lack of testamentary capacity

D.   Ethical Considerations

There is a presumption that the attorney-client relationship is a confidential relationship. Because of the nature of the confidential relationship, attorneys are held to a higher standard when it comes to undue influence claims. Accordingly, many courts presume there was undue influence in instances where the attorney drafted the will. See, for example, *Carter v. Williams*, 431 S.E.2d 297 (Va. 1993); *In re Will of Moses*, 227 So.2d 829 (Miss. 1969); *In re Estate of Keeley*, 167 Minn. 120, 208 N.W. 535 (1926); and *In re Estate of Peterson*, 283 Minn. 446, 168 N.W.2d 502 (1969). In Texas, the probate code contains a specific law that causes a bequest to be void that the attorney writes to himself or herself, a parent, employee, or spouse unless the attorney is related to the testator. See, Tex. Prob. Code §58B. Attorneys must be very cautious when preparing any will in which the attorney benefits.

There are often occasions when an attorney is asked if he or she would serve as the client's personal representative. Canon 5-6 of the ABA Code of Professional Responsibility states a lawyer should not consciously influence a client to name him or her as executor, trustee, or lawyer in an instrument. In those cases where a client wishes to name his or her lawyer as such, care should be taken by the lawyer to avoid even the appearance of impropriety. The Code of Professional Responsibility, adopted by the American Bar Association, states that "other than in exceptional circumstances, a lawyer should insist that an instrument in which his client desires to name him beneficially be prepared by another lawyer selected by the client." See, EC 5-5. If a situation arises in which a client wants the attorney to prepare a will in which the attorney is a beneficiary, the attorney should insist that another attorney prepare the document.

E. Case Study

As indicated before, the claims of lack of testamentary capacity and undue influence go hand in hand. The basis of the allegation is often that the testator was in a weakened mental or physical condition, lacked testamentary capacity, and was therefore more susceptible to undue influence. Let us look at a fact pattern that could give rise to a claim of lack of testamentary capacity and undue influence.

A new client, Roger Coven, comes to the office shortly after his mother Edna passed away. Roger has the original will that Edna prepared 12 years ago, after her husband passed away. The will names Roger as the executor or personal representative of the estate and divides Edna's entire estate equally between Roger and his younger brother Roy. Roger indicates that he is concerned because he has seen very little of his mother in the past year and a half. He was previously very close to his mother, spending every holiday with her, serving as her power of attorney and medical directive agent, and keeping in touch with her several times a week by phone. Edna spent time with Roger's family enjoying watching his daughter grow up. Edna had a stroke about two years ago, and during her recovery she became a bit more dependent on Roger.

Roger tells you that about a year and a half ago a man named Steven Varish befriended his mother in a chat room of an Internet gaming site. Edna would spend hours sitting at home playing various card games on the Internet. Varish and Edna began chatting, beyond the typical strategizing needed as teammates. They soon shared their real names instead of their user IDs, and Varish discovered that Edna's maiden name was Varish. Both thought it to be a very unusual last name. They discussed their family histories. Edna told Varish about where she lived and found out he lived nearby. They met in person, becoming "fast friends," with Varish coming to Edna's home several times a week.

One day while visiting his mother, Edna announced to Roger that Steven was her half-brother. She said that after a few weeks of talking about their families, Edna and Steven discovered that they both had a father named Alfred. Even though Steven did not produce a birth certificate, Edna felt that Steven must be telling her the truth. She was overjoyed to find another family member, as her parents divorced when she was young, and she knew very little about her father or her father's family. Soon she began spending all of her time with Varish to the exclusion of her family. Roger was suspicious, but when he questioned his mother about Varish, she became very angry with him. Within a month, Roger found that he could not spend time with his mother without Varish present. When Roger tried to speak to his mother about how much time she was spending with Varish, Edna cut off most communication with him and his brother.

About one year after she met Varish, Edna had a second very serious stroke that left her significantly debilitated. She went to a rehabilitation facility. Roger continued to try to interact with his mother, but she was very distant, claiming that Varish was her only "real" family. While his mother was in the rehabilitation facility, Roger had many conversations with her during which she appeared to be very confused, not remembering who he was or what they were discussing. Three months after the stroke, Edna fell, striking her head severely. She suffered a brain bleed and was in a coma for several days. Varish did not tell Roger his mother was in the hospital or give any information about the fall. Roger went to the rehab facility to visit his mother only to discover she was not there. The staff would not tell him anything about what happened, or even what hospital Edna was in because a new medical directive was on file naming Varish as Edna's agent for medical decisions. Edna did not regain consciousness and died one week after falling. Varish told Roger of his mother's death on the day of the funeral. Roger is concerned because he thinks his mother might have written a new will at the same time she made a new medical directive, which leaves everything to Varish.

What are the immediate concerns? Roger should consider filing a caveat to prevent the probate of any other will. He can also attempt to submit the will he has to probate, because he is unsure if another will exists. A call can be placed to the probate clerk to determine if a will in the Estate of Edna Coven has been probated. If Roger had evidence that a newer will had been prepared, he should not attempt to probate the previous will that he has.

Let us assume for purposes of our example that another will, prepared only a few months ago, has been submitted for probate. Roger obtains a copy of this will, and his worst fears are true: Varish is the sole beneficiary of his mother's estate. Roger and his brother Raymond are not even mentioned in the will. In examining the will, it appears to be some kind of "form" will or will template that can be completed online or purchased in an office supply store.

The elements of undue influence that are already present in the limited fact to this point are the following:

1. Edna is a vulnerable person. She has had a stroke with possible brain damage within the last year.
2. Varish has caused Edna to be isolated from her family, and he is in a position to exert influence on Edna.
3. Varish stands to benefit from the influence he has exerted because he is now the sole beneficiary of Edna's estate.
4. The distribution to Varish is "unnatural" because a testator's children and other family members are the natural beneficiaries.
5. There are suspicious circumstances in Varish's claim to be Edna's half-brother and his failure to tell Roger that Edna was in the hospital.

It appears that Roger has a valid claim against the estate that Edna lacked testamentary capacity and that her will was the product of undue influence. Proving this claim will still require that additional factors be present. Roger and Roy will have to prove that Varish was in a confidential relationship with Edna, thereby being in a position that he could influence Edna, and Edna would listen to his influence. It will be necessary to subpoena Edna's medical records to determine her mental status on the date the will was signed. Even though the will might appear to be a form, it will be necessary to confirm that it was not prepared by an attorney. If the will was prepared by an attorney, the attorney will have to be questioned, provide his or her notes file, and provide any other information about the preparation of the will. If the will was a form, it will be necessary to find out how the form was obtained, how it was completed, who paid for the form if payment was required, and who was present when it was signed.

A sample complaint that would be used to file a claim that the will is void because the testator lacked testamentary capacity and was subject to undue influence is provided in Figure 3-1.

DIANA L. ANDERSON, ESQ.
ID#021251991
CARLUCCIO, LEONE, DIMON,
DOYLE & SACKS, LLC
9 Robbins Street
Toms River, New Jersey 08753
(732) 797-1600
Attorney for Plaintiff

_____

IN THE MATTER OF THE ESTATE   SUPERIOR COURT OF NEW JERSEY
OF EDNA COVEN, Deceased   CHANCERY DIVISION
                                     PROBATE PART
                                     OCEAN COUNTY

                                     DOCKET NO. 2394 - 13

                                          Civil Action

                                       COMPLAINT

_____

    Plaintiff, **ROGER COVEN**, residing at 284 Bradley Court, Toms River, Ocean County, New Jersey 08757 by way of Complaint, says:

Figure 3-1. Sample Complaint

Figure 3-1. Continued

FIRST COUNT—BACKGROUND

1. Plaintiff is the son of the decedent Edna Coven. Plaintiff also has a brother, Raymond Coven

2. Decedent died on September 19, 2013.

3. Defendant, Steven Varish, was unknown to decedent throughout her lifetime. Defendant was introduced to decedent approximately two (2) years prior to her death and previously had no contact with decedent.

4. Decedent enjoyed playing an online bridge game that included an online "chat" room component for discussion among players. While playing an Internet game, decedent was contacted by a player who indicated he had the same last name as her maiden name, and lived in Toms River. A meeting between the decedent and defendant occurred. Defendant did not know decedent prior to this encounter.

5. Defendant now claims to be related to decedent.

6. Defendant has offered no proof of the alleged relationship between him and the decedent.

7. Defendant unduly influenced decedent into executing a new will dated August 16, 2013, a mere three weeks prior to her death in which Defendant was the sole beneficiary of decedent's estate to the exclusion of decedent's son. Decedent lacked testamentary capacity to execute a will.

WHEREFORE, Plaintiff, Roger Coven, demands judgment as follows:

    A. Declaring the Last Will and Testament of Edna Coven dated August 16, 2013, which was submitted for probate null and void and of no force and effect.

    B. Permitting for probate the Last Will and Testament of Edna Coven dated June 24, 2005, and allowing Plaintiff Roger Coven to continue to serve as Executor.

    C. Compelling the Defendant, Steven Varish, to immediately turn over all of the Decedent's possessions, including but not limited to any and all documents, keys, money, bank accounts, personal property, life insurance documents, Deeds, and other possessions.

    D. Prohibiting Defendant Steven Varish from interfering.

    E. Requiring Defendant to provide an accounting of any and all assets.

    F. Granting such other and further relief as the Court may deem just and equitable.

SECOND COUNT—UNDUE INFLUENCE

8. Plaintiff repeats and reiterates the allegations contain in the First Count as if set forth at length herein.

9. From the first meeting between Defendant and decedent, Defendant began unduly influencing decedent, isolating her from her family, and causing disagreements among family members.

10. Decedent became emotionally dependent on Defendant because Defendant prevented decedent from seeing either of her sons.

11. Plaintiff has always maintained a close relationship with his mother. He has cared for decedent, paid bills, helped her to relocate from Florida when her husband died, and assisted her when she went to rehabilitation.

(continued)

Figure 3-1. Continued

Decedent enjoyed time at Plaintiff's home, celebrated all holidays and birthdays with Plaintiff, and spoke on the phone with Plaintiff several times per week.

12. It is generally presumed that the testator was of sound mind and competent when she executed the will, however, decedent's will is tainted by undue influence and is subject to being found void.

13. Defendant subjected decedent to mental, moral, or physical exertion which had destroyed her free agency by preventing the decedent from following the dictates of her own mind and will and accepting instead the domination and influence of Defendant.

14. Defendant and decedent had a confidential relationship whereby Defendant was in a position of trust by reason of the decedent's weakness or dependence on defendant. Defendant isolated decedent from her family, led her to believe he was the only one who cared for her, took over control of her finances, and made decedent dependent on him.

15. There are suspicious circumstances such as Defendant's sudden appearance in decedent's life within two years of her death, his complete isolation of decedent from her family, his failure to notify decedent's son of her hospitalization and her death, which, in combination with the confidential relationship, shift the burden of proof to the Defendant.

WHEREFORE, Plaintiff, Roger Coven, demands judgment as follows:

A. Declaring the Last Will and Testament of Edna Coven dated August 16, 2013, which was submitted for probate null and void and of no force and effect.

B. Permitting for probate the Last Will and Testament of Edna Coven dated June 24, 2005, and allowing Plaintiff Roger Coven to continue to serve as Executor.

C. Compelling the Defendant, Steven Varish, to immediately turn over all of the Decedent's possessions, including but not limited to any and all documents, keys, money, bank accounts, personal property, life insurance documents, Deeds and other possessions.

D. Prohibiting Defendant Steven Varish from interfering.

E. Requiring Defendant to provide an accounting of any and all assets.

F. Granting such other and further relief as the Court may deem just and `equitable.

THIRD COUNT—LACK OF TESTAMENTARY CAPACITY

16. Plaintiff repeats and reiterates the allegations contain in the First Count and Second Count as if set forth at length herein.

17. In February/March 2012, decedent suffered a blood clot in her brain. She was unable to maintain her own finances, and Plaintiff began paying bills and assisting her more. Medical records will indicate that she was incapable of making her own decisions at that time.

18. Decedent went to a rehabilitation facility. She was unable to think clearly and had difficulty with short- and long-term memory. She often called Plaintiff in a confused state, unable to remember the day or time of

Figure 3-1. Continued

She was disoriented and unable to provide for her own care.

19. The legal presumption is that testator was of sound mind and competent when she executed the will. This legal presumption can be overcome in this matter as there is medical evidence that decedent's memory and judgment were impaired, and that she lacked the testamentary capacity necessary to prepare and execute a will after the date of the blood clot.

20. The gauge of testamentary capacity is whether the testator can comprehend the property she is about to dispose; the natural objects of his bounty; the meaning of the business in which she is engaged; the relation of each of these factors to the other; and the manner of distribution that is set forth in the will.

21. Decedent lacked testamentary capacity due to her medical condition and was unduly influenced by Defendant to change her will to only benefit Defendant.

WHEREFORE, Plaintiff, Roger Coven, demands judgment as follows:

A. Declaring the Last Will and Testament of Edna Coven dated August 16, 2013, which was submitted for probate null and void and of no force and effect.

B. Permitting for probate the Last Will and Testament of Edna Coven dated June 24, 2005, and allowing Plaintiff Roger Coven to continue to serve as Executor.

C. Compelling the Defendant, Steven Varish, to immediately turn over all of the Decedent's possessions, including but not limited to any and all documents, keys, money, bank accounts, personal property, life insurance documents, Deeds, and other possessions.

D. Prohibiting Defendant Steven Varish from interfering.

E. Requiring Defendant to provide an accounting of any and all assets.

F. Granting such other and further relief as the Court may deem just and `equitable.

CARLUCCIO, LEONE, DIMON,
DOYLE & SACKS, LLC

DATED:

BY:_____

DIANA L. ANDERSON, ESQ.
Attorney for Plaintiff

The sample complaint in Figure 3-1 is in the format used in the state of New Jersey; however, the elements of alleging undue influence and lack of testamentary capacity are common to many states.

Lack of testamentary capacity and undue influence are claims that arise after the testator has passed away. Facts pertaining to these allegations can be found in the file of the attorney who drafted the will. Careful notes about who made the appointment, who was present at the appointment, the attorney's observations about the client's capacity, and the interaction between the client and other family members who might be present could become evidence in a claim against the will. A paralegal should keep all of the attorney's notes pertaining to a will in the file in case such a claim is made years after the will was prepared.

Summary

Lack of testamentary capacity and undue influence are two challenges that are often alleged in an attempt to invalidate a will. Initially, the burden of proof will be on the party making the allegation, but if suspicious circumstances exist, the burden can switch. The allegation of lack of capacity must pertain to the time the testator made the will, not at the time of death. The challenge to the will is brought to court by filing a complaint to have the will declared invalid.

Review Questions

1. What are the elements of undue influence?

2. What is the difference between case law and statutory law?

3. Who has the burden of proof in a will challenge?

4. How can an attorney determine if a client has testamentary capacity?

5. When does the issue of lack of testamentary capacity arise?

True or False

1. T   F   Anyone can challenge the validity of a will.

2. T   F   A client with Alzheimer's lacks testamentary capacity.

3. T   F   An attorney is presumed to have a confidential relationship with a client.

4. T   F   Suspicious circumstances can shift the burden of proof in a will challenge.

5. T   F   If a testator leaves all of his property to a charity, that could be evidence of lack of testamentary capacity.

Drafting Exercise

Using the form complaint given as an example, and the following fact pattern, compose a draft complaint alleging lack of testamentary capacity and undue influence, and a list of additional information that is needed:

Elizabeth Martin is an 89-year-old widow who lived in New Jersey. Her husband passed away about ten years ago. She has three sons, Christopher, Andrew, and Robert. Christopher and Andrew are married, and each have two children. Christopher is in the Navy, currently stationed in San Diego. Andrew lives in Maryland, but travels extensively for business. Although both Christopher and Andrew live far from their mother, they have always had a good relationship, speaking to the mother several times each month on the phone, and visiting as often as possible. Robert was married but went through a very difficult divorce. Robert has been living in Elizabeth's home for the past two years. Andrew contacted the office because he has just found out that his mother died more than two weeks ago and his brother never told him or Christopher. As you talk more to Andrew, you learn that over the last year, he has been having more and more difficulty with his brother Robert. The issues came to a head at Christmas when Andrew stopped at his mother's house unexpectedly and Robert would not let him in. He says that Robert has been answering the phone and is reluctant to let him speak to his mother, often telling him "Mom does not want to speak to you." When Andrew questioned Robert about his mother's death, the only answer he received was "I did what mom wanted me to do." The first notice he received of his mother's death was a notice of probate filed by his brother, and a copy of his mother's will indicating that Elizabeth had left her estate to Robert. Christopher and Andrew are not even mentioned in the will.

Key Terms

Beyond a reasonable doubt
Burden of proof
Case law
Clear and convincing evidence
Contestant

Preponderance of evidence
Statutory law
Suspicious circumstances
Testamentary capacity
Undue influence

4

Basic Wills

This chapter will provide an overview of each of the sections of a basic will. Some of these sections will be explored in more detail in the following chapters. For now, let us just identify each section of a will, the purpose for the section, and some examples of language that is commonly used. For this chapter, we will be examining the last will and testament of a client, Frank Bryce. Frank is married and has three children. He is a new client who came to the office by way of some Internet advertising. He has never had a will or any other estate-planning documents. We will look at Frank's estate-planning needs and then change the facts to suggest different needs, while providing solutions to how to address those needs.

A.   Clauses in the Will

1.   Preamble

The first section of the will is usually referred to as the **preamble**. It identifies the **testator**, or person who is making the will, and where he lives. Frank is married, and when we write a will for Frank's wife, she will be referred to as the **testatrix**. If the testator is known by more than one name, the alternate names should also be listed in the will with the initials "a.k.a." for also known as, listed before the alternate name. The preamble also acknowledges that the testator intends the document to be his last will and testament, and that by making this will he is revoking all prior wills. The revocation of prior will is important, especially if there are several prior wills.

> **Preamble:** the first section of the will that identifies the testator and states that the testator intends the document to be his last will and testament

> **Testator:** a male who is making a will

> **Testatrix:** a female who is making a will

The language used in the preamble of the will is as follows:

> I, **FRANK BRYCE** of 1313 Main Street, Hangleton, New Jersey, make this as my LAST WILL AND TESTAMENT, and revoke all prior wills and codicils.

The word **codicil** is the term used to describe an amendment to a will. Frank is expressing the intent that this current document is the only document that is his will,

> **Codicil:** an amendment to a will

and if there are any other documents, or amendments to those documents, those should be ignored, and this document should be considered as his will.

If Frank is a nickname for "Francis," then Frank's will should include the following:

> I, **FRANCIS BRYCE (a.k.a. FRANK BRYCE)** *of 1313 Main Street, Hangleton, New Jersey, make this as my LAST WILL AND TESTAMENT, and revoke all prior wills and codicils.*

Practice Tip

If the attorney prepares a lot of wills, the paralegal will be using a combination of forms, wills of previous clients, and new language. Putting the clients' names in capital letter and in bold print will help to ensure that the names are changed for each client. It will help avoid the embarrassing mistake of sending a draft will to a client for review that contains another person's name.

Some older wills contain very elaborate or formal language in the preamble. However, most of the old, formal language has been abandoned in favor of simple, more easily understood language. For example, there are old wills that are drafted on preprinted will paper with engraved calligraphy writing at the top that says, "*Last Will and Testament.*" The will paper is then blank leaving space for the will to be printed in normal text. Using this type of will paper requires inputting the proper settings on the printer to begin the text in the correct location. Many attorneys have abandoned this type of paper and use blank, legal-sized paper. However, many still use a very formal-looking cover page (also known as a backer) for the will such as the preprinted papers shown in Figure 4-1.

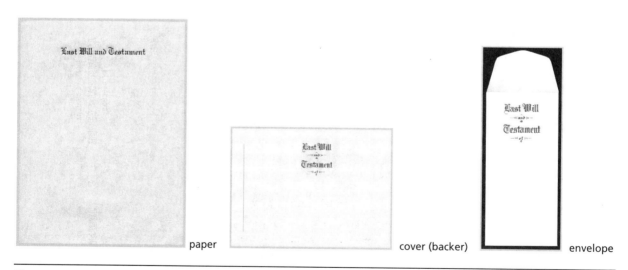

paper   cover (backer)   envelope

Figure 4-1. Preprinted Papers

A video demonstrating how to put the will together, secure the top with staples, fold it, and place it in the envelope can be found on the companion Web site.

A testator can revoke a will by tearing it up, physically destroying it, writing the word "VOID" across it, or disposing of it. Very often, clients keep their old wills, and when they die, there are several versions still around. The most recent will, which includes the phrase, "I am revoking all prior wills," is the only will that is valid.

Practice Tip

Encourage your clients to return the draft versions of the will to your office and have those drafts shredded. Instruct them to destroy their old wills, or to write "void" on the will to avoid confusion as to which will is valid.

In the next section of the will, the testator names each member of his immediate family and identifies his or her relationship to the testator.

2.   Family Members

After the testator is identified, the next person usually identified is the testator's spouse, if the testator is married. Let us add to our facts that Frank's wife is named Ava:

> My spouse's name is **AVA BRYCE**. All references in this will to my "spouse" is to said named spouse.

If Frank's wife had predeceased him, or died before him, that could be referenced in this section as follows:

> My spouse, **AVA BRYCE**, has predeceased me.

Naming the person, and that person's relationship to the testator is important in interpreting and applying the provisions of the will.

Practice Tip

It is not necessary to name a deceased spouse; however, many clients want to have the spouse named in recognition of that person.

If the testator gets divorced, the rights of the ex-spouse will be determined by how the person is identified in the will. In some states, the law treats the ex-spouse as if he or she died before the testator, meaning the ex-spouse is excluded from the will. If the will was drafted after the divorce, and the testator has identified the ex-spouse by name and specifically leaves assets to the ex-spouse, those assets will still pass to the ex-spouse. For example,

> *My ex-spouse's name is **AVA BRYCE**. All references in this will to my "ex-spouse" are to **AVA BRYCE**, and she shall be entitled to all distributions set forth in this will.*

Next, the testator's will identifies the testator's children and lists all of the names of the children. The will must list all of the children, regardless of whether or not every child is receiving a distribution from the will. Because Frank and his wife are somewhat younger, language will be included that the will pertains to all of his current children and any additional children he and his wife may have in the future:

> *I have three (3) children, **JOHN BRYCE, JANE BRYCE, and MARY BRYCE**. All references in my will to my "child" or "children" are to said named child or children and all children born after the date of this will.*

The most easily understood way to identify the children is to list all of the children by name, and then to include language that acknowledges any additional children who are born to the testator after the date of signing the will. Identifying the children in this manner avoids any mistakes that unintentionally leave a child out of the will. Although language regarding children born after the date the will is executed is not always necessary for every client, for some clients it is crucial. Some clients think of the birth of a child or a grandchild as a time to update their estate plan. Unfortunately, many clients do not remember to do so. A well-drafted will provides for the testator's additional children who may be born after the date the will is signed even if the testator forgets to update his will.

If a testator drafts a will intending to leave assets to all of his children and then has another child after the date of the will, the new child will be included in the distribution unless there is a clause specifically excluding any additional children. A person who would have been a beneficiary under a will, but the testator did not know about that person is called a **pretermitted heir**. The most common type of pretermitted heir is a **pretermitted child**, or a child born after the execution of the will.

The identification of family could be done in a much less formal manner such as the following:

> *My family consists of my spouse, **AVA BRYCE**, and my three (3) children, **JOHN BRYCE, JANE BRYCE, and MARY BRYCE**. All references to my "family" should be interpreted to mean only these members of my family.*

What if the testator does not want to leave his estate to all of his children? What if the testator wants to purposefully exclude one child? Excluding one or more children from a will is very common. There are a variety of reasons why a client may want to exclude one or more of his children. One child may have already been given a large sum of money to buy a house or start a business, and the parents want the remainder

Pretermitted heir: a person who would have been a beneficiary under a will, but the testator did not know about that person

Pretermitted child: a child born after the execution of the will of their assets to go to the other children. Or, one child may be financially very well off and the others more in need of funds. It is very often the case that one child is estranged from the family, or the parents may disagree with the way the child is living, or whom the child has married, and as a result the child is excluded from the will. To exclude a child from the will is to **disinherit** that child. The excluded child should still be named in the will regardless of the reasons for the exclusion. A statement should be included explaining that one child is excluded, and possibly provide the reasons why that child is to be excluded. For example,

> I have three (3) children, **JOHN BRYCE, JANE BRYCE, and MARY BRYCE**. *It is my intention to make no provision for my son JOHN BRYCE for reasons known to him. All references in this will to my "child" or "children" are only to my children JANE and MARY BRYCE.*

Including this statement shows that the **scrivener**, or person writing the will, was aware that there were three children and one was purposefully left out. If the excluded child was not listed, an argument could be made that the scrivener simply made a mistake and forgot to list one child. An alternate way to draft this paragraph would be as follows:

> I leave my estate to two (2) of my three (3) living children, **JOHN BRYCE and JANE BRYCE**. *I am excluding my daughter **MARY BRYCE**, and making no provision for her in my will because I have had no contact with her for many years.*

Parents may need to exclude a disabled child who is receiving government benefits because if the child received a distribution from the estate, the benefits might be stopped. In our example, let us assume that Frank's son John is disabled and receiving Medicaid. If John were to get a distribution from the estate, he would no longer be eligible for Medicaid, so Frank and Ava need to leave him out of the will. If that is the reason the child is disinherited, the following language could be used:

> I have three (3) children, **JOHN BRYCE, JANE BRYCE, and MARY BRYCE**. *It is my intention to make no distribution to my son **JOHN BRYCE** that would cause him to be ineligible for any and all governmental benefits.*

Disinherit: to exclude someone from the will

Scrivener: the person who writes the will (usually an attorney) for the testator

Practice Tip

It is always helpful to carefully, and tactfully, question a client about why the client wants to exclude one child and make note of those reasons in the file in case an issue about the will comes up at a later time.

It is interesting to note that while a testator can purposefully exclude a child from the will and can disinherit any one of his children or all of his children, it is not possible to disinherit a spouse. Many clients seek to have a new will prepared because they are separated from their spouse and want to exclude their spouse from their estate. Every state provides for some minimum portion of the estate that will pass to the surviving spouse. It is important to know the specific law in your state as to the minimum share that will be given to a spouse, even if the spouse is excluded from the will. If the will does attempt to disinherit the spouse, the surviving spouse can challenge the will in court and make claim to the allowable share. It is only possible to completely disinherit a spouse if the surviving spouse consents to being left out of the deceased spouse's estate. The document the disinherited spouse needs to sign is called a marital disclaimer. The law pertaining to the spouse's share will be discussed in more detail in Chapter 10.

3. Payment of Estate Debts

The will should contain a paragraph that addresses the payment of all estate debts. Payment of estate debts can include final medical expenses, funeral expenses, attorney's fees, and any expenses incurred in the administration of the estate, such as the executor or personal representative's phone calls to beneficiaries, postage, probate costs, mileage for going to secure the decedent's assets, or any other expense incurred in the administration of the estate.

Sample langauge for the payment of debts is as follows:

> *I direct my executor to pay my funeral expenses, my medical expenses, the costs of administration of my estate, and all of my enforceable debts, other than those secured by property specifically devised under this will, or secured by property passing outside of this will, as my executor, with sole discretion, determines shall be paid.*

Mortgage: a debt secured by real property

Funeral and medical expenses include anything related to the decedent's last illness, and the funeral, including the funeral itself, publishing an obituary, paying for a meal after the funeral, or for any type of religious service in addition to the funeral. Debts that are secured by property are mortgages. A **mortgage** is usually not considered an estate debt because the mortgage will be paid when the property is sold. The testator can specifically state that he wants a piece of real property to pass free and clear of any mortgages, but the assets of the estate are not usually used to pay off a mortgage secured by real property. If the testator wants the mortgage paid off, the following language could be used:

> *I direct my executor to pay my funeral expenses, my medical expenses, the costs of administration of my estate and all of my enforceable debts, including any mortgages or encumbrances secured by real property specifically devised under this will.*

In some states, a paragraph can be included that requires the payment of estate and/or inheritance taxes to be made from estate assets. Estate taxes will be discussed in Chapter 13. Sample language for the payment of taxes includes the following:

I direct that any and all estate, inheritance, or other death taxes due and owing pursuant to the laws of any jurisdiction by reason of my death shall be paid by my estate, without contribution, reimbursement, or apportionment by any beneficiary.

If the will does not specifically direct the payment of estate or inheritance taxes, then each beneficiary is responsible for the taxes due on the monies he or she receives. Who is responsible for the estate taxes can have a big impact on the amount of money each beneficiary receives. Examples of how it can impact each beneficiary are provided in Chapter 13.

4. Personal Memorandum

A will often makes reference to a **personal memorandum** written by the testator. The memorandum gives the testator the opportunity to make distributions of personal property and sentimental items by way of a memorandum written in his or her own handwriting. The memo directs the executor to distribute certain personal items to specific people, but it is only guide for the personal representative to follow. The personal memo is not legally enforceable.

Personal memorandum: a memorandum written by the testator that makes distributions of personal property

The items that are typically included in the memo are items that have more of a sentimental value than a dollar value. For example, the testator may request that his pocket watch be given to his oldest son or a collectible figurine to his granddaughter. The memo should not be used to distribute things that are worth a lot of money, like a car, real property, or very valuable jewelry.

Sample language for such a memorandum can be as follows:

I devise all my personal belongings in accordance with a memorandum which I may have executed. If no such memorandum can be found within 60 days after the probate of the will, my executor named in the will can conclude that no memorandum exists, and shall dispose of all personal items in accordance with this will.

Making reference to a personal memorandum avoids a situation where a testator wants to list every piece of personal property as going to a specific person.

The personal memorandum should not include funeral arrangements. In many jurisdictions, there is a waiting period before the will can be admitted to probate, which can be as long as ten days after the date of death. The funeral arrangements will need to be made immediately, without waiting for the will to be admitted to probate. Many states allow for a separate document to be executed that appoints a funeral representative with the authority to make funeral arrangements. A form of funeral directive can be found on the companion Web site.

5. Bequests

After the memorandum, if one is included, the next series of clauses in the will distribute the decedent's assets. The distribution of assets is accomplished through

Bequest: a provision in the will that directs the distribution of assets to a beneficiary

different types of **bequests**. In the previous chapter, we learned that there are four types of testamentary bequests: *specific, demonstrative, general,* and *residuary*. A *specific bequest* is a specific item or amount of money. Frank, our testator, could specifically bequest an item to his son:

> *I hereby give and bequest my diamond cufflinks to my son, JOHN BRYCE.*

A *demonstrative bequest* is a gift of a certain amount of property from a specific source. For example, Frank could direct that each of his grandchildren be given $10,000 from a specific account:

> *I hereby give and bequest the sum of $10,000 from my Merrill Lynch stock account to each grandchild of mine, born as of the date of my death.*

A *general bequest* is a gift of property payable from any asset in the testator's estate. For example, Frank can make a bequest to each of his grandchildren without specifying the source of the funds:

> *I hereby give and bequest the sum of $10,000 to each grandchild of mine, born as of the date of my death.*

Residuary estate: the amount remaining after payment of estate expenses, taxes, and the specific, demonstrative, and general bequests

Per stirpes: by representation, distribution of a beneficiary's share to the heirs of a beneficiary, if the beneficiary has predeceased the testator

Per capita: a per capita distribution of an estate to the residuary beneficiaries and the heirs of a deceased beneficiary

The final type of bequest is a *residuary bequest*. Residuary bequests distribute the money and assets remaining in the **residuary estate**, which is the amount remaining after payment of estate expenses, taxes, and the specific, demonstrative, and general bequests.

The distribution to the residuary beneficiaries can be either **per stirpes**, or **per capita**. A *per stirpes* distribution means by representation, so that if any one of the residuary beneficiaries predeceases (or dies before) the testator, then that residuary beneficiary's share goes to his or her heirs. A *per capita* distribution means that the distribution is made to each issue or child of the deceased heir. *Per capita* is also known as by representation. For example,

> *I bequest the residuary amounts in my estate to my three children **JOHN BRYCE, JANE BRYCE, and MARY BRYCE** in equal shares, share and share alike, per stirpes.*

If John dies before his father, John's share of his father's estate goes to John's children. For purposes of this example, let us assume John has three children. John's children will divide John's one-third of the residuary estate. Jane and Mary will still each receive one-third of the residuary estate (Figure 4-2).

If the distribution were to be made per capita, the result would be much different:

> *I bequest the residuary amounts in my estate to my three children **JOHN BRYCE, JANE BRYCE, and MARY BRYCE** in equal shares, share and share alike, per capita.*

Figure 4-2. Example of *Per Stirpes* Distribution to Residuary Beneficiaries

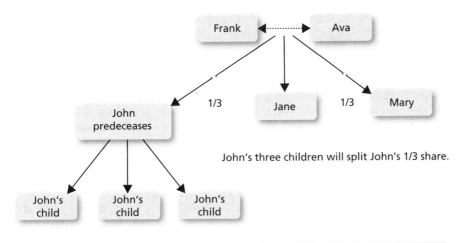

John's three children will split John's 1/3 share.

Let us assume John has three children of his own, and that John dies before his father. Using the per capita distribution scheme, each of John's three children gets his or her own share of the estate, along with Jane and Mary. Instead of the residuary estate being divided into three equal parts, the estate will be divided into five shares: one share for each one of John's three children, one share for Jane, and one share for Mary. Each of the residuary beneficiaries will receive one-fifth of Frank's estate.

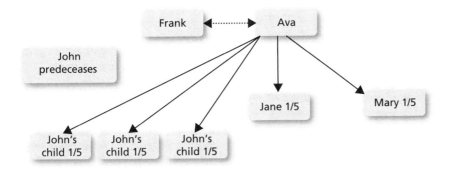

Figure 4-3. Example of *Per Capita* Distribution to Residuary Beneficiaries

In a per capita distribution, it is as if John's children move up one generation and take John's place, causing the distribution to be recalculated to one-fifth for each beneficiary. Most states have a default provision that will govern the method of distribution if the will does not state "per stirpes" or "per capita" (or by representation).

The residuary bequest is very important. If the testator's will contains specific bequests and then does not provide for the distribution of the remainder of the estate, the executor may also have to do an intestate administration. For example, let us assume Frank and Ava prepared detailed wills. Frank dies, and some years after his death, Ava goes to another attorney to have a new will prepared. The other attorney prepares a will that makes specific bequests of $20,000 to each child and grandchild. At the time of her death, Ava has three children and six grandchildren who will receive a total of $180,000. After distributing the $180,000 the executor has no direction as to the distribution of the remainder of Ava's estate and must distribute the estate in accordance with the intestate laws of the state.

6.   Fiduciary Appointments

Fiduciary: someone who is responsible for the property or assets of another person

Executor: the fiduciary appointed in a will who is responsible for marshaling, or gathering, the decedent's assets, paying all of the decedent's debts, and then distributing the assets to the beneficiaries named in the will

A **fiduciary** is someone who is responsible for the property or assets of another person. The fiduciary has a responsibility to invest assets prudently or hold the assets for the benefit of another person. The fiduciary must at all times act in the sole interest of the person for whom the assets are held. The **executor** is a fiduciary appointed in a will and is responsible for marshaling, or gathering, the decedent's assets, paying all of the decedent's debts, and then distributing the assets to the beneficiaries named in the will. A will usually names a second executor in case the first one cannot serve or declines to serve. Sample language for the appointment of an executor and a substitute executor is as follows:

> *I appoint my wife, **AVA BRYCE**, to be executor of my will. If **AVA BRYCE** should fail to qualify or otherwise cease to act as executor, then I appoint my son, **JOHN BRYCE**.*

If Ava is unable or unwilling to serve, for any reason, then John, the substitute executor, can serve. If both Ava and John cannot or will not serve as executor, then a court procedure to appoint another fiduciary for the estate will be required. A fiduciary for an estate that is appointed by the court is called an *administrator*. The various aspects of administration of the estate will be discussed in Chapter 10. Frank can also appoint co-executors:

> *I appoint my wife, **AVA BRYCE**, and my son, **JOHN BRYCE**, to be co-executors of my will. If either of them should predecease me, or fail to qualify or otherwise cease to act as executor, then either one of them shall continue to serve as the sole executor.*
> *— OR —*
> *I appoint my wife, **AVA BRYCE**, and my son, **JOHN BRYCE**, to be co-executors of my will. If either of them should predecease me, or fail to qualify or otherwise cease to act as executor, then I appoint my daughter, **JANE BRYCE**, to serve in place of either of them.*
> *— OR —*

*I appoint my wife, **AVA BRYCE**, to be executor of my will. If **AVA BRYCE** should fail to qualify or otherwise cease to act as executor, then I appoint my son, **JOHN BRYCE**, and my daughter, **JANE BRYCE**, to serve as co-executors.*

Practice Tip

It is often very difficult for two people to serve as co-executors because both executors have to be able to work together and do all of the tasks necessary together. Encourage clients to list multiple executors and backup executors but no co-executors.

The executor, or administrator, is entitled to be paid a fee, called a **commission**, which is based on the total value of the estate. The *commission* is an estate expense. The testator can also specify that the executor is to serve without compensation:

*I appoint my wife, **AVA BRYCE**, to be executor of my will. If **AVA BRYCE** should fail to qualify or otherwise cease to act as executor, then I appoint my son, **JOHN BRYCE**. My executor or substitute executor shall serve without compensation.*

Many clients feel that having the executor serve without compensation, especially if the executor is one of the children, keeps the distribution of the estate equal.

Commission: a fee paid to the executor or administrator; based on the total value of the estate; an estate expense

7.   Creation of a Trust

Sometimes a testator requests that the assets given to a beneficiary be held in trust. A **trust** is a type of legal document that establishes rules for the use of funds and protects those funds. A trust can be used when the beneficiary is too young to receive the funds, or if the testator feels that the beneficiary will spend the funds too quickly. The creation of a trust, and the different types of trusts, will be discussed in Chapter 6. Creation of a trust can be as simple as designating that the assets be held in trust as follows:

Trust: a legal document that establishes the rules for the use of funds

*I hereby bequest all the rest and residue of my estate to my children, **JOHN BRYCE, JANE BRYCE, and MARY BRYCE**, in equal shares, share and share alike, with the share going to **MARY BRYCE**, to be held in trust until her 21st birthday.*

If the will requires that any of the assets be placed into trust, then the testator also needs to put language in the will appointing a **trustee** and a substitute trustee. A *trustee* is a fiduciary who is responsible for the assets held in trust. Sample language for the appointment of a trustee is similar to that for appointment of an executor:

Trustee: an individual or institution named that is given control of assets to be used for the benefit of another person

*I appoint my sister, **SALLY SMITH**, to be the trustee of any trust formed pursuant to my will. If **SALLY SMITH** should fail to qualify or otherwise cease to act as trustee, then I appoint my brother-in-law, **SAMUEL SMITH**.*

In this example, an assumption is made that the only reason a trustee would be necessary is if both Frank and Ava have passed away, leaving assets to Mary, who is under age 21. Frank is naming someone other than his spouse Ava to serve as a trustee because the trust will only be formed if Ava has predeceased him. The trustee will control Mary's share of the estate until Mary has reached the age of 21. If the original trustee cannot or will not serve, for any reason, the substitute trustee can serve. If the substitute trustee cannot or will not serve, the appointment of another trustee is usually provided for in the trust document itself.

8.   Appointing a Guardian

Guardian: someone who is legally responsible for the person and property of a minor or an incapacitated adult

If Frank and Ava's children are minors, they will want to appoint a **guardian** for the children. A guardian is someone who is responsible for the person and property of a minor child or someone who is incapacitated. If the guardian is also in control of a minor child's assets, then the guardian is also a fiduciary.

> *I appoint my sister,* **SALLY SMITH**, *to be the Guardian of the person and property of my minor children. If* **SALLY SMITH** *should fail to qualify or otherwise cease to act as Guardian, then I appoint my brother-in-law,* **SAMUEL SMITH**.

Choosing a guardian can be one of the most difficult decisions a testator can make and is very often one of the decisions that is later changed as the minor child gets older. Parents often choose a husband and wife, and later find that the couple they have chosen as guardians has gotten divorced, thereby necessitating a change in the will to name new guardians. It is also common that parents will name an older child as a guardian for the younger children:

> *I appoint my sister,* **SALLY SMITH**, *and my brother-in-law,* **SAMUEL SMITH**, *to be the Co-Guardians of the person and property of daughter* **MARY BRYCE**. *If either* **SALLY SMITH** *or* **SAMUEL SMITH** *should fail to qualify or otherwise cease to act as Guardian, then I appoint my son,* **JOHN BRYCE**, *to serve in their place.*

It is not necessary to change a will simply because a minor child is now an adult. If a will names a guardian, and the child has already reached the age of majority, that portion of the will is not enforced.

9.   Choosing Fiduciaries

A testator will occasionally be unsure whom to appoint for each of the fiduciary roles. He may not have close family members or does not trust the family members he does have. Parents may be concerned about choosing one child over another and of potentially causing conflicts among the beneficiaries. Many testators will require assistance in making their choice. It can be helpful to ask the testator to consider where each person lives, what the children do for a living, if one child has more time to complete the tasks than another child, and so forth. Is there one child who has a knack for details? Does a child have time constraints or travel a lot for business? Is there anything that would make it difficult for one child or another to attend to the duties of an executor? These are all questions to ask to assist the testator in choosing the fiduciaries needed in the will.

Some parents automatically choose the oldest child, while others choose the child who lives in the same state. There is no "right" or "wrong" choice. If the person doing the will has young children, there can be a conflict between whether the mother's family or the father's family is chosen as the guardian. Consideration also has to be given to the age of the person chosen as the guardian and the age of the children. Choosing a grandparent as a guardian may not always be the best choice based on the age of the child and the age of the grandparent.

Not only does the testator have to potentially choose three fiduciaries, one each for the executor, trustee, and guardian, the testator could potentially have to choose six fiduciaries, in case any one of the three original fiduciaries cannot serve. It is not necessary, however, to choose different people for each role. One person can serve in all three roles. One person can serve as both the trustee and guardian, with a different person serving as the executor. There can be different combinations and different people serving in different roles.

The testator can also choose to appoint someone as a **co-fiduciary**, or two people to serve together. The testator can choose co-executors, co-trustees, and co-guardians. Any position for which a co-fiduciary is appointed requires the cooperation of both people appointed. This forced cooperation can be problematic if the two co-fiduciaries cannot get along or disagree over how things should be handled. For that reason, a co-fiduciary arrangement should be used only when the testator can say with certainty that the two people appointed can cooperate with each other.

Co-fiduciary: two people to serve together in being responsible for the property or assets of another person

A testator can also choose a professional, such as an attorney, or an institution, such as a bank, to serve as the executor and/or trustee. Often, an elderly testator who does not have any close family will ask the attorney to serve as his executor. Most states allow the attorney to serve as executor if the attorney has had a signficant attorney-client relationship with the testator. An attorney should not, under any circumstances, write a will in which the attorney is a beneficiary of the estate. This is a conflict of interest and would be considered an ethical violation and must be avoided. If a testator is a family member and is insistent on leaving a bequest to the attorney, then the attorney should refer the testator to another attorney.

10. Bond

The will can require that any fiduciary appointed under the will is required to obtain a **surety bond**. This is a special type of insurance policy that insures the proper performance of the duties of the fiduciary. The amount of the bond is determined by the amount of funds that are under the control of the fiduciary. If the executor misappropriates or steals the money in the estate, the surety bond will be available to pay the beneficiaries. The company that issued the bond will seek contribution from the executor.

Surety bond: a type of insurance that will protect an asset if a fiduciary fails to fufill his or her fiduciary duty

Many testators choose to waive the bond requirement if the executor of the estate is also a beneficiary of the estate, because the executor is actually responsible for what will become his or her own money. However, if the executor is a family friend and is not one of the beneficiaries, a testator can require the bond to insure that the estate is handled properly. Sample language that waives the bond requirement is as follows:

No executor or trustee or substitute executor or substitute trustee shall be required to furnish bond or other security in any jurisdiction.

In the absence of this language, the fiduciary will be required to obtain a bond.

Practice Tip

It is helpful to have the contact information for several surety companies available to provide to the client. Surety companies offer different rates, so it will be necessary to shop around for the best price.

---

11.   Simultaneous Death

Reciprocal will: a will in which each spouse leaves his or her assets to the surviving spouse

One of the last provisions of the will is language addressing the distribution of an estate in the event of the simultaneous death of both a husband and wife. Many married couples own property and assets jointly, so that if one passes away, the surviving spouse inherits the property or assets. What happens to joint assets if both spouses die at the same time, or under circumstances where it cannot be determined who died first? Or what if the wills are reciprocal and both spouses die at the same time? A **reciprocal will** is one in which each spouse leaves his or her assets to the surviving spouse. The husband leaves his estate to his wife, and the wife leaves her estate to her husband. If both spouses have passed away, what happens to the assets?

Survival presumption clause: a clause used in a reciprocal will that establishes a presumption that one spouse died first and the other survived, even if it is not possible to determine which spouse died first

Many states have adopted the Uniform Simultaneous Death Act to address this problem. The law states that each spouse will be treated as though he or she predeceased the other if they die within 120 hours of one another, unless a specific clause in the will deals with this particular possibility. The clause that addresses the simultaneous death of both spouses is called the **survival presumption clause** or simultaneous death clause. This clause establishes a presumption that one spouse died first and the other survived, even if it is not possible to determine which spouse died first. If, as the result of an accident, for example, a husband and wife die together, the survival presumption clause will govern to determine who died first. In our example, if Frank and Ava died in a plane crash at the same time, their combined estate may be impossible to administer without a survival presumption clause. Sample language to be used in one will is the following:

If my spouse and I shall die simultaneously, or under circumstances that make it impossible to determine the order of death, then my spouse shall be deemed to have survived me.

This clause would be inserted in one spouse's will, and the opposite presumption would be inserted into the other spouse's will.

If my spouse and I shall die simultaneously, or under circumstances that make it impossible to determine the order of death, then my spouse shall be deemed to have predeceased me.

It is critical that one will contain a survival presumption, and the other will contain a presumption that the party predeceased, and that no mistake is made and the same clause inserted into both wills. With the proper survival presumption, even if both parties die simultaneously, the law will allow a presumption that one spouse died, leaving his or her assets to the surviving spouse, and then the will of the surviving spouse can be used to administer both estates.

Deaths may be treated as simultaneous under the law even when one spouse dies within five days after the other one if both died due to a common accident. Some states have modified the Act and require the surviving spouse to survive for 120 hours or be deemed to have predeceased. Under no circumstances can a husband and wife have only one will. Each person needs his or her own will.

12. In Terrorem Clauses

A clause in a will threatening to disinherit anyone who challenges the will is called an **in terrorem**, or no contest, clause. In general, an *in terrorem* clause threatens that if any beneficiary challenges the will, then that beneficiary will receive nothing from the estate, or instead will receive only one dollar. Only a few states recognize and enforce *in terrorem* clauses. Most states do not recognize an *in terrorem* clause, and if such a clause is included in the will, the clause is declared "null" and void, and given no effect. Even in states that recognize an *in terrorem* clause, the clause does not always operate the way a testator may have intended. If a beneficiary successfully challenges the will, the will might be found to be invalid. If the whole will is invalid, then the *in terrorem* clause is also invalid.

In terrorem clause: a clause in a will threatening to disinherit anyone who challenges the will

13. Precatory Language

A testator may want to direct how the assets in his estate are used by the beneficiaries. For example, Frank Bryce could leave his son John $50,000 and state that the money is to be used to buy a house. The will could state the following:

> *I hereby give the sum of fifty thousand dollars ($50,000) to my son **JOHN BRYCE** so that he can use it as a down payment to buy a house.*

The langauge in the will stating that the money is to be used as a down payment on a house is interpreted as a hope or wish but is not a specific direction from the testator. This type of langauge is known as **precatory language**. *Precatory language* in a will is usually interpreted as something the testator would like to occur but is not enforceable. If the client is insistent that the suggestion be followed, the bequest should be placed into a trust that can more tightly control the use of the funds.

Precatory language: usually interpreted as something the testator would like to occur but is not enforceable

Practice Tip

Clients very often want precatory language in the will, and it is perfectly fine to put any such suggestion or hope for use of the assets into the will with the bequest. The client should be cautioned that the executor has no authority to enforece such a provision.

B. Executing the Will

Executing the will: the process of signing and witnessing the signature of the will

Each state has specific requirements that have to be followed as to the proper way that a will has to be signed and who must witness the signature. The process of signing and witnessing the signature of the will is called **executing the will**. Failure to follow the specific state requirements for executing the will can result in the will being ruled invalid or having to take extra steps in order to be able to use the will.

Typically a will needs to be signed by the testator, and two witnesses need to be present to watch the testator sign the will. Sample language for the signature portion of the will is as follows:

IN WITNESS WHEREOF, I subscribe my name this _____ day of _____, 201___.

_____

FRANK BRYCE

Practice Tip

The pages of a will should be adjusted so that the testator's signature line appears on the same page as the statement above. For example, do not allow the page break to be located in such a way that a page contains only the testator's signature without the additional langauge.

The will must have a statement that is signed by the witnesses indicating that they have identified the testator, that the testator is a competent adult, and that they saw the testator sign the will. Sample language for the statement of the witnesses is as follows:

SIGNED, SEALED, PUBLISHED, and DECLARED by the Testator to be his Last Will and Testament, in our presence and in the presence of each of us, we all being present at the same time; and we, at his request, in his presence, and in the presence of each other, have hereunto signed our names as attesting witnesses.

_____*residing at*_____
Witness

_____*residing at*_____
Witness

Some states require two witnesses, and some states require three witnesses. Many attorneys now routinely include three witness signatures, even if the state in which they practice requires only two, in order to make sure the will is more acceptable in another state.

Many states allow for a **self-proving affidavit** to be part of the will. A *self-proving affidavit* is signed by a notary, and it attests to the fact that the witnesses were present and the will was properly signed by the testator. (See also UPC §2-504.) Without a self-proving affidavit, it may be necessary to find the witnesses after the testator dies in order to prove the validity of the witnesses' signatures.

A sample of the language of a self-proving affidavit is as follows.

Self-proving affidavit: a section of the will that is signed by a notary, attesting to the fact that the witnesses were present when the will was signed by the testator

STATE OF _____)

*   ) SS.*

COUNTY OF _____)

*   I, FRANK BRYCE, the Testator, sign my name to this instrument this _____ day of _____, 201___, and being first duly sworn, do hereby declare to the undersigned authority that I sign and execute this instrument as my Last Will and Testament and that I sign it willingly, and that I execute it as my free and voluntary act for the purposes therein expressed, and that I am 18 years of age or older, of sound mind, and under no constraint or undue influence.*

_____

FRANK BRYCE
*   Subscribed, sworn to, and acknowledged before me by **FRANK BRYCE** the Testator, and subscribed and sworn to before me by _____ and _____ , witnesses, this _____ day of _____ , 201___ .*

_____

NOTARY PUBLIC (or Attorney)

It is always necessary to follow the formalities of the state in which the estate is located for signing the will in order to complete the document.

Practice Tip

Although it is not necessary, it is good practice to have the testator sign or initial the bottom or side of each page of the will. This prevents someone from changing one of the pages and is an acknowledgment by the testator that he has read each page of the will. A signature on the bottom of a page can prevent a challenge to a will after the testator has passed away.

There will be circumstances in which a testator cannot physically sign his name on the document. This can occur for many reasons, such as illness, injury, or paralysis. If the testator cannot sign his name but can only make a mark for a signature, a specific type of notary statement is needed, such as the following:

STATE OF _____)

                        ss:

COUNTY OF _____)

         BE IT REMEMBERED *that on this _____ day of _____, 201___, before me, the subscribed, a Notary Public of the State of _____, personally appeared FRANK BRYCE, who I am satisfied is the person mentioned in the within document, and I having first made known to him the contents thereof, he did place his mark upon this document, intending to give legal effect to same, and did acknowledge that he signed, sealed, and delivered the same as and for his voluntary act and deed for the uses and purposes therein expressed.*

                                                        _____

                                                               NOTARY PUBLIC

If a will is to be signed with a mark instead of a full signature, it is important to keep additional notes regarding the testator's competency, that the full contents of the will were read to him, that he understood the contents of the will, and that he verbally acknowledged that he wished the document to serve as his last will and testament.

If the attorney does a lot of estate planning, or considers it his or her specialty, the paralegal will find it necessary to schedule documents signings outside of the office. Will signings may need to take place in the client's home, hospital room, rehabilitation facility, or another location other than the attorney's office because of the client's health.

Practice Tip

Whenever a document signing occurs outside of the office, prepare and take a second set of documents in case there is an error in signing or the document gets damaged. Having the second set available for when a problem inevitably occurs will save a lot of frustration in getting the client's signature.

C.   Changing the Will

Codicil: an amendment to a will

An amendment to a will is known as a **codicil**. A codicil is a separate document attached to the will that changes some provision in the will. Any changes made to the will by way of a codicil must be signed and witnessed in the same specific way that the will is signed. Many attorneys (the author included) do not usually prepare codicils. With the availability of word-processing software, if the attorney has prepared the will, the attorney can simply insert the new language into the existing will and reprint the entire document, instead of preparing an amendment that is attached to the will. If the attorney did not prepare the will, the attorney may opt to prepare a separate codicil to avoid having the paralegal re-type the entire will.

A codicil must reference the date on which the original will was signed and the portion of the will that is being amended. For example, Frank Bryce included the following paragraph in his will appointing a guardian:

I appoint my sister, SALLY SMITH, to be the Guardian of the person and property of my minor children. If SALLY SMITH should fail to qualify or otherwise cease to act as Guardian, then I appoint my brother-in-law, SAMUEL SMITH.

Two years after the will is executed, Sally and Samuel get divorced. Frank wants to amend his will. The amendment, or codicil, is going to state the following:

CODICIL

This codicil is made to the Last Will and Testament of Frank Bryce dated August 18, 2012, to amend paragraph four, wherein the guardians were appointed, to delete same in its entirety and replace with the following:

I appoint my sister, SALLY SMITH, to be the Guardian of the person and property of my minor children. If SALLY SMITH should fail to qualify or otherwise cease to act as Guardian, then I appoint my brother, THOMAS BRYCE.

STATE OF _____)

) SS.

COUNTY OF _____)

I, FRANK BRYCE, the Testator, sign my name to this instrument this _____ day of _____, 201___, and being first duly sworn, do hereby declare to the undersigned authority that I sign and execute this instrument as my Last Will and Testament and that I sign it willingly, and that I execute it as my free and voluntary act for the purposes therein expressed, and that I am 18 years of age or older, of sound mind and under no constraint or undue influence.

_____
FRANK BRYCE

*Subscribed, sworn to, and acknowledged before me by **FRANK BRYCE** the Testator, and subscribed and sworn to before me by _____ and _____,
witnesses, this _____ day of _____, 201___.*

_____
NOTARY PUBLIC (or Attorney)

The codicil should be kept with the original will. The danger of codicils is that they could get separated from the original will, and then any changes intended by the testator are not followed. The codicil may also be purposefully ignored, especially if the executor does not like the contents of the codicil. For example, Frank gets into an argument with his daughter Jane and writes a codicil disinheriting Jane. The executor of Frank's estate finds the will and codicil after Frank's death but feels it is not right that Frank felt that way about Jane and destroys the codicil. If no one knew about the existence of the codicil, the will could be probated without it, and Jane would take her inheritance.

A testator may also inadvertently cause an amendment to the will by selling or otherwise disposing of an asset that is listed in the will. For example, the will might state the following:

> *I hereby bequeath and bequest my home located at 123 Main Street, Hangleton, New Jersey, to my son JOHN BRYCE.*

If the testator sells that particular piece of property, then John Bryce does not receive that piece of property. In some state, John may not even receive the money that Frank received when that piece of property was sold. In other states, John would be entitled to the remainder of the proceeds of the property that was sold.

If the property is sold by the testator prior to death and is therefore not owned by the testator as of the date of death, it is called **ademption by extinction**. If the testator gives the beneficiary the asset prior to death, then it is referred to as **ademption by satisfaction**. In our example, Frank may decide to give John the house. Frank does not change his will. When Frank dies, the gift of the house is deemed to satisfy the bequest of the house in the will. This is ademption by satisfaction.

A testator may also change the ownership of assets so that the assets do not pass through the will. A testator might also not understand how joint ownership can affect assets that would otherwise pass to his heirs. As discussed in Chapter 2, assets that are owned jointly with others sometimes pass to the surviving owner. If the form of ownership gives each owner a right of survivorship, and one owner dies, the deceased owner's share passes to the surviving owners. Any asset that is owned jointly, with right of survivorship, does not pass through the estate and is not controlled by the will. Clients may sometimes find it convenient to put one of their children's names on an account so that someone else can access the account without realizing how that ownership affects the estate.

Ademption by extinction: property is sold by the testator prior to death and is therefore not owned by the testator as of the date of death

Ademption by satisfaction: the testator has already given the beneficiary the asset prior to death

D. Revocation of the Will

As discussed previously, a will can be revoked by physically destroying the will, tearing it in half, burning it, or destroying it. Writing the word "revoked" or "void" on the will can also revoke a will. A will can also be revoked by the execution of a new will. In some states, writing anything on the will can cause the will to be considered revoked or deemed to be rendered void. It is not uncommon for a client to attempt to "correct" a will by manually writing on the original. For example, a testator may write in the name of a new grandchild, or change the last name of his daughter when she gets married. Any of these handwritten additions to a will could be good intentioned but could result in the whole will being found invalid. It is important to remind clients not to write on the original will.

Practice Tip

The original last will and testament should be folded and placed inside of a will envelope, if the attorney uses those. The client should be provided with a copy, along with the reminder to make any notes on the copy, but never the original.

A complete simple will that would be created from the facts set forth in this chapter, using the sample language described would be the following:

I, **FRANK BRYCE**, *of 1313 Main Street, Hangleton, New Jersey, make this my LAST WILL AND TESTAMENT and revoke all prior wills and Codicil.*

My spouse's name is **AVA BRYCE**. *All references in this will to my "spouse" are to said named spouse. I have three (3) children,* **JOHN BRYCE, JANE BRYCE, and MARY BRYCE**. *All references in this will to my "child" or "children" are to said named child or children, and all children hereafter born.*

I direct my executor to pay my funeral expenses, my medical expenses, the costs of administration of my estate and all of my enforceable debts, other than those secured by property specifically devised under this will, or secured by property passing outside of this will, as my executor, with sole discretion, determines shall be paid.

I direct that any and all estate, inheritance, or other death taxes due and owing pursuant to the laws of any jurisdiction by reason of my death, shall be paid by my estate, without contribution, reimbursement, or apportionment by any beneficiary.

I devise all my personal belongings in accordance with a memorandum which I may have executed and which is in existence at the time of my death. If no such memorandum can be found within 60 days after the probate of the will, my executor named in the will can conclude that no memorandum exists, and shall dispose of all personal items in accordance with this will.

I hereby make the following bequests:

1. *The sum of ten thousand dollars ($10,000) to the Boy Scouts of America*
2. *The sum of ten thousand dollars ($10,000) to the American Cancer Society*
3. *The sum of ten thousand dollars ($10,000) to my alma mater*

I bequest my residuary estate to my wife **AVA BRYCE**. *If my wife* **AVA BRYCE** *shall predecease me, I give, devise, and bequest my residuary estate to my three children in equal shares, share and share alike.*

*I appoint my wife, **AVA BRYCE**, to be executor of my will. If **AVA BRYCE** should fail to qualify or otherwise cease to act as executor, then I appoint my son, **JOHN BRYCE**.*

*I appoint my sister, **SALLY SMITH**, to be the trustee of any trust formed pursuant to my will. If **SALLY SMITH** should fail to qualify or otherwise cease to act as trustee, then I appoint my son, **JOHN BRYCE**.*

*I appoint my sister, **SALLY SMITH**, to be the Guardian of the person and property of my minor children. If **SALLY SMITH** should fail to qualify or otherwise cease to act as Guardian, then I appoint my brother-in-law, **SAMUEL SMITH**.*

No executor or trustee or substitute executor or substitute trustee shall be required to furnish bond or other security in any jurisdiction.

If my spouse and I shall die simultaneously, or under circumstances that make it impossible to determine the order of death, then my spouse shall be deemed to have survived me.

IN WITNESS WHEREOF, I subscribe my name this _____ day of _____, 201___.

_____

FRANK BRYCE

SIGNED, SEALED, PUBLISHED, and DECLARED by the Testator to be his Last Will and Testament, in our presence and in the presence of each of us, we all being present at the same time; and we, at his request, in his presence, and in the presence of each other, have hereunto signed our names as attesting witnesses.

_____*residing at*_____

Witness

_____*residing at*_____

Witness

STATE OF _____)

) *SS.*

COUNTY OF _____)

I, FRANK BRYCE, the Testator, sign my name to this instrument this _____ day of _____, 201___, and being first duly sworn, do hereby declare that I sign and execute this instrument as my Last Will and Testament, and that I sign it willingly, and that I execute it as my free and voluntary act for the purposes therein expressed, and that I am 18 years of age or older, of sound mind, and under no constraint or undue influence.

_____

FRANK BRYCE

Subscribed, sworn to, and acknowledged before me by **FRANK BRYCE** *the Testator, and subscribed and sworn to before me by* _____ *and* _____, *witnesses, this* _____ *day of* _____, *201___.*

_____
NOTARY PUBLIC (or Attorney)

Summary

Each clause in a last will and testament plays an important role in recording and effectuating a client's estate plan. There are clauses to identify family, beneficiaries, payment of debts, distribution of the estate, and so on. It is important to pay attention to details such as the spelling of each beneficiary's name and the percentage of the distribution. It is also important to become familiar with state requirements for making a will self-proving and to follow those requirements carefully.

Review Questions

1. James and Mary Bryce want to draft new wills. They have four children but do not speak to their son. They want to leave him out of the will. Can they do that? If "yes," what language would be used ? If "no," why not?

2. How is a prior will revoked?

3. What is paid first — a specific bequest or a residuary bequest?

4. Can a husband and wife draft one will that disposes of their combined estate?

True or False

1. T   F   A will does not need to be witnessed.

2. T   F   Per stirpes is another term for per capita.

3. T   F   *In terrorem* clauses are generally disregarded.

4. T   F   Witnesses cannot be interested parties.

5. T   F   The testator can disinherit his children.

Drafting Exercises

In this chapter, we prepared simple wills for clients Frank and Ava Bryce. Use Frank and Ava as examples for the following different facts:

1. Draft a paragraph identifying family members for Frank if Ava predeceased him.

2. Draft a paragraph identifying family members if Frank was unmarried and had no children.

3. Draft a paragraph identifying family members for Frank if he and Ava had no children.

4. Draft a paragraph identifying family members for Frank if he is married to Ava. They have three children: Frank has one child from a first marriage and has adopted Ava's two children.

5. Draft a paragraph identifying family members if Frank and Ava are married with three children but one child has predeceased them, leaving a grandchild whom Frank and Ava are raising.

6. Draft a specific bequest for Frank leaving his car to his son John.

7. Draft specific bequests for Frank leaving $1,000 each to the Juvenile Diabetes Funds, Rutgers University, and his church, Hangleton Church.

8. Draft a residuary bequest for Frank if Ava has already predeceased him.

9. Draft a residuary bequest for Frank so that the residue of the estate goes to Ava, and if Ava predeceases him, to his three children.

10. Draft a residuary bequest for Frank so that the residue of the estate goes to Ava, and if Ava predeceases him, to his daughter, but not to his son John, because Frank is disinheriting John.

11. Draft a residuary bequest for Frank so that the residue of the estate goes to Ava, and if Ava predeceases him, to his three children or to the survivor among them.

12. Draft the appointment of an executor if Frank wants his wife and son to serve as co-executors.

13. Draft the appointment of an executor if Ava has predeceased Frank and Frank wants all of his kids named as substitute executors.

14. Frank and Ava have been separate for many years but have never been divorced. Frank wants to leave Ava nothing, but he knows he cannot disinherit his spouse. Draft a sample paragraph leaving Ava only the elective (or marital) share.

Will Signing Checklist

1. Ask the testator to review the will and be sure he understands the document, and that the will has been done the way he instructed.

2. Get two competent adults to serve as witnesses. If the witnesses are people obtained by the testator, ask the witnesses if they are related to the testator. If they are, determine if they are beneficiaries of the testator's estate.

3. Get a notary public or an attorney to sign the self-proving affidavit of the witnesses after the will has been signed. All parties, the two witnesses, the notary, and the testator must be present when the testator signs the will.

4. Have the testator sign the bottom of each page of the will. This serves two purposes: It acknowledges that the testator has read each page, and it prevents someone from tampering with the will by drafting a new page and inserting it into the will.

5. Have the testator sign and date the will on the last page in each place, where indicated.

6. Ask the witnesses to sign the will where indicated.

7. The notary or attorney completes and signs the self-proving affidavit.

8. Make copies of the will for the client.

9. Instruct the client not to write on the original of the will, because in many states, writing on the will causes it to become invalid.

10. If the client is taking the original will, mark on the file that the client has taken the original. If the attorney is going to retain the original, store the original file where the attorney stores all original documents, and record that the Bryce will is stored with the attorney. Mark the copies of the will given to the client with a stamp indicating that the attorney retained the original, or write those words on the copy.

Key Terms

Ademption by extinction	Executing the will
Ademption by satisfaction	Executor
Bequest	Fiduciary
Codicil	Guardian
Co-fiduciary	In terrorem clause
Commission	Mortgage
Disinherit	Per capita

Personal memorandum

Per stirpes

Preamble

Precatory language

Pretermitted child

Pretermitted heir

Reciprocal will

Residuary estate

Scrivener

Self-proving affidavit

Surety bond

Survival presumtion clause

Testator

Testatrix

Trust

Trustee

What Is a Trust?

This chapter will explore the various elements required to form a trust and the general operation of a trust. In the next chapter we will explore the actual language needed to create different types of trusts.

A. Introduction

A **trust** is an arrangement that allows a third party to hold and control assets on behalf of a beneficiary. The third party in control of the trust is a type of fiduciary called a **trustee**. The person who places the assets into trust is called the *grantor*, **settlor**, or *trust maker*. The person, or group of people, who receives a distribution of assets from the trust is called the **beneficiary** (or beneficiaries). Where a trust is located or what assets the trust holds is irrelevant. Trust assets can be held in a simple savings account or an investment account. A trust can own a piece of real property. Where the trust assets are held is not important. What is important is following the terms of the trust in spending, using, or distributing the assets. A trust can be thought of as a list of rules that govern when to distribute the trust assets and to whom those assets are given. A trustee for the beneficiaries, whether in a bank account, investment account, real property, or any combination of different assets owned in the name of the trust, manages the trust assets.

For example, the attorney has a client, Carl Burke. Carl's grandson, Jeffrey, is very smart and says he wants to be an engineer like Carl when he grows up. Carl has set up a trust for Jeffrey, who is 12 years old. Carl has opened a bank account in the name of the "Jeffrey Burke Trust" and had a trust document written that restricts payments from the trust for Jeffrey's college education. Carl is the grantor or settlor of the trust; Jeffrey is the beneficiary. Carl is also serving as the trustee. When Jeffrey turns 18 he demands to be given the money but is surprised to find the answer is "no," that the money will only be paid to the college he is attending. This is an example of a very simple trust.

Trust: an arrangement that allows a third party to hold and control assets on behalf of a beneficiary

Trustee: the person who maintains the trust property and makes distributions to the beneficiary or beneficiaries according to the terms of the trust

Grantor, settlor, or trust maker: the person who typically directs the creation of the trust and provides the assets that are placed into the trust

Beneficiary: recipient of the trust's assets

B.   Creating a Trust

There are five essential elements to the creation of a trust: a valid trust purpose, a grantor, a beneficiary or class of beneficiaries, a trustee, and property to place into the trust. Each of these five elements must be present for the trust to be valid or legal.

Valid trust purpose: any legal purpose

First, every trust must have a **valid trust purpose**. A *valid trust purpose* is defined as any legal purpose. Examples include the purpose of protecting assets from creditors, providing for support of a child or disabled person, or supporting charities. Valid trust purposes also include estate planning and tax planning. A trust cannot be used to provide funding for an illegal purpose. For example, Carl's son Martin had a very bitter divorce. Martin resents paying his ex-wife child support even though the money is used to support his only child, Jeffrey. Martin cannot take all of his assets and income and create a trust with himself as the beneficiary for the sole purpose of avoiding having to pay court-ordered child support.

Second, the grantor or settlor of the trust must fund the trust. The grantor or settlor is the person who typically directs the creation of the trust and puts the assets into the trust. The terms *grantor* or *settlor* can be used interchangeably, depending on the language used in the state in which the trust is written. The grantor or settlor of the trust can be an estate if the will directs that a trust must be created. A trust created in a will is called a **testamentary trust**.

Testamentary trust: a trust created in a Last Will and Estate

Third, the trust must be for the benefit of a beneficiary or class of beneficiaries. The beneficiaries of the trust are the recipients of the trust assets distributed by the trustee in accordance with the terms of the trust. In Chapter 2 we learned that the term *beneficiary* also describes the person or class of people who receive a distribution from an estate. The term *beneficiary* is the same whether used to describe those who receive distributions from a trust, those who receive distributions from an estate, or those who receive the proceeds of a life insurance policy.

A beneficiary can be a single person or a class of people. For example, a trust can be created for one grandchild, and name that grandchild specifically, or a trust can be created for all of the grandchildren as a class of people. By identifying a class of beneficiaries, a trust can be created for beneficiaries who are not alive at the time the trust is formed. For example, a grantor names all of his or her grandchildren as beneficiaries of a trust. The class of beneficiaries could include all of the grandchildren alive at the time the distribution is made, not just those who were alive at the time the trust was created.

Practice Tip

The paralegal and/or the attorney should have the same type of discussion with a grantor when naming beneficiaries for the trust as is required when a testator chooses beneficiaries of his estate. Are all of the children included as beneficiaries? If one child is excluded, why? Careful documentation of the grantor's intent can avoid litigation in the future.

Fourth, the trust must name a *trustee*. A *trustee* maintains the trust property and makes distributions to the beneficiary or beneficiaries according to the terms of the trust. A trustee may be a person or a legal entity, such as a bank. In a will, the testator can name an executor or co-executors. Similarly, in a trust the grantor can name a trustee or co-trustees. The trust should name a **successor trustee** in case the named trustee cannot complete the requirements. The *successor trustee* is the trustee who takes over if the initial trustee can no longer fulfill the duties of serving as trustee.

Successor trustee: takes over if the initial trustee can no longer fulfill the duties of serving as trustee

---

Practice Tip

Clients should be strongly encouraged to name a substitute or successor trustee to avoid the need for court intervention in the event the named trustee is unable or unwilling to serve.

The trustee owes a **fiduciary duty** to all of the beneficiaries. The trustee's *fiduciary duty* is a legal and moral obligation to manage the trust property in a responsible and productive manner. A trustee is under an absolute obligation to act solely for the benefit of the trust's beneficiaries. The fiduciary duties include protecting the trust assets, investing prudently, and making distributions in accordance with the terms of the trust. The role of the trustee is similar to the role of the executor that was discussed in Chapter 2. The trustee must comply with the terms of the trust in the same manner as an executor must comply with the terms of the will.

Fiduciary duty: a legal and moral obligation to manage the trust property in a responsible and productive manner

The fifth and final element to form a trust is **trust property or trust assets**. Trust property can be any type of real property or personal property, whether a tangible asset or an intangible asset. Trust assets can be held in a simple checking or savings account. The assets can be in an investment account, or the trust can own real property. It is irrelevant where the assets are held. It is only relevant that the assets are owned by the trust.

Trust property or trust assets: any type of real property, personal property, whether a tangible asset or an intangible asset

The money or assets in the trust is known as the **corpus** or *principal* of the trust. If the principal is invested in something that earns interest, or dividends, or pays rent, then the money coming into the trust is **income** to the trust. Added together, the income and principal of the trust equal the **trust fund**. There are tax implications for certain types of trusts that earn income, and they must be discussed with a tax professional. If the trust is irrevocable and earns income, the income may need to be reported on a trust tax return.

Corpus or principal: the money or assets in the trust

Income: interest, dividends, or rent earned on the principal, coming into the trust

Trust fund: the income and principal added together

C.   Funding a Trust

A trust is funded when the grantor turns assets over to the trustee, and those assets come under the ownership of the trust. Turning the assets over to a trust, or "granting" the assets to the trust, occurs in many different ways. How the asset is actually turned over to the trust depends on the nature of the asset and the nature of the ownership of the asset by the grantor.

For most assets, funding the trust requires changing the title to how the asset is owned. For example, Gwen Jones has a bank account in a local bank. The bank account is in the name of Gwen Jones and is identified by her name and her Social Security number. Ms. Jones wishes to create a **revocable trust** for the benefit of her nephew, Harold Jones, using her bank account. A *revocable trust* is one that can be revoked, and the provisions of the trust can be altered or amended by the grantor. Choosing whether a trust should be revocable or irrevocable and the reasons for that choice will be discussed later in this chapter.

Revocable trust: a trust that is able to be revoked, modified, or amended

To create a revocable trust for Harold, a trust would be drafted outlining who is to serve as trustee, who would be the successor trustee, what happens to the funds while in the trust, and when the trust is to make distributions to Harold. Once the trust is finalized, the owner of the bank account would then be changed from Gwen Jones to the "Harold Jones Revocable Trust." Because the trust is a *revocable trust*, Gwen can still keep control of the bank account. Even though the title is the Harold Jones Revocable Trust, Gwen still owns the bank account and, as the Grantor and Trustee, can revoke the trust at any time.

Irrevocable trust: may not be revoked, modified, or amended

If the trust created by Gwen Jones is an **irrevocable trust**, then Gwen, as the grantor, will no longer own the asset; it will be owned by the trust. An *irrevocable trust* is one that cannot be revoked, altered, or amended by the grantor. Assets in an irrevocable trust are out of the control and ownership of the grantor. If the Harold Jones Trust is irrevocable, then the trust would be required to get a special taxpayer identification number known as an Employer Identification Number (EIN), by filing an SS-4 application with the Internal Revenue Service (IRS). A copy of this form can be found at the on the companion Web site. The owner of the bank account is the Harold Jones Irrevocable Trust. Any taxable income earned by the assets in the trust is reported on a trust tax return using the EIN obtained for the trust.

Practice Tip

Suggest to the client that the EIN should be obtained immediately and offer to assist with that process while the client is in the office signing the trust. Doing it immediately ensures that it is done properly.

As another example of how a trust is funded, let us consider the use of real property owned by Gwen to fund the trust. To fund a trust with real property, a new deed would be prepared with Gwen as the grantor, and the new owner as the Harold Jones Irrevocable Trust. The deed would be prepared in accordance with state requirements for preparation of deed and recorded in the county register of deeds.

> ## *Practice Tip*
>
> A client who needs a trust may also need assistance with transferring assets to the trust in order to fund the trust. In addition to suggesting that the EIN be obtained immediately, suggest that the attorney's office ensure that the trust is properly funded.

D. When to Create a Trust

Trusts can be created at two different times. First, a trust can be created during a client's lifetime and is referred to as an **inter vivos trust** or *living trust*. Second, a trust can be created in a Last Will and Estate and is referred to as a *testamentary trust*. In an *inter vivos* or living trust, the grantor can serve as the trustee. In a testamentary trust, the will must name someone to serve as trustee, because the grantor is the decedent and cannot serve. The executor will be responsible for causing the assets to pass from the grantor's estate into the testamentary trust.

Inter vivos or living trust: a trust created during the client's lifetime

If the trust is revocable and the grantor serves as the trustee, the trust document is called a **declaration of trust**. The grantor creates the trust, decides on the terms, and serves as the trustee. Because the grantor is also the trustee, the assets in a living trust remain under the control of the grantor. A trust that is a revocable declaration of trust does not require an EIN, as the grantor's Social Security number can be used.

Declaration of trust: a trust document in which the trust is revocable and where the grantor serves as the trustee

If the grantor appoints someone else to serve as the trustee, then the trust is called a **trust agreement**. In a trust agreement, the trustee must agree to comply with the terms of the trust. The trustee is required to sign the trust agreement, along with the grantor or grantors, as proof of the trustee's agreement to comply with the terms of the trust. An irrevocable trust agreement requires an EIN.

Trust agreement: a trust in which the grantor appoints the trustee

Inter vivos trusts can be revocable or irrevocable. The example used above, the Harold Jones Trust, is an *inter vivos* trust. Whether the trust is revocable or irrevocable is determined by the grantor and depends on the goals the grantor has for the trust. For example, if Gwen wants to be able to control the distribution of assets to her nephew Harold and wants to retain the right to stop funding the trust if her nephew does not behave, then the trust would be revocable. If Gwen is willing to give up control of the assets in trust, and has no desire to change or terminate the trust, then the trust can be irrevocable. There are various reasons why a grantor may choose to have a trust be revocable or irrevocable, and these will be explored later in this chapter.

Testamentary trusts can never be amended or modified by the grantor because in a testamentary trust the grantor is the testator. The testamentary trust does not come into being until the Last Will and Testament is admitted to probate, which occurs after the testator is deceased. Because the grantor of the property into the trust is the estate of the deceased, the grantor can no longer make any amendments to the trust. Therefore, testamentary trusts are always considered irrevocable.

An example of a testamentary trust would be a bequest in a will to a grandchild who is a minor. The bequest could simply state that the money is left to the grandchild, in trust, until the child reaches age 21. For example, a will could contain the following language:

> *I hereby give the remainder of my estate to my granddaughter Alyssa to be held IN TRUST until her 21st birthday.*

This simple statement could be the basis for the creation of a trust. The testator will have to be reminded to choose a trustee for the trust in his will.

A testamentary trust can also be more elaborate and leave certain terms and conditions for the distribution of the funds:

> *I hereby give the remainder of my estate to my grandchildren to be administered and distributed as provided in this Article.*

The testator would then put into the will the conditions for administration of the trust such as various ages for distributions, whether or not the beneficiaries can receive income distributions, and so forth. The various provisions that can be included in a testamentary trust will be discussed in Chapter 8.

Testamentary trusts become public because the trust is created in the will and cannot be formed or funded until the will is probated. Probate of a will requires that the will be registered and subject to public inspection. The terms of the trust and the funding for the trust are set forth in the will which becomes accessible to the public just as the contents of the will become public information. The desire to have the trust remain private is one reason why an *inter vivos* trust would be preferable for some clients.

E.   Trustee's Powers

The trustee's powers can be derived from four different sources. First, the trust can specifically set forth the powers allocated to the trustee. Second, the trustee can look to the provisions of the Uniform Trust Code (UTC) if the state has adopted the UTC. If the state has not adopted the UTC, or has adopted only certain provisions, the trustee's powers will be defined by the state's statutes. Third, the trustee's duties can be implied by the goals of the trust. Fourth, the trustee may need to look to the court for guidance. The wording needed to establish the trustee's powers within the trust document will be discussed in Chapter 8.

The trust can set forth the specific powers granted to the trustee, and the powers can also be incorporated by reference to the UTC or state statutes. The trust does not necessarily have to list all of the powers, if reference to the powers contained in the state's statutes is sufficient. Powers that are implied by the trust goals can come up in a variety of circumstances. For example, a trust could be the owner of an apartment building that has many tenants who pay rent. The trust requires the trustee to make a distribution of income to each of the beneficiaries every year. The trust does not specifically state that the trustee is given the authority to collect the rents. The authority to collect the rents can be implied because the goal of the trust is to make income distributions to the beneficiaries. Without the authority to collect the rents, the trustee has no funds to maintain the building, pay taxes, utilities, or other expenses, and cannot make distributions to the beneficiaries. Even though the trust did not specifically state that the trustee has the authority to collect rents, that authority could still be implied. The grantor must have intended that the trustee have that authority in order to accomplish the goal of making an annual income distribution to the beneficiaries. If the trustee was uncertain whether he or she had the necessary authority, the trustee could seek court approval for the actions needed.

If the provisions of the trust are vague, ambiguous, or silent as to whether a trustee can do something to accomplish the goals of the trust, then the trustee can apply to the court for the authority needed to fulfill the trust purposes. For example, an elderly client serves as the trustee of a family trust. She is in poor health and is concerned about her ability to continue to serve as trustee. When the trust is reviewed, it is discovered that it makes no provision for a successor trustee. In addition, the trust does not give the trustee authority to appoint a successor, or provide any other method to have a successor appointed. Because the trust does not provide for a method by which a new trustee is to be appointed, the original trustee must apply to the court for direction. Notice will be given to all of the beneficiaries, who will have the opportunity to weigh in on who is appointed as the new trustee. This could be a costly and time-consuming process, which may lead to disagreement between the beneficiaries that could have been avoided by including a successor trustee.

Practice Tip

Always encourage clients to appoint a second fiduciary, whether it is an executor, trustee, or guardian, to avoid potentially costly litigation that would be required for the court to appoint a fiduciary if the first one cannot continue.

There are two different names for the trustee who is appointed or serves after the original trustee. If the trustee has qualified and served as a trustee, then the second trustee is a **successor trustee**. If the first trustee fails to ever qualify, and never serves, then the next trustee is called the **substitute trustee**.

Successor trustee: the trustee who serves after the original trustee

Substitute trustee: the trustee who takes over if the initial trustee cannot serve as trustee

F. Trustee's Duties and Responsibilities

The duties of the trustee are fiduciary responsibilities. A trustee's duties include many things, and each state's laws contain a list of regulations governing a trustee's duty to the trust. In general, a trustee must become fully familiar with and agree to abide by the terms of the trust. The trustee has ongoing responsibilities to the beneficiaries, and if the trustee fails to fulfill those responsibilities, the trustee may be subject to liability. There are many common duties that were codified in the Uniform Trust Code. Section eight of the UTC summarizes the duties and responsibilities of the trustee as the duty to "administer the trust in good faith, in accordance with its terms and purposes and the interests of the beneficiaries, and in accordance with this Code." The UTC also requires a duty of loyalty, impartiality, and prudent administration.

A trustee has a duty to make any distributions from the trust to the correct person. If the beneficiary to whom a distribution is intended is a minor, or is incapacitated, the trustee may be required to make distributions to a guardian on behalf of the beneficiary. If the beneficiary of the trust is a minor or is incapacitated, the guardian of the beneficiary can enforce all of the rights afforded under the trust on behalf of that beneficiary. Many trusts could potentially have minors as beneficiaries. It is very common to include a clause in a trust to allow for ease or facility of payment of the distribution. A sample of the language for such a clause would be the following:

> *Facility of Payment. The Trustee may make distributions and payments of income or principal to or for the benefit of any beneficiary who is a minor, or who is incapacitated directly to such beneficiary or to his or her attorney-in-fact, guardian, or parent. The Trustee may also make distributions directly to pay the debts or expenses of the beneficiary.*

If there is any potential, no matter how remote, that one of the original beneficiaries could die before the trust is fully distributed, and distributions would then be made to a minor, it is imperative that this type of clause be included.

The Uniform Prudent Investor Act (UPIA) governs the trustee's duties and responsibilities, in most states. The UPIA can be found at the end of this chapter companion Web site. The UPIA was drafted at the National Conference of Commissioners on Uniform State Laws in 1994 and has been adopted by 44 states. Section 2(b) of the UPIA sets forth a list of factors that a trustee must consider when making investment decisions for the assets in a trust:

(1) general economic conditions;
(2) the possible effect of inflation or deflation;
(3) the expected tax consequences of investment decisions or strategies;
(4) the role that each investment or course of action plays within the overall trust portfolio, which may include financial assets, interests in closely held enterprises, tangible and intangible personal property, and real property;
(5) the expected total return from income and the appreciation of capital;

The UPIA allows the trustee to delegate responsibility for investment and management of the trust assets to an investment advisor or financial representative. However, the trustee continues to be responsible for complying with the terms of the trust.

Diversify the investments: invest in a number of different types of things

One of the requirements of the UPIA is that the trustee must **diversify the investments** in which the trust assets are placed. *Diversifying the investments* means to invest in a number of different types of things, so that the potential risk is reduced. The UPIA measures the trustee's performance on the basis of the performance of the entire portfolio of investment, not the performance of an individual investment. If the trustee does not diversify the investments and invests in only one thing, such as a specific stock, and that investment fails, then the trustee has not fulfilled his or her fiduciary duties and could be liable to the beneficiaries. The easiest way for the trustee to diversify the investments within the trust is to invest in a **mutual fund.**

The Securities and Exchange Commission (SEC) defines a *mutual fund* as a company that brings together money from many people and invests it in stocks, bonds, or other assets. The stocks, bonds, or other assets in the mutual fund are known as the **portfolio**. The different investments held by a trust are also known as the **trust's portfolio**. If a trustee invests trust assets in a mutual fund, the trust will own shares of the mutual fund. The number of shares owned represents the amount of interest the trust owns in the mutual fund.

A mutual fund takes care of the trustee's requirement to diversify because the mutual fund itself is made up of a number of different types of investments. There are thousands of different mutual funds available, and the funds are rated according to the investment goals that each fund tries to meet. A mutual fund is often a good option for a trustee who has only a small amount of money in the trust because the mutual fund is professionally managed and provides necessary diversification without the need for the trustee to spread the assets over a number of different investments.

Mutual fund: a company that brings together money from many people and invests it in stocks, bonds, or other assets

Portfolio: the stocks, bonds, or other assets in a mutual fund

Trust's portfolio: the different investments held by a trust

Practice Tip

Clients will often ask for investment advice. It is good practice to have available contact information for two or three different financial advisors that can be given to clients with the caveat that no recommendation is being made about the performance of the financial advisor.

The trustee is responsible for the assets in the trust and is liable to the beneficiaries for the prudent investment of those assets. One of the risks that the trustee must avoid is the loss of value of the assets due to inflation. If the assets in the trust are not invested in something that provides a rate of return that keeps up with inflation, the assets are going to lose value. When the distributions are made to the beneficiaries, the beneficiaries may receive less than what the grantor expected. The trustee must find a balance between a completely safe investment that produces no income and a risky investment that could potentially produce a higher rate of return.

The trustee has a duty to be loyal to the trust, and not to engage in self-dealing. The trustee cannot use the trust assets for his or her own use. The trustee must never commingle his or her own funds with those of the trust and must never enter into any transaction with the trust, or even borrow assets from the trust. For example, if a trustee holds a trust at the same local bank where the trustee has his or her own accounts, the trustee cannot deposit personal checks into the trust. Any of these activities would split the trustee's loyalty between his or her own investment and what is best for the trust, resulting in a conflict of interest for the trustee.

The trustee must ensure that the trust assets are held according to the terms of the trust. The trustee must perform the trustee duties without charging any fee except if a commission is allowed by the terms of the trust and in accordance with state law. The trustee cannot delegate any of his or her duties or fiduciary responsibilities to another person, unless it is to a co-trustee and is specifically permitted by the terms of the trust. The trustee must act impartially, treat all beneficiaries equally, and always act in the best interest of all beneficiaries.

A trustee is legally and morally bound to manage the trust property in a responsible and productive manner, acting solely for the benefit of the trust's beneficiaries. A trustee who fails to fulfill his or her duties, or breaches those duties, can be removed as the trustee. The trust document can contain the method by which the beneficiaries can vote to remove a trustee for cause. If the trust document does not contain instructions on how to remove a trustee, it may be necessary for the beneficiaries to file a petition with the court asking to have the trustee removed for breach of fiduciary duties. Figure 5-1 provides examples of some common fiduciary duties and breaches, or violations, of those duties.

Fiduciary Duty	Example of Breach of Duty
- Duty to make distributions from trust to correct person	- Making distributions to anyone other than the beneficiary such as paying the spouse, a creditor, or a parent
- Duty to act prudently in investing and managing trust assets	- Failing to diversify the investments or investing in a "get rich quick" scheme or risky investment
- Duty of loyalty to the trust and not engaging in self-dealing	- Buying a piece of property from the trust for half of the market value. The trustee then sells the property for full value, retaining the additional money earned on the sale
- Duty not to commingle funds	- Using a single bank account or investment account for both the trust funds and the trustee's personal funds

Figure 5-1. Examples of Some Common Fiduciary Duties and Breaches

G. **Express or Implied Trusts**

Trusts can be **express trusts** or **implied trusts**. An *express trust* is one that is specifically created by the expressed intentions of the grantor or settlor and is evidenced by a written document setting forth the grantor's goals for use of the trust monies. The document includes the terms and conditions of distributions and the identities of the beneficiaries. The intention of the parties to create the trust is shown by the language in the trust agreement or declaration of trust or in the parties' conduct. The trusts discussed previously in this chapter, such as testamentary trusts or inter vivos trusts, are examples of express trusts.

An *implied trust* is one that comes about by operation of law. The terms and conditions of the trust are developed from the intent of the parties. It is created by a court of equity because of actions of the parties. There are two types of implied trusts: **resulting trust** and **constructive trust**. A *resulting trust* is created by a court based on what the law presumes to be the intent of the parties but does not take into consideration the expressed intent of the parties. In a resulting trust, a person holds title to property as a trustee for the rightful owner, who is considered the beneficiary of the resulting trust. An example of a resulting trust would be the following: Rose plans an extended vacation in Europe. She asks her friend Lily to house sit for her while she is away. Rose gives Lily $100,000 to buy the vacant property next door if it goes on the market. The property goes on the market, and Lily buys the property but has the deed and title put into her own name. When Rose takes Lily to court, the court finds that that property will be held in a resulting trust for Lily.

A *constructive trust* is a trust created by a court regardless of the parties' intentions and is an equitable remedy. A constructive trust will be formed for the benefit of a party that has been wrongfully deprived of its rights. A court imposes it when a party is holding legal right to property that was obtained by **unjust enrichment**. *Unjust enrichment* is when a person unfairly benefits from another person's mistake or at another person's expense. In common terms, it is when something unfair occurs, and the court tries to correct the unfairness. Many times unjust enrichment occurs in the context of a contract. For example, Katie Bell signs a contract for the completion of some home improvements. She wants to have an addition put on with a new bedroom and bathroom. After the contractor has completed framing the addition, Katie decides that she no longer wants to have the addition completed. She refuses to pay the contractor for the work that was completed, and the contractor is unable to complete the job. Katie gets the benefit of the portion of the addition that was completed. If the contractor sued Katie, the court would require that the fee for the work that was completed be placed into a constructive trust to be held until the matter is resolved. The constructive trust would serve to protect the funds until the dispute was resolved. A constructive trust is not created by a trust agreement or declaration of trust. The court imposes it to correct some wrongdoing.

The types of trusts under each category are shown in Figure 5-2.

Express trust: trust specifically created by the expressed intentions of the grantor or settlor and evidenced by written documents setting forth the grantor's goal for use of the trust monies, the terms and conditions of distribution, and identification of the beneficiaries

Implied trust: trust that comes about by operation of law; terms and conditions of the trust are developed from the intent of the parties

Resulting trust: a trust created by a court based on what the law presumes to be the intent of the parties, but does not take into consideration the expressed intent of the parties

Constructive trust: a trust created by a court regardless of the parties' intentions and is an equitable remedy imposed by a court

Unjust enrichment: when a person unfairly benefits from another person's mistake or at another person's expense; when something unfair occurs, and the court tries to correct the unfairness

Figure 5-2. Types of Trusts

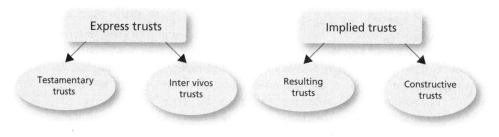

H. Laws Governing Trusts

Common law: the law that is developed in the courts through the decisions of judges

Statutory law: the law that is set forth in the statutes or laws of a state

Codified: collected and organized into a code

The law governing trusts is specific to the state in which the trust was formed. Trusts formed in New Jersey, for example, are subject to interpretation according to New Jersey law. The law of trusts for each state was developed from what is known as **common law**. *Common law* is the law that is developed in the courts through the decisions of judges. Common law is distinguished from **statutory law** that is the law that is set forth in the statutes or laws of a state. Statutory law in a state can be **codified**, or organized into a code.

An example of uniform codified law that has been adopted by many states is the Uniform Trust Code. In 2000, the Uniform Law Commission looked at all of the common laws and statutory laws of the 50 states pertaining to trusts. The Commission developed the Uniform Trust Code, or UTC, which was an attempt to create a uniform codified set of rules to govern trusts. The UTC has been adopted by Alabama, Arizona, Arkansas, District of Columbia, Florida, Kansas, Maine, Massachusetts, Michigan, Missouri, Nebraska, New Hampshire, New Mexico, North Carolina, North Dakota, Ohio, Oregon, Pennsylvania, South Carolina, Tennessee, Utah, Vermont, Virginia, West Virginia, and Wyoming. It was introduced for adoption in New Jersey in 2013. A copy of the Uniform Trust Code can be found on the companion Web site.

In states that have adopted the UTC, trusts are governed by the UTC. In states that have not adopted the UTC, trusts are governed by a collection of state statutes and the common law found in case law.

I. Cy-près

Cy-près doctrine: requires that when a trust or bequest in a will cannot be completed, the funds in the trust or bequest be used to the nearest possible purpose

There is a specific legal doctrine that governs trusts that is called the cy-près doctrine (pronounced "sigh - press".) The **cy-près doctrine** is an abbreviated form of the French term *cy-près comme possible*, which means "as near as possible." The doctrine, in general, requires that when a trust or a bequest in a will cannot be completed, the funds in the trust or bequest be used to the nearest possible purpose. The cy-près doctrine was first developed by a court that had to address a bequest from the estate of Francis Jackson, an abolitionist from Boston. Jackson set aside money in his estate to be placed in a trust for the purposes of abolishing slavery. The trust was created after Jackson's death and continued to operate for many years. Slavery was finally abolished by adoption of the Thirteenth Amendment. Therefore, the funds in Jackson's trust could no longer be used for that purpose. The courts determined that the next best use of the money would be to use the funds for the needs of African Americans in the Boston region.

Cy-près also governs the distribution of unclaimed settlement funds resulting from a class action. Class actions can take years to resolve. During the litigation, some class members may have moved and cannot be located or may have died. The settlement fund created by the class action may not be able to be fully distributed. The cy-près doctrine would allow the distribution of some or all of those unclaimed monies to charities.

Summary

A trust is an arrangement in which a grantor allows a fiduciary to hold and control assets on behalf of a beneficiary. There are five essential elements to creating a trust. The trust can be revocable, irrevocable, formed by a declaration or agreement, or by order of the court. The trustee is a fiduciary and his or her powers are found in state law and/or the Uniform Trust Code.

Review Questions

1. What are the differences between a revocable trust and an irrevocable trust?

2. What types of duties does a trustee have?

3. Can a grantor serve as the trustee of his or her own trust?

4. What kinds of property can be held by a trust?

5. What are the five essential elements to creating a trust?

6. What is an EIN and when is it required?

7. Can the attorney apply for the EIN on behalf of the Trustee?

True or False

1. T   F   Inter vivos trusts can be revocable or irrevocable.

2. T   F   The trustee owes a fiduciary duty to all of the beneficiaries.

3. T   F   An example of the corpus or principal of the trust is interest income.

4. T   F   If the provisions of the trust are vague, or ambiguous, the trust must be dissolved.

5. T   F   Every trust should provide for a trustee and a substitute or successor trustee.

6. T   F   An example of an implied trust is a testamentary trust.

7. T   F   A trustee can borrow money from a trust.

8. T   F   The cy-près doctrine governs all types of trusts.

9. T   F   A trustee can delegate administrative duties.

10. T   F   An implied trust is one created by a court.

Key Terms

Beneficiary
Codified
Common law
Constructive trust
Corpus or principal
Cy-près doctrine
Declaration of trust
Diversify the investments
Express trust
Fiduciary duty
Grantor, settlor, or trust maker
Implied trust
Income
Inter vivos or living trust
Irrevocable trust
Mutual fund

Portfolio
Resulting trust
Revocable trust
Statutory law
Substitute trustee
Successor trustee
Testamentary trust
Trust
Trust agreement
Trust fund
Trust property or trust assets
Trustee
Trust's portfolio
Unjust enrichment
Valid trust purpose

Drafting a Trust

In Chapter 4 we examined each provision within a hypothetical will created for a client. In this chapter we will create a trust for John Jones and his wife, Linda, for the benefit of the couple's children, John Jones, age 8, and twins Grace and Lily Jones, age 4. John and Linda are 38 and 36 years old, respectively. They have been married for 15 years.

A.   Trust Purpose

John and Linda Jones are considering a trust to provide funding for their children's college education if both John and Linda pass away before the children complete college. The couple wants John's brother, Robert, to serve as the trustee. For purposes of this example, we will assume the trust is **inter vivos**, that it is being created during John and Linda Jones' lifetime, and that the trust is going to be a revocable trust because John and Linda may want to revoke the trust if the original purpose is no longer relevant. The trust will be called the "Jones Family Revocable Trust."

Inter vivos: trust created during the grantor's lifetime

The first meeting with the clients will be used to gather all of the information about their goals for the trust, the beneficiaries, the proposed trustee, and the substitute trustee. In order to complete the trust, there will likely be several subsequent meetings to review the trust language and finalize how the goals of the trust will be accomplished.

> ### *Practice Tip*
>
> Creating a trust requires multiple drafts and revisions of the trust document. It is important to keep the drafts organized so that the correct version of the document is sent out to the client for review. Develop a system of numbering and/or dating the drafts to aid in keeping track of the changes.

B.   Identify Parties and Type of Trust

Grantors: the people who are gifting, or granting, the assets that will be used to fund the trust

Settlor or trustor: a grantor may also be known as settlor or trustor depending on the state in which the trust is being formed

The first provision in the trust is the preamble, identifying the document as a trust created by John and Linda Jones, who are known as the **grantors**. The *grantors* of a trust are the people who are gifting, or granting, the assets that will be used to fund the trust. The grantor can also be known as the **settlor** or *trustor* depending on the terminology used in the state in which the trust is being formed. The preamble also includes the date on which the trust was created and identifies that the trust is being created in cooperation with the trustee who is named in the preamble. The sample language would be as follows:

> *We, John Jones and Linda Jones as Grantors, enter into this trust agreement this* _____ *day of* _____, *20* _____, *with Robert Jones, as Trustee (hereinafter called the "Trustee").*

Trust formation date: the date the trust was signed

Trust agreement: a trust that requires that the trustee agree to abide by the terms of the trust

The grantors usually fill in the date of the trust when it is signed. This date is referred to as the **trust formation date**. The language of the preamble indicates that this trust is going to be a **trust agreement** because it requires Robert to agree to serve as the trustee pursuant to the terms of the trust. A *trust agreement* requires that the trustee agree to abide by the terms of the trust. Unlike a will, where the testator chooses an executor but the executor does not have to sign the will, a trustee is required to sign a trust agreement indicating that he or she agrees to abide by the terms of the trust.

> ### Practice Tip
>
> The choice of trustee is important. Often clients find it difficult to choose a trustee and therefore may delay in finalizing the trust document. Create some kind of follow-up system so that completed documents get signed and finalized by the clients.

Declaration of trust: a trust in which the grantor or grantors serve as the trustee

Instead of a trust agreement, the trust could be a **declaration of trust**. A *declaration of trust* is one in which the grantor or grantors serve as the trustee. In our example, if John and/or Linda were both the grantors and the trustees, the trust would be a declaration of trust because John and Linda are not asking a trustee to agree to abide by the terms of the trust. The sample language for a declaration of trust would be as follows:

> *This Declaration of Trust is made by John Jones and Linda Jones as Grantors and Trustees as set forth herein this* _____ *day of* _____, *20* _____.

Trusts in which the grantors also serve as the trustees are usually revocable trusts because the grantors are not giving up control over the use of the assets placed into the trust. If a grantor is going to act as a trustee for an irrevocable trust, there will most likely be a provision in the trust that the grantor cannot act as the sole trustee.

Practice Tip

Irrevocable trusts are treated very differently from revocable trusts because the trust cannot be revoked. When the trust documents are mailed to the client, the cover letter should include a statement that the trust is irrevocable. The attorney may also want the client to acknowledge, in writing, that the client understands the trust is irrevocable. Copies of the cover letter and/or the client acknowledgement that the trust is irrevocable should be kept in the file. No matter how many times the irrevocable nature of the trust is explained to a client, there will always be the client who calls years after an irrevocable trust is formed and asks if the trust can be changed.

The next paragraph of the trust identifies the parties that are the beneficiaries, in our example, the children of John and Linda Jones:

Child or Children. We have three children, John Jones, Grace Jones, and Lily Jones. All references in this Trust to our "child or children" are to said named child or children, and any after borne children.

In our example, the Jones family is making a provision for any additional children who may be born after the date of the formation of the trust. This reference to "after borne" children would be omitted if the couple was beyond child-bearing age.

The trust could also create a class of beneficiaries, instead of naming specific people as beneficiaries. For example, John and Linda can create a class of beneficiaries and identify who belongs to the class.

Beneficiaries. The purpose of this trust is to benefit a group of persons consisting solely of our three children, John Jones, Grace Jones, and Lily Jones, our grandchildren, and any other issue of ours who are living at the time of final distribution of this trust.

Creating a class of beneficiaries is most often done when the trust is going to be in existence for a long time and the grantors want distributions to go on for several generations.

C. Identify Assets and Management of Assets

The next set of provisions in the trust document identify the assets that John and Linda want to place into the trust and how those assets are to be managed. The assets to be placed in the trust do not have to be specifically identified at the time the trust is formed. The assets are also not limited to assets currently owned by John and Linda. The assets that will be placed into the trust are listed on a separate page titled "Schedule A" that is attached to the back of the trust. In this manner, the schedule can be amended as assets are added to the trust or removed from the trust without having to amend the trust.

> **Assets.** *We have transferred, or we will transfer, those assets listed on Schedule A. The grantors may, with the consent of the Trustee, transfer or assign, additional assets or property to the Trustee to be added to Schedule A.*

The assets listed on Schedule A can be anything, including a specific piece of real property, a bank account, or any other asset that has value. The assets in the trust can also be something the grantors intend to acquire but do not own at the time the trust is formed.

The next paragraphs, or series of paragraphs, describe how the grantors want the assets to be managed. The content of these paragraphs is going to depend on the grantors' goals. The grantors in our example are setting up the trust to provide for their children's college education in the event that both of them pass away. There are many other purposes for trusts that will be discussed in the next chapter. The language for the administration of different types of trusts will change depending on the purpose of the trust.

> **Administration of Trust.** *During our lifetime, the Trustee will accumulate all the income and principal of the assets placed into this trust and maintain same for the benefit of our children as the Trustee in his sole and absolute discretion deems advisable to provide adequately and properly for the secondary education of our children. With respect to such assets, the Trustee shall invest, reinvest, and administer such assets in accordance with the terms of this Trust Agreement.*

In this example, the trust assets are to be held and all of the income earned by the assets in the trust is to be accumulated and put back into the trust until such time as the trust is needed for one of the children to attend college. In this example, any income earned by the assets in the trust is kept within the trust. John and Linda may fund the trust by granting an investment account to the trust. As that investment account grows, all of the interest and income earned by the investment account will be reinvested and held by the trust so that the amount of money in the trust continues to grow.

The trust could, as an alternative, allow for the use of the income generated by the trust. John and Linda could require that the interest income earned by the assets in the trust be used every year for the benefit of their children. Income to the trust can include any monies earned by the assets in the trust. Examples of income include rent from real property, interest from bank accounts or bonds, or dividends from stocks. A provision allowing the income from the trust to be used on an annual basis is usually included in a trust set up for the support and maintenance of the beneficiaries. An example of language that would allow the trustee to use the income from the trust for the beneficiaries would be as follows:

> **Administration of Trust.** *During our lifetime, the Trustee may distribute the net income of the assets placed into this trust, for the benefit of our children, as the Trustee in his sole and*

absolute discretion deems advisable to provide adequately and properly for the secondary education of our children. Trustee shall add any income not so distributed to principal.

In our example, the trust purpose is education, so the trustee's discretion is limited to using the funds in the trust for that purpose. If the purpose of the trust were more general, such as to provide income for the support of the beneficiaries, the trustee's discretion could also be more general.

The trust could also allow for the payment of **principal** from the trust. Principal is the actual asset in the trust. Examples of principal include real property, a bank account, bonds, or stock. An example of language that would allow the trustee to use principal from the trust for the beneficiaries would be the following:

Principal: the actual assets in a trust

> **Administration of Trust.** *During our lifetime, the Trustee may use any or all of the principal of this trust for the purpose of paying for the college education of our children.*

The payment of income and/or principal from the trust can be either by a defined standard, such as a specific amount or percentage, or can be left to the discretion of the trustee. If the trustee has discretion to pay out or accumulate income, the type of trust is called a **sprinkling trust** or *spray trust* or *discretionary trust*. An example of sample language for this type of trustee discretion is the following:

Sprinkling trust or spray trust or discretionary trust: a trust that gives the trustee discretion to pay out or accumulate income

> *The Trustee shall hold, manage, invest, and reinvest the trust estate, shall collect the income thereof, and shall pay over or apply the net income and principal thereof, to such extent, including the whole thereof, and in such manner and at such time or times as the Trustee, in the exercise of sole and absolute discretion, may deem advisable.*

The choice of a trustee becomes even more important in this type of trust because the trustee has broad discretion and can make unequal distributions to the beneficiaries that could lead to discontent.

If the trust calls for payment to a minor child or someone who is incapacitated, the distribution may have to be made to the beneficiary's guardian. If the grantor knows the beneficiaries are minors or incapacitated, the grantor of the trust can allow for payments to be made for the benefit of a beneficiary, or on behalf of a beneficiary. Sample language for payment to another person on behalf of a beneficiary would be the following:

> *The Trustee shall pay over the net income and principal of the trust to, or for the benefit of, the Beneficiary until the Beneficiary attains the age of twenty-one (21) years.*

The trustee may also have to comply with the Uniform Gifts to Minors Act or other state statutes that permit payment to someone other than a beneficiary. The Uniform Gifts to Minors Act (UGMA) is a law pertaining to the ownership of certain types of investments by minors. Some investments, like annuities, mutual funds, or securities, require the owner to sign a contract. Someone who is a minor does not have the legal capacity to sign a contract. A UGMA account is a type of custodial account that allows a minor to own securities without a formal trust.

D.   Revocable or Irrevocable

Revocable trust: a trust in which the grantors have reserved for themselves the right to make changes to the trust or to revoke the trust in its entirety

The next paragraph will address the ability of the grantors to alter or amend the trust. As initially stated, the trust that is being drafted for the Jones family is a **revocable trust**, meaning the grantors have reserved for themselves the right to make changes to the trust or to revoke the trust in its entirety. Reserving this right is consistent with the purposes of this trust because if the couple's children are grown and are living independent lives, there is no further need for the trust. When the need for the trust is no longer relevant, the Jones' may want to revoke the trust or change the beneficiaries of the trust to their grandchildren instead of their children. The language that makes the trust revocable is as follows:

> *Amendment and Revocation. We the Grantors reserve the right and power to alter, amend, or revoke this Agreement, at any time and from time to time, during our lifetimes either in whole or in part, without the consent of the Trustee or any beneficiary hereunder by written notice, acknowledged and delivered to the Trustee other than by Will; provided, however, that the duties, responsibilities, and rate of compensation of the Trustee shall not be altered or modified without the Trustee's written consent.*

Section 602 of the Uniform Trust Code provides that the settlor of a trust can revoke the trust by substantial compliance with the method of revocation found in the trust. In our example above, the settlor (or grantor) can revoke the trust by providing written notice, acknowledged and delivered to the trustee. This means the grantor can simply write a letter to the trustee, indicating that as of a specific date, the trust is revoked.

If the trust in our example were irrevocable, this paragraph would not be added. Instead, there would be a paragraph describing the terms of the trust as irrevocable, what it means to be irrevocable, and that the grantors are acknowledging that the trust cannot be altered, amended, or revoked. An example of the language used in an irrevocable trust is the following:

> *Trust Irrevocable. We have been fully informed as to the distinction between a revocable and irrevocable trust, and declare this to be irrevocable and hereby surrender all rights to revoke same or to alter, amend, or modify any of the provisions of this agreement.*

John and Linda Jones asked to have a trust drafted that would pay for their children's college education if they pass away before their children have finished with college. The trust may be in place for several years before it is needed, but it may never be needed if John and Linda live to see their children graduate from college. In the event that both John and Linda die leaving one or more of their children who have not finished college, the trust will then provide the funds for the child or children to attend college.

Practice Tip

A new client coming in to discuss a trust is a good opportunity to bring up other estate-planning documents such as a will, especially if the trust is for the benefit of minor children. When making the appointment for the new client, the paralegal can ask if the client has a will or would like to discuss preparing a will with the attorney.

E. Distributions from the Trust

The trust must be carefully drafted to address the distributions and to conform to John and Linda's goals. There are two ways to address distribution: dividing the trust into separate shares or keeping the trust in one pool or pot of assets. If John and Linda want each of their children to have equal access to trust assets, the trust would direct that the assets be divided into separate shares at the time of John and Linda's deaths. The following paragraph would address the division of the trust among the beneficiaries:

> ***Division into Separate Children's Shares.*** *Upon the second of the grantors to die, the balance of the Trust shall be divided into equal shares, one each for our children who have not completed college. In the event that any of our children predecease us, or have already completed college, the Trustee shall divide the balance of the Trust among the remaining children. The Trustee shall hold the assets as separate trusts for the benefit of each child and shall pay to or apply for his or her benefit all the net income and so much of the principal at any time and from time to time as the Trustee with sole discretion believes advisable to provide adequately for the child's secondary education.*

Upon the deaths of both John and Linda, the trust is divided into equal shares, and each child who has not completed college gets one equal share of the trust. In this manner each child gets an equal share to go to college and must either choose a college that is within the budget of the trust or must find another way to pay the difference.

The alternative to dividing the trust equally among the children is keeping the funds in one "pool" of assets, known as a **one-pot trust**. A *one-pot trust* keeps all of the assets in the trust together and directs the trustee to make distributions as needed, in our example, for college. Making the distributions from one pool of money could lead to inequities among the beneficiaries. For example, if the first child who reaches college age chooses an expensive out-of-state college and takes five years to graduate, the first child could use most of the trust, leaving little or nothing for the remaining children. An example of language that would be used if the trust funds were not to be divided into equal shares is the following:

One-pot trust: a trust that keeps all of the assets together in one pool and directs the trustee to make distributions as needed

> ***Administration of Trust:*** *The Trustee shall hold the Jones Family Revocable Trust for the benefit of our children until the first child is ready to begin college education. The Trustee shall pay to or apply for the use and benefit of each of our children as much of the income and*

principal as the Trustee shall deem necessary for each of our children's college education. The Trustee does not need to make equal payments to our children. Any income not so distributed shall be accumulated and added to principal.

In this one-pot trust, the trustee is directed to hold the funds until the first child is ready to go to college, and then is directed to use the funds in the trust, as needed, for each child without regard to whether the payments are equal. The difference between dividing the trust into equal shares at the time of death and having a one-pot trust can often have unintended consequences in the same way that the choice of using a percentage or a specific dollar amount in a will has in the distribution of a residuary estate.

In our example, an assumption is made that the specific goal of the trust is college education, and that other funds are available for the day-to-day care of the children. If John and Linda are alive, they fully intend to pay for their children's college education. If, however, they both die before their children have finished college, they want to be sure that money has been set aside for that purpose. Because the goal is college education, any child who has already completed college at the time of John and Linda's deaths would not be entitled to a distribution from the trust. John and Linda's three children are different ages, each with a potential need for a distribution from the trust occurring at different times. The trust may have to be used for some, all, or none of the children.

F. Appointment of Trustee

Trustee's commission: a statutory fee to which the trustee is entitled that is a percentage of the corpus and the income of the trust

The next set of provisions addresses the trustee. The trust could include direction that provides for compensation to the trustee in the form of a **trustee's commission**. The *trustee's commission* is a statutory fee to which the trustee is entitled that is a percentage of the corpus and the income of the trust.

> ***Compensation of Fiduciaries.*** *The Trustee shall be entitled to reasonable compensation for services hereunder in accordance with the statutory rate then prevailing. Every fiduciary shall be reimbursed for the reasonable costs and expenses incurred in connection with the administration of the Trusts. The Trustee, and any successor Trustee, shall serve without bond.*

Surety bond: bond obtained by an executor of an estate; ensures the proper performance of the trustee and ensures against theft or misappropriation of trust assets

If the trustee is a corporate entity, like a bank or a financial institution, then compensation will have to be paid. If the trustee is a family member or private individual, the grantors can direct that the trust require the trustee serve without compensation. The trust will also direct whether the trustee has to obtain a **surety bond**. A *surety bond* for a trustee is the same type of bond discussed in Chapter 4 that is obtained by an executor of an estate. The bond ensures the proper performance of the trustee and ensures against theft or misappropriation of trust assets. In our example, John's brother, Robert, is proposed as the trustee. John and Linda will have to decide if they want to require Robert to obtain a bond.

> ## Practice Tip
>
> Trustees often serve for long periods of time and are responsible for investing the assets of the trust. Trusts that give the trustee these additional responsibilities make it more likely that the trustee will be required to obtain a bond.

The trust must also set forth the methodology for choosing a new trustee should Robert Jones, the original named trustee, resign or be unwilling or unable to complete the role of the trustee:

> **Trustee Resignation.** *The Trustee has the right to resign at any time by thirty (30) days written notice to the grantors. The resignation of a Trustee shall become effective upon the appointment and written acceptance of the successor Trustee. If no successor is appointed, then a successor Trustee shall be appointed by a majority of the current adult beneficiaries. The appointment must be made in writing.*

If Robert qualifies and acts as the trustee but then cannot complete his duties, the next trustee is the **successor trustee**. If Robert does not qualify and never acts as trustee, and a new trustee is chosen, the second trustee is called the **substitute trustee**. Any successor or substitute trustee succeeds to all the powers and duties conferred upon the original trustee. If the original trustee was required to obtain a bond, any successor or substitute trustee will also be required to obtain a bond.

Successor trustee: the next trustee who is chosen if the original named trustee qualifies and acts as the trustee but then cannot complete his or her duties

Substitute trustee: new trustee who is chosen if the named trustee does not qualify and never acts as trustee and a new trustee is chosen

It is common to have a clause in the trust that prohibits anyone who is a beneficiary of the trust from serving as trustee. It is also common to have a "backup plan" in case a successor trustee does not get appointed. Some grantors like to choose alternative trustees; some choose instead to put a method of choosing the alternative trustee into the trust. If a new trustee is not appointed by the prior trustee, the trust could include language that the beneficiaries can vote on a new trustee or they can apply to court to have one appointed. If the Jones' agree that none of their children should serve as trustee and want to provide a means by which a successor trustee could be appointed by the court, if necessary, then the following paragraph would be included:

> *It is our intention that no individual who is a beneficiary shall act as sole Trustee hereunder. If no successor is appointed and qualifies within thirty (30) days of the resignation of the Trustee, then the resigning Trustee or any adult beneficiary may apply to a court of competent jurisdiction for the appointment of a successor Trustee.*

This paragraph will allow for any of the beneficiaries to ask the court of the state in which the trust was formed to appoint a trustee if no successor trustee has been appointed.

> ## Practice Tip
>
> If a court has to appoint a new trustee, that can be very costly to the trust. Always remind and encourage clients to choose several successor trustees when possible.

G. Trustee Powers

The Jones' are considering the trust in our example to pay for their children's college expenses in the event that they both die before all of their children finish college. As stated previously, it is possible that the Jones' will outlive the purpose of the trust. If that happens, then they have reserved for themselves the right to dissolve or revoke the trust. If the Jones' unfortunately die before their children complete college, it will be up to the trustee to use the money in the trust in accordance with the provisions of the trust. The trustee may expend the money for the college education of each of the Jones' children and may spend all of the money in the trust for that purpose. If the children do not need all of the money in the trust or if there is money remaining in the trust after they have completed college, the trust has to provide for the distribution of that money:

> **Residuary.** *Any funds remaining in this Trust after all of our children have reached age 30 or have completed college, whichever comes first, shall be distributed to our children free of trust, in equal shares, share and share alike.*

The trust should contain a provision that allows the trustee to dissolve the trust if there is only a small amount of money remaining in trust or if it is uneconomical to continue to hold the money in trust. The trust usually sets forth a specific dollar amount at which the trust would be considered uneconomical:

> **Trust Uneconomical.** *If at any time the fair market value of the Trust is TEN THOUSAND ($10,000) DOLLARS or less, the Trustee may, within his sole discretion, terminate and distribute the funds remaining in the Trust to the beneficiaries in equal shares.*

This provision gives the trustee a means by which the trust can be terminated, the final distribution made to the beneficiaries.

The wording of the powers entrusted to the trustee is unique to each state, but sample language setting forth some specific powers given to the trustee is as follows:

> **Trustee Powers.** *The Trustee, Substitute Trustee, or Successor Trustee shall have the following powers, in addition to those powers set forth in state law:*
> (a) *To hold any stocks, securities, or other real or personal property that is delivered to the trust;*
> (b) *To sell any such real or personal property held by the trust, and invest and reinvest the monies held in trust;*
> (c) *To employ such professionals and advisors as the Trustee shall require.*

The powers and duties of the trustee are going to be defined by the goals of the trust.

Practice Tip

Review the general duties and responsibilities of the trustee with the grantors to assist them in choosing the right person for the trustee. Also, make sure that the trustee understands his or her responsibilities when signing the trust if the attorney is not present during the finalization of the trust.

H. Miscellaneous Provisions

In our example John and Linda do not want any portion of the trust to become public and do not want Robert, the trustee, to have to pay an accountant and/or an attorney to prepare an **accounting** of the trust. An *accounting* is a report of income and expenditures in which the total balance remaining is determined for a certain period of time. For example, a monthly accounting would indicate the income received during the month, the expenses incurred during that same month, followed by the total balance remaining. The following paragraph would be added to avoid the requirement of an accounting:

Accounting: a report of income and expenditures in which the total balance remaining is determined for a certain period of time

> ***Accounting.*** *It is my desire to avoid the expense and delay of a public or judicial accounting of the administration of the Trusts created hereunder. An accounting of my Trustee approved in writing by all shall be conclusive and binding upon all persons having an interest in the Trusts. This shall not preclude any fiduciary from electing to submit an account for judicial settlement.*

The trust must also provide for the survival presumptions to be made if any beneficiary fails to survive the grantors:

> ***Survival Presumptions.*** *If any beneficiary fails to survive me by thirty (30) days, then such beneficiary shall be deemed to have predeceased me. This Agreement and the Trust established hereunder shall be governed by the laws of this State.*

The survival presumptions vary from state to state with some states requiring survival for only 120 hours in order to qualify for a distribution.

I. Signature

As shown below, there are signature lines for the grantors, John and Linda, and a signature line for Robert Jones accepting his role as the trustee. It is important that John, Linda, and Robert sign the trust document at the same time to make the trust binding on John and Linda as grantors, and Robert as trustee. Although circumstances often arise that require the trust to be executed by each person at a different time, it is preferable that everyone be present at the same time to ensure that all parties are aware of their responsibilities under the terms of the trust.

IN WITNESS WHEREOF. We, John Jones and Linda Jones, as Grantors, and Robert Jones, as Trustee, have set our hands and seals on the _____ day of _____, 20_____.

————————————————————
John Jones, Grantor

————————————————————
Linda Jones, Grantor

————————————————————
Robert Jones, Trustee

Following the signatures of the grantors, the trust would include a clause attesting to the signatures and providing for the signatures of the witnesses or notary depending on the requirements of the state in which the trust is formed. The requirements for the execution of the trust vary from state to state. A form of an attestation clause would be as follows:

*Subscribed, sworn to, and acknowledged before me by **JOHN JONES and LINDA JONES** the Grantors, this_____ day of _____, 201___.*

————————————————————
NOTARY PUBLIC (or Attorney)

*Subscribed, sworn to, and acknowledged before me by **ROBERT JONES** the Trustee, this_____ day of _____, 201___.*

————————————————————
NOTARY PUBLIC (or Attorney)

Finally, the last part of the trust would be "Schedule A" listing the assets that are included in the trust. The form of Schedule A is relatively simple, and sample language would be the following:

SCHEDULE A

The property under the foregoing Trust Agreement shall consist of the following:

TEN ($10.00) DOLLARS CASH

The schedule at the end of the trust can be amended from time to time to reflect the assets owned by the trust. Amending Schedule A can be accomplished without amending the entire trust.

Practice Tip

As each trust is drafted, create a "form bank" using the unique provisions of that trust so that the new language can be included in future trusts with a similar purpose.

Summary

Each paragraph in a trust plays an important role in the creation of a trust. The client will have to identify the trustee, the beneficiaries, the amount and timing of the distribution, and decide whether the trust is going to be revocable, or irrevocable. A sample trust document, created from the paragraphs outlined above, is included at the end of the chapter. Finalization of the trust may take many revisions, requiring careful numbering of each subsequent version of the trust.

Review Questions

1. John and Linda Jones want to serve as the trustees of a trust they are creating. Is it a trust agreement or a declaration of trust? Why?

2. When is a trustee required to obtain a surety bond?

3. When does a trust terminate?

4. Can Robert, as the trustee, be the owner of a piece of real property that is in a trust?

5. How is a successor trustee appointed?

6. Does the trustee have to pay each of the beneficiaries the same amount?

True or False

1. T   F   In a one-pot trust, the trustee is directed to use the funds in the trust for all the beneficiaries, without regard to whether the payments to each beneficiary are equal.

2. T   F   The terms grantor, settlor, and trustor are interchangeable.

3. T   F   A trustee is not required to sign a trust agreement.

4. T   F   If a trustee qualifies and acts as the trustee but then cannot complete his or her duties, the next trustee is the substitute trustee.

5. T   F   If the trustee has discretion to pay out or accumulate income, the trust is known as a sprinkling trust.

6. T   F   A trust can be both revocable and irrevocable.

7. T   F   The assets used to fund the trust are listed in Schedule Λ.

8. T   F   An inter vivos trust is created during the grantor's lifetime.

9. T   F   A UGMA account allows a minor to own securities without a trust.

10. T   F   A grantor can finalize a trust without naming a trustee.

Drafting Exercise

Arnold and Alice Peasgood have three adult sons: Arnold Jr., Andrew, and Alex. Arnold Jr. and Alex are both married and both have two children. Andrew has been married three times, has three children (one with each wife), and has recently moved back home to his parents' house after losing his house to foreclosure. The Peasgoods have a very substantial estate. Arnold recently passed away, leaving Alice as the executor of his estate. Alice has come to the office to talk about making some gifts to her sons, and possibly creating a trust for Andrew, and Andrew's three children, Denise, Jonathan, and Annemarie. Andrew tends to spend money without thinking. His mother is concerned that he will never save enough to own a home, pay for his children's college education, or retire. Alice wants to give all of her sons yearly gifts but wants to control the money that goes to Andrew so that he can use some during his lifetime, but some will be saved for his children. She thinks that she and Arnold Jr. should be trustees, but when she dies, Arnold Jr. can take over.

1. Should this trust be revocable or irrevocable?

2. Can Alice serve as a trustee?

3. Who will be the beneficiaries?

4. What additional information needs to be discussed with Alice?

5. Draft a proposed form of trust for Alice.

Key Terms

Accounting	Sprinkling trust or spray trust
Declaration of trust	or discretionary trust
Grantors	Substitute trustee
Inter vivos	Successor trustee
One-pot trust	Surety bond
Principal	Trust agreement
Revocable trust	Trust formation date
Settlor or trustor	Trustee's commission

Sample Trust Document

We, John Jones and Linda Jones as Grantors, enter into this trust agreement this _____ day of _____, 20_____, with Robert Jones, as Trustee (hereinafter called the "Trustee").

John Jones and Linda Jones make this Declaration of Trust as Grantors, and Trustees as set forth herein this _____ day of _____, 20_____.

Child or Children. *We have three children, John Jones, Grace Jones, and Lily Jones. All references in this Trust to our "child or children" are to said named child or children, and any after borne children.*

Assets. *We have transferred, or we will transfer, those assets listed on Schedule A. The grantors may, with the consent of the Trustee, transfer or assign additional assets or property to the Trustee to be added to Schedule A.*

Administration of Trust. *During our lifetime, the Trustee will accumulate all the income and principal of the assets placed into this Trust, and maintain same for the benefit of my children, as the Trustee in his sole and absolute discretion deems advisable to provide adequately and properly for the secondary education of my children. With respect to such assets, the Trustee shall invest, reinvest, and administer such assets in accordance with the terms of this Trust Agreement.*

Administration of Trust. *During our lifetime, the Trustee may distribute the net income of the assets placed into this Trust, for the benefit of my children, as the Trustee in his sole and absolute discretion deems advisable to provide adequately and properly for the secondary education of my children. Trustee shall add any income not so distributed to principal.*

Amendment and Revocation. *We the Grantors reserve the right and power to alter, amend, or revoke this Agreement, at any time and from time to time, during our lifetimes either in whole or in part, without the consent of the Trustee or any beneficiary hereunder by written notice, acknowledged and delivered to the Trustee other than by Will; provided, however, that the duties, responsibilities, and rate of compensation of the Trustee shall not be altered or modified without the Trustee's written consent.*

Trust Irrevocable. *We have been fully informed as to the distinction between a revocable and irrevocable Trust and declare this to be irrevocable and hereby surrender all rights to revoke same or to alter, amend, or modify any of the provisions of this agreement.*

Division into Separate Children's Shares. *Upon the second of the grantors to die, the balance of the Trust shall be divided into equal shares, one each for our children who have not completed college. In the event that any of our children predecease us, or have already completed college, the Trustee shall divide the balance of the Trust among the remaining children. The Trustee shall hold the assets as separate Trusts for the benefit of each child and shall pay to or apply for his or her benefit all the net income and so much of the principal at any time and from time to time as the Trustee with sole discretion believes advisable to provide adequately for the child's secondary education.*

Compensation of Fiduciaries. *The Trustee shall be entitled to reasonable compensation for services hereunder in accordance with the statutory rate then prevailing. Every fiduciary shall be reimbursed for the reasonable costs and expenses incurred in connection with the administration of the Trusts. The Trustee and any successor Trustee shall serve without bond.*

Trustee Resignation. *The Trustee has the right to resign at any time by thirty (30) days written notice to the grantors. The resignation of a Trustee shall become effective* *upon the appointment and written acceptance of the successor Trustee. If no successor is appointed, then a successor Trustee shall be appointed by a majority of the current adult beneficiaries. The appointment must be made in writing.*

MAY BE INCLUDED — would be used if you do not want one of the beneficiaries to be a trustee

It is our intention that no individual who is a beneficiary shall act as sole Trustee hereunder. If no successor is appointed and qualifies within thirty (30) days of the resignation of the Trustee, then the resigning Trustee or any adult beneficiary may apply to a court of competent jurisdiction for the appointment of a successor Trustee.

Residuary. *Any funds remaining in this Trust after all of my children have reached age 30 or have completed college, whichever comes first, shall be distributed to my children free of Trust, in equal shares, share and share alike.*

Trust Uneconomical. *If at any time the fair market value of the Trust is TEN THOUSAND ($10,000) DOLLARS or less, the Trustee may, within his sole discretion, terminate and distribute the funds remaining in the Trust to the beneficiaries in equal shares.*

Accounting. *It is my desire to avoid the expense and delay of a public or judicial accounting of the administration of the Trusts created hereunder. An accounting of my Trustee approved in writing by all shall be conclusive and binding upon all persons having an interest in the Trusts. This shall not preclude any fiduciary from electing to submit an account for judicial settlement.*

Survival Presumptions. *If any beneficiary fails to survive me by thirty (30) days, then such beneficiary shall be deemed to have predeceased me. This Agreement and the Trust established hereunder shall be governed by the laws of this State.*

IN WITNESS WHEREOF. *We, John Jones and Linda Jones, as Grantors, and Robert Jones, as Trustee, have set our hands and seals on the _____ day of _____, 20_____.*

_____

John Jones, Grantor

_____

Linda Jones, Grantor

_____

Robert Jones, Trustee

*Subscribed, sworn to, and acknowledged before me by **JOHN JONES and LINDA JONES** the Grantors, this _____ day of _____, 201__.*

_____

NOTARY PUBLIC (or Attorney)

*Subscribed, sworn to, and acknowledged before me by **ROBERT JONES** the Trustee, this _____ day of _____, 201__.*

_____

NOTARY PUBLIC (or Attorney)

7

Complex Wills

An estate that is considered "complex" is one in which estate taxes, federal or state estate taxes, will be due. The concept of the complex will is to try to maximize the deductions available and minimize the taxes due. This chapter will outline how a complex will operates to reduce taxes. Complex wills are just that — complex. Learning to draft the provisions of a tax-wise will is beyond the scope of this text. Instead of learning how to draft this type of will, this chapter will focus on understanding the reasoning and the basic operations of a complex will.

A.   What Is a Complex Will?

A basic, or "simple" will devises, or distributes, the decedent's assets to family members, charities, or persons of the decedent's choosing. The term "simple will" is used to describe a will that devises only real and personal property but does not address federal or state inheritance or estate taxes. A complex will or **tax-wise will** is one that is appropriate for estates that will be subject to federal and/or state estate or inheritance taxes because of the size, or value, of the estate. A complex will can also address the issues that arise in estate planning for a couple in their second marriage, when one or both spouses have children from their first marriage.

Tax-wise will: will that is appropriate for estates that will be subject to federal and/or state estate or inheritance taxes because of the size, or value, of the estate

When interviewing a client in preparation for an estate-planning consultation, it is necessary to ask the estimated size of the estate. If the clients are husband and wife, the consultation needs to include determining the size of each individual estate and the couple's combined estate. It is helpful to record the asset information in three columns: one column for the estimated value of all assets in the husband's name, a second column for the estimated value of assets in the wife's name, and a third column with the estimated value of assets that are held jointly in both names. Married couples frequently hold the majority of their assets in joint names. It is common that a couple owns the home jointly, and for many people, their home is the largest asset that they own. It is also important to make careful notes as to children from a previous marriage and whether or not those children will be included in the current will.

In this chapter, we will address two types of complex wills: those done for tax purposes, and those for married couples with children from previous marriages. Complex wills contain various forms of trusts. In Chapter 1 we learned that a will is formally known as a last will and testament. If a will contains a trust, such as a credit shelter trust, bypass trust, or marital trust, that trust is said to be a **testamentary trust**, because it is formed in the will and only becomes valid after the testator has passed away. Trusts that are formed while the person is alive are known as **inter vivos trusts** or **living trusts**. Both types of trusts were discussed in complete detail in Chapters 5 and 6. For now it is important to note that a trust can be formed in a will and can be used to reduce federal or state estate tax, to protect assets going to a beneficiary, or to set out rules as to when a beneficiary can gain access to the assets he or she is to receive.

Testamentary trust: a trust that is formed in a last will and testament

Inter vivos trusts or living trusts: trusts that are formed while the person is alive

B. Federal Gift and Estate Tax

Unified Gift and Estate Tax: Title 26 of the United States Code, a combination of gift tax and estate tax

Estates that have a gross value over a certain limit will incur federal estate tax. A *tax-wise will* is one that takes maximum advantage of the tax credits available to reduce the potential estate tax. In order to understand the operation of a tax-wise will, it is necessary to understand a little bit about how estates are taxed. Estates are taxed pursuant to the federal **Unified Gift and Estate Tax**. The laws for estate tax and gift tax can be found in Chapters 11 and 12 of Title 26 of the United States Code.[1] Title 26 is also where the Internal Revenue Code (IRC) is found. The *Unified Gift and Estate Tax* is a combination of gift tax and estate tax.

The first part of the tax is a gift tax that is imposed on all gifts made above a specific amount. In 2014, the maximum amount that can be gifted without payment of the gift tax is $14,000 per person/per year. Married couples can make what are known as "split gifts" and can make gifts of up to $28,000 per person/per year.

> Example: A married couple with four children wishes to make the maximum amount of gifts allowed per year without paying gift taxes. Mom and Dad can gift $26,000 to each of their four children every year, for a total of $104,000 each year ($13,000 × 2 [mom and dad] × 4 children). If each of their children is married, mom and dad can also gift $26,000 to each of their children's spouses, to each of the grandchildren, and to any other family members.

The gift tax imposes a tax on all gifts, or transfers, of property made during a person's life that are above the maximum amount that is exempt from gift tax. If a gift above $14,000 per person/per year is made, a gift tax is imposed on that gift. The gift tax increases periodically due to inflation adjustments.

There are many types of gifts that are not subject to gift taxes. A gift that is below the maximum amount of $14,000 per year is exempt from tax. Gifts of tuition or

---

1. 26 U.S.C. Subtitle B, Chapter 11, Estate Tax §§2001-2210; 26 U.S.C. Subtitle B, Chapter 12, Gift Tax §§2501-2524.

medical expenses paid directly to an educational or medical institution for someone else, gifts to your spouse, gifts to a political organization for its use, and gifts to charities are also exempt from gift taxes.

The second part of the Unified Gift and Estate Tax is the federal estate tax. Federal estate tax is imposed on the transfer of the **taxable estate** of the decedent if the taxable estate is above a certain amount. In 2014, the maximum size of an estate that can pass free of federal estate tax is $5,340,000. The estate passes tax free because the Unified Gift and Estate Tax law contains a credit for taxes due, which is known as the **unified credit**. In 2014, the unified credit is $2,081,800, which exempts an estate of $5,340,000 from tax. A tax credit reduces the amount of tax owed. A taxable estate of $5,340,000 results in an estate tax of $2,081,800. Therefore, if the tax bill is $2,081,800, and there is a credit for both estate taxes and gift taxes of $2,081,800, then the tax bill is reduced to zero.

The *taxable estate* is composed of all of the decedent's real and personal property that is transferred from the decedent to a beneficiary by way of the decedent's will, by intestate succession, through a trust, or by the distribution of investment accounts directly to beneficiaries. The *taxable estate* is the gross estate, all of the property owned at the time of death, less certain allowable deductions. Calculation of the gross estate and the taxable estate will be discussed in more detail in Chapter 9.

Through a combination of gift taxes and estate taxes, the federal government has tried to ensure that taxes are still paid even if the decedent makes gifts prior to death in an attempt to avoid the estate tax. If a person has an estate that would otherwise be taxed and attempts to gift their assets to their heirs before death to avoid the estate tax, a gift tax will be imposed on the gifts made just prior to death. There are also provisions in the estate tax law and gift tax law that look at how close to a person's death the gifts were made, and whether or not the amounts gifted should be brought back into the estate, and then taxed as part of the estate.

Taxable estate: all of the decedent's real and personal property that is transferred from the decedent to a beneficiary by way of the decedent's will, by intestate succession, through a trust, or by the distribution of investment accounts directly to beneficiaries

Unified credit: a credit for gift and estate taxes due

C.   Credit Shelter Trust Will

The main purpose of a tax-wise will is to limit the amount of estate taxes by taking maximum advantage of the tax credit available. This is accomplished by way of a **credit shelter trust**. A *credit shelter trust* is a trust created in the will that shelters assets from estate tax. A will containing a credit shelter trust is often referred to as a credit shelter will. A tax-wise will is the general name used for a more complex will used for married couples with a combined estate that will exceed the amount covered by the unified credit. The estate tax is imposed on the estate of the second spouse to die. There are no federal estate taxes imposed between a husband and wife. This is known as the **unlimited marital deduction.** All of the deceased spouse's assets, and assets that the couple own jointly, pass to the surviving spouse tax free. No matter how large the estate is, all of the assets in the estate can pass from the first spouse to die to the surviving spouse, and the surviving spouse does not have to pay any taxes. When the surviving spouse (or second to die spouse) passes, the second estate is subject to tax. The tax is paid by the beneficiaries of the second estate, usually the couple's children. Some estates, such as those including businesses, firms, or real

Credit shelter trust: a trust created in the will into which assets from the first spouse to die are placed, thereby sheltering those assets from estate tax

Unlimited marital deduction: no federal estate taxes are imposed between spouses; the surviving spouse does not pay federal estate taxes property investments, do not have enough cash to pay the taxes, requiring assets to be sold.

By way of example, let us look at the estate of Trevor and Katherine Bell who have three children and a very large estate:

Joint assets: Home, estimated value	$2,500,000	
Investment accounts	$2,000,000	
	$4,500,000 Total joint assets	

Trevor's assets: 401(k) from employer	$2,000,000	
Investment property	$1,500,000	
	$3,500,000 Total Trevor's assets	

Katherine's assets: 401(k) from employer	$400,000	
Vacation home	$500,000	
	$950,000 Total Katherine's assets	

When Trevor passes away, the assets held in his name alone, totaling $3,500,000, pass to Katherine tax free. The jointly owned assets, worth $4,500,000, also pass to Katherine tax free for a total of $8,000,000. Add this amount to Katherine's existing assets for an estimated total for Katherine's estate of $8,950,000. If Katherine does no further estate planning after Trevor's death, and assuming her estate is not significantly depleted before her death, her estate will be over the amount that can be sheltered by the unified credit. Katherine's heirs (the couple's three children) will incur significant estate taxes. The federal tax on an estate is 40 percent. In our example, Katherine's estate is $8,950,000 and will therefore incur a tax of $3,580,000. Katherine's estate is entitled to a tax credit of $2,081,800. Therefore, the remaining tax owed is $1,498,200.

Total estate value = $8,950,000
$\times$ 40 percent
$3, 580,000 taxes owed before credit
$-$2,081,800 unified credit
$1,498,200 remaining taxes owed

The remaining tax owed, $1,498,000, must be paid by the couple's three children upon Katherine's death. This tax could be avoided if the couple had a credit shelter trust in their will.

The credit shelter trust operates by preserving the tax credit of the first spouse to die by placing the assets of the first spouse to die into a trust. Each person receives a unified credit that can be used for estate and gift taxes. The unified tax credit is considered to be **portable**, meaning that the credit, or any portion of the credit, not used by the first spouse to die can be preserved and used by the second spouse to die.

Portable: the surviving spouse can use any portion of the $5,000,000 exemption not used by the first spouse to die

At the death of the first spouse, in our example Trevor, the assets go into the credit shelter trust. Those assets are not subject to estate tax because Trevor's unified credit covers the taxes that would have been incurred. Upon the death of the second spouse, Katherine, the assets pass to the children from Katherine's estate covered by Katherine's unified credit, and pass from the trust to the children, without tax because the tax was covered by Trevor's unified credit. (See Figure 7-1.)

Figure 7-1. Example: Credit Shelter Trust

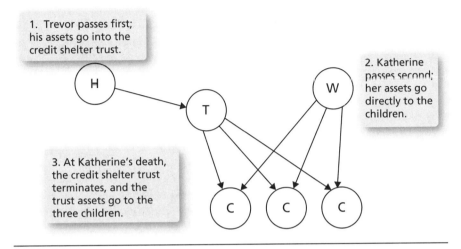

1. Trevor passes first; his assets go into the credit shelter trust.

2. Katherine passes second; her assets go directly to the children.

3. At Katherine's death, the credit shelter trust terminates, and the trust assets go to the three children.

A credit shelter operates by putting the assets of the first spouse to die into a credit shelter trust instead of having those assets pass to the surviving spouse. Assets passing between a husband and wife are not taxed, but if instead those assets pass to a trust, estate taxes would be incurred. The unified tax credit of the first spouse to die is used for the taxes incurred by putting his assets into trust instead of passing those assets to the surviving spouse. When the surviving spouse passes away, the assets in the credit shelter trust pass to the couple's children, and the assets from the surviving spouse pass to the children, protected by the surviving spouse's unified credit. Using the credit of each spouse, the couple can shelter an estate of up to $10,680,000.

Let us look at how a credit shelter trust would operate for our clients Trevor and Katherine with three children, with the large estate, from our previous example:

Joint assets:	Home, estimated value	$2,500,000
	Investment accounts	$2,000,000
		$4,500,000 Total joint assets
Trevor's assets:	401(k) from employer	$2,000,000
	Investment property	$1,500,000
		$3,500,000 Total Trevor's assets
Katherine's assets:	401(k) from employer	$400,000
	Vacation home	$500,000
		$950,000 Total Katherine's assets

Let us assume again that Trevor passes away first. The assets that are in Trevor's name alone, $3,500,000, will pass into a credit shelter trust, and Trevor's unified credit will cover the estate taxes owed. The jointly held assets, $4,500,000, will pass to Katherine. Remember, there is no tax between a husband and wife, so Katherine will not owe federal estate tax. Upon Katherine's death, Katherine's estate, which now consists of the jointly held assets of $4,500,000 and the assets she held, $950,000, for a total of $5,450,000, will pass to the couple's children. Katherine's

Figure 7-2. Credit Shelter Trust

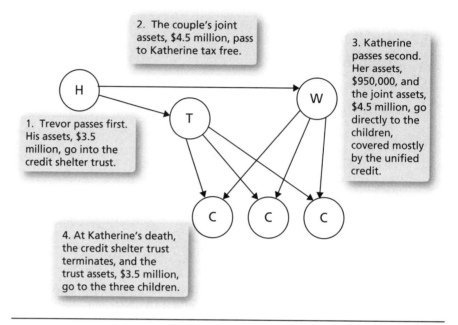

2. The couple's joint assets, $4.5 million, pass to Katherine tax free.

3. Katherine passes second. Her assets, $950,000, and the joint assets, $4.5 million, go directly to the children, covered mostly by the unified credit.

1. Trevor passes first. His assets, $3.5 million, go into the credit shelter trust.

4. At Katherine's death, the credit shelter trust terminates, and the trust assets, $3.5 million, go to the three children.

estate will incur a tax of $2,180,000 ($5,450,000 × 40 percent), which is mostly covered by the unified credit of $2,081,800, leaving a tax of only $98,200. The assets from the credit shelter trust will pass to the children tax free because of Trevor's unified credit. By using a credit shelter in the will, the estate tax is significantly reduced and/or eliminated. (See Figure 7-2.)

A credit shelter will provides significant tax savings to the beneficiaries of the second spouse to die. A credit shelter trust is also often called a **bypass trust** because the property placed in this type of trust is not subject to federal estate tax in the surviving spouse's estate. In other words, the assets placed into the trust "bypass" the surviving spouse and "bypass" the tax.

The surviving spouse can be given some limited access to the trust assets. The surviving spouse can receive all of the trust's income for life. The surviving spouse can also get principal from the trust to pay for health costs, education, maintenance, and support. If the trustee is an independent trustee, meaning it is not a family member and not a beneficiary of the trust, the trust can be written to give the trustee discretion to give unlimited amounts of trust principal to the surviving spouse. The surviving spouse can have what is known as a **power of appointment** over trust assets. This means that the surviving spouse can direct, either during his or her lifetime or in his or her will, that trust assets should go to his or her children or grandchildren. The surviving spouse cannot use this power of appointment to make gifts to him- or herself, or to his or her own estate. The surviving spouse can also be given the right to make annual withdrawals from the trust of the greater of $5,000 or 5 percent of the value of trust. This right of withdrawal is

Bypass trust: also known as a credit shelter; trust property placed in this type of trust is not subject to federal estate tax in the surviving spouse's estate; assets placed into the trust "bypass" the surviving spouse and "bypass" the tax

Power of appointment: surviving spouse can direct, either during his or her lifetime or in his or her will, that trust assets should go to his or her children or grandchildren noncumulative, meaning if the surviving spouse does not exercise this right in one year, he or she may not take two years' worth of withdrawals the following year. Using these rights, the surviving spouse can gain access to a good portion of the trust assets if the trustee agrees.

D. A/B Trusts Will

In the example we used above, the will of the first spouse to die contains a credit shelter trust. When the first spouse dies, his or her assets go into the credit shelter trust and are sheltered from taxation. The remaining assets pass to the surviving spouse free of trust. However, many times, the will contains two trusts. Another type of will that addresses estate tax issues is an **A/B will**. An *A/B will* contains two trusts: the first trust, or the "A" trust, is a marital trust, and the second trust is the "B" trust, which is known as the credit shelter or bypass marital trust. The joint assets passing to the surviving spouse go into the marital trust and qualify for the marital deduction from estate tax. Assets in the decedent's name alone can be used to fund the credit shelter trust. The credit shelter trust is usually funded up to the maximum amount that can be sheltered by the unified credit. (See Figure 7-3.)

A/B will: type of will that addresses estate tax issues; contains two trusts: the first trust, or the "A" trust, is a marital trust, and the second trust is the "B" trust, which is known as the credit shelter or bypass marital trust

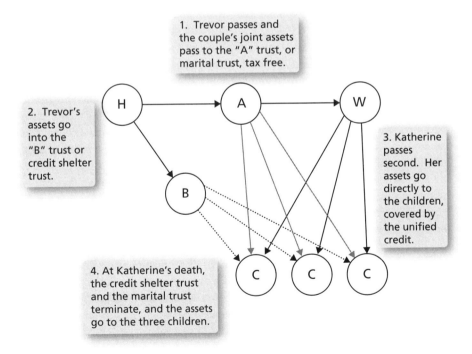

1. Trevor passes and the couple's joint assets pass to the "A" trust, or marital trust, tax free.

2. Trevor's assets go into the "B" trust or credit shelter trust.

3. Katherine passes second. Her assets go directly to the children, covered by the unified credit.

4. At Katherine's death, the credit shelter trust and the marital trust terminate, and the assets go to the three children.

Figure 7-3. Example: A/B Trust

E.   QTIP Trust Wills

Qualified terminable interest property (QTIP): a type of trust created in a will that allows income to the spouse for life, but restricts the spouse's ability to redirect the assets in the trust after his or her death; typically used in second marriages

In our example, Trevor, or Katherine, or both, may have children from a prior marriage. They may each have children from a first marriage, and they may have children together. Each spouse may have accumulated real and personal property from his or her former spouse that he or she may want to preserve for children of the prior marriage. A complex will is also useful in doing estate planning for couples that are in second marriages and have children from their first marriage. Where a simple will would pass most or all of the assets to the surviving spouse, a more complex will, containing a specific type of trust, can pass certain assets to the surviving spouse for use during his or her lifetime and then ensure that those assets pass to the children from a first marriage. For a married couple that has potential estate tax concerns and has children from first marriages, it may be appropriate to use a specific type of trust called a **qualified terminable interest property** (QTIP) trust. A QTIP trust works in conjunction with a credit shelter trust in the same way as the A/B trust will operates. However, in a marital trust, the surviving spouse can have control over the trust assets. When the A trust is a QTIP trust, the surviving spouse gets income from the QTIP trust, but he or she cannot withdraw the principal of the trust and cannot change who will receive the benefits of the trust upon his or her death. The QTIP trust is used when there is concern that the surviving spouse will remarry or where there is a second marriage and one or both spouses are concerned about the surviving spouse disinheriting the children from a first marriage in favor of his or her own children.

F.   Equalize Asset Ownership

As noted, it is important when first interviewing a married couple to take note of the total amount of assets and to note the amount of assets held in the husband's name alone, the amount in the wife's name alone, and the amount held in joint names. This asset list becomes part of the client's file. If the joint assets are not divided and the total assets not equalized, the estate tax planning that was attempted by drafting a tax-wise will could potentially fail. A careful record must be made that the clients were advised to do the division of assets, and the reason why they were instructed to divide the assets. If the clients do not follow through on the advice and their estate incurs significant taxes, the heirs will want an explanation of what advice was given. In most cases, in order to take maximum advantage of the tax credits and tax shelters, it is necessary to sever joint interests between a husband and wife. Assets that are held jointly by a husband and wife pass automatically to the surviving spouse and usually cannot be used to fund the credit shelter trust.

For some clients, the asset ownership may be disproportional, with one party having significantly more than the other party. This requires a reallocation of assets so that each party has enough assets in each party's own name to fund the credit shelter trust. If, for example, the majority of the couple's assets were held in Trevor's name alone, and Katherine passed first, the unified credit that was available to Katherine is not used because there are insufficient assets in Katherine's estate. The reverse can also be true. Trevor could hold a great deal more assets, and he could pass first. The assets in his estate could be more than what could be sheltered by the unified credit.

In order to illustrate the need to split the assets equally, let us change our example to husband and wife clients with a large combined estate, with the wife, Katherine, holding a disproportionately smaller amount of the assets:

Joint assets: Home, estimated value	$2,500,000
Various investment accounts	$4,000,000
Vacation home	$500,000
	$7,000,000 Total joint assets
Trevor's assets: 401(k) from employer	$1,500,000
Investment property	$1,500,000
	$3,000,000 Total Trevor's assets
Katherine's assets: 401(k) from employer	$100,000
Bank account	$50,000
	$150,000 Total Katherine's assets

In this example, if Trevor passes away first, Katherine will inherit the jointly owned property worth $7,000,000. Trevor's assets, worth $3,000,000, would be used to fund the credit shelter trust. When Katherine passes away, her estate consists of the $7,000,000 of joint assets and her own $150,000 of assets for a total of $7,150,000. An estate tax of $2,502,500 will be owed. The unified credit of $2,081,800 will be applied, leaving an estate tax owed of $420,700. A portion of the unified credit that could have been used is wasted. (See Figure 7-4.)

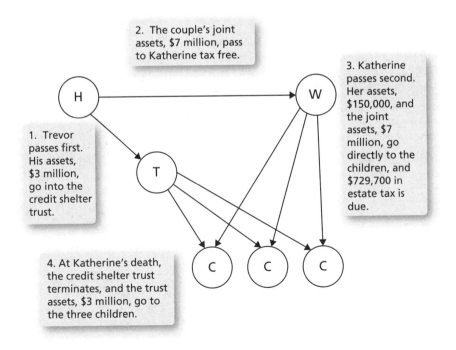

Figure 7-4. Example: Unequal Assets

Figure 7-5. Example: Unequal Assets

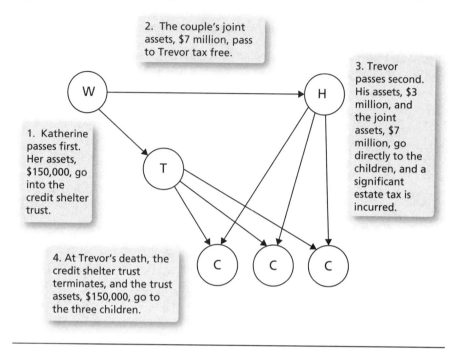

2. The couple's joint assets, $7 million, pass to Trevor tax free.

3. Trevor passes second. His assets, $3 million, and the joint assets, $7 million, go directly to the children, and a significant estate tax is incurred.

1. Katherine passes first. Her assets, $150,000, go into the credit shelter trust.

4. At Trevor's death, the credit shelter trust terminates, and the trust assets, $150,000, go to the three children.

Or the reverse can occur. If Katherine passes first, the only assets in her name alone are those worth $150,000. Those assets can be used to fund a credit shelter trust, but the majority of the unified credit that could be used by her estate is wasted. Trevor's estate, consisting of the assets in his name and the joint assets, would then be worth $10,000,000. The estate would generate a tax of $4,000, ($10,000,000 × 40 percent), and the unified credit will cover only $2,081,800 of the estate taxes due, leaving an estate tax bill of $1,918,200. (See Figure 7-5.)

The estate tax in this example could have been avoided if the assets were equally split between the husband and wife. In many cases, it may be necessary to transfer the house and other assets from being jointly held by the husband and wife into just the wife's name in order to equalize the amount of assets each holds. Reallocating assets among the spouses is often something that a client is reluctant to do, even if it would result in less estate tax being owed.

The same estate tax result happens if our wealthy couple owns all of their assets jointly, because when one spouse passes, the surviving spouse automatically owns all of the assets and there is no opportunity to place these assets into a trust. (See Figure 7-6.)

Joint assets: Home, estimated value	$2,500,000
Various investment accounts	$4,000,000
Vacation home	$500,000
Investment property	$1,500,000
	$8,500,000 Total joint assets

Figure 7-6. Example: Jointly Owned Assets

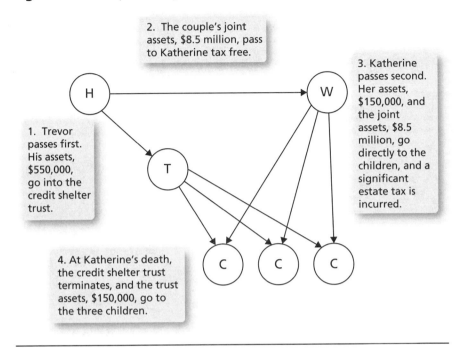

2. The couple's joint assets, $8.5 million, pass to Katherine tax free.

3. Katherine passes second. Her assets, $150,000, and the joint assets, $8.5 million, go directly to the children, and a significant estate tax is incurred.

1. Trevor passes first. His assets, $550,000, go into the credit shelter trust.

4. At Katherine's death, the credit shelter trust terminates, and the trust assets, $150,000, go to the three children.

Trevor's assets: 401(k) from employer	$500,000
Bank account	$50,000
	$550,000 Total Trevor's assets
Katherine's assets: 401(k) from employer	$100,000
Bank account	$50,000
	$150,000 Total Katherine's assets

In this example, the bulk of the couple's assets are owned jointly. Those assets automatically pass to the surviving spouse and usually cannot be used to fund a credit shelter trust. Therefore, if Trevor passes first, Katherine inherits $8,500,000 of joint assets and can only use Trevor's assets totaling $550,000 to fund a credit shelter trust. Most of the unified credit will be wasted. A similar result occurs if Katherine passes first, and Trevor inherits $8,500,000 of joint assets and can only use Katherine's assets totaling $150,000 to fund the credit shelter trust. In order for the credit shelter trust within the will to work properly, it is imperative that the couple not only split their assets, but that the split be equal.

There are many occasions when the benefit of a credit shelter trust is explained to a couple, and the couple chooses not to use this type of complex will to reduce or eliminate their potential estate taxes. The use of a credit shelter trust is complex and requires the appointment of a trustee. The surviving spouse can serve as the sole trustee and cannot have complete control over the assets in the trust. If the surviving spouse were to have complete control over the assets in the trust, then those assets would be included in the surviving spouse's estate when he or she passed away. The assets are kept out of the surviving spouse's estate because the surviving spouse does not have complete control over those assets.

There is always a fear (or even the very real possibility) that the trustee will refuse to turn over trust assets or that the surviving spouse will be left without sufficient assets to provide for care. Despite the various rights that are given to the surviving spouse, the surviving spouse does not have complete control. This requirement of giving up control of the assets is often the reason why a couple chooses not to use a credit shelter trust.

G. Funding the Trust or Trusts

Pecuniary share: the smallest amount that, if allowed as a marital deduction, would result in the least possible federal estate tax

Fractional share formula: funds both the marital trust and the credit shelter trust proportionally, allocating a portion of each asset to the marital trust in the proportion that each trust bears to the total value

Up-front marital formula: funds the marital trust first and then uses the remaining assets to fund the credit shelter trust

Reverse marital formula: funds the credit shelter first, and the remaining assets go into the marital trust

The amount that is placed into the credit shelter trust and how those funds can be used by the surviving spouse are determined in a number of different ways. Often the language used in the will does not require that a specific dollar amount be placed into trust but instead provides the method of calculating the amount placed into trust. Regardless of how the amount is calculated, the goal is to reduce or eliminate federal estate tax, and possibly state estate tax, by taking maximum advantage of the unified credit, or state tax credit.

There are two methods, or formulas used, to calculate the amount that is placed in a marital trust: a **pecuniary share formula** and a **fractional share formula**. A *pecuniary share formula* funds a specific dollar amount. A *pecuniary share* would be the smallest amount that, if allowed as a marital deduction, would result in the least possible federal estate tax. The remainder of the decedent's estate will go into a credit shelter trust. A *fractional share formula* funds both the marital trust and the credit shelter trust proportionally. A fractional formula allocates a portion of each asset to the marital trust in the proportion that each trust bears to the total value.

There are a variety of pecuniary formulas available. Some formulas fund the marital trust first and then use the remaining assets to fund the credit shelter trust. This type of formula is called an **up-front marital formula**. Other formulas fund the credit shelter first, and the remaining assets go into the marital trust. This type of formula is called a **reverse marital formula**.

Sample language for a pecuniary share would be the following:

If my spouse survives me, I devise to my spouse, outright and free of trust, the minimum amount necessary to reduce the federal estate tax to zero, or as close thereto as possible, by utilizing the unlimited marital deduction available under the federal estate tax law in effect at the time of my death, but only after taking into account all credits for federal estate tax purposes available to my estate and all other assets which pass to my said spouse under this Will or otherwise and which qualify for the marital deduction.

The fractional formula uses a fraction to determine how much goes into the trust. The numerator of the fraction is the amount of the marital share, and the denominator of the fraction is the residue of the estate:

If my spouse survives me, I devise to my Trustee, that fractional share of my residuary estate which is the minimum portion necessary to reduce the federal estate tax for my estate to zero, or as close to zero as possible.

Whether using the pecuniary share or fractional share formulas, the accountant and/or attorney who are responsible for completing the estate tax return usually calculate the amount to go into the credit shelter trust.

H.   State Estate Tax

The majority of states do not have a state estate tax. However, there are, as of January 1, 2014, 17 states that impose an estate tax based on the size of the estate. There are also states that impose an inheritance tax, which is mostly based on the nature of the relationship of the beneficiary to the decedent. Beneficiaries who are farther down the family tree are typically taxed higher than the immediate family. For example, in New Jersey, the inheritance tax is not applied to **lineal descendants**. A *lineal descendant* is one up or down from the decedent, like a parent or a child. An inheritance tax is imposed on nonlineal descendants like siblings, nieces and nephews, cousins, and so forth. The extent of the estate tax and the calculation of the amount due will be discussed in full detail in Chapter 9. Figure 7-7 shows the states that currently have an estate tax, the states with an inheritance tax, and those states with both taxes, as of December 2013.

Lineal descendant: a descendant who is one up or down from the decedent, like a parent or a child

Estate Tax	Inheritance tax	Both Estate Tax and Inheritance Tax
Connecticut	Iowa	Maryland
Delaware	Kentucky	New Jersey
District of Columbia	Nebraska	
Illinois	Pennsylvania	
Maine	Tennessee	
Massachusetts		
Minnesota		
New York		
Oregon		
Rhode Island		
Vermont		
Washington		

Figure 7-7. States with Estate Tax and Inheritance Tax

Obviously, this type of estate planning is reserved for clients with very large estates that need to address estate tax issues. There are attorneys who have developed a specialty in drafting very complex wills and estate plans for very wealthy clients. For most attorneys, drafting a complex or tax-wise will is not common, as most clients' estates are not large enough to require sheltering from federal tax. However, in those states that have a state estate tax, the complex or tax-wise will can also be used to shelter a portion of the estate of the first spouse to die from state estate taxes in the same manner as it operates for an estate subject to federal estate taxes.

I. Tax Planning for Same-Sex Couples

The complex or tax-wise wills discussed in this chapter are useful only for federal estate tax planning for married couples. Previously, the term "married" was defined in the Defense of Marriage Act (DOMA) [Pub. L. No. 104-199, 110 Stat. 2419 (1996); 1 U.S.C. §7 (1996); 28 U.S.C. §1738C (1996)] as the "legal union between one man and one woman as husband and wife" and the word "spouse" as "a person of the opposite sex who is a husband or a wife" [1 U.S.C. §7 (1996)]. DOMA prevented the federal government from recognizing same-sex marriages and left it up to each individual state to determine if that state will recognize it. Therefore, federal tax exemptions or credits that are available for husbands and wives in an opposite-sex marriage were not available for persons in same-sex marriages, civil unions, or domestic partnerships. In 2013 there were a number of cases before the U.S. Supreme Court addressing same-sex marriage rights. In the case of *United States v. Windsor*, the Supreme Court specifically looked at the DOMA. The Supreme Court ruled, by a vote of five to four, that the law was unconstitutional. This ruling opened the door for each state to adopt legislation recognizing same-sex marriages and affording people in those marriages the same tax benefits available to different-sex marriages.

Now there are many states in which there is some recognition of same-sex relationships, either through same-sex marriage, domestic partnership, or civil union. In those states that have legislative recognition of a same-sex marriage, there is a corresponding recognition of a more favorable state tax treatment for the surviving spouse of a same-sex relationship. State tax deductions and exemptions that are available to an opposite-sex spouse are also available to a same-sex spouse.

As of this writing, the states that recognize same-sex marriages either by court decision, state law, or popular vote are the following: California, Connecticut, Delaware, Hawaii, Illinois, Iowa, Maine, Maryland, Massachusetts, Minnesota, Nevada, New Hampshire, New Jersey, New Mexico, New York, Oregon, Pennsylvania, Rhode Island, Vermont, and Washington. These states provide the same state estate tax treatment to same-sex spouses as to opposite-sex spouses. Federal estate tax exemptions should be applied to same-sex spouses who have been married in those states where the same-sex marriage is permitted by law.

Summary

A complex will is used to minimize taxes and maximize use of tax credit. It is used for very large estates, for those that will be subject to federal estate taxes, or in those few states in which state estate tax is imposed. A complex will contains a specific type of trust that preserves the tax credit of the first spouse to die, thereby maximizing the credit available. Failing to draft the correct terms within a complex will can result in the heirs owing significant additional taxes.

Review Questions

1. What type of will is best for a husband and wife with a large estate, where the husband has two children from his first marriage?

2. What is the federal estate tax for property owned jointly by a husband and wife when the husband dies and the property passes to the wife as the surviving spouse?

3. What is the unified credit, and how is it applied to federal estate taxes?

4. How should a married couple own their assets in order to take full advantage of the tax credits and shelters available?

5. What are the names of the two different methods or formulas used to calculate the amount that goes into a marital trust?

6. A credit shelter trust is also known as a _____ trust.

7. Are same-sex couples entitled to an unlimited marital deduction?

True or False

1. T   F   A tax-wise will can be used for same-sex couples.

2. T   F   Certain types of gifts are exempt from taxation.

3. T   F   QTIP trusts allow full access to all of the assets.

4. T   F   If property is held jointly, it can be used to fund a credit shelter trust.

5. T   F   A credit shelter trust in a will is a testamentary trust.

6. T   F   A married couple can make a split gift of $28,000 per person per year.

7. T   F   Pecuniary share and fractional share are two methods of calculating the amount to go into a marital trust.

8. T   F   A very wealthy client says that he can gift away all of his assets, and as long as he does not die within one year, no taxes are due.

9. T   F   The term "unlimited marital deduction" describes the fact that there are no estate taxes between a husband and wife.

10. T   F   A portable tax credit means the first spouse to die carries the credit with him or her to the grave.

11. T   F   A complex will can also address the issues that arise in estate planning for a couple in their second marriage.

12. T   F   The surviving spouse has no access to any assets in a credit shelter trust.

13. T   F   QTIP trusts are best used by clients who are in their first marriage and have no children.

14. T   F   In 2014, the Unified Gift and Estate Tax credit was $2,081,800.

Key Terms

A/B will
Bypass trust
Credit shelter trust
Fractional share formula
Inter vivos trusts or living
   trusts
Lineal descendant
Pecuniary share
Portable
Power of appointment

Qualified terminable interest property
   (QTIP)
Reverse marital formula
Taxable estate
Tax-wise will
Testamentary trust
Unified credit
Unified Gift and Estate Tax
Unlimited marital deduction
Up-front marital formula

8

Complex Trusts

In Chapter 5 we learned that trusts could be revocable or irrevocable. Trusts can be created during a person's lifetime, *inter vivos* or living trusts, or in a person's will, testamentary trusts. The goals of the trust will dictate whether a trust is revocable or irrevocable, or if it is created immediately or only after death. For example, if the goal of the trust is asset protection, then the trust must be irrevocable, and the grantor must give up the right to control the funds placed in the trust. By giving up control and making the trustee responsible for managing the asset pursuant to the terms of the trust, the asset is no longer owned by the grantor and is therefore not subject to taxes that the grantor might incur. Asset protection can mean protection from taxes or liability.

Another factor governing the choice of a trust is the desire for privacy. A client may prefer to distribute assets in a trust instead of a will because a trust can be kept private, whereas a will has to be admitted to probate and then it becomes a public document. The goal of this chapter is to explain the different types of trusts and the reasons for choosing different types of trusts. However, the choice of trust and the language included in each trust are the responsibility of the attorney drafting the trust.

Practice Tip

Clients will often come in with a preconceived notion of the type of trust they want, but after discussion about the goals of the trust, it will be determined that an entirely different type of trust is required. Remember, the goals of the trust govern the type of trust, not what the neighbor next door has in his or her trust, or what is being advertised on TV, or any other outside factor.

A.   Marital Trusts and Family Trusts

Marital trusts and family trusts are used in large estates to minimize the amount of federal estate tax due. These two types of trusts are often used together in very large

Marital trust: allows for assets to pass from the decedent spouse to the surviving spouse without being taxed

Unlimited marital deduction: because there is no estate tax between a husband and wife, the amount of the estate tax deduction is referred to as "unlimited"

Family trust: generally funded by the assets left in the decedent's estate that are not included in the marital trust; grantor decides the terms of the trust, chooses the beneficiaries, and appoints a trustee to administer the trust

General power of appointment: the surviving spouse has the ability to name the beneficiaries of the marital trust assets that remain at his or her death

estates. A **marital trust** allows for assets to pass from the decedent spouse to the surviving spouse without being taxed. There is no tax between a husband and wife — this is known as the **unlimited marital deduction**. A **family trust** is generally funded by the assets left in the decedent's estate that are not included in the marital trust. The grantor decides the terms of the trust, chooses the beneficiaries, and appoints a trustee to administer the trust.

The marital trust operates by ensuring that assets from the decedent spouse pass only to the surviving spouse, thereby qualifying for the marital deduction. The marital trust can also include provisions that prevent the surviving spouse from disposing of all of the assets in the trust during his or her lifetime. In order for the assets passing into the trust to qualify for the unlimited marital deduction, two conditions must exist: first, the surviving spouse must have a right to receive the income from the trust; and second, the surviving spouse must have a **general power of appointment** over the principal of the trust. A *general power of appointment* means that the surviving spouse has the ability to name the beneficiaries of the marital trust assets that remain at his or her death. If these two conditions do not exist within the trust, the IRS will not allow the use of the marital deduction on the estate tax return of the decedent spouse, resulting in the assets being brought back into the decedent estate for tax purposes.

A family trust allows a very wealthy grantor to pass some of that wealth to other family members, but to control how those funds are used. Typically, the marital trust is funded first, and a provision is included in the will that the remaining assets, or some portion of those assets, are then placed into the family trust. Typically the decedent's children are named as the beneficiaries, although the surviving spouse can also be a beneficiary of a family trust. Assets in a testamentary family trust are not included in the surviving spouse's estate, even if the surviving spouse is a beneficiary, because the surviving spouse does not control those assets.

Using a family trust is not always necessary for tax planning. Instead, family trusts are often used to pass assets to children from a first marriage, or to control the use of the assets. Provisions can be included in the family trust to allow for payments of principal and/or income, restrict the ages at which payments from the trust can be made, or add any other controls or limits the grantor wants to place on the distribution of funds from the family trust.

B.   Credit Shelter Trusts

Credit shelter trust: trust created in the will that shelters assets from estate tax

Credit shelter will or A/B will: a will containing a credit shelter trust

A **credit shelter trust** is a trust created in the will that shelters assets from estate tax. It is used in more complex estate planning for married couples who have a combined estate that will exceed the amount covered by the unified credit. A will containing a *credit shelter trust* is often referred to as a **credit shelter will** or *A/B will*. The will contains two trusts: the first trust, or the "A" trust, is a marital trust, and the second trust is the "B" trust, which is known as the credit shelter, or bypass marital trust. The joint assets passing to the surviving spouse go into the marital trust and qualify for the marital deduction from estate tax. Assets in the decedent's name alone can be used to fund the credit shelter trust. The credit shelter trust is usually funded up to the maximum amount that can be sheltered by the unified credit.

Credit shelter trusts can also be created during a person's lifetime but are usually not funded until the death of the first spouse. The provisions of the credit shelter trust are similar whether the trust is created *inter vivos* or as a testamentary trust. Assets are passed from the decedent to the trust, protected by the decedent's estate tax credit. The remaining assets pass to the surviving spouse. The credit shelter trust distributes the assets after the death of the second spouse. The circumstances under which a credit shelter trust is needed will be discussed further in Chapters 12 and 13.

C. QTIP Trusts

For a married couple that has potential estate tax concerns and has children from first marriages, it may be appropriate to use a specific type of trust call a **qualified terminable interest property** (QTIP) trust. A QTIP trust works in conjunction with a credit shelter trust in the same way as the A/B trust will operates. However, in a marital trust, the surviving spouse can have control over the trust assets. When the A trust is a QTIP trust, the surviving spouse gets income from the QTIP trust, but he or she cannot withdraw the principal of the trust and cannot change who will receive the benefits of the trust upon his or her death.

A QTIP trust can be written to provide the greater of $5,000 or 5 percent of the trust assets to the surviving spouse every year. The trust must provide that the surviving spouse receive all of the income from the trust annually for the rest of his or her life. But the surviving spouse cannot designate what happens to the assets upon his or her death. Upon the death of the surviving spouse, the trust is distributed according to the beneficiaries named by the first spouse to die. The executor of the estate can make an election to claim the marital deduction for amounts transferred to a QTIP trust so that those assets also pass without federal estate taxation.

A QTIP trust allows a testator to take advantage of the marital deduction for transfers made to the surviving spouse while still limiting the ownership rights the surviving spouse has over assets in the trust. This restriction ensures that the trust will ultimately pass to the beneficiaries named by the first spouse to die and not the children or family of the surviving spouse. The QTIP trust is used when there is concern that the surviving spouse will remarry or where there is a second marriage and one or both spouses are concerned about the surviving spouse disinheriting the children from a first marriage in favor of his or her own children.

Qualified terminable interest property (QTIP) trust: a type of trust that allows the surviving spouse to receive income but does not allow the surviving spouse to either withdraw the principal of the trust or change who will receive the benefits of the trust upon death

D. Special Needs Trusts

A **special needs trust** (SNT) is a trust formed for the benefit of a disabled person which will allow the disabled person to hold assets while continuing to qualify for income- or asset-based governmental benefits. The authority to create SNTs comes from 42 U.S.C. 1396p(d)(4)(A), which is why SNTs are also known as (d)(4)(A) trusts. In order to create a special needs trust, the beneficiary must be under age 65 and disabled as that term is used in the social security regulations. For a minor, a

Special needs trust (SNT): a trust formed for the benefit of a disabled person which will allow the disabled person to hold assets while continuing to qualify for income- or asset-based governmental benefits person would be considered disabled if he or she "has a medically determinable physical or mental impairment, which results in marked and severe functional limitations, and which can be expected to result in death or which has lasted or can be expected to last for a continuous period of not less than 12 months." An individual age 18 and older is "disabled" if he or she has a medically determinable physical or mental impairment that results in the inability to do any substantial gainful activity, and can be expected to result in death, or has lasted or can be expected to last for a continuous period of not less than 12 months. A parent, grandparent, or legal guardian of the beneficiary, or a court are the only parties that can establish an SNT. All expenditures from the SNT must be for the sole benefit of the disabled beneficiary.

A SNT is specifically designed to allow a person to benefit from assets held in a trust for him or her, while allowing the person to continue to be eligible for governmental benefits such as Medicaid. Medicaid is a governmental healthcare program for individuals and families that meet income- and assets-based tests. It is found in Social Security Act, Title XIX, 42 U.S.C. §§1396, et seq. Medicaid provides health insurance to the parents or caretakers and dependent children, pregnant women, and people who are aged, blind, or disabled. Medicaid can provide payment for hospital services, doctor visits, prescriptions, nursing home care, and other healthcare needs, if the person receiving Medicaid is eligible for those programs. Medicaid has strict limits on the amount of income and assets that a person can have and continue to be eligible for benefits.

The specific eligibility requirements for Medicaid are unique to each state. Many states include residency requirements and citizenship requirements. In order to be eligible for Medicaid a person must be a parent or caretaker of dependent children, over 65, blind, or permanently disabled, or pregnant. Eligibility is also determined by specific standards for income and resources or assets.

Medicaid should not be confused with Medicare which is the federal health insurance program for workers who have paid into the Medicare system, Social Security Act, Title XVIII, 42 U.S.C. §§1395 et seq. Eligibility for Medicare requires payment into the Medicare system for 40 quarters or obtaining 40 "credits." As of the date of publication of this text, a worker paying into the Medicare system earns one credit per $920 of salary earned and can earn up to four credits per year. Earning the 40 credits required for Medicare eligibility requires at least ten years of employment. A married person can also qualify on the basis of his or her spouse's work history.

Medicare is medical insurance and requires the payment of premiums and co-pays. Certain prescription drugs are covered only in part, and there are many costs that are not covered by Medicare. If a person is disabled, requires care, and has no assets, that person can become eligible for Medicaid, which covers all necessary medical services. A SNT is a specific type of trust for disabled persons who are receiving Medicaid or other governmental benefits.

Eligibility for Medicaid is based on the factors listed above and certain financial criteria. In order to be eligible for Medicaid, a person must be receiving very little income and, in most cases, have less than $2,000 in assets. Social security income, veterans' benefits, pensions, annuities, interest, dividends, payments from trust funds, and rental income from real property all qualify as income and can cause a person to be ineligible for Medicaid. Assets that are held in a SNT are not included as income or resources in determining if a person is eligible for Medicaid. If a disabled person has assets or income that exceeds the limits, he or she will be ineligible to receive Medicaid. If a person is already receiving Medicaid and inherits assets, then he or she may be ineligible to continue to receive benefits. For example, the Thomas' have a son, Dean, who was born with cerebral palsy. Dean requires full-time care and lives in a group home that provides housing, medical care, education, and social activities. The cost of Dean's care is paid by Medicaid because Dean has never been able to work, receives a small amount of money from Social Security disability, and has no assets. When Dean's grandfather dies, he leaves Dean $10,000 in his will. The $10,000 is distributed to Dean, and the next month Dean is found by Medicaid to be over the resource limits of Medicaid. Dean would then be ineligible for Medicaid. Because Dean requires full-time care, the $10,000 bequest from his grandfather was quickly used up paying for Dean's healthcare costs. When the inheritance money runs out, Dean must requalify for Medicaid. This gap in eligibility can result in loss of services or inability to afford medications or treatments. To avoid this difficulty, the will should have directed that funds go into a special needs trust.

Practice Tip

As part of the initial interview with a client regarding a new will, the client should be asked if any of the beneficiaries of the proposed will are disabled or have special needs so that a trust can be suggested if necessary.

There are two types of special needs trusts: **first party special needs trusts** and **third party special needs trusts**. In a first party special needs trust the source of the funds is the disabled person's own money, such as the settlement from a personal injury action. Special needs trusts funded with the disabled person's own funds are also known as "self-settled" or "first person" trusts. This type of special needs trust is often established by the court as part of the settlement of personal injury litigation, and the monies received from the litigation are placed into the trust. An example of a first party trust would be if Dean's parents had filed personal injury litigation for Dean claiming that the reason dean has cerebral palsy is because of a birth injury. If Dean were to be awarded money damages, that money could be placed in a SNT for Dean. The creation of the SNT and the order placing the funds into the trust would be part of the final settlement of the litigation.

First party special needs trusts: a special needs trust where the source of the funds is the disabled person's own money

Third party special needs trust: a special needs trust where the source of the funds can be gifts or bequests from various friends and family members or the trust can be set up in the last will and testament of the disabled person under a parent or other family member

Practice Tip

Many personal injury attorneys are unaware of the impact of Medicaid and the benefit of SNTs. Working with a personal injury attorney on SNTs can be a good source for mutual referrals.

A third party special needs trust is one in which the source of the funds is bequests from friends or family members. A third party special needs trust can be set up in the last will and testament of the disabled person's parent or other family member. The testamentary SNT is funded when the testator dies, and the trust receives funds from the decedent's estate and holds those funds on behalf of the disabled person. The trust created for Dean in his grandfather's will from our example above is a third party SNT because it is funded by a bequest from Dean's grandfather.

The main difference between a first party and a third party SNT is what happens to any funds remaining in the trust after the death of the disabled person and whether or not those funds must be used to reimburse any benefits that were paid. In a first party or self-settled trust, any funds remaining in the trust after the death of the disabled person must be used to reimburse Medicaid for any monies expended for medical care provided to the disabled person while the trust was in existence. Medical care includes home healthcare or nursing home care of the disabled person. After Medicaid is paid back in full, any other public assistance programs that have a right of reimbursement under any state or federal law must be repaid. If, after all of these entities have been repaid, there are any funds remaining in the trust, then those remaining funds can be disbursed to family members.

In a third party trust, after the death of the disabled person, any funds remaining in the trust can pass to whomever the grantor has designated at the time the trust was established. These secondary beneficiaries can be siblings or other family members of the person with special needs. There is no requirement to pay back Medicaid or any other governmental benefits before the assets pass to the beneficiaries.

Whether a third party SNT is set up during someone's lifetime or under someone's will, the basic terms of the trust are the same. Third party trusts provide that during the lifetime of the person with special needs, the trustee can use trust assets to provide for the disabled person's well-being. The trustee is directed to use the assets for the person's special needs, such as any goods or services that will maintain or improve comfort, welfare, and care. The SNT is for expenditures beyond basic needs and must be used in coordination with the benefits provided by government assistance. The trustee can use assets to supplement basic healthcare services, to pay the expenses of vacations, or to make improvements to real estate that would provide suitable housing for the disabled person. The purpose of the trust is to preserve a person's eligibility for whatever governmental benefits may be available under the law of the state where the person with special needs resides.

There are also many reporting requirements for a first party SNT that are not required for a third party SNT. The trustee must file annually an informal accounting of the administration of the trust's assets, income, and expenses with the agency charged with the beneficiary's Medicaid eligibility redetermination. Finally, subsequent additions to the trust must be reported to the appropriate determination agency (any agencies from which the beneficiary is receiving benefits, such as Medicaid).

> ## Practice Tip
>
> A SNT is very complex, and the trustee has many more duties than the trustee of
> other types of trusts. Clients needing a SNT will often continue to require assistance
> if they are the trustee of the SNT. The person preparing the SNT must become
> familiar with the state's annual reporting and accounting requirements and be
> prepared to guide the client in meeting these requirements.

E. Irrevocable Life Insurance Trusts

An **irrevocable life insurance trust** is a trust that owns a life insurance policy as a
means of distributing the proceeds of the policy outside of the decedent's estate and
is therefore not subject to estate taxes. An irrevocable life insurance trust is often
referred to as an ILIT, pronounced "eye-lit." Typically, an individual or a married
couple will initiate an application for life insurance. The policy is usually a whole life
policy that accumulates value. The trust is drafted so that the trust becomes the
owner of the life insurance policy. The insured person, or persons, is the client
who wants the trust. The clients then make a gift of the cost of paying the premium
to the trust. The trustee of the ILIT is responsible for paying the premium on the life
insurance policy each year. When the insured dies, the proceeds of the life insurance
policy are paid into the trust and distributed in accordance with the provisions of the
trust. The life insurance used in this type of trust is frequently a **second-to-die
policy** in which both the husband and wife are insured, and the policy pays out
only after the second of them passes away. In the second-to-die policy, the premium
costs are often lower because two lives are insured, and the risks are lower than when
only one life is insured.

> **Irrevocable life insurance trust:** a trust that owns a life insurance policy

> **Second-to-die policy:** both husband and wife are insured and policy pays a death benefit only after the second spouse dies

    In Chapter 6 we drafted a revocable trust for John and Linda Jones. Let us exam-
ine how an ILIT for John and Linda would work. Assume that John and Linda have
an estate that is larger than the exclusion amount of $5,250,000 that is applicable for
2014. John owns a life insurance policy on his own life that pays a death benefit of
$1,000,000. If John dies owning that life insurance policy, then John's estate will
owe estate tax on the $1,000,000 death benefit because the total estate is already over
the exclusion amount. The current estate tax rate is 40 percent, which will result in a
tax of $400,000 on the $1,000,000 death benefit. By using an ILIT, John and Linda
can avoid paying tax on the death benefit. John and Linda can either purchase life
insurance through the ILIT or obtain a policy and then transfer it to the ILIT.
The ILIT is the owner of the policy. Because John and Linda do not own the policy,
the death benefit is not subject to estate tax when John dies.

    The ILIT could also be used for a *second-to-die policy* that would insure both John
and Linda. A second-to-die policy would pay a death benefit only after both John
and Linda have passed. The policy pays a death benefit only after the second of them
passes away. If John dies first, Linda does not receive the benefits of the policy. When
Linda dies, the proceeds of the policy are paid to the ILIT and distributed to their

children John Jones, Grace Jones, and Lily Jones. The proceeds or benefits of the policy are not included in John and Linda's estate because the ILIT owns the policy. Therefore, no estate tax is paid on the proceeds.

Practice Tip

In Chapter 7 we learned about the need for complex or tax-wise wills. Clients who need complex wills to maximize the use of the unified gift and estate tax credit may also need or want an ILIT but may not be aware of that type of trust.

The asset or assets held by an ILIT are life insurance policies. The policies are listed in a schedule attached to the back of the trust, just as other assets are listed in other types of trusts. One difference between an ILIT and other types of trusts is that the trustee is given specific directions regarding collection of the proceeds from the policy and whether to hold or distribute the proceeds according to the terms of the trust.

Liquid asset: cash or cash equivalent

Another purpose for creating an ILIT is to provide cash to pay estate taxes on other assets in the estate that are not liquid. A **liquid asset** is cash or cash equivalent. For example, if estate tax is owed on a bank account, money from the account is withdrawn and used to pay the estate tax. If estate tax were owed on real property, the real property would have to be sold to pay the tax. Real property is an example of a nonliquid asset because it would take time to market and sell the real property. If John and Linda own a valuable piece of real estate that they want their children to inherit, they may want an ILIT to provide the cash to pay the estate taxes that would be due on the real property to allow their children to keep the real property. An ILIT can be used to either hold an asset outside of the estate so it is not subject to estate taxes, or the death benefit of the life insurance policy can be earmarked to pay for estate taxes due on nonliquid estate assets.

F. Spendthrift Trusts

Spendthrift trust: a trust in which no beneficiary has the right or power to receive any income or principal from the trust

In a **spendthrift trust**, no beneficiary has the right or power to receive any income or principal from the trust. The beneficiary or beneficiaries do not have the right to sell, assign, grant, transfer, mortgage, pledge, or in any way encumber his or her share of the income or principal of the trust. The trust will not become liable for the debts of any of the beneficiaries, and the trust assets will not have to be used to satisfy any debts of the beneficiaries. A spendthrift trust is used for beneficiaries who have a history of bad financial decisions or have a lot of outstanding debts. Sample language to include in a spendthrift trust would be the following:

> *No beneficiary of this trust has the right to sell, assign, grant, transfer, mortgage, or encumber his or her share of the income or principal of this trust. Any share of the income or principal of*

this trust will not be liable for the debts of any beneficiary or the claims of any creditors of any beneficiary, or be subject to any bankruptcy proceedings filed by any beneficiary. The income and/or principal of this trust are not subject to any attachments, garnishments, creditor's bills, or any other legal process. The interest of each beneficiary will also be free from the control or interference of any creditor of any spouse of a beneficiary.

As indicated in the sample language, the purpose of the trust is to protect the proceeds of the trust in case any of the beneficiaries of the trust have credit problems, outstanding debts, bankruptcies, or any other legal claims against assets. Spendthrift provisions can be added to most trusts to protect beneficiaries from creditors. However, a grantor cannot create a spendthrift trust for him or her if the intent of that trust is to defraud creditors. A spendthrift trust created by the grantor to protect the grantor's assets from the grantor's creditors is known as a **self-settled spendthrift trust**. In most states, spendthrift trusts created by the grantor for the grantor's assets are not permitted. A few states, such as Alaska and Nevada, have adopted specific statutes that allow for domestic asset protection trusts, which allow for self-settled spendthrift trusts.

Self-settled spendthrift trust: a spendthrift trust created by the grantor to protect the grantor's assets from the grantor's creditors

G.   Generation-Skipping Trusts (GSTs)

A **generation-skipping trust (GST)** is one in which the assets placed in the trust are passed down to the grantor's grandchildren, not the grantor's children, thereby skipping over a generation. The purpose of skipping a generation is to avoid the estate taxes that would be incurred by the children if the assets were transferred to them. The trust transfers assets from the estate of the grantor to the grantor's grandchildren. The grantor's children do not take title to the assets in the trust. If the assets that were placed in the trust went to the grantor's children first, and then the grandchildren, the children would incur estate tax. There is currently a generation-skipping tax exemption that allows the assets in a GST to pass to a "skip generation" without estate tax.

Generation-skipping trust: one in which the contributed assets are passed down to the grantor's grandchildren, not the grantor's children

A GST can be created during a grantor's lifetime, or it can be created as part of a will. The GST can be a "stand-alone" trust for the benefit of a grandchild or a person in a skip generation, or it can be used in conjunction with other trusts for the grantor's children or spouse. There are some advantages to using exemptions from the tax. Many individuals allocate their generation-skipping exemption to a generation-skipping trust for the benefit of their children and grandchildren. The trust is funded with cash or property that has a value up to the available generation-skipping transfer tax exemption. The trust is not taxed when the children die and will pass tax-free to the grandchildren. The trust may also be drafted in such a way as to protect the assets from creditors. If the trust assets had been left to the children outright, the assets would have been subject to creditors' claims.

In a GST, the child can serve as a trustee and would then be able to control how the assets in the trust are invested. However, if the child is the trustee, the trust must contain language limiting the child's ability to make distributions of income and

Ascertainable standard: a standard that governs the use of trust assets and prevents the assets from being considered part of the trustee's assets for estate tax purposes

principal. The distribution must meet an **ascertainable standard** in order to avoid subjecting the trust to federal estate taxation at the child's death. An *ascertainable standard*, as that term is used in estate taxation, is a standard that governs the use of trust assets and prevents the assets from being considered part of the trustee's assets for estate tax purposes. The Internal Revenue Code recognizes several ascertainable standards, including health, maintenance, support, and education.

H. Charitable Remainder Trusts (CRTs)

A charitable remainder trust (CRT) is a type of trust that provides for a charitable gift, and income to the grantor or someone designated by the grantor, over a period of years. At the end of the trust term, the remaining principal in the trust goes to a charitable organization chosen by the grantor. CRTs come in two basic forms: charitable remainder annuity trusts (CRATs) and charitable remainder unitrusts (CRUTs). The major difference lies in the formula used to calculate payments to the income beneficiary.

> ### *Practice Tip*
>
> **The various types of trusts are most often referred to by the initials, or by the words formed by the initials. It is necessary to be familiar enough with the types of trusts to know the differences between CRATs and CRUTs, and ILITs and SNTs.**

Charitable remainder annuity trust: one that annually pays the donor a fixed percentage of the value of the donated assets at the time those assets were placed in the trust

Charitable remainder unitrust: a trust with a fixed annual percentage payout but a variable dollar amount as the assets are revalued each year

A **charitable remainder annuity trust (CRAT)** pays the donor a fixed percentage of the value of the donated assets at the time those assets were placed in the trust. In other words, the income stream is stable over the life of the trust. For example, a donor creating a 20-year CRAT worth $100,000 would receive an annual income of $5,000, assuming the minimum required yearly payout of 5 percent. A **charitable remainder unitrust (CRUT)** has a fixed annual payout ratio of at least 5 percent, but the actual dollar amount will fluctuate instead of remaining consistent because the assets held in a CRUT are revalued each year.

I. Medicaid Qualifying Trusts

As discussed previously, a SNT can be used to hold assets for a disabled person who is receiving Medicaid benefits. An irrevocable trust can also be used to take assets out of a person's name in order to make them eligible for Medicaid without having to spend the assets in the trust. Elderly persons frequently use irrevocable trusts in an effort to avoid paying the high cost of a nursing home stay by making it appear that they have no assets remaining to pay for care. For example, an elderly person could transfer assets to an irrevocable trust before applying for Medicaid.

In order to qualify, the assets must be transferred to an irrevocable trust at least 5 years prior to filing the Medicaid application. Transferring assets to an irrevocable trust is the equivalent of making a complete gift of the asset. The grantor does not have any right to get the asset back or to alter or affect the assets use in any way once the transfer is made. During the grantor's life, the asset is not counted as belonging to the grantor in determining if the grantor is eligible for Medicaid.

Here is an example of how an asset protection trust works when making application for Medicaid. Clients Zechariahs and Zelda Smith are 70 and 68 years old, respectively. They are interested in an "asset protection" trust because Mr. Smith says he does not want the government to take all of his money if he needs to go into a nursing home. Of course, the government will not take all of Mr. Smith's money if he needs to go into a nursing home. What will happen is that Mr. Smith will be required to use his money to pay for the care he is receiving in the nursing home, and when his money runs outs, he will continue to receive care, but the government will pay for that care. The cost of nursing home care can quickly deplete a client's savings and investment accounts leaving nothing for the heirs.

Mr. Smith is particularly concerned because his mother had been in a nursing home for the last two years of her life, and instead of inheriting his mother's estate, Zechariahs used the money to provide care for his mother. When the money ran out, his mother's care was provided through Medicaid. He wants to avoid that result by preserving assets for his wife and/or children.

An asset protection trust for Mr. and Mrs. Smith would have to be an irrevocable trust agreement. They would have to appoint someone to serve as their trustee, probably one of their children, and any assets that they placed into the trust would have to remain in the trust. Any asset that the Smiths want to protect is an asset over which they must be willing to give up control. The asset protection occurs because the asset is owned, irrevocably, by the trust, not by the Smiths. Mr. Smith cannot direct when to receive payments from the trust and cannot direct the trustee how to act. There can be some limited right to withdraw income from the trust, but for the most part, assets placed in the trust are within the control of the trustee. Mr. and Mrs. Smith must be ready to give up what is known as all **indicia of ownership**, meaning they are not able to exercise any of the ownership rights such as the right to sell the asset, the right to gift or otherwise transfer the asset, or the right to obtain income from the asset. Transferring property to an irrevocable trust is the equivalent of making a complete gift of the property, and Mr. and Mrs. Smith will not have any right to get the property back or to alter or affect its use in any way once the transfer is made.

Indicia of ownership: signs that the grantor still possesses the asset; no indicia of ownership means the grantor is not able to exercise any ownership rights to assets

This type of asset protection trust would have the goal of allowing Mr. and Mrs. Smith to direct where certain assets are distributed, most likely to their children, and allowing them to become eligible for Medicaid benefits without spending those assets for their own care. In order to become eligible for Medicaid, Mr. Smith would most likely be allowed to own no more than $2,000 in assets. All of his other assets had to have been used for his care. Because Mr. Smith is married, Mrs. Smith would be allowed to keep about half of the couple's assets, up to a certain limit, but the majority of Mr. Smith's assets have to be used to pay for any care he would require. When the assets run out, Mr. Smith would then become eligible for

Medicaid. Assets that Mr. Smith transferred to an irrevocable trust are owned by the trust and are not owned by Mr. Smith. Therefore, the assets in the trust would not have been spent for Mr. Smith's care.

This type of asset protection can be very effective, but clients must be advised that assets have to be transferred to an irrevocable trust at least 5 years prior to filing an application for Medicaid, and certain other requirements must be met as well. One specific type of trust used in preserving assets while qualifying for Medicaid is a **qualified personal residence trust (QPRT)**. A QPRT places a residence in a trust either for the benefit of one's spouse and children or for a charity. After the trust is created, the grantor who owns the house transfers the house to the trust. The grantor reserves the right to live in the house for a certain period of time. At the end of that period of time, the house is transferred to the beneficiaries. The interest that the grantor retains is known as the **retained interest**. The interest that goes to the beneficiaries is known as the **remainder interest**. The transfer of the property to the trust is treated as a gift to the beneficiaries of the trust. A qualified personal residence trust can apply to a primary or secondary residence, but only one house, or personal residence can be held in the trust. Because the house is no longer owned by the grantor, the house does not have to be sold, and the proceeds are made available to pay for care, allowing the grantor to be eligible for Medicaid.

An asset protection trust is also effective in protecting a client from the claims of a creditor. Many people with high incomes, who could be subject to claims of creditors or could be subject to liability-related lawsuits, create irrevocable trusts to protect their assets from these types of claims.

J. Testamentary Trusts

Qualified personal residence trust: one that places a residence in a trust either for the benefit of one's spouse and children or for a charity

Retained interest: the interest that the grantor retains

Remainder interest: the interest that goes to the beneficiaries

Testamentary trust: any trust created in a last will and testament

As discussed previously, a **testamentary trust** is any trust created in a last will and testament. Because the grantor, or creator, of the trust is deceased, the trust is irrevocable, as the grantor cannot change any of the provisions after death. Testamentary trusts are included in wills for various reasons, but the most common is that the proposed beneficiary is a minor, and the assets are going to be held until the minor reaches the age of majority or until some other specified age. In our example of the will created for John and Linda Jones, the couple would make their wills reciprocal, meaning John would leave his estate to his wife Linda, and Linda would leave her estate to her husband John. If both John and Linda died at the same time, or under circumstances where it was not possible to determine who died first, the Jones' estate would pass to the couple's three children in equal shares, share and share alike. Because the children are minor, the Jones' would have a testamentary trust that provided for the money distributed to the children to be held in trust.

A testamentary trust for a minor child can provide for keeping the child's funds in trust beyond the age of majority, which in most states is age 18. Many times, a parent will request that the funds be held longer, or that various smaller distributions be made from the trust. A testamentary trust for the benefit of a minor child may allow the trust monies to be used for the care and maintenance of the child, for secondary school or medical expenses, even to the point of totally depleting the trust. Thereafter, the trust can provide for distributions at a certain age or even two or three different ages. Sample language could include the following:

> *In addition to income, the Trustee is to pay for the benefit of my child from the principal of the child's share of the trust, even to the point of completely exhausting the same, such amounts as the trustee deems reasonable to provide the maintenance, support, health and education of my child. After my child has reached any following ages, the child shall have the right to request from the trust one third of the fair market value after 25 years of age; one third of the fair market value of the balance thereof after 30 years of years of age; and all of the balance after 35 years of age. The Trustee's determination as to the assets to be distributed shall be conclusive.*

In this type of provision, the distributions from the trust are spread out over the child's lifetime, to hopefully coincide with the timing of typical "life events" such as a marriage, birth of a child, purchase of a house, or start of a business.

Testamentary trusts for children must also address the issue of when each child gets paid from the trust, if there is more than one child benefiting from a single trust, and whether the trust is divided at the time the first child gets a distribution. A trust can be treated as a single trust for purposes of holding and investing the assets, and then upon the first distribution from the trust, usually when the oldest child reaches the first age of distribution, the trust is divided into equal shares, with one share for each child. Thereafter, each child's distribution is calculated from the child's individual share.

Testamentary trusts can also include marital trusts and family trusts. In most cases the marital trust is the credit shelter trust, and then the remaining assets of the estate in excess of the credit shelter amount pass to the family trust. The complexities of testamentary family trusts found in complex wills which restrict the distributions of assets were discussed in Chapter 3.

K.   Clifford Trusts

A **Clifford trust** is a type of irrevocable inter vivos trust that was previously used to shelter income-producing assets. The income for the trust was paid to the beneficiaries, but the assets reverted back to the grantors. Prior to the Tax Reform Act of 1986, there was a loophole that allowed parents to transfer income-producing assets to a trust for the benefit of their children. The income would be taxed to the children, at the children's lower tax rate. When the trust expired, the parents, as grantors, would take the assets back. The trust had to be in place for a minimum of ten years. After the Act of 1986, the loophole was closed, and the grantor of the trust was taxed on the income instead of the beneficiary. Because the Tax Reform Act of 1986 eliminated most of the tax advantages of the Clifford Trust, few Clifford Trusts are created today.

Clifford trust: a type of irrevocable inter vivos trust that was previously used to shelter income-producing assets

L. Dynasty Trusts

A dynasty trust is a long-term, irrevocable trust designed to pass wealth from generation to generation without incurring estate taxes on each transfer. The trust operates by holding the assets transferred to the trust by the grantor and allowing distributions from the trust to the beneficiaries each year. The beneficiaries of a dynasty trust are typically the grantor's child, grandchildren, and great-grandchildren. By making annual distributions from the trust, the value of the trust is not subject to estate taxes when the grantor dies, and when each generation subsequently dies. The trust can last for more than 100 years if used in a state that does not have any restrictions on how long a trust can last. Some states have a law known as the "rule against perpetuities." This rule requires that a trust end no longer than 21 years after the death of the last person who was alive at the time the trust was created. The rule against perpetuities means that the trust has to end and cannot continue in perpetuity. It is applied by looking at the beneficiaries who are alive at the time the trust was created — when the last of those beneficiaries dies, the trust can only last for 21 more years.

For example, Walden MacNair lost his wife last year. When Mrs. MacNair died, she had only a simple will and left her entire estate to her husband. MacNair has two children, a son and a daughter, three grandchildren, and one great-grandchild. MacNair has a net worth over $15 million. MacNair wants to leave his entire estate to his two children, in equal shares, share and share alike. Each of MacNair's children would inherit $7.5 million, and the children would pay federal estate tax on the portion of the estate over $5 million. Most likely, MacNair's children will not spend all of that money during their lifetimes, and then MacNair's children will leave the money to their children, MacNair's grandchildren, and estate tax will once again be owed on any amount over $5 million. Instead of leaving the money to his children in his will, MacNair can establish a dynasty trust. The trust can stay in place for several generations but must end within 21 years of the death of MacNair's great-grandchild because of the rule against perpetuities. MacNair can transfer $5 million to the trust without incurring generation-skipping tax, or gift tax, as there is currently a $5 million exemption for both taxes. The trust would then make annual distributions to MacNair's children, and when the children pass, the trust would make annual distributions to the grandchildren, and would keep making distributions to each subsequent generation.

One unique problem of a dynasty trust is that the trust will most likely outlive any individual trustee appointed for the trust. For this reason, and because the trust assets are often very large, most dynasty trusts have professional or corporate trustees such as banks or financial institutions. Having a professional trustee will ensure that the provisions of the trust are followed, and the trust is properly administered.

Summary

Complex trusts are used for asset protection. The assets in the trust can be protected from taxes, protected from being included as an available resource for Medicaid purposes, or protected from being disbursed to the surviving spouse's new spouse.

A complex trust can be a stand-alone trust or be can be found in a last will and testament. The various types of trusts are often referred to by the initials of the types of trust such as SNT (special needs trust) or ILIT (irrevocable life insurance trust).

Review Questions

1. What are the two purposes that can be served using an ILIT?

2. Can an elderly person set up an SNT for himself or herself to protect assets and become qualified for Medicaid? Why or why not?

3. Are asset protection trusts revocable or irrevocable? Why?

4. Does a credit shelter trust have to be in a will or can it be an *inter vivos* trust?

5. What is the difference between a CRAT and a CRUT?

6. The trustee named in the trust wants to resign and allow the next trustee named to take over. Is the second trustee the substitute trustee or the successor trustee?

7. Are trusts used in Medicaid planning revocable or irrevocable?

True or False

1. T F Testamentary trusts are irrevocable.

2. T F A grantor can give up all indicia of ownership and still retain the right to sell the asset.

3. T F The source of funds in a first party special needs trust is the disabled person's own money.

4. T F Transferring assets to an irrevocable trust is the equivalent of making a complete gift of the asset.

5. T F A special needs trust is a testamentary trust.

6. T F Testamentary trusts can include marital trusts and family trusts

7. T F An irrevocable life insurance trust is a good trust for a child with a disability.

8. T F A CRAT or CRUT is good for a client who wants to leave money to a charity.

9. T F A QTIP trust can own a life insurance policy to get the proceeds of the policy out of the client's estate.

10. T F Dynasty trusts are long-term trusts that usually involve a very large estate or a lot of money.

Key Terms

Ascertainable standard
Charitable remainder annuity trust
Charitable remainder unitrust
Clifford trust
Credit shelter will or A/B will
Family trust
First party special needs trusts
General power of appointment
Generation-skipping trust
Indicia of ownership
Irrevocable life insurance trust
Liquid asset
Marital trust

Qualified personal residence trust
Qualified terminable interest property
   (QTIP) trust
Remainder interest
Retained interest
Second-to-die policy
Self-settled spendthrift trust
Special needs trust (SNT)
Spendthrift trust
Testamentary trust
Third party special needs trust
Unlimited marital deduction

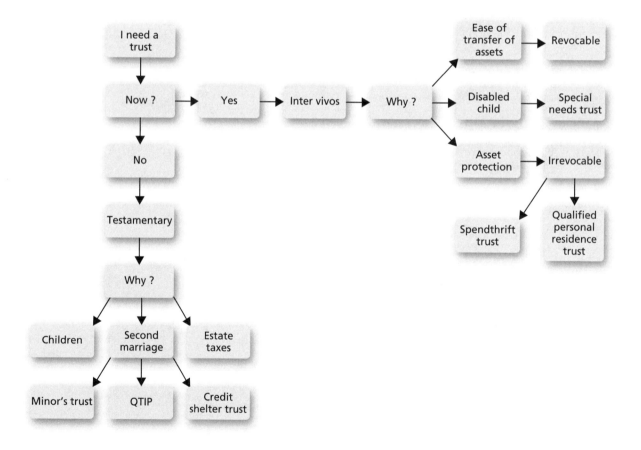

Figure 8-1. What Kind of Trust Is Needed?

Estate Tax

In Chapter 7 we learned about complex wills that help reduce the federal estate tax that is imposed on very large estates, such as those combined estates of a married couple that are over $10 million. In this chapter we will review each of the taxes to which an estate and/or a decedent could be subject. There are potentially five areas of taxation in an estate: (1) federal estate tax; (2) state estate taxation, if the state in which the estate is located imposes an estate tax; (3) state inheritance taxation, if the state in which the estate is located imposes an inheritance tax; (4) income tax incurred by the decedent for the portion of the tax year prior to death; and (5) income tax incurred by income earned on the assets held by the estate during the administration.

This chapter will examine the federal and state estate tax, state inheritance tax and income taxes, and the paralegal's role in assisting the personal representative and/or the tax preparer in completing the documentation necessary to file the appropriate tax returns for each applicable tax.

A. Federal Estate Taxes

1. History of Federal Estate Taxes

In order to understand federal estate taxes, it is necessary to understand a little of the history of how those taxes developed. In Chapter 7 we learned that estates are taxed pursuant to the federal **unified gift and estate tax**. The laws for estate tax and gift tax can be found in Chapters 11 and 12 of Title 26 of the United States Code.[1] Title 26 is also where the Internal Revenue Code (IRC) is found. The *unified gift and estate tax* is a combination of a gift tax and an estate tax. In previous years the exemption rose a little each year to keep up with inflation. The tax law expired in 2010, leaving nothing in its place. For the year 2010 there was no federal gift or estate tax on any

Unified gift and estate tax: a combination of a gift tax and an estate tax

---

1. 26 U.S.C. Subtitle B, Chapter 11, Estate Tax §§2001-2210; 26 U.S.C. Subtitle B, Chapter 12, Gift Tax §§2501-2524.

gift or estate of any size. A temporary tax was put into place for the years 2011 and 2012 but was set to expire at the end of 2012. Without some act of Congress there would once again be no federal gift or estate tax in 2013. The expiration of the gift and estate tax was part of the fiscal cliff that dominated the news in early 2013. On January 2, 2013, President Obama signed the American Taxpayer Relief Act (ATRA) into law. The law made the temporary tax provisions adopted in 2010 permanent and established a combined gift and estate tax exemption of $5,000,000. The exemption, which continues to increase annually due to inflation, was $5,250,000 in 2013 and $5,340,000 in 2014.

The federal gift tax is now permanently unified with the federal estate tax. The word "unified," as it is used in this context, means that the taxes are combined. Both the gift tax and the estate tax use the same rates and schedules, including the 40 percent maximum tax rate. In this chapter we will review some of the pertinent sections of ATRA to the extent that the law impacts estate planning considerations for a paralegal. Those students who are truly having difficulty sleeping should try reading all 59 pages of the act, which can be found here: http://www.gpo.gov/fdsys/pkg/BILLS-112hr8enr/pdf/BILLS-112hr8enr.pdf. The important part of this history for the paralegal to remember is that a combination of gifts given and the size of an estate could result in an estate being subject to federal estate taxation.

Practice Tip

Review the information about estate taxes on the IRS Web site at http://www.irs.gov/pub/irs-pdf/p559.pdf.

2. Coordination of Gift Tax and Estate Tax

As indicated above, the estate and gift taxes are combined, or unified. The first part of the unified gift and estate tax is a gift tax that is imposed on all gifts made above a specific amount. In 2014 the maximum amount that can be gifted without payment of the gift tax is $14,000 per person/per year. Any gift over $14,000 incurs a gift tax that must be paid by the donor, or person giving the gift. Married couples can make what are known as "split gifts" of up to $28,000 per person/per year.

Example

Marie Edgecombe gives a $50,000 gift to her daughter to help with the down payment for a new home. This is the first time Marie has given a gift in excess of the annual exclusion of $14,000 per person/per year. Marie's gift exceeds the annual exclusion by $36,000 if the gift was made in 2014.

$50,000	Gift
–$14,000	Annual exclusion
$36,000	Taxable portion of gift

The tax implications would be different if Mr. and Mrs. Edgecombe gave a combined gift. For example, Mr. and Mrs. Edgecombe give their daughter and son-in-law a gift of $50,000 as a down payment for their new home. The gift does not exceed the annual exclusion because Mr. and Mrs. Edgecombe each have an exclusion of $14,000 for a combined exclusion of $28,000. The Edgecombe's gift of $50,000 to their daughter and son-in-law is less than the annual exclusion.

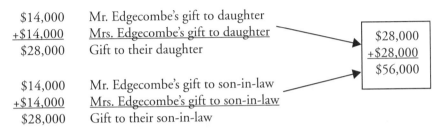

The combined gift exclusion would be $56,000 for Mr. and Mrs. Edgecombe's gifts to their daughter and son-in-law, which covers the $50,000 gift that was made.

There are many types of gifts that are not subject to gift taxes. As we already learned, a gift that is below the maximum amount of $14,000 per person per year is exempt from tax. Gifts of tuition or medical expenses paid directly to an educational or medical institution for someone else are exempt from tax. Gifts to a spouse, gifts to a political organization for its use, and gifts to charities are also exempt from gift taxes.

The second part of the unified gift and estate tax is the federal estate tax. Federal estate tax is imposed on the transfer of the **taxable estate** of the decedent if the taxable estate is, for 2014, above $5,340,000. The taxable estate is the value of the estate, less certain allowable deductions that will be discussed further in this chapter. If the estate is valued at $5,340,000 or less, the estate passes tax free because the unified gift and estate tax law contains a credit for taxes due. This credit is called the **unified credit**.

Taxable estate: gross estate less certain allowable deductions resulting in the net estate or the taxable estate

Unified credit: a credit for taxes due; in 2014 this credit is $2,081,800, which exempts an estate of $5,340,000 from tax

Example

Frank Bryce dies with a $5,000,000 estate in 2014. He did not make any gifts during his lifetime and did not use any of his lifetime exemption. Frank's available lifetime exemption is $5,340,000, which is greater than the value of Frank's estate. Frank's heirs will owe no federal estate tax.

The tax credit available is for gift taxes, estate taxes, or a combination of the two taxes. In 2014, the unified credit amount was $2,081,800, which covers the taxes that would be due on either an estate of $5,340,000 or a combination of a taxable estate and taxable gifts that does not exceed $5,340,000. The amount of the combined total of taxable gifts and the taxable estate that is exempt from taxation is called the **lifetime exemption**. In 2014, the lifetime exemption was $5,340,000 but will continue to increase each year because of inflation.

Lifetime exemption: the amount of the combined total of taxable gifts and the taxable estate that is exempt from taxation

As discussed above, taxable gifts are those that exceed the annual exclusion amount of $14,000 per person/per year. If gifts are given that are over the annual exclusion and incur a gift tax, the amount that the gift is over the annual exclusion is deducted from the donor's lifetime exemption.

Example

Steven Black gives gifts of $500,000 each to his three nephews for a total gift of $1,500,000. Each of these gifts exceeds the annual exclusion by $486,000 and is taxable.

$500,000	Gift
–$ 14,000	Annual exclusion
$486,000	Taxable gift × 3 nephews = $1,458,000 total taxable gifts

The amount of the taxable gift is deducted from the donor's lifetime exemption:

$5,340,000	Donor's lifetime exemption
–1,458,000	Amount of taxable gift
$3,882,000	Excess exemption

Because the amount of the taxable gifts does not exceed Steven's lifetime exemption, no gift tax is due. The excess exemption could potentially be needed by Steven to cover taxes due on his remaining estate.

Let us look at an example of what would happen if the donor makes a gift that exceeds his or her lifetime exemption.

Example

Gilbert Wimple gives a cash gift of $3,000,000 to each of his two children for a total of $6,000,000. Gilbert has never given any previous gifts that exceeded the annual exclusion, so in 2014 he still has his entire lifetime exemption of $5,340,000. Each of Gilbert's $3,000,000 gifts exceeds the $14,000 annual exclusion by $2,986,000.

$3,000,000	Gift to child
–$ 14,000	Annual exclusion
$2,986,000	Taxable gift per child × 2 children = $5,972,000

Gilbert has a lifetime exemption of $5,340,000. The amount of the gifts that is in excess of Gilbert's lifetime exemption is $632,000.

$5,972,000	Total taxable gifts
–$5,340,000	Lifetime exclusion
$ 632,000	Taxable gift × 40 percent gift tax rate = $252,800 of taxes due

The portion of the gift that is not exempt from gift taxation is subject to tax at the maximum rate of 40 percent. Therefore, Gilbert will owe $252,800 in gift taxes.

So far we have looked at estates that are below and above the taxable amount, and gifts that are below and above the taxable amount. Now let us look at a situation in which there is a taxable estate and the decedent made taxable gifts. If a decedent has given taxable gifts, thereby reducing his or her lifetime exclusion, and also has a sizable estate, the result may be that the heirs will owe a considerable amount of federal estate tax.

Example

Frank Bryce's estate is worth $6,000,000 at the time of his death in 2014. Frank gave generous gifts to his three children during his lifetime. He has used $1,250,000 of his lifetime exemption on the gifts to his children. Frank's lifetime exemption is reduced by the amount used.

$5,340,000	Lifetime exemption
-$1,250,000	Exemption used on gifts
$4,090,000	Remaining exemption

$6,000,000
−$4,090,000
$1,910,000 × 40 percent = $764,000

Frank's estate of $6,000,000 is greater than the amount of his remaining exemption. As a result, Frank's heirs will owe federal estate taxes of approximately $764,000. Frank's children may need to sell or liquidate assets to pay the estate tax.

As previously stated, the federal gift and estate tax exemption for 2014 is $5,340,000. The exemption will continue to be indexed for inflation in 2015 and later years. If the decedent made any taxable gifts during his or her lifetime, then the available estate tax exemption will be equal to the difference between the total exemption available and the value of the lifetime gifts made. Let us look at three examples to further illustrate the operation of the combined estate tax and gift tax.

Example 1

Lou Bagman dies in 2014. He has made no lifetime gifts. His gross estate is $5,500,000. His estate has $500,000 of allowable debts, expenses, and deductions. His net estate is $5,000,000. In 2014 the available estate tax exemption is $5,340,000. The taxable estate equals the net estate less the available tax exemption.

$5,000,000	Total estate value
-$5,340,000	Lifetime exemption
$ 160,000	Excess tax exemption

Lou's taxable estate is zero.

Example 2

Lou Bagman dies in 2014. He has made no lifetime gifts. His gross estate is $6,000,000. His estate has $500,000 of allowable debts, expenses, and deductions.

His net estate is $5,500,000. In 2014 the available estate tax exemption is $5,340,000.

$5,500,000   Net estate
−$5,340,000   Lifetime exemption
$ 160,000   Taxable estate × 40 percent = $64,000 estate tax liability

Example 3

Lou Bagman dies in 2014. He has made $1,000,000 in lifetime gifts and paid no taxes on these gifts. Lou's gross estate is $5,500,000. His estate has $500,000 of allowable debts, expenses, and deductions. His net estate is $5,000,000.

$5,340,000   Lifetime exemption
−$1,000,000   Lifetime gifts
$4,340,000   Remaining exemption

→

$5,000,000   Estate value
−$4,340,000   Available exemption
$660,000 × 40 percent = $264,000 estate taxes

Lou's heirs will have to pay approximately $264,000 in federal estate tax.

To this point, all of the examples explain the operation of the lifetime exemption for gift and estate taxes available to a single person who has passed. In the next section, we will examine how that lifetime exemption operates for a married couple.

3.   Portability of Exemption

Portable: this means that any unused portion of the exemption (or exclusion) can be transported to the surviving spouse

Unlimited marital deduction: for married couples, the first spouse to die can leave his or her entire estate to the surviving spouse tax free

ATRA, the new tax law, makes the tax deduction available for estate taxes **portable**. This means that any unused portion of the exemption (or exclusion) can be transported from the deceased spouse to the surviving spouse. For married couples, the first spouse to die can leave his or her entire estate to the surviving spouse tax free. This is also known as the **unlimited marital deduction**. When the second spouse dies, the second spouse gets his or her own tax deduction, plus the unused deduction of the first spouse's tax deduction. The unused exclusion is known as the deceased spouse unused exclusion (DSUE).

Example

Frank Bryce and his wife Ava have a very large estate worth $10,250,000. The estate consists of $7,000,000 in Ava's name and $3,250,000 in Frank's name. Frank dies, leaving his $3,250,000 of assets to his children. Frank had a lifetime exemption of $5,340,000; therefore, Frank's estate still has $2,090,000 of his exemption or DSUE remaining.

$5,340,000   Lifetime exemption
−$3,250,000   Estate taxes on transfers made to his children
$2,090,000   Excess exemption of DSUE

Ava, as the executor of Frank's estate, would need to file a federal estate tax return, Form 706, in order to be able to preserve the $2,090,000 of remaining exemption, or

DSUE, not used in Frank's estate. Ava has a $5,250,000 exclusion of her own, which is added to the remaining $2,000,000 from Frank's estate. Ava will be able to shelter $7,250,000 of taxable gifts or inheritance from her estate.

$5,340,000	Ava's lifetime exemption
+$2,000,000	Frank's remaining exemption
$7,340,000	Available exemption

$7,000,000	Estate value
-$7,340,000	Available exemption
($340,000)	Excess exemption—no tax

Ava has $7,000,000 of assets in her name that will pass to her children, exempted from tax because of the $7,340,000 in exemption available. No estate tax is imposed.

Consider in the above example what would have happened if Frank had left his assets to Ava instead of to his children. Frank's assets, $3,250,000, pass to Ava tax free due to the unlimited marital deduction. Frank's exclusion is not used, so it is lost. When Ava dies, her estate consists of her own $7,000,000 plus Frank's $3,250,000 for a total estate of $10,250,000. Ava's exclusion is only $5,340,000.

$10,250,000	Estate value
-$ 5,340,000	Ava's exemption
$ 4,910,000	× 40 percent = $1,964,000 estate tax liability

Ava's children will have to pay a significant amount of estate tax that could have been avoided with careful planning.

4.   Application of Federal Taxes to Same-Sex Couples

The portability of the tax exclusion was previously limited to married couples and was not available to same-sex couples in a civil union or domestic partnership. Section 3 of the Defense of Marriage Act (DOMA) defined the term "marriage" as the "legal union between one man and one woman as husband and wife" and the word "spouse" as "a person of the opposite sex who is a husband or a wife." DOMA also stated that no state or territory shall be required to recognize as a marriage a same-sex relationship that is recognized as a marriage in another state. DOMA prevented the federal government from recognizing same-sex marriages and left it up to each individual state to determine if that state will recognize them. Because of DOMA, the federal estate tax exemption available to married couples was not available to same-sex couples who were legally married according to the state in which they resided.

DOMA stated the following:

> No State, territory, or possession of the United States, or Indian tribe, shall be required to give effect to any public act, record, or judicial proceeding of any other State, territory, possession, or tribe respecting a relationship between persons of the same sex that is treated as a marriage under the laws of such other State, territory, possession, or tribe, or a right or claim arising from such relationship. [Defense of Marriage Act, Pub. L. No. 104-199, 110 Stat. 2419 (1996); 1 U.S.C. §7 (1996); 28 U.S.C. §1738C (1996)]

The application of DOMA meant that a civil union or domestic partnership, which may have been valid under state law, did not have to be recognized by another state and did not have to be recognized by the federal government. Therefore, the federal estate tax exemptions that were applicable to married couples did not apply to same-sex couples because the federal government did not recognize a marriage between two people of the same sex.

In 2013 there were a number of cases before the U.S. Supreme Court addressing same-sex marriage rights. In the case of *United States v. Windsor*, the Supreme Court looked at the DOMA in the context of estate taxes. Edith Windsor tried to claim the unlimited marital deduction when her partner, Thea Spyer, passed away. The deduction was denied, giving rise to the litigation wherein Windsor claimed DOMA was unconstitutional. The Supreme Court ruled, by a vote of five to four, that the law was unconstitutional. The Supreme Court explained that the states have always had the responsibility of regulating and defining marriage. For example, a state-issued marriage license is required in order to get married. Some states have chosen to allow same-sex couples to marry. The Court found that the federal law discriminated against same-sex couples who are legally married according to state law. Laws that are found to be discriminatory violate the U.S. Constitution and are deemed invalid as unconstitutional. The holding in the *Windsor* case meant that same-sex couples who are legally married must now be treated the same under federal law as married opposite-sex couples. For federal estate tax purposes, this means that the portability of the estate tax exclusion between married couples is also available to persons in states that recognize same-sex marriages. Although the *Windsor* case initially focused on the availability of estate taxes, it ultimately led to DOMA being declared unconstitutional.

5. How to Calculate the Estate Tax

The federal tax is calculated and reported using IRS Form 706. The form and the instructions on how to fill it out are included on the companion Web site. Also included on the companion Web site is a copy of IRS Publication 559, entitled Survivors, Executors and Administrators. Publication 559 provides a lot of useful information for the personal representative of an estate as to the various taxes that could affect an estate. To calculate the estate tax, it is necessary to first determine all of the assets in the **gross estate**, and then subtract certain allowable **deductions**. The *gross estate* consists of all of the decedent's real and personal property that will be transferred from the decedent to a beneficiary. The *deductions* are amounts taken out of the gross estate that reduce the value of the gross estate. After determining the value of the *gross estate*, the *deductions* are subtracted, resulting in the **net estate**. Subtract the available federal estate tax exemption from the net estate to determine the taxable estate.

This information is provided as background only, as the calculation of estate taxes is something best left to tax professionals. The paralegal's role in the calculation of potential estate taxes will be meeting with the executor or personal representative of the estate, gathering all of the documentation regarding the value of assets in the estate, gathering estate expenses incurred, and organizing the information for the tax preparer. Gathering the necessary information may take several weeks over the

Gross estate: all of a decedent's real and personal property that will be transferred from the decedent to a beneficiary

Deductions: amounts taken out of the gross estate that reduce its value

Net estate: deductions subtracted from the value of the gross estate course of the estate administration with the total of attorney's fees charged and estimated to be needed to finish the estate being the final expenses incurred.

The gross estate also includes assets that are transferred by way of the decedent's will, by intestate succession, through a trust, or by operation of law such as an account with a POD (payable on death) or TOD (transferable on death) designation. POD and TOD were discussed in Chapter 1 and are ways of designating a bank account or brokerage account as payable on death or transferable on death. Because the gross estate includes all property transferred, regardless of how it is transferred, the gross estate may include assets that are not part of the **probate estate**, or the estate that passes to the beneficiaries by way of the will. The gross estate also includes property interests that are not owned by the decedent at the time of death, such as the **dower** and **curtesy** rights of a surviving spouse. Dower and curtesy rights arise upon the death of a spouse. *Dower* is a wife's interest in her husband's property upon his death. *Curtesy* is a husband's entitlement to a life estate property that his wife possessed at her death. (See Chapter 10 for a more detailed discussion of dower and curtesy rights.) Also included in the gross estate might be the value of certain items of property that the decedent had transferred during the three years immediately preceding the date of death.

The net estate is calculated by subtracting certain allowable deductions from the gross estate. The allowable deductions fall into three general categories: debt, expenses, and nontaxable transfers. Deductions for debt include all of the debts of the decedent, such as mortgage, credit cards, medical bills from the last illness, and funeral expenses. Expenses that are deducted from the taxable estate include the costs of estate administration such as probate fees; professional fees for the attorney, accountant, and appraiser; and carrying cost for any real property such as insurance, utilities, and property taxes. The final category of deductions includes transfers or distributions that are not taxed such as charitable bequests, and transfers to a surviving spouse that qualify for the unlimited marital deduction.

As an example, let us look at the estate of Frank and Ava. Their combined estate was $10,250,000. Frank died, leaving his estate of $3,250,000 to his children. The estate consists of several investment accounts and a large commercial rental property.

Probate estate: estate that passes to the beneficiaries by way of the will

Dower: a wife's interest in her husband's property upon his death

Curtesy: a husband's entitlement to a life estate property that his wife possessed at her death.

$ 3,250,000 Gross estate

–$500	Probate fees	
–$10,000	Attorney's fees	Expenses
–$10,000	Accountant's fees	
–$39,000	Utilities, taxes, insurance on rental property	

–$15,000	Funeral expenses	
–$22,000	Medical expenses	
–$5,700	Credit card debt	Debts
–$750,000	Mortgage	
–$5,000	Charitable bequest	
$2,393,000	Net estate	

The total amount of all of the deductions is subtracted from the gross estate, resulting in the net estate. From the net estate, subtract the available federal estate tax exemption to arrive at the taxable estate.

6.   Reporting the Estate Tax — Form 706

The federal estate taxes are calculated and reported using IRS Form 706. A complete copy of the form and the IRS's instructions on how to complete the form are included on the companion Web site. The executor, administrator, or personal representative of the decedent's estate is responsible for filing the estate tax return. The personal representative is required to complete and file Form 706 if the gross estate is larger than the applicable exclusion amount for the year in question, or if the personal representative wants to preserve the unused exclusion of the deceased spouse (DSUE). The estate tax return must be filed within nine months of the decedent's death. The personal representative may request an extension of time in which to file, allowing for an automatic six-month extension. If the personal representative misses the deadline or fails to file an estate tax return, interest and penalties will accrue.

The estate tax return is very complicated. Many elder law and estate attorneys do not do estate tax returns, relying instead on the services of a tax professional such as an accountant. There are different types of estate tax software available that can be used to assist with the calculation of the estate tax and preparation of Form 706. Even when special tax preparation software is used, however, completion of the estate tax form can be difficult. It takes time and experience with estates to properly learn how to complete Form 706.

The paralegal will be responsible for gathering and organizing the documents necessary for the tax professional to complete Form 706. The form includes a number of different schedules onto which the decedent's assets must be listed. It is important that the assets be listed in the correct schedule. Some assets may appear to fit into more than one schedule. A brief overview of what goes on each schedule is given below.

Gross value: the fair market value of a property, not reduced by any mortgages or liabilities

Fair market value: the price at which the property would sell in an arm's-length transaction between a willing buyer and a willing seller

Arm's-length transaction: one in which there is no relationship between the parties

SCHEDULE A-1 — Section 2032A Valuation: Schedule A includes the *gross value* of all real property owned by the decedent. The **gross value** is the fair market value not reduced by any mortgages or liabilities on the property. If there is a mortgage, that information is included on Schedule K. **Fair market value** is established by an appraiser and is the value that the property would sell for at an arm's-length transaction between a willing buyer and a willing seller. An **arm's-length transaction** is one in which there is no relationship between the parties. For example, if the estate were to sell the property to one of the beneficiaries, without using a realtor, the transaction would not be considered arm's length. The value would be as of the date of death and should be established by obtaining an appraisal report. If the property is jointly owned, then the value of the property is included in Schedule E.

SCHEDULE B — Stocks and Bonds: Stocks must be valued as of the date of death. If the stock portfolio is large, it is important that the date of death valuations are accurate. There are different ways to calculate the fair market value. The fair market value of the stock is going to be the average of the high and low selling prices on the date of the decedent's death. The value of publicly traded stocks can be found using an online pricing service. If the decedent died on a weekend, when the stock market is closed, it will be necessary to find the average value on Friday, and the average value on Monday, and then prorate the difference depending on whether the decedent died on Saturday or Sunday.

SCHEDULE C — Mortgages, Notes, and Cash: Mortgages referenced on this schedule are mortgages owed to the decedent in which someone else is making payments to the decedent for a loan given by the decedent. Mortgages that are liabilities to the decedent are listed in Schedule K. Copies of the actual mortgages or notes should be maintained with the schedule.

SCHEDULE D — Insurance on the Decedent's Life: Insurance can be excluded from the value of the decedent's estate using an ILIT, or irrevocable life insurance trust. This was discussed in Chapter 8. The value must still be listed on the return. The executor must provide an explanation as to why the value should not be included and attach a copy of the ILIT. The proceeds paid from a life insurance policy may also be included in the gross estate if the benefits are payable to the estate or if the policy was supposed to be paid to a beneficiary and the beneficiary died before the insured and there was no contingent beneficiary named. If the decedent retained any of the **incidents of ownership**, then the policy is includable in the decedent's taxable estate. *Incidents of ownership* include the right to name a beneficiary or change the beneficiary, the right to cash in the policy, the right to use the policy as collateral for a loan, or the right to assign the policy to another person.

Incidents of ownership: proof that a person owns an insurance policy can be found if the person exercises certain rights

SCHEDULE E — Jointly Owned Property: Part 1 is for surviving spouses owning property as joint tenancy with right of survivorship (JTWROS). One-half, or 50 percent of the value of the property is included. Part 2 is used if the joint tenant can prove contribution to ownership and there is some other distribution of the ownership, for example, if a joint owner can show that he or she paid 75 percent of the purchase price of the property. An appraisal of the property should be obtained and kept with the schedule.

SCHEDULE F — Other Miscellaneous Property Not Reportable Under Any Other Schedule: This would include the decedent's personal property. Failing to list any personal property is a red flag to the IRS and would cause questions to be raised. If for some reason the decedent truly had no personal property, then an explanation of the circumstances would need to be provided. For example, if the decedent died in a fire that also destroyed his home and all his personal property, a statement should be attached to Form 706 indicating those events. Coins owned by the decedent would also go onto this schedule and not on Schedule C as cash if the coins were rare coins where the collector's value is more than the face value.

SCHEDULE G — Transfers During Decedent's Life: This schedule includes transfers made by the decedent within three years of the date of death. The amount of any gifts made by decedent within three years prior to death will be brought back into the estate for estate tax purposes. If this did not occur, would not everyone "give away" all of their assets as "death bed" gifts to avoid estate tax?

Annuity: a form of insurance or investment product that is designed to pay out a stream of payments to the owner at a later point in time

SCHEDULE I — Annuities: An **annuity** is a form of insurance or investment product that is designed to pay out a stream of payments to the owner at a later point in time. The payments may be equal or unequal, conditional or unconditional, periodic or sporadic. The term *annuity* can include pension plans, individual retirement arrangements, purchased commercial annuities, and private annuities. A copy of the investment statement for the annuity should be provided.

SCHEDULE J — Funeral Expenses and Expenses Incurred in Administering Property Subject to Claims: The expenses included on Schedule J are limited to the type and amount allowed by each state's law. Expenses include attorney's fees, accountant's fees, funeral expenses, costs of administration of the estate such as probate fees, and the executor's commission. Copies of invoices and receipts showing payment, including copies of checks from the estate account or other documentation of each expense paid, must be kept with the schedule.

SCHEDULE K — Debts of the Decedent — Mortgages and Liens: Any mortgages or liens on real property owned by the decedent that need to be paid as part of the administration of the estate are listed in Schedule K. The paralegal should obtain a copy of the recorded mortgage and mortgage note to include with Form 706.

SCHEDULE L — Net Losses During Administration and Expenses Incurred in Administering Property Not Subject to Claims: The type of losses included on Schedule L include only things referred to as casualty losses, such as losses from fire or theft, that are not reimbursed by insurance. Documentation supporting this entry could include appraisal reports, police reports if property was stolen, copies of the insurance denial letters, or receipts from the purchase of items.

SCHEDULE M — Bequests, etc., to Surviving Spouse: This includes everything going to the surviving spouse that is included in the gross estate. The paralegal should prepare an inventory of these items for inclusion on the schedule.

SCHEDULE O — Charitable, Public, and Similar Gifts and Bequests: Any bequests made to charities are listed on Schedule O. Qualifying charities include, according to the IRS, any corporation or association organized and operated exclusively for religious, charitable, scientific, literary, or educational purposes, including the encouragement of art, or to foster national or international amateur sports competition, or for the prevention of cruelty to children and animals. A receipt from the charity or cancelled check would be required.

SCHEDULE P — Credit for Foreign Death Taxes: If the decedent was a U.S. citizen but owed death taxes to a foreign government pursuant to a tax treaty with a foreign government, those taxes are listed on Schedule P. A list of countries with which the United States has tax treaties is included in the instructions to Form 706. Proof of payment of the taxes would be required.

SCHEDULE Q — Credit for Tax on Prior Transfers: Schedule Q includes a credit for taxes paid on previous transfers if those transfers occurred during a certain period of time.

SCHEDULE R — Generation-Skipping Transfer Tax: Form 706 is also used to compute the generation-skipping transfer (GSTT) tax that is imposed by Chapter 13 of the Internal Revenue Code. Further explanation of this tax is provided below.

SCHEDULE U — Qualified Conservation Easement Exclusion: Schedule U allows for the deduction of the value of a qualified conservation easement.

A conservation easement is a restriction placed on the land to preserve it for outdoor recreation, protection of natural habitat of fish, wildlife, or plants, or preservation of open space including farmland and forestland. If any of the decedent's property is subject to this type of easement, the easement will be recorded as a restriction on the property in the same way that a deed is recorded. A copy of the recorded easement should be included with the schedule.

7. Paralegal's Role

Much of the information presented in this chapter should be reviewed with the intent of providing background information so that a paralegal can have an understanding of how the tax system works. It is not intended to provide a guide for the completion of the tax reporting forms that an estate may require. The paralegal's role is obtaining and organizing the information necessary to complete the forms. The paralegal should create some type of reminder and/or tracking system to be sure to follow up on each document needed to complete the estate tax return. On the front of each estate file, it is useful to have a sheet with information noting the decedent's name, date of death, the date of the nine-month deadline in which the estate tax return should be filed, and the EIN for the estate. Preparing this type of form with all of the important information provides a good visual reminder of what is required to be done and when. A paralegal will often customize this form to include the information most often requested by the attorney in the administration of the estate, so that the necessary information is quickly accessible. The important dates and information can also be included in Time Matters or other similar scheduling software used by attorneys.

As we have learned, the personal representative of the estate must sign the tax returns. A copy of the letter testamentary or letter of administration must be included with the return. The paralegal will be responsible for coordinating the signature or the personal representative or corepresentatives. This will include setting up an appointment to meet with the personal representative or corepresentatives, following up with each person whose signature is required, and providing each person with a copy of the signed return when same is filed.

An original letter or certificate appointing the representative or corepresentatives will also have to be included with the tax reporting forms. If the forms are prepared by a tax professional, the personal representative is still responsible for signing the return. A meeting between the attorney, the tax professional, and the clients may be necessary to review the forms prior to signature. Coordinating all of the attachments, including the letter testamentary or letter of administration, is typically the paralegal's responsibility even if Form 706 is prepared by a tax professional.

If federal estate taxes are owed, the taxes must be paid when Form 706 is filed. When the return is accepted by the IRS, a release will be sent indicating that the correct amount of taxes has been paid. If no taxes are due, a release will be sent indicating no taxes are due.

8. Generation-Skipping Transfer Tax

The generation-skipping transfer tax (GSTTT) is an extra tax charged on transfers made to the decedent's grandchildren or great-grandchildren which are greater than the lifetime exemption of $5,250,000. The GSTTT is imposed on outright gifts to **skip persons**, and also applies to transfers to a trust for the benefit of a *skip person*. There are two categories of skip persons. The recipient of a gift or transfer is a skip person if the person is related to the decedent but is two or more generations below the decedent, for example, a grandchild or great-grandchild. A skip person can also be someone who is not related to the decedent but is more than 37.5 years younger than the decedent. The generation-skipping tax will be imposed only if the transfer avoids incurring a gift or estate tax at each generation level. The maximum tax rate is 40 percent.

Skip person: a transferee who is a member of a generation that is two or more generations below the generation of the decedent

For example, the decedent created a trust for her child and grandchildren. The trust allows for income generated by the trust assets to be distributed between the child and grandchildren. The principal of the trust is to be distributed outright to the grandchildren following the child's death. If the trust property is not subject to estate tax at the child's death, a generation-skipping tax will be imposed on the grandchildren when the child dies.

B. State Estate and Inheritance Tax

As previously discussed, the assets in an estate can be subject to different state taxes in addition to the federal estate tax. An estate may be subject to state estate and/or inheritance taxes in addition to federal estate tax. Estate tax is based on the size of the decedent's estate. Inheritance tax is based on the familial relationship between the beneficiary and the decedent. Some states, like Maine, Washington, and Oregon, impose a state estate tax. Other states, like Nebraska or Iowa, impose a state inheritance tax. Still others, like New Jersey and Maryland, impose both an estate tax and an inheritance tax.

Practice Tip

Research your state's estate tax or inheritance tax laws. At a minimum a paralegal should be aware of whether or not the state in which he or she is working has an estate tax, an inheritance tax, or both. *Forbes* magazine did an article with a map illustrating the individual state's laws (http://www.forbes.com/sites/ashleaebeling/2013/01/28/where-not-to-die-in-2013/).

Who is responsible for paying state estate and inheritance taxes should be addressed in the decedent's will if the state in which the decedent lived imposes either tax. The will should indicate whether any taxes due are to be paid from the estate, or should be paid by the beneficiaries who receive the distribution. Who pays the tax can often be a source of controversy between the beneficiaries, depending on who is responsible for the payment of the tax. The issue that arises is similar to the problems that can potentially arise from specific bequests that were discussed in Chapter 2. Look at how payment of estate taxes affects the beneficiaries in a state like New Jersey that imposes both an estate tax and an inheritance tax.

Decedent's will states the following:

My estate, prior to the distribution of any bequest, shall pay all estate taxes, from whatever source.

The decedent's will makes several significant specific bequests to grandchildren, her brother, a niece, and one to a person who was unrelated to her. The residuary estate is designated for the decedent's three children:

I make the following specific bequests:
1. *Ten Thousand Dollars ($10,000) to my granddaughter*
2. *Ten Thousand Dollars ($10,000) to my grandson*
3. *Ten Thousand Dollars ($10,000) to my niece*
4. *Twenty-five Thousand Dollars ($25,000) to my brother*
5. *Twenty-five Thousand Dollars ($25,000) to my dear friend and neighbor.*

Each of the categories of beneficiaries listed in the specific bequests is treated differently for New Jersey inheritance tax purposes. In New Jersey, inheritance taxes are imposed on beneficiaries who are not lineal descendants. The tax rate is a **sliding scale**, meaning that it starts at one level and increases as the value of the estate increases. There is no tax imposed if the beneficiary is the decedent's father, mother, grandparent, spouse/civil union partner, child, or stepchild. A tax starting at 11 percent is imposed if the beneficiary is the decedent's brother or sister. A tax starting at 15 percent is imposed on all other beneficiaries. The tax consequences of our decedent's bequests are as follows:

Sliding scale: a tax rate that starts at one level and then increases as the value of the estate increases

1. $10,000 to the decedent's granddaughter — no tax
2. $10,000 to the decedent's grandson — no tax
3. $10,000 to the decedent's niece — 15 percent tax or $1,500
4. $25,000 to the decedent's brother — 11 percent tax or $2,750
5. $25,000 to decedent's friend — <u>15 percent tax or $3,750</u>
   Total inheritance tax due = $8,000

Because the decedent's will specified that the estate is to pay all of the taxes due, each beneficiary will receive the full bequest, and the estate will be responsible for payment of the $8,000 of taxes that are due. The $8,000 is deducted from the estate value as an estate expense and reduces the amount of the residuary estate that is available for distribution to the residuary beneficiaries. The residuary beneficiaries in our example are the decedent's children, who are not taxed. This type of distribution can cause resentment because not only is the decedent giving money to beneficiaries other than her children, but also the children's residuary share is reduced by the amount of the taxes on those distributions.

The distribution would have been different if the decedent specified that each beneficiary is responsible for his or her own taxes:

1. $10,000 to the decedent's granddaughter — no tax = $10,000
2. $10,000 to the decedent's grandson — no tax = $10,000
3. $10,000 to the decedent's niece — 15 percent tax or $1,500 = $8,500
4. $25,000 to the decedent's brother — 11 percent tax or $2,750 = $22,250
5. $25,000 to decedent's friend — 15 percent tax or $3,750 = $21,250

Each individual would have been responsible for the payment of inheritance taxes due, and the amount of the tax would have been deducted from his or her distribution, leaving only the net amount going to the beneficiary. The residuary beneficiaries would not be impacted by the inheritance taxes due.

C.   Decedent's Last Income Tax Return

The personal representative of an estate is also responsible for filing the decedent's last income tax return. The first step is to determine whether or not the decedent was required to file income tax returns in the years prior to his or her death. Generally, an income tax return would be required for individuals earning a gross income of $10,950 and above. If the decedent did not earn sufficient income to file an income tax return in the year prior to death, then an income tax return does not have to be filed in the year of death. If the decedent was very elderly, and perhaps lost capacity prior to death, the decedent might have neglected to file a return even though a return was required. The personal representative can file IRS Form 4506 to request a copy of the previous year's tax return. The executor can retain an accountant to provide this service.

D.   Income Tax on the Estate

Income earned on the assets held in an estate is subject to taxation. The executor is responsible for maintaining the assets and collecting any income earned on those assets. There could be federal and state tax imposed on that income. The Fiduciary Income Tax Return, Form 1041, must be filed if the estate earns more than $6,000 in income or if any of the beneficiaries of the estate are nonresident aliens. The paralegal will be responsible for obtaining the correct names and addresses of all beneficiaries as well as their relationships to the decedent. The paralegal must also confirm the citizenship of all of the beneficiaries. The paralegal will be responsible for keeping track of the amount of income earned on the assets. If the income reaches $6,000, the tax professional responsible for preparing Form 706 should be alerted that a Fiduciary Income Tax Return, Form 1041, is required. The paralegal will have to organize all of the documentation received for the estate so that end-of-year statements indicating income earned are identified and set aside for the tax professional's review.

Summary

The decedent and the estate can be subject to various federal and state taxes. The decedent's estate may be affected by gifts given by the decedent prior to death. It is the executor's fiduciary responsibility to ensure that all of the applicable taxes are paid before any money is distributed to the beneficiaries. All of the federal tax exemptions that are available to married couples are also available to same-sex married couples who live in states allowing same-sex marriage.

Review Questions

1. What are the taxes that an estate might have to pay?

2. What are some types of gifts that are not subject to gift taxes?

3. Who is responsible for signing an estate tax return?

4. Are some estates subject to both a federal estate tax and state estate tax?

5. What is the maximum amount per person, per year that a married couple can give as a gift?

6. Under what schedule on Form 706 should the following assets be listed?

- Real property owned as joint tenants
- Real property that is part of a partnership interest
- Ownership in a co-op
- Money market account
- Money market account connected to a trading account
- Tax refunds received as a result of the filing of the decedent's last income tax return
- Life insurance owned by the decedent that insures another's life
- Life insurance owned by an ILIT that was previously owned by the decedent and transferred to the ILIT within three years of the decedent's death
- Mortgages owed by the decedent

True or False

1. T F The federal estate tax will always be imposed on an estate over $5,340,000.

2. T F Estate taxes have to be paid by the surviving spouse immediately after the first spouse dies.

3. T   F   The total estate of a husband and wife that can be exempt from taxation is as much as $10,680,000 in 2014.

4. T   F   If taxable gifts are given during a lifetime, the amount of available tax credit at death is reduced.

5. T   F   Some states impose an estate tax and an inheritance tax.

6. T   F   After a person dies, there is no need to file any more income tax returns for the person.

7. T   F   Estate taxes are calculated and filed using IRS Form 706.

8. T   F   *DSUE* stands for *deceased spouse unused exclusion.*

9. T   F   The gross estate minus deductions equals the net estate.

10. T   F   An arm's-length transaction is when the administrator of an estate sells an estate property to a relative.

Sample Estate Exercise

Review the facts presented below, and suggest the organizational and administrative tasks the paralegal needs to complete to prepare this estate to be turned over to the attorney or accountant for preparation of the estate tax return.

Arnold and Molly Bode are very wealthy. Arnold died in April 2013. Mr. and Mrs. Bode have two adult children, one grandchild, and one grandchild on the way. When Mr. Bode dies, Mrs. Bode comes to the office for assistance with probate, administration of the estate, and preparation of the estate tax return. She brings with her some financial statements, their tax returns, the original will, and a file box full of other documents with the explanation, "I don't know what all of this is; I just took it all out of Arnold's desk." Arnold's will is a complex will that takes maximum advantage of the federal tax credits available to him and his wife. In the will, Arnold makes a specific bequest of $100,000 each to Boston University, his alma mater, and the American Red Cross, and a $250,000 specific bequest to his grandchild. The remainder of his estate goes directly to his wife, if she survives him, and if not, to his two children in equal shares.

In the file box, the paralegal finds documents pertaining to the following assets:

- Deeds to two properties — one deed is for the couple's home; it is in the names of Arnold and Molly Bode, joint tenants with right of survivorship. The other deed is for Arnold's grandparents' home that is located in Mantoloking, New Jersey. The property was used as a vacation home and was significantly damaged during Hurricane Sandy. The deed is in the name of Arnold and Arnold's late brother, Avery, as joint tenants.
- Mortgage note — Arnold loaned a friend's daughter $500,000 to start a business. The mortgage is secured by a commercial property and has been recorded as a lien

against the property. The friend's daughter has been making regular payments, with interest, on the mortgage.

- ILIT—Mr. and Mrs. Bode created an ILIT approximately eight years ago. The ILIT is the owner of a second-to-die policy with a death benefit of $3,000,000.
- Rare coin collection—Arnold had the collection appraised recently, for insurance purposes, and included the value of the collection as a rider to his homeowner's insurance.
- Google, Facebook, and Starbucks stock held in an E-Trade account.
- Annuities—There were several different annuities purchased from different investment companies.
- IRA/401(k)—This was held by Morgan Stanley.
- Stock accounts—One is working at Merrill Lynch and one at Edward Jones.
- Money market account, checking account, savings account—All are found at a local bank.
- Two life insurance policies—There is one from his former employer and one from Prudential.

After reviewing the documents in the file box, it appears that there are a number of things that Arnold could possibly own for which documentation was not included. Draft a memo to the attorney with suggestions as to additional documents the client will need to bring in.

Key Terms

Annuity	Net estate
Arm's-length transaction	Portable
Curtesy	Probate estate
Deductions	Skip person
Dower	Sliding scale
Fair market value	Taxable estate
Gross estate	Unified credit
Gross value	Unified gift and estate tax
Incidents of ownership	Unlimited marital deduction
Lifetime exemption	

10

Probate Process

As we learned in Chapter 2, a will is formally known as a last will and testament. A person who dies with a valid will is said to have died **testate**. A person who dies without a valid will has died **intestate**. If a person dies without having a valid will, the laws of the state in which the person lived will provide regulations as to the distribution of their assets. The laws governing the distribution of an intestate estate are called the **laws of intestate succession** or the **laws of intestacy**. If a person dies with a will, the will is registered, or admitted to probate.

This chapter will examine the process by which a person is appointed to serve as the personal representative of the decedent's estate. After a person gets appointed, the estate gets administered, which includes things like paying the decedent's last bills, selling assets, and distributing the estate to the beneficiaries. Estate administration will be examined in detail in Chapter 11. The first section of this chapter will examine the probate process for a testate estate, in which a will gets admitted to probate and the personal representative gets appointed. The second section will examine the probate process for an intestate estate, in which there is no will and an administrator of the estate must be appointed.

Testate: a person who dies with a valid will

Intestate: a person who dies without a valid will

Laws of intestate succession or the laws of intestacy: laws that govern the distribution of an intestate estate

A. Testate Estate

1. Types of Personal Representatives

The personal representative of the estate can be appointed in one of two ways: through the will or through the court. If the decedent died with a valid will, the person appointed as the representative of the estate is the person named in the will as the **executor**. If the decedent died intestate, the person appointed to serve as the representative of the estate is called an **administrator**. An administrator can also be appointed in situations where there is a problem with the will, or if the person named as the executor in the will is unavailable, or unable to serve, and no backup person is named. The probate court is the state court with jurisdiction to appoint the administrator of an estate.

Executor: the person named in a will as the representative of the estate

Administrator: the person appointed as the representative of the estate when there is no will, or if the executor appointed in the will cannot serve or if there is some problem with the will

Administrator ad litem: an administrator "during the litigation"; appointed by the court when there is any court proceeding in which the estate of a deceased person must be represented and there is no executor or administrator for the estate

Administrator ad prosequendum: an administrator appointed for the purposes of prosecuting a wrongful death

There are two other specific types of administrators of estates: (1) **administrator ad litem** and (2) **administrator ad prosequendum**. An *administrator ad litem* is Latin for an administrator "during the litigation." An administrator ad litem is appointed by the court when there is any court proceeding in which the estate of a deceased person must be represented and there is no executor or administrator for the estate. An administrator ad litem is appointed only if there is no existing executor or administrator of the estate, or if the executor or administrator has conflicting interests. Figure 10-1 presents an application for the appointment of an administrator ad litem that is used in the state courts of Hamilton County, Tennessee.

An *administrator ad prosequendum* is an administrator appointed by the court for the specific purposes of bringing a wrongful death claim. The translation of the Latin term *ad prosequendum* is the administrator "for the prosecution." The administrator ad prosequendum prosecutes the wrongful death on behalf of the heirs of the estate. For example, if the decedent died as the result of another person's negligence, the surviving family members may want to bring a wrongful death claim. One of the decedent's relatives could be appointed as the administrator ad prosequendum for purposes of bringing that claim. In some states, such as New Jersey, an administrator ad prosequendum is required for wrongful death litigation even if another executor or administrator has been put into place for the estate. If the decedent had a will, the executor brings an application to the court to be appointed as the administrator ad prosequendum after he or she is appointed as executor.

Practice Tip

Many clients seeking assistance with probate are very emotional, especially if the decedent passed away very suddenly under circumstances that give rise to the appointment of an administrator ad prosequendum. The surviving family members may not understand their rights and responsibilities, and it may be necessary to explain the process several times. Patience and understanding are essential.

2.   Uniform Probate Code

Each state has its own regulations and laws pertaining to probate of estates. Some states have adopted the Uniform Probate Code, a uniform set of laws established by the National Committee on Uniform Laws. The Uniform Probate Code (UPC), was intended to establish uniformity in the area of estates, wills, and the laws of intestacy. The first UPC was drafted in 1969, and in 1990, the UPC was revised and then amended a second time in 1993. As of the date of publication, only 18 states have adopted the UPC so the goal of uniformity among all of the states' laws has not been achieved. Some states have adopted portions of the UPC or have modeled their own laws after the UPC, but it has not been adopted in its entirety by all of the states. Therefore, each state's laws pertaining to probate can be different, with some

Figure 10-1. Application for the Appointment of an Administrator Ad Litem

IN THE CHANCERY COURT OF HAMILTON COUNTY, TENNESSEE	**APPLICATION FOR APPOINTMENT OF ADMINISTRATOR AD LITEM FOR CAUSE OF ACTION ONLY** T.C.A. § 30-1-109	PART 2 PROBATE DIVISION FILE NO.

IN THE MATTER OF THE ESTATE OF

DECEDENT

ITEM 1. APPLICANT.

_____,

requests the Court to appoint Applicant as Administrator *ad litem* of this estate for the limited purpose of a cause of action.

ITEM 2. AVERMENTS.

Applicant would show that Decedent died on _____ at the age of _____ at _____.
                                                    Date   *City & State*

Decedent's residence at time of death was:

_____, _____, _____ _____
        Street and Number   *City*   *State*   *Zip Code*

Applicant's relationship to Decedent is _____

For legal action against_____

_____

Applicant avers: these facts are true to the best knowledge, information, and belief of Applicant; no person is currently serving as administrator or executor for this estate; Applicant is aware of no person interested in the estate or willing to serve as administrator; Applicant is ready, willing, and qualified to serve as administrator *ad litem* according to law; the Administrator *ad litem*'s sole duty and function will be to provide a nominal party for a legal cause of action; and where it becomes necessary for Applicant to take control and custody of property or assets of this estate, Applicant shall execute a bond with good security before taking control and custody of such property or assets.

ITEM 3. PREMISES CONSIDERED, APPLICANT PRAYS:

1. That facts have been shown herein, or will be made known by the testimony or affidavit of an interested person, to support the appointment of a limited administrator.

2. That Applicant be appointed administrator *ad litem* of this estate pursuant to T.C.A. § 30-1-109.

3. That the CLERK & MASTER qualify Applicant and issue Letters of Administration for Cause of Action Only.

_____
        Applicant's Address

_____   _____
                                                                Applicant Signature

_____

STATE OF TENNESSEE
CHANCERY COURT OF HAMILTON COUNTY   S. LEE AKERS, CLERK & MASTER

Sworn to and subscribed before me on _____   By_____
                                                          date   *Deputy Probate Clerk*

_____
Attorneys for Applicant
BY_____
                                        BPR#

_____
Address

_____
Telephone NO.   *Fax NO.*

(continued)

Figure 10-1. Continued

MASTER'S ORDER

From an examination of Applicant and witnesses under oath it appears the facts stated in the Application are true, and that after proper qualification and payment of costs and pursuant to T.C.A. § 16-16-201 letters of limited administration for an administrator *ad litem* are to be issued for cause of action only to:

_____

Court costs are paid.

No further reports are required by the COURT.

5-YEAR CAUSE OF ACTION? ☒ NO ☒ YES   If yes, this estate shall remain open for a period of five (5) years after which it shall be closed unless requested by Administrator *ad litem*. Additional letters shall be issued as necessary upon payment of additional costs.

This _____ day of _____, 20____.

_____

S. LEE AKERS, CLERK & MASTER

similarity among the states that have either adopted all or part of the UPC. A full copy of the UPC can be found on the companion Web site.

3.   Death Certificate

The first task to be accomplished after someone dies is to obtain a copy of the death certificate. The death certificate will need to be submitted to the surrogate's office with the will when the application for probate is made. The death certificate must be a certified original and contain the raised seal of the Registrar of Vital Statistics of the state in which the person died. The informant, or person who gives the information pertaining to the decedent, should carefully check that all of the information contained in the death certificate is correct, including the spelling of the person's name and the state where the person was a resident on the date of death.

If any of the information in the death certificate is incorrect, the executor must make corrections. Most states limit the people who can have access to the death certificate to the immediate family and the representative of the estate. There may be a delay in issuing the death certificate if the death was suspicious or was unattended (meaning the person died alone), or if an autopsy is required.

4. Domicile

A will must be probated in the state the decedent declared as his or her **legal residence or domicile**. The *legal residence or domicile* is the state in which the decedent votes, has a driver's license, and pays state taxes. There are many people who have more than one residence, or who were visiting another state or county at the time of death. A person can have more than one residence but can have only one domicile. For example, someone can own a home in New Jersey and a home in Florida and spend part of the year in each residence, but the person would only declare one of those states as the decedent's domicile.

Clients often choose which state to declare as their legal residence based on estate tax laws, choosing the state with the most favorable tax treatment. Different states have different taxes, including estate taxes, inheritance taxes, or property transfer taxes. For example, only three states—New Jersey, Delaware, and Maryland—have both an estate tax and an inheritance tax. North Carolina has a state estate tax but no inheritance tax. South Carolina does not have an estate tax or an inheritance tax. In Florida, there is a unique set of rules called the Florida Homestead, which affects the transfer of Florida property for Florida residents. States may have taxes on nonresident beneficiaries or nonresident decedents, so it is important to have the state of residence correct on the death certificate. Estate taxes are discussed in more detail in Chapter 9.

For example, Olympia was traveling to her home in Florida when she was severely injured in a terrible car accident in Raleigh, North Carolina. After about two weeks in the hospital, she died from her injuries. Her driver's license was issued by the State of New York. The death certificate, issued by the vital statistics office of the City of Raleigh, indicated that her last residence was unknown. Some investigation may be necessary, but there is a good chance that Olympia was a resident of the State of New York because that is where she had her driver's license. She could also have done estate planning that included establishing Florida as her home state, so it will be important to talk to her accountant and/or her attorney to see where she had her estate-planning documents prepared.

5. Obtain the Original Will

If there is a valid will, the executor must obtain the original for submission to the probate office. We will look at what to do if there is no will or if there is a problem with the will, in the next section of this chapter. Locating the will, or determining if there is a will to look for, is often very difficult. If the decedent passed unexpectedly or if the decedent was very private about his or her affairs, family members may not even know where to look for the will. Some investigation by the family and/or the attorney may be necessary.

Legal residence or domicile: the state in which the individual votes, has a driver's license, and pays state taxes

Practice Tip

A paralegal will often get calls asking if an attorney in the office has any record of having prepared a will for a recently deceased person. Careful records of all of the wills prepared in the office must be maintained, including paper copies and digital copies of the completed wills. Once the client signs the will, scan the will as a PDF so that there is easy access to a signed copy.

Keeping accurate records of all of the wills prepared in the office is essential as the family members of the decedent will often go back to the attorney who prepared the will when help is needed to probate the will. The paralegal should develop some system for organizing and updating the list of wills, including which clients have taken their original wills and which clients have asked the attorney to retain the original will.

Example

Percy Dore was in his late 80s. His wife Kendra had been experiencing symptoms of dementia for years. Approximately one year ago, Percy had to place Kendra in a nursing home because he was unable to continue to care for her. They had no children and no close relatives other than some distant grandnieces and grandnephews who lived out of the country. Percy went to the nursing home to visit his wife every day, and when he did not show up for a few days, the staff of the home called the police, and it was discovered that Percy had died. Percy and his wife had some close friends who lived in the area where they lived before Percy retired. Their friends had a son who was a lawyer, and the nursing home knew that the lawyer had visited Kendra. The police contacted the lawyer. The lawyer's records showed that he had prepared a will for Percy and Kendra, but he only had a copy of the will in his file. Fortunately, the file also contained a note indicating that the original will was stored in Percy's safe deposit box. A court-appointed administrator was needed to open the safe deposit box, retrieve the will, and submit it to the probate court. The will was valid and appointed the longtime friend as executor.

If the family of the decedent has a reason to believe the will is in a safe deposit box, it may be necessary to make application to the court for permission to search the safe deposit box. The application usually involves presenting some evidence to the court that gives rise to a reasonable belief that the will may be located in the safe deposit box, such as a receipt for the rental fees for the box or a notation from the lawyer who prepared the will that the client took the original.

Practice Tip

After the will is signed, the file should be marked indicating either "Client retained original documents" or "Original documents retained by lawyer." Self-inking stamps can be obtained from office supply stores that contain these statements so that the stamp can be placed on the documents and file.

If the lawyer prepares a great number of wills, the lawyer will often provide for the safe storage of original documents that are retained, such as an office safe or other secure location. The paralegal will be responsible for maintaining the records of the wills that are stored in the law firm's safe. This record does not have to be elaborate. A simple word document stored on a computer, with a backup printed copy in the lawyer's files, and another in the safe, would be sufficient.

6. Admitting a Will to Probate

Once the original will and death certificate have been obtained, the next step is to have the original will admitted to **probate**. Probate means to prove, validate, and register a will. Probate is not the process of administration of the estate, although many people use the two terms interchangeably. To probate means simply to register the will. What the executor does after the will has been registered is the actual estate administration.

Probate: to prove, validate, and register a will

Most states have special courts, usually called probate courts, that deal with probating wills. The probate court also hears cases involving challenges to wills, and addresses wills that cannot be probated because of problems with the will. The probate court appoints administrators for estates where there is no will, or if the executor named in the will cannot serve. The probate court also provides ongoing supervision of the personal representatives appointed for estates. In many states, the forms necessary to probate an estate can be found online. For example, the majority of California's probate documents can be found online (http://www.courts.ca.gov/forms.htm).

The time in which the will must be submitted to probate starts to run at the testator's death. Many states establish a date or number of days after death during which the will must be submitted or the person holding the will faces penalty. Anytime the law requires something to be done within a specific time period, the time period is referred to as the **statute of limitations**. For example, Texas law requires that a will be probated within four years of the date of decedent's death. In Massachusetts, the will must be presented for probate within three years of the decedent's death. Failure to present the will for probate within the statute of limitations will result in the will being barred from probate. Many states require a waiting period between the date of death and the date on which the will can be submitted to probate. For example, in Maine there is a five-day waiting period after a decedent's death before any probate matter can be initiated. In New Jersey, the waiting period is ten days.

Statute of limitations: state law requiring that an action be brought within a certain time

Practice Tip

The paralegal is on the front line when it comes to receiving the phone calls from clients. When dealing with the probate of a will, the client is often a grieving family member who has just lost a loved one. As obvious as it sounds, it is always appropriate to first offer condolences for the loss of the loved one before moving on to providing information about probate. The caller may not know what to do, or may believe that something needs to be done immediately. It is helpful to prepare a checklist of items needed that can be sent to the client when the call is first received that someone has passed away.

The will is probated in the county where the decedent lived at the time of death, UPC §3-201. That may be different from where the death occurred, especially if the decedent was in a long-term care facility prior to death. If, for example, the decedent still owned a home at the date of death in one county, but died after residing in a long-term care facility in different county, then the decedent's residence was where the home was located, not the location of the long-term care facility.

Common form: the process by which a will is admitted to probate when the will conforms to all of the state's requirements, also known as informal probate

There are two ways that a will can be admitted to probate: in **common form** and in **solemn form**. Probate in *common form* is used in states in which the will is considered "self-proving." This means that the state's requirements for the preparation of the will have been properly followed. Two witnesses have signed the statement indicating that they saw the testator sign the will, and that the testator said that it was his or her will. In some states, such as California, a will is self-proving when it contains the signature of the testator and the witnesses. In other states, such as Louisiana and New Jersey, the witnesses' signatures must be attested to, or sworn to, a notary public or an attorney. A clause known as an **attestation clause** is included in the will after the witnesses' signatures.

Solemn form: the probate process that is required when there is some defect of problem with the will, also known as formal probate

Attestation clause: a statement indicating that the notary swears or affirms an oath that the signatures are of the people identified in the document

In states that allow for self-proving wills, the probate process is simple. The probate court will typically accept the will for probate without any court proceeding. The witnesses to the testator's signature do not have to testify, and nothing other than the death certificate has to be presented in order for the will to be admitted to probate. The probate court does not require the person submitting the will for probate to notify any of the beneficiaries or creditors that the will is being submitted. The procedure for probating a self-proving, valid will is brief and simple.

Probate in *solemn form* is usually required when there is some defect or problem with the will. For example, if the state requires an attestation clause to be used, and it was not included in the will, solemn probate will be needed. In a solemn form probate, the witnesses who watched the testator sign will have to give sworn testimony in probate court that they witnessed the testator signing. Solemn probate can also be used if the executor is unable to find the original will, or if the will was written on, damaged, or there is some other problem with the will. Probate in solemn form is a court proceeding, and notice to all interested parties, including creditors and beneficiaries, is required.

7.   Preventing Probate

Caveat: a warning against allowing probate of a will

During the waiting period, if the state requires a waiting period, any person who wants to prevent the probate of the will can file a **caveat** with the probate court. A *caveat* is a warning against allowing probate of a will. A caveat can be a simple form, filed immediately after a person dies, that prevents a will from being admitted to probate. A caveat is often the first step in a will challenge. Figure 10-2 shows a sample of a caveat used in the State of Florida.

A caveat can be used in situations in which it is believed the will is fraudulent, or not valid, or if it is believed that a later will has been prepared, but the later will cannot be located. Some states require that the caveat is filed before the will is admitted to probate. For example, in New Jersey, which has a ten-day waiting period, a caveat must be filed during the ten-day period, or before the will is admitted to

Figure 10-2. Sample Caveat (Florida)

IN THE CIRCUIT COURT FOR _____COUNTY,
FLORIDA   PROBATE DIVISION

IN RE: ESTATE OF

                    File No. _____

                    Division _____
                    Deceased.

CAVEAT BY INTERESTED PERSON
(other than creditor)

    1. The interest of the caveator is _____,
of _____ deceased, whose last known residence address is
_____,
the last four digits of whose social security number, if known, are _____, whose year of birth,
if known, is _____, and who died on or about _____, _____.

    2. Caveator's name, mailing address, and residence are: _____
_____
_____.

    3. Caveator, a nonresident of the state of Florida, who is not represented by an attorney admitted to practice
in Florida, hereby designates_____, who (is)(is not) a member of The Florida
Bar, a resident of _____County, Florida, whose mailing address is _____
_____as caveator's agent for the service of notice and consents
that service of notice on the agent shall bind the caveator.

(delete paragraph 3 if not applicable)

    Caveator requests that the court not admit a will of the decedent to probate or appoint a Personal representative without formal notice on caveator or his or her designated agent, and that caveator be given such additional notice as the Florida Probate Rules require.

    Under penalties of perjury, I declare that I have read the foregoing, and the facts alleged are true, to the best of my knowledge and belief.

    Signed on _____,_____

                                                        _____
                                                        Caveator

---

(continued)

Figure 10-2. Continued

ACCEPTANCE

I CERTIFY that I am a resident of _____ County, Florida, and my (residence)(office) address is indicated above. I hereby accept the foregoing designation as Resident Agent.

Signed on _____, _____.

_____
Resident Agent

probate. In North Carolina, someone challenging the will has up to three years to file a caveat, and can do so after the will has been admitted to probate. It is important to know the state's requirements for the timing of filing a caveat, so that it can be explained to the frantic client who calls claiming another relative "stole grandma's will."

Example

New Jersey has a ten-day waiting period before a will can be admitted to probate. Angie Johnson calls the office on June 3 indicating that her grandmother, Irma, passed away over the weekend. There has been some controversy within the family, and many of Irma's important documents are missing. Angie cannot find the most recent copy of Irma's will. She is concerned that another family member has taken the will or had her grandmother prepare a new will. It is determined that Irma died on Saturday, June 1. This date is the beginning of the ten-day waiting period required by New Jersey statutes. The will cannot be admitted to probate until the 11th day after the date of death or until June 11. The attorney recommends Angie file a caveat because the will could not be probated during this waiting period. If someone does try to probate a will for Irma, the caveat will prevent probate and will require that Angie receive notice that someone is trying to probate. If Angie had called after the ten-day waiting period had expired, but no one had tried to probate a will, the caveat can still be filed. In New Jersey, the time in which a caveat can be filed is within the ten-day waiting period, or until someone files a will, whichever comes first. The New Jersey form of caveat is much simpler than that in Florida and requires only the information shown in Figure 10-3.

The caveat is signed and filed with the surrogate's clerk, thereby preventing the filing of any document purporting to be the last will and testament of Martin Shaun.

If a beneficiary of an estate has reason to believe the will is not valid or there is some problem with the estate, the first challenge that can be made is filing a caveat.

Figure 10-3. Sample Caveat (New Jersey)

CARLUCCIO, LEONE, DIMON, DOYLE & SACKS, L.L.C.

9 Robbins Street

Toms River, New Jersey 08753

(732) 797-1600

IN THE MATTER OF THE ESTATE

OF MARTIN SHAUN, Deceased

: SUPERIOR COURT OF NEW JERSEY

: CHANCERY DIVISION

: OCEAN COUNTY

: SURROGATE'S COURT:PROBATE PART

: DOCKET NO.

:

:   **Civil Action**

:   **CAVEAT AGAINST THE**

   PROBATE OF WILL

   I, ANTHONY CAPIZZI, next of kin of MARTIN SHAUN, late of the Township of Berkeley, County of Ocean, New Jersey, who died on October 27, 2013, do hereby caveat and protest against admitting to probate any paper writing purporting to be the Will of MARTIN SHAUN.

Dated: _____

_____

ANTHONY CAPIZZI

If the person making the challenge does not file a caveat, or is out of time to do so, the administration of the estate, or the will itself, can always be challenged in other ways. Other types of estate litigation will be discussed in Chapter 12.

8. Ancillary Probate

For those decedents who own real property in another jurisdiction, another probate proceeding must take place in that location to distribute that property. This is known as **ancillary probate** or *ancillary administration*. A decedent's will is probated in the state in which the decedent was domiciled at the time of death. This probate is sometimes referred to as the **domiciliary probate**. For example, Roger Alvarez died a resident of the state of New York. His primary home was located in New York, but

Ancillary probate or ancillary administration: to prove, validate, and register a will in another jurisdiction where real property is owned

Domiciliary probate: the fact that a decedent's will is probated in the state in which he or she was domiciled

Foreign executor: an executor from another state

he also owned a vacation home in North Carolina. The decedent's will is first admitted to probate in New York (domiciliary probate), and then an ancillary probate proceeding is conducted in North Carolina with regard to the North Carolina property. Ancillary probate is secondary or supplemental to the domiciliary probate.

Ancillary probate can be time consuming and costly. The executor may be required to hire an attorney in the second state to assist with ancillary probate. Some states allow an executor from another state, sometimes called a **foreign executor**, to simply file the letter testamentary from the domiciliary state along with a copy of the will. Other states require full probate of the will. Ancillary probate can only be granted after the domiciliary probate. If the will is being challenged in the domiciliary state, the ancillary probate cannot be accomplished until that challenge is resolved.

Many clients own property in more than one state. Clients who are "snow birds" and go to warmer states in the south, routinely travel north as summer approaches. Clients owning property in more than one state may wish to take steps to avoid ancillary probate. In Chapter 1 we learned that there are several ways in which property can pass from the decedent to the designated beneficiary without passing through the probate estate. Remember, only those assets that are in the decedent's name alone become part of the probate estate and are distributed in accordance with the will. Any asset that is jointly held passes by way of a TOD (transferable on death) or POD (payable on death) order. Any asset that has a beneficiary designation, such as a life insurance policy, is not a probate asset. If a client owns out-of-state property, the attorney may suggest putting the property into trust or owning the property jointly, with the right of survivorship, so that a method of distributing the property exists independent of the will.

For example, our client, Roger Alvarez, is domiciled in New York but owns real property in North Carolina. Roger is recently married and wants to change his will to include his wife, Maria. The attorney is aware that Roger owns real property in North Carolina and suggests that the deed to the North Carolina property be changed from Roger's name to the name of Roger and Maria Alvarez, husband and wife, as joint tenants with right of survivorship (JTWROS). If either Roger or Maria dies, the North Carolina property passes to the surviving spouse by operation of law without going through ancillary probate. Let us take this example one step farther to see what happens many years later when Roger passes away. An attorney has assisted Maria in getting Roger's will admitted to probate and administering the estate. The issue of the North Carolina property has come up. Roger and Maria have two adult children, sons Fred and George. Their sons are both married, and each has children. The extended family lives in various states, but they enjoy gathering at the North Carolina property several times each year. Maria could change the deed to the North Carolina property to take Roger's name off and add Fred and George as joint tenants with right of survivorship. Maria may also want to place the property into a revocable trust with Fred and George and their heirs as beneficiaries of the trust. Property passing to a beneficiary or beneficiaries by way of a trust does not require ancillary probate.

9. Small Estate or Informal Probate

If the size of the estate is less than the current amount set by state law, then the estate may be able to be probated using a simplified procedure. **Small estate probate** or **informal probate** is a simplified probate process by which a personal representative is appointed to administer an estate in an abbreviated procedure that costs less money and takes less time. The request for informal probate can be made whether or not there is a will. It requires someone being willing to serve as the personal representative of the estate and submitting the necessary application and supporting affidavits to the probate court in the county in which the decedent lived.

Small estate probate or informal probate: a simplified probate process by which a personal representative is appointed to administer an estate in an abbreviated procedure

The right to use the small estate probate process is usually limited to estates under a certain dollar amount. For example, in New Jersey, small estate probate is available for those estates of $10,000 or less where the surviving spouse or domestic partner is entitled to all of the assets, or for estates of $5,000 or less where there is no surviving spouse or domestic partner (N.J. Stat. Ann. §3B:10-3 and 4). In other states, such as Oregon, the estate can be much larger and still be eligible for small estate probate. The Oregon statute provides for small estate probate when $75,000 or less of the fair market value of the estate is from personal property, and $200,000 or less of the fair market value of the estate is from real property. Estates that are administered in accordance with the state's laws on informal probate are not under the continued monitoring of the probate court.

The exact process used for small estate probate will vary from state to state, but there are certain common elements. Usually an affidavit is required from either the executor or a beneficiary stating who is entitled to receive an asset. The executor or beneficiary files with the court an inventory and something proving the value of the asset. Proof of value can be an appraisal report for real property or a statement from a bank or financial institution indicating the date of death balance. Notice of the small estate probate must be provided to all distributors and creditors. For example, on the date of her death, our client, Maria Alvarez, owns very few assets. She has transferred her ownership in the North Carolina property to a trust for her sons, Fred and George. She sold the home in New York and used the proceeds to pay for care in an assisted living facility. On the date of her death, Maria's estate consisted of a checking account with $5,000 and a savings account with $22,000. Fred and George can follow the New York procedure for small estate probate.

10. Letters Testamentary

When the will is admitted to probate, the executor of the estate is given a certificate referred to as a Letter Testamentary or Executor's Certificate that acts as proof that the executor has authority to act on behalf of the estate. The executor needs to obtain an original sealed certificate for each bank account, financial institution, or asset that needs to be liquidated. If the decedent has a savings account and checking account in one bank, an investment account with a financial institution, a home, and a car, the executor will need four certificates, one for the checking and savings account, one for

Figure 10-4. Sample Letter Testamentary

```
                         LETTERS TESTAMENTARY
_____, whose address is _____, having been appointed and qualified as
[executor] [executrix] of the will of _____, deceased, who died on or about
[date], is hereby authorized to act as [executor] [executrix] for and in behalf of
the estate and to take possession of the estate's property as authorized by law.
Issued this date: _____, ____.
_____, Clerk.
By: _____, Deputy Clerk.
      (Seal)
```

the investment account, one to sell the house, and one to sell the car. Every time the Executor takes an action on behalf of the estate, whether selling an asset or liquidating an account, one of the original probate certificates must be used. The probate court will issue a certain number of certificates as standard with the probate of a will, but additional certificates can be requested. Figure 10-4 shows a sample of a letter testamentary issued by the probate court of Kansas:

The letter testamentary is issued by the court and is not a form a paralegal will be expected to draft.

How many certificates are needed? Let us look at an example: The decedent died owning a home located at 11 Holiday Road, Anytown. She had a 2009 Ford Escape, a savings and checking account at Anytown Bank, a local savings and loan. She also had a money market account with Bank of America, a retirement account with Merrill Lynch, and an E-Trade investment account. A minimum of six certificates should be requested:

1. Savings and Checking accounts — one certificate can be used for two accounts at the same bank
2. Money market account
3. Retirement account
4. Investment account
5. One certificate will be needed to sell the house
6. One certificate will be needed to sell the car

If more accounts or assets are discovered, additional certificates can be obtained from the probate court.

The executor is required to give notice of probate following the rules of the state and county in which the will has been probated. Notice must be given to all of the beneficiaries of the estate, and each beneficiary must be provided with a copy

Figure 10-5. Sample Notification Letter

```
To all Beneficiaries of the Estate of Olive Hornby

Please be advised that the Executor of the Estate of Olive Hornby has retained
this office. Enclosed please find a notice of probate as required by state law.
You will receive additional information as the administration of the estate
progresses. If you have any questions regarding this matter, please feel free to
call my office.
```

of the will. Some states have a requirement that if there are charities named in the will, the attorney general also receives notice of probate, so that the attorney general can protect the interests of the charity. Notice is usually given by mailing a letter or a specific notice form, along with a copy of the will, to each person named in the will. For an example a form go to http://www .supremecourt.ohio.gov/LegalResources/Rules/superintendence/probate_forms/ and look at form 2.2. That is the form used in Ohio to notify beneficiaries of the probate of a decedent's will.

The notices should be sent by certified mail, return receipt requested. The recipient of the notice signs the receipt, which is a green card attached to the outside of the envelope. The receipt is returned to the executor or the attorney representing the executor. Copies of the green receipt cards, along with the notice or letter sent to each beneficiary, should be kept as proof that notice was provided. Notice must be provided within the time specified in the state statutes. If the attorney is representing the executor and is taking responsibility for mailing out the notices, the form letter in Figure 10-5 can be included with the notice of probate.

If state law requires that the beneficiaries also receive a copy of the will along with the notice of probate, a copy of the will would also be included. Remember, once the will is admitted to probate, it becomes a public document, and anyone can obtain a copy from the probate office.

In many states, probate is relatively easy and relatively inexpensive. No formal court procedure is required. In some states, a tax on probate is imposed, or the state has fees that make probating a will more expensive. For example, Virginia has a probate tax that is assessed at the rate of 10 cents per $100 on estates valued at more than $15,000, including the first $15,000 of assets. The tax must be paid at the time the will is presented for probate. In those states where there is a probate tax, or fees are excessively high, many estate planners will recommend the use of a living trust or inter vivos trust instead of a will. A living trust is also preferable to those clients who wish to keep the estate private, because unlike a will, a trust is not made public after death. A living trust is a type of trust created during the life of the decedent. Remember from Chapter 5 that trusts created in the will are testamentary trusts. The trust directs that the property held in the trust be distributed to the beneficiaries at the death of the grantor, thereby avoiding probate. In other states, the cost of probate is relatively low compared to the cost of creating an inter vivos trust, and it is far preferable (and less costly) to use a will instead of a trust. It is important to know not only the estate laws of the state in which you are working, but also the effect of various taxes and the preferred ways of avoiding those taxes if possible.

B.   Intestate Estate

1.   Appointing an Administrator

Probate is the first step when a decedent dies with a valid will. If the decedent dies without a will, the estate is considered intestate, and a personal representative for the estate must be appointed. The personal representative of the estate is called an *administrator* and is appointed by the court. An administrator may also be appointed if there is a will, but the executor named in the will cannot serve. For example, refer back to our client Maria Alvarez. On the date of her death, she had a valid will but named her late husband Roger as the executor. She never changed her will after Roger's death, and no substitute executor was named. One or both of her sons will have to apply to be the administrator of their mother's estate. Most states have an order of priority for appointment of an administrator of an intestate estate. For example, under the UPC, the order of the persons who are entitled to be appointed as the administrator is as follows:

- The person named in the will as executor
- The surviving spouse
- Other heirs of the decedent
- If 45 days have passed since the decedent's death, any creditor (UPC §3-203)

Heirs, next of kin, distributees: persons who by operation of law — the application of the established rules of law — inherit or succeed to the property of a person intestate on his or her death

Degree of consanguinity: the blood relationship of the heirs to the decedent

The terms **heirs, next of kin, distributees,** and *devisees* all refer to the people who, by operation of law, inherit the property of a person who died intestate. A chart that is useful in determining the degree of relationship was introduced in Chapter 1. This chart is used to determine the **degree of consanguinity**, or blood relationship of the heirs to the decedent.

The relative that is the closest degree of relationship has the right to serve as administrator of the estate. In our example above, both Fred and George have the right to serve as the administrator of their mother's estate. The closest relative might not be one or two people, but an entire class of people. In Chapter 1 we looked at the example of a client who had a distant cousin named Marjorie who died intestate. We determined that the client's grandfather and Marjorie's father were brothers. Therefore, using the chart showing the degree of consanguinity, we determined that the client and Marjorie are first cousins once removed. All of the first cousins once removed will have an equal right to serve as the administrator of Marjorie's estate. The identities of all the persons who qualify as first cousins will have to be determined. This may require some investigation. It will be necessary to determine if Marjorie's father had any other brothers or sisters, and, if he did, if they had any other children. It will also be necessary to track down Marjorie's mother's family and determine if any of the maternal relatives are within the same degree of kinship.

After all of the next of kin are identified and those who are all on the same degree of kinship as Marjorie are located, the application for appointment of an administrator can be made. There are two ways the application can be made: first, by notice to all the parties, or second, with **renunciations** from other family members. A *renunciation* is a form by which a potential beneficiary of an estate either waives the right to serve as a fiduciary or waives the right to take from the estate. In some states the renunciation form is also called a waiver. In our example, Marjorie discovers that her father had a brother whom she never knew about. Marjorie never kept in touch with that side of her family, so none of the younger generations were aware of the other cousins. Our client would have to locate those relatives because they are all entitled to serve as administrator. The attorney would have to contact those relatives and determine if they would be willing to sign renunciations allowing our client to serve as administrator. If the attorney was able to get renunciations from all of the relatives with the right to serve as administrator, the renunciations, along with an application for appointment of an administrator, can be submitted. The state's specific rules will have to be consulted as to the form of the application. If the attorney cannot get the necessary renunciations, a complaint will have to be filed in the probate court seeking the appointment of an administrator. Notice would be provided to all of the next of kin in accordance with the state's requirements.

Completing the appointment of an administrator for an intestate estate can mean months of research tracking down heirs and determining the degree of relationship. The court may appoint an interim administrator who is given the job of finding and notifying all of the heirs. The interim administrator may also be given the job of securing all of the decedent's assets and preparing an inventory in preparation of the administration.

As another example, look at our client Brian whose mother has passed away, and who needs assistance with probate. The client's mother, Alice, had two children, Brian and his brother Christopher. Alice died intestate. Each of Alice's children has an equal right to serve as administrator. If Brian had no desire to serve as the administrator of Alice's estate, he could **renounce**, or disclaim, his right to serve in favor of Christopher. A sample of the language needed for a renunciation, as used in the District of Columbia, is shown in Figure 10-6.

Each state may have its own form or procedure for renouncing or disclaiming the right to serve as administrator. It is important to submit all of the necessary renunciations with the application for the appointment of an administrator. For example, if Alice had five children instead of just two, Christopher would need to get renunciations from all of his brothers and sisters in order to be appointed as the administrator of the estate. If any one of the people eligible to serve as administrator refuses to sign a renunciation, then it may be necessary to have a hearing to determine who should be appointed.

There are also rare occasions when no heirs to the decedent's estate can be found. When a person dies intestate and no next of kin, no matter how remotely related,

Renunciation: a form by which a potential beneficiary of an estate either gives up the right to serve as a fiduciary, or gives up the right to take from the estate, also known as a waiver

Renounce: to give up or disclaim the right to receive from the estate, or to serve as the personal representative

Figure 10-6. Sample Renunciation

SUPERIOR COURT OF THE DISTRICT OF COLUMBIA

PROBATE DIVISION

Estate of ________ ADM ________

____

Deceased

RENUNCIATION

I, ______________________________, being a competent adult, and being familiar with the petition of ______________________________, for Letters of Administration, and being aware of the fact that according to D.C. Code, sec. 20-303, I have priority to serve as personal representative of the instant estate in that I am the ____________________ (relationship to decedent such as heir, legatee, personal representative or alternate personal representative nominated in the will) of the deceased, hereby renounce my right to serve as the personal representative of this estate.

____

Date

____

Signature

____

Address

____

____

____

Telephone Number

Escheat: when a person dies intestate without any other person capable of taking the property as an heir, the assets in the estate are transferred to the state in which the decedent lived at the time of death

can be found, the assets in the estate **escheat**, or are transferred to the state in which the decedent lived. Escheat can also occur when money is left unclaimed in a bank account. If the owner cannot be located, the funds in the account escheat to the state but can be reclaimed by the rightful owner.

2. Determining the Intestate Distribution

The degree of relationship is used to determine who has the right to serve as the administrator of the estate and who is entitled to share in the estate. All of the relatives who are in an equal degree of relationship to the deceased, such as children, all share equally in the estate. If any person predeceased the decedent,

Figure 10-7. Example: Distribution of Alice's Estate

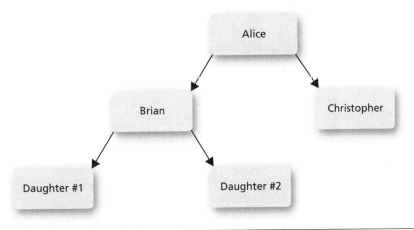

that person's share is then divided among the predeceased person's heirs. If a person predeceased leaving no heirs, that person's share lapses, and the estate is then divided among the survivors. This can easily become very confusing. It is often necessary to draw family tree charts to correctly identify the relatives, as well as their right to take from the estate.

In our example above, Brian and Christopher are both equal heirs of Alice's estate. They would share in her estate equally because they both occupy the same degree of kinship or consanguinity, to their mother. If Alice had other children, those children would also occupy the same degree of kinship with regard to their mother, even if those children had a different father than Brian and Christopher.

The degree of relationship is used to determine the distribution of the estate. All of the relatives on the same level or at the same degree of relationship to the decedent get an equal share of the estate. But what happens if someone on the same degree of kinship predeceases the decedent? By way of explanation, let us change the facts in our example. As we already know, Alice died intestate. She had two children, Brian and Christopher, who each receive equal distributions from her estate. Now let us see what happens if Brian predeceased her. Assume Brian had two young daughters. The distribution of Alice's estate is shown in Figure 10-7.

Because Brian predeceased his mother, his 50 percent share of his mother's estate will pass to his two daughters, who will equally share Brian's distribution from the estate. This is an easy example. The situations that a paralegal can encounter can be much more complicated. In an intestate estate, there will be additional cousins, predeceased heirs, lost relatives, and unknown family members. At the end of the chapter is a portion of a family tree used in a recent intestate case. The intestate succession laws are very confusing. For example, look at each section of the New Jersey intestate succession statute. New Jersey Statute 3B:5-3 lists the intestate share of decedent's surviving spouse as the entire intestate estate if

(1) No descendant or parent of the decedent survives the decedent; or

(2) All of the decedent's surviving descendants are also descendants of the surviving spouse and there is no other descendant of the surviving spouse who survives the decedent

The statute indicates that the surviving spouse gets all of the decedent's assets, if the decedent did not have any descendants, and the decedent's parents have predeceased. For example, Alex and Amy Carrow have no children. Alex passes away without a will. Alex's parents have already passed away. Therefore, Alex's entire estate is distributed to Amy, his surviving wife.

The next part of the statute addresses the distribution if one of Alex's parents survived:

> The first 25% of the intestate estate, but not less than $50,000.00 nor more than $200,000.00, plus three-fourths of any balance of the intestate estate, if no descendant of the decedent survives the decedent, but a parent of the decedent survives the decedent;

If one of Alex's parents, say his father, survives Alex, he is entitled to a distribution from Alex's estate. Amy receives 25 percent of Alex's estate and three-fourths of the balance of the estate. The remainder goes to Alex's father. If Alex's entire estate is worth $200,000, applying the statute results in the following:

Amy's share of the estate is 25 percent of $200,000 = $50,000.
The balance of the intestate estate is $200,000 − $50,000 = $150,000.
Amy's additional share is three-fourths (or 75 percent) of $150,000 = $122,500.
$50,000 + $122,500 = $172,500 for Amy and $28,500 for Alex's father.

The third and final part of the New Jersey statute addresses the distribution of an intestate estate if there are surviving descendants. Let us change our facts to include two children for Alex and Amy. The statute states that Amy will receive the following distribution:

> The first 25% of the intestate estate, but not less than $50,000.00 nor more than $200,000.00, plus one-half of the balance of the intestate estate:
>
> **(1)** If all of the decedent's surviving descendants are also descendants of the surviving spouse and the surviving spouse has one or more surviving descendants who are not descendants of the descendent; or
>
> **(2)** If one or more of the decedent's surviving descendants is not a descendant of the surviving spouse.

Amy receives 25 percent of the estate and one-half of the balance if both of the children are her children, or if one of the children is Alex's child from a previous marriage. The remainder of the estate is divided among the children. There are additional statutes that similarly describe the intestate share of the surviving children, or other descendants, or other heirs.

If a person dies testate, or with a will, the only assets that pass according to the will are probate assets. If a person dies without a will, a similar result occurs. Any of the decedent's assets that pass by operation of law are not included in the intestate estate.

Assets such as jointly owned property, joint bank accounts, accounts that are marked payable on death (POD) or transferable on death (TOD), pass to the surviving owner, or designated beneficiary, regardless of the degree of relationship of the beneficiary to the decedent. For example, if the person dies intestate, but had a joint bank account with her brother, the joint account still goes to the brother and is not distributed according to the intestate laws. When an asset is owned only in the name of the decedent, and there is no other way that this asset will pass to a joint owner or surviving owner, then the asset will go to the heirs according to the intestacy laws of the state in which the decedent lived. Another example of a family tree that was created for the distribution of an intestate estate can be found on the companion Web site.

3.   Dower and Curtesy

In some states, there are specific rules used to distribute the assets of a spouse to the surviving spouse. Those laws are known as **dower** and **curtesy**. Dower and curtesy are a set of laws that evolved from common law that govern the distribution of marital property to the surviving spouse. Dower is a wife's interest in her husband's property upon his death. It comes from the same root word used for dowry, or the money or goods that a woman brings to the marriage. Curtesy is the husband's interest in property that his wife owned at her death. Dower and curtesy rights have been abolished in most states and replaced with laws pertaining to the marital share. One of the few states that maintains dower and curtesy rights is Arkansas. The surviving spouse's share of the estate is known as a **statutory share, marital share**, or **elective share**. Different states use different terms to describe the portion of a deceased person's estate that the surviving spouse is entitled to claim under state law. In many states, the elective share or statutory share is about one-third of a deceased spouse's property. If the deceased spouse left a will, the surviving spouse can claim an elective share of the estate if it is larger than the share left in the will.

Dower: a wife's interest in her husband's property upon his death

Curtesy: the husband's interest in property that his wife owned at her death

Statutory share, marital share, or elective share: the share of the deceased spouse's estate to which the surviving spouse is entitled

Summary

The probate process begins with obtaining the original will if the decedent died testate or applying to be appointed as the administrator if the decedent died intestate. Probate is easy if the will is self-proving and if a caveat has not been filed. Probate may be done using an informal process if the estate meets the state requirements for informal probate. Ancillary probate may be necessary if there is out of state property. If the estate is intestate, the administrator must follow the state's rules for intestate succession.

Review Questions

1. What happens when a person dies with no heirs and no will?

2. What is the difference between an executor and an administrator of an estate?

3. Can a person disinherit a spouse? Can parents disinherit their children?

4. A client had a will prepared in Wisconsin, where she owns a home. She also owns a home in Arizona. She was in a car accident in Wichita, Kansas, while driving from Wisconsin to her home in Arizona. She spent three weeks in the hospital in Kansas and another six weeks in a rehabilitation hospital, but died in the rehabilitation facility from a sudden stroke. Her death certificate states place of residence at date of death as the rehabilitation facility located in Wichita.

    a. What is the client's state of residence?
    b. What happens to the death certificate?
    c. Where will the will be admitted to probate?

5. The person appointed to administer an intestate estate is called:

    a. Executor
    b. Personal representative
    c. Administrator
    d. Both b and c

6. The person appointed to bring a wrongful death claim is called:

    a. Administrator ad litem
    b. Executor
    c. Personal representative
    d. Administrator ad prosequendum

7. Each state has its own rules for small estate administration. Go to this link to research your state's laws: http://www.nolo.com/legal-encyclopedia/probate-shortcuts-in-your-state-31020.html.

Using your state's laws, determine whether the estate in the following fact pattern can be administered by way of the small estate administration procedure:

Marvin Riddle has died with a will but a very small estate. He was married, but his wife passed away many years ago. He has one child, a daughter Marilyn, who lives in a different state. Marilyn advises that her father's estate consists of his car, a very small condo in an adult community valued at approximately $45,000, a checking account with $1,800, and a savings account with $10,000. Her father received a pension of $3,000 per month, which ended with his death.

    a. How many certificates or letters of administration will Marilyn need to administer her father's estate?

8. Use the following information and the family tree chart in Figure 10-8 to answer the questions below.

A new client named George comes to the office regarding his Uncle Ben, who has died intestate at age 103. George is able to provide you with a portion of Uncle Ben's family tree. All of the people in the green boxes have predeceased Ben. There are additional family members in the fifth generation, but since all of the members of the fourth generation are surviving, we will not be including any additional family members.

    a. Which people have the first right to serve as administrator of Uncle Ben's estate?

Figure 10-8. Family Tree Chart

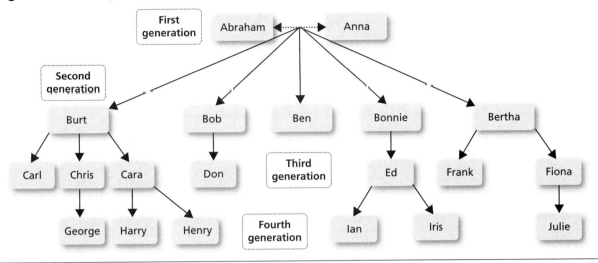

b. What form is necessary if only one of the people who is eligible to serve as administrator wants to serve, and all of the others are willing to let that person serve? Go to the Ohio probate form Web site, and using the appropriate form, draft the necessary document.

c. Who is entitled to a portion of the intestate estate? What is the portion or percentage that would go to each person?

d. What is George's relationship to Ben? To Fiona? To Ian?

Key Terms

Administrator
Administrator ad litem
Administrator ad prosequendum
Ancillary probate or ancillary administration
Attestation clause
Caveat
Common form
Curtesy
Degree of consanguinity
Domiciliary probate
Dower
Escheat
Executor
Foreign executor

Heirs, next of kin, distributees
Intestate
Laws of intestate succession or the laws of intestacy
Legal residence or domicile
Probate
Renounce
Renunciation
Small estate probate or informal probate
Solemn form
Statute of limitations
Statutory share, marital share, or elective share
Testate

Estate Administration

This chapter will discuss all of the tasks the representative needs to complete the administration of the estate. The estate administration process is relatively simple, but there are many steps involved. It can take several months and sometimes years to complete the administration of an estate. The beneficiaries are often impatient and demanding. They will call the office, demanding to know when they are going to get "their" money. The paralegal will need to be able to update the beneficiaries when they call, and keep the executor on track in completing each of the necessary tasks. Attention to detail and some type of reminder or "tickler system" for follow-up are the two main skills that are needed. The paralegal will be working very independently in the administration of an estate, and it is important that every detail is addressed.

A. Overview of Estate Administration

As we learned previously, the personal representative of the estate is the executor, if appointed in the will. The personal representative is an administrator, if appointed by the court. For the remainder of this chapter, the personal representative will be referred to as the executor, even though the tasks listed in this chapter can be completed by an executor or an administrator. As a very general overview, estate administration involves the liquidation and consolidation of all of the decedent's assets, payment of estate debts and expenses, and distribution of the estate assets to the beneficiaries. An example of a checklist used in estate administration is included at the end of the chapter in Figure 11-5. The consolidation of the estate assets is known as **marshaling the assets**. Finding the assets of the decedent can often require a good bit of detective work. If the decedent was very elderly at the time of death, he or she may not have maintained good financial records. There may be old bank accounts that were forgotten or retirement accounts from previous employment. There may be employer-paid life insurance that was part of a retirement package, or stock options or dividends that were not recorded. The executor is responsible for gathering all of the information about the decedent's assets. The executor is also responsible for gathering all of the decedent's last bills, including any outstanding credit cards, expenses of last illness, funeral expenses, and other debts.

Marshaling the assets: consolidation of the estate assets

Commission: payment to the personal representative for all of the work that is required, calculated as a percentage of the principal and income of the estate

The executor is entitled to a **commission**, or fee, in payment of all of the work that is required. The commission is calculated from the value of the estate. The fee is usually based on a percentage of the value of the assets in the estate, plus a percentage of the income generated by those assets while they are under the control of the executor. The executor's commission is a debt of the estate that must be paid. The executor is permitted to hire whatever professionals are needed and to pay those professionals from the estate.

An executor can turn over all of the administrative duties of serving as executor to the attorney, who will then turn many of those duties over to the paralegal. Other executors will attempt to administer the estate on their own, only to run into stumbling blocks that cause them to give up. The worst position for the paralegal is to take over an estate that an executor has been neglecting. The paralegal will then have to untangle the mess while dealing with frustrated beneficiaries.

B.   Estates of Percy and Kendra Dore

In this chapter, we will go through the steps of estate administration for the estate of our late client, Percy Dore. You will recall from previous chapters that Percy Dore was in his late 80s. His wife Kendra was residing in a local nursing home when Percy passed away. Percy and Kendra have no children and no close relatives other than some distant grandnieces and grandnephews who lived out of the country. A court-appointed administrator was needed to open Percy's safe-deposit box, retrieve the will, and submit the will to the probate court. The will was valid and appointed the Dores' longtime friend as executor. Shortly after Percy passed away, Kendra's health declined, and she also passed away. Percy's estate passes to his wife Kendra, and then immediately passes from Kendra's estate to the beneficiaries named in Kendra's will.

C.   Probate and Appointment of Personal Representative

The first steps that have to be completed are those involving the probate of the will and appointment of the personal representative, whether that representative is an executor or an administrator.

1.   Obtain the Death Certificate

In most states, a death certificate can only be obtained by the next-of-kin. As was discussed in Chapter 9, it is important the executor check the accuracy of all of the information on the death certificate. Is the place of residence correct? Is the decedent's name spelled correctly? If it is not correct, the executor should take the necessary steps to correct the information on the death certificate. The correction may need to be submitted by the next-of-kin who gave the information on the death certificate.

2.   Locate the Decedent's Will, If There Is a Will

As discussed in the previous chapter, locating the will may require a petition to the probate court for permission to enter the decedent's safe-deposit box. In Percy's case, the attorney who drafted the will had notes indicating that the will was located in Percy's safe-deposit box. A court order was required to gain access to the box and retrieve the original will.

3.   Probate the Decedent's Will — If There Is No Will, Apply for Administration

Probate was covered in detail in Chapter 10. In states that allow for self-proving wills, probate is relatively simple and inexpensive. The executor of the estate takes the will, an original death certificate, and some form of payment to the probate court. It is not a formal court as one would normally think of a court. Instead, the executor simply presents the will to the clerk of the court, completes a questionnaire identifying the decedent, the beneficiaries, and the assets in the estate, and then signs paperwork indicating that he or she is taking on the responsibilities of serving as the executor. Different states require different information to be presented to the probate clerk. The paralegal should research his or her home state and determine if a probate application form used within that state is available for download.

4.   Arrange for Bond If Necessary

Surety bonds, ensuring that the executor or administrator completes his or her duties, were discussed at length in Chapter 4. If the will requires a surety bond, the executor must obtain the bond in order to complete the probate process. If an administrator must be appointed, a bond will usually be required. It is helpful to have the contact information for a few bond companies to provide to clients. Percy's will indicated that no executor or substitute executor would be required to obtain a bond.

5.   Notify Beneficiaries and Creditors as Required by State Law

The notice requirements vary from state to state. The paralegal should be aware of the notice requirements in the state in which he or she is working, and what is required to comply with those requirements. The notice requirement may include supplying each beneficiary with a copy of the will, and proving that the beneficiary received the copy of the will. In the State of Texas, the form in Figure 11-1 is used, which is a good example of the language necessary to notify the beneficiaries.

Figure 11-1. Example: Notifying Beneficiaries

CERTIFIED MAIL

RETURN RECEIPT REQUESTED #_____

[Beneficiary Name]

[Beneficiary Address]

      Re: Estate of [Decedent's Name], Deceased; Cause No. [Number] in the Probate Court No. 1 of Travis County, Texas

Dear [Beneficiary Name]:

[Executor Name] has retained this firm to represent her in her capacity as Independent Executor of the Estate of [Decedent Name], Deceased (referred to in this letter as the "Estate"). I am writing this letter to you on behalf of [Executor Name]. Section 128A of the Texas Probate Code requires the independent executor of an estate to notify all beneficiaries of the Estate that the will has been probated. Accordingly, you are hereby notified that:

1.   [Decedent Name]s will dated [Date of Will] was admitted to probate in the Probate Court No. 1 of Travis County, Texas, under Cause No. [Number], and [Executor Name] was appointed as and qualified as independent executor of the Estate on [Date of Qualification].

2.   [Beneficiary Name] is named as a beneficiary in the will.

3.   The name and address of [Executor Name] is: [Executor Name], Estate of [Decedent Name], c/o [Firm Name], [Firm Address].

4.   A copy of the will and order admitting it to probate are attached.

This firm represents [Executor Name]. It does not represent you or the Estate.

                            Very truly yours,

                            [Lawyer Name]

Enclosures

As indicated in the notice, the document is sent to the beneficiaries by certified mail, return receipt requested. If the probate court requires the executor to prove that a copy of the will was provided to each beneficiary, the paralegal will be required to provide copies of the green cards that come back from the U.S. Postal Service as the certified mail receipts.

Percy's relatives did not live in the United States. Fortunately, the executor could speak the same language as the beneficiaries, which made communication possible. Using e-mail, the beneficiaries were notified of Percy's death and provided copies of the will and the court documents.

D. Administrative Duties

The first set of duties listed above were items that the paralegal can typically assist the executor, administrator, or personal representative in completing but involve tasks that cannot be delegated to the paralegal to complete without supervision. For example, the paralegal may assist the executor in probating the will in order to have the executor appointed, but the executor must sign all of the documents necessary. The next set of tasks can be delegated to the paralegal who can then work independently.

1. Request Post Office Forward Decedent's Mail to Executor

The U.S. post office utilizes a specific form for forwarding mail. The form can be completed online (https://moversguide.usps.com/icoa/icoa-main-flow.do?execution= e1s1). Mail can be forwarded directly to the executor or to the attorney's office if the attorney is assisting with the administration of the estate. The forwarded mail will be the source of a lot of information about the decedent's assets and debts. Separate subfiles should be set within the main file for credit card statements, medical expenses, funeral expenses, utility bills from the decedent's home, and so forth.

2. Secure the Decedent's Home and Real Property

The executor must take control of the decedent's real property. If the executor lives out of state, this task can often fall on the attorney and/or paralegal to complete. Make sure the decedent's home is locked and no one else is improperly living in the home. Turn the heat up to the proper level to avoid frozen pipes in the winter if the house is located in a state where that is an issue. Make sure that utility bills necessary to keep heat in the home continue to be paid. All of these tasks are administrative in nature and can be delegated to the paralegal.

Securing the home is sometimes not as easy as it sounds. Another relative may be living in the home, or a home health aide may be living there. What is needed to secure the home is going to be very fact sensitive. Obviously, the decedent's immediate family such as surviving spouse and children will continue to live in the home. However, more distant relatives, such as a niece or nephew who was temporarily living with an elderly relative, may need to move out after the decedent's death. If someone who is not a beneficiary is living in the decedent's house, it may be necessary to have that person pay rent and carry costs of the property if the person is unable to obtain alternative housing.

Waste: occurs when an asset that has value is diminished because of some action or inaction of the representative of the estate

The executor's job is to avoid **waste** of estate assets. *Waste* occurs when an asset that has value is diminished because of some action or inaction of the representative of the estate. For example, Percy Dore had a neighbor who looked in on him from time to time. When the neighbor saw that Percy had died, the neighbor told a friend, the friend told someone else, and suddenly one day when the executor went to the house, there were trespassers living in there. The executor did not want to do anything to get the neighbor in trouble, so he allowed the trespassers to continue living there, even though they were not paying rent, were using the utilities, and were damaging the house. Percy's executor is guilty of waste, because he is allowing the value of the house to be diminished.

3. Give Notice of Appointment as Representative to Banks, Investment Brokers, and Others

Copies of the probate documents should be provided to each of the decedent's banks, financial institutions, brokers, and so forth. Each of these places will want an original certificate, and if necessary, more certificates can be obtained from the probate clerks. The probate document is known as a letter testamentary or letter of administration. It is proof that the executor or administrator is the person given the authority to act on behalf of the estate. The probate certificate, also known as a letter testamentary or letter of administration, can be sent to the various banks with a cover letter explaining the status of the situation. A sample of the language used in such a letter is shown in Figure 11-2.

```
Bank of America


            Re:    Estate of Percy Dore
                   Account #123-34-4567


Dear Sir/Madam:


     Please be advised that this office represents the executor of the Estate of
Percy Dore. Enclosed please find a copy of the letter testamentary appointing my
client as the executor of the estate and a copy of the decedent's death certifi-
cate. Kindly provide the date of death balance at your earliest convenience. Thank
you for your attention to this matter.
```

Figure 11-2. Sample Cover Letter

Figure 11-3. Power of Attorney to Authorize Banking Activities

> The Agent named herein is specifically authorized to sign and deliver any and all documents necessary to liquidate all investment accounts, bank accounts, or other assets, to access, inspect, and remove the contents of any safe-deposit box, to apply for an Employer Identification Number (EIN) on behalf of the estate, and to take any measures necessary for the purposes of administering the estate.

Major financial institutions all have specific departments that deal with estates, and the addresses of the proper place to send correspondence can be found on the Internet, or by calling the phone numbers listed on the decedent's financial statements.

4. Obtain an EIN and Open an Estate Bank Account

The executor of the estate will need to open an estate account, or perhaps even two accounts: a checking account and some type of interest-bearing savings or money market account. The executor will be finding and liquidating assets, which will result in checks being sent to the executor made out to the Estate of Percy Dore. In order to open a bank account for the estate, the executor must first obtain an employer identification number (EIN) for the estate. The EIN is obtained from the IRS using Form SS-4. The form can be completed and mailed or faxed to the IRS. The EIN can also be obtained from the IRS Web site (https://sa2.www4.irs.gov/modiein/individual/index.jsp). The executor can obtain this number or can delegate the authority to obtain this number to the attorney handling the estate by way of a power of attorney.

In cases where the executor has turned the administration of the estate over to the attorney, it is helpful to have the executor sign a power of attorney giving the attorney the authority to obtain an EIN, open an estate account, and do whatever other banking activities are necessary on behalf of the executor. An example of language that can be included in a power of attorney to specifically authorize banking activities is shown in Figure 11-3.

The executor can sign a power of attorney that will delegate the authority to complete these administrative tasks to the attorney.

E. Marshaling the Assets

After the representative of the estate is appointed and the administrative tasks are complete, the assets of the estate have to be gathered or marshaled together to be under the control of the executor. It will be necessary to determine which assets are going to be liquidated and which are going to be either held by the estate or given directly to a beneficiary as a specific gift. But first, it will be necessary to find the assets.

1. Search for Assets

The search for a decedent's assets can often involve a good bit of detective work. If the executor knows nothing about the decedent's finances, finding all of the assets can be challenging. The executor will have to search around the decedent's house for old bank statements, investment records, or other financial information. Once the executor begins to receive the decedent's mail, more information about the decedent's finances will become available. Separate files should be kept for bills, correspondence, account statements, and so forth. For example, if the executor has been receiving the decedent's mail for a few weeks, the executor may have accumulated bank statements from different banks; credit card bills; mortgage statements; property tax invoices; notices of premiums due for life, health, or auto insurance; or other types of financial information. The documents should be separated so that all of the statements from one bank are all in one file, in date order. Bills from the decedent's last illness and records of other estate debts should be separated from the assets.

Another good place to obtain information about the decedent's finances is with the decedent's last income tax return filed with the IRS and/or with the state, if the state where the decedent resided has an income tax. The income tax return will contain interest earned on investments and bank accounts, as well as the identity of those accounts. Interest income is reported on a form called a 1099. Each bank or investment company issues its own 1099, and the forms will be attached to the federal income tax return. If the executor does not have any other information, such as bank statements or investment records, the executor must write to each financial institution that issued a 1099 to determine if the decedent still has an account there. The executor will need to find each source of income for each 1099 form on the decedent's income tax return.

Dividend: a distribution of money made to a shareholder of stock of a company

A link to a sample 1099 form can be found on the IRS Web site (http://www.irs.gov/pub/irs-pdf/f1099k.pdf). The 1099 form will also reveal income from dividends and investments, and may lead to the discovery of additional assets. A **dividend** is a distribution of money made to a shareholder of stock of a company. For example, if Percy owned shares of telephone company stock, that stock might pay $1.00 in dividends each year for each share of stock owned. If Percy had a 1099 showing receipt of $10.00 in dividends from the telephone company, then he must have owned 10 shares of telephone company stock. It will be necessary for the executor to track down the account where the stock is held or find the actual stock certificates.

Today, most stocks and investments are held electronically, or in stock accounts with a financial institution. Years ago, companies issued actual stock certificates, indicating the number of shares of stock purchased. These certificates might be in a safe-deposit box at a bank or in a home safe or lockbox. If the decedent had actual stock certificates, the executor will need to contact each of the companies for which the decedent owned stock and find out about the liquidation process.

2. List Contents of All Safe-Deposit Boxes

An inventory of the contents of the box should be made as soon as possible. The safe-deposit box will often contain additional information about the decedent's assets.

Safe-deposit boxes are used by people of a certain generation to store documents that are perceived to be "important." It is not uncommon to find birth and death certificates, burial plot ownership documents, stock certificates, jewelry, passports, or other things one would not think of needing to be kept in a safe-deposit box. As a matter of practice, it is helpful to have two people make the inventory of the box, so that there is no chance that the executor can be accused of removing anything from the box. Not everyone has a safe-deposit box, but a clue as to whether or not a decedent has a safe-deposit box can be found by looking at the bank statements. The rental fee for the box is usually automatically deducted from one of the accounts held at the bank where the box is located. Also, the key for a safe-deposit box is usually very distinctive, being larger and having more square-looking teeth than a household key. If a key is found, but there is no information pertaining to the location of a safe-deposit box, it may be necessary to go to each of the decedent's banks, in person, and inquire if the decedent had a safe-deposit box located in that bank. The opposite can also occur. The executor could be aware that the decedent had a safe-deposit box but is unable to locate the key. In that case, the bank must be notified, and the bank will make arrangements to have the lock to the box drilled open. The bank will charge the estate for the cost of drilling the lock open.

3. Have Assets Appraised by a Qualified Appraiser When Advisable or Required by Law to Establish Value of Assets in Estate

Real property needs to be appraised by a real property appraiser. The value of the real property must be established as of the date of death for estate tax purposes and for future tax purposes. Real property should be appraised as of the date of death, even if the property is specifically bequeathed to a certain person. For example, Percy Dore leaves any home owned by him at the date of death to his wife, Kendra. In Kendra's will the house is left to Percy, and if Percy predeceases her, the value of the house is to be divided among his nieces and nephews. On the date of his death, Percy owned a home in New Jersey. Percy and Kendra purchased the property many years ago for approximately $100,000. As of the date of Kendra's death, the property is worth $200,000. It is important to establish that date of death value for purposes of potential capital gains taxes. A real property appraiser establishes the value of the house. A copy of the appraisal should be maintained in the file and will be attached to any estate tax returns that the executor is required to file. Capital gains tax is that tax that is imposed on the gain in value. Capital gains taxes, and other taxes affecting an estate, were discussed in Chapter 9. Other assets besides real property may also need to be appraised. Jewelry, coins, antiques, and other collectables are some examples of personal property that needs to be appraised.

4. File Claims for Any Veteran's or Social Security Benefits That Are Due

Very often the funeral home where the decedent's funeral is held will notify Social Security. Social Security benefits received by the decedent may have to be paid back, depending on the date of death. If monies are owed, Social Security will reverse the payments, and funds will be withdrawn. It is important not to close the decedent's bank into which the Social Security payment is made. Most, if not all, Social Security benefits are directly deposited in the recipient's bank account. If the account is closed. and monies need to be repaid to Social Security because of an overpayment, the estate will be billed for that amount. If the funeral home has not notified Social Security, the death of a Social Security recipient can be reported by a family member. A link to useful information, including the contact phone numbers, can be found at http://www.ssa.gov/pubs/EN-05-10008.pdf.

5.   File Claim for Life Insurance Payable to the Estate

The forms necessary to file life insurance claims can usually be downloaded from each company that insured the decedent. Finding the decedent's actual policy is helpful, but if the executor does not locate any policies, an assumption should not be made that the decedent did not have any life insurance. Evidence that the decedent had an insurance policy can be found from the check register or bank statements showing the premium payments, or the information can be found on the income tax return in the form of dividend being paid for certain types of policies.

6.   Determine if the Real Property Will Be Sold and Hire a Realtor

Listing agreement: a contract between the realtor and the estate setting forth the terms of the sale

If the decedent's home or other real property is to be sold, it is recommended that a licensed realtor be hired to list and sell the property. The executor of the estate will sign a **listing agreement** with the realtor. The *listing agreement* is a contract between the realtor and the estate setting forth the terms of the sale. The sales price, realtor's commission, and items to be included and excluded from the sale will be listed in the listing agreement. The executor signs the listing agreement as a representative of the estate. The property will be listed as an estate sale.

In our example, Percy left his home to his wife, Kendra, and if Kendra predeceased then the property was to be sold. Kendra is in a skilled nursing facility and will not be returning to the home, so in our example, the home should be sold. How would the matter be handled if instead, Percy left the house to Kendra, and if Kendra predeceased, the house was given to one of his nieces as a specific bequest? If the decedent left real property as a specific bequest, the executor will have to take the necessary steps to transfer the real property to the correct beneficiary and will not list the property for sale. The mechanics of how to transfer the property, and the tax consequences of that transfer, will be discussed later.

7.   Review Any Lease or Mortgages Held by the Decedent

Mortgage: any type of loan that is secured by a recorded lien against real property

If the decedent held any mortgages, the executor must review those mortgages and make sure that the payments are being made. A **mortgage** is any type of loan that is secured by a recorded lien against real property. The mortgages referred to here are mortgages in which the decedent is the mortgagee, or payee, the one who receives the money. If there are any mortgages, the payments must be made to the executor and deposited into the estate account.

It is common for the will to specifically address a mortgage. For example, a parent might lend money to an adult child for the purchase of a house. The parents hold the mortgage that the adult child then pays off. The mortgage may have been recorded as a lien against the property. The parents could choose to put a provision in each of their wills that states that any remaining amount on the mortgage is forgiven, or the adult child is not required to pay the mortgage back. The unpaid portion of the loan could be reconciled against the share that child was to receive. For example, consider the estate of Frank Bryce. A draft will was prepared for Frank in Chapter 2 when he was single. Many years later, he comes back to the firm to have a new will prepared. Frank is now married and has three children, John, Jane, and Mary. Frank and his wife Ava lent their son John $50,000 as a down payment on a new home. John agreed to pay Frank and Ava $500 a month, with no interest, until the loan was repaid. Frank drew up a mortgage agreement, and Frank, Ava, and John signed the agreement. Frank's wife Ava has predeceased him. Frank's will contains the following clause:

> *I have lent my son John Bryce the sum of $50,000 as a down payment on his home. He has faithfully repaid me every month as required. I hereby forgive any payment remaining outstanding as of the date of my death, and direct that my executor reconcile same against any distribution John would have received from my estate.*

Any distribution going to John at the conclusion of the estate administration will take into account the outstanding balance due on the loan to John. If John had made 10 payments of $500, or paid $5,000, then the remaining balance due on the loan would be $45,000. John will be deemed to have already received a $45,000 distribution from the estate, and the remaining assets in the estate will be divided accordingly.

8.   Examine All Insurance Policies on Real Estate and Personal Property and Have the Insured's Name Changed to the Estate

If the decedent owned real property at the time of death, the executor will need to make sure that the homeowner's insurance is notified of the decedent's death. The homeowner's company may require that the home be secured and may discontinue coverage if the property is vacant. When the contents of the decedent's home are appraised, it may be necessary to increase the amount of insurance coverage or to have a special rider or amendment to the homeowner's policy to cover the personal property. In our example, we know that Percy and Kendra owned a home, and we can assume they carried homeowner's insurance to cover any loss of the property. The homeowner's insurance policy should be changed to the name of the Estate of Percy Dore.

9.   Collect All Income Due the Decedent or the Estate

Income to the decedent and/or the estate could be due from several sources including employment contracts, rent, or deferred compensation. Collection of income is another area where collecting the decedent's mail can be helpful. The executor will have to also review the deposits made to the decedent's bank accounts which will reveal sources of income. The source of all income checks received by the decedent and deposits made to the decedent's accounts should be identified. It is the executor's duty to track down all income sources and determine if those income sources should continue payment or if payment terminated upon the decedent's death.

F.   Pay Estate Expenses and Debts

The payment of expenses and debts will begin as soon as there are assets available in the estate account to pay those items. It is not necessary to completely find and liquidate all of the decedent's assets in order to begin paying the debts. For example, as indicated earlier, it will be necessary to keep the heat on in the decedent's home, so it will be necessary to pay the gas and/or electric bills at the decedent's home. Some services, such as the phone, cable, Internet, newspaper delivery, and so forth, can be discontinued and the final bill paid. Other expenses will be ongoing. A simple letter like the one in Figure 11-4 should be sent to all service providers where service is to be discontinued.

1.   Review Each Claim Against the Estate, and Debt of the Estate

After the decedent's death, there will most likely be many outstanding bills generated by the decedent's last illness. These bills will all have to be reviewed by the executor. The executor must make sure that any available medical insurance, including Medicare, was billed if appropriate. Depending on the circumstances of the decedent's death, it may be necessary to submit bills to an auto insurance carrier or other liability insurance company, for example, if the decedent passed as the result of a car accident, or some other type of accident that might give rise to a wrongful death claim.

It is the executor's responsibility to pay all of the debts of the estate, but only the legitimate debts. If there is any other source of payment, such as third party liability, that source should be notified.

2.   Defend Against Any Lawsuit Against the Decedent or the Estate

If there is any litigation that was ongoing at the time of the decedent's death, that litigation will continue with the estate being substituted in as either the plaintiff or

> Please be advised that this office represents the executor of the estate of Percy Dore. Please discontinue service to the decedent's property, and send all future correspondence to this office at the address listed above. If you have any questions, please feel free to contact my office.

Figure 11-4. Sample Letter for Discontinuation of Service defendant. The executor will have to notify the parties involved in the litigation. For example, prior to his death, Percy brought a lawsuit against the contractor who built his house because all of the windows on the south side of the house leaked during a recent storm. He named the builder and the window manufacturer as defendants. Now that Percy has died, the plaintiff of the lawsuit is changed from Percy Dore to the Estate of Percy Dore.

3.   Estimate Cash Needed for Legacies, Taxes, and Other Costs of Administering the Estate

The calculation and payment of estate and inheritance taxes were discussed in detail in Chapter 9. For purposes of this chapter, let us assume the amount of estate taxes has been calculated. In addition to the payment of taxes, the estate is going to need sufficient cash to pay the costs of administration, such as attorney's fees, accountant's fees, and appraiser's fees. The executor will also have to continue to pay utility bills and carrying costs for the house.

The following is a list of potential costs of administration:

- Attorney fees
- Accountant fees
- Realtor fees
- Final utility bills for decedent's home
- Cost of final medical care
- Funeral expenses, including purchase of a burial plot
- Costs of storing and/or maintaining decedent's personal property
- Costs of shipping personal property to beneficiaries

If the decedent does not have adequate cash to pay costs and expenses, the executor must then choose the assets that will be sold to raise cash. It might be necessary to involve an accountant and possibly a financial advisor to determine which assets are best to liquidate. The executor will have to determine if there are tax consequences to liquidating assets and try to minimize those consequences.

G.   Finalization of Estate

The final set of tasks are those required to finalize the estate. As soon as all of the assets are identified and liquidated if needed, and debts and expenses of the estate are paid, the executor can begin calculating the distributions to the beneficiaries.

1.   Make Partial Distributions Before the Estate Is Finalized, If Possible

It may be possible during the administration to make a partial distribution of assets, especially if the estate is large, or the administration spans many months. Partial distributions can also be made if the decedent made specific bequests. For example, the decedent's will contains the following specific bequests:

> *I hereby bequeath and bequest the sum of $1,000 to the Boy Scouts of America.*
> *I hereby bequeath and bequest the sum of $1,000 to my church.*
> *I hereby bequeath and bequest the sum of $1,000 to All American College.*

Assume that the decedent has more than sufficient assets to pay all of the estate debt, the specific bequests, and still pay the residuary beneficiaries a large sum of money. The executor might choose to pay the three specific bequests long before the estate is totally resolved. The issue of paying partial bequests requires an analysis of many factors including the size of the estate, the amount of any estate debts, the size of the specific bequests, and the nature of the estate assets. Before any monies are paid to any beneficiary, the executor must get a release from the beneficiary.

2. Prepare Data for Final Accounting; Show All Assets, Income, and Disbursements

The will may or may not require a formal accounting of the assets and income of the estate. The state law of the state in which the decedent passed may also have certain accounting requirements that the executor must follow. Even if not required by the will or by state law, the beneficiaries may demand an accounting. The executor will be responsible for preparing any accounting that is required; however, the executor is allowed to hire any professional needed to complete his or her duties. Any income generated by Percy's stock accounts, reimbursement checks from insurance, rental payment from property, and all other income to the estate must be recorded. A careful record of the distributions made from the estate assets, all bills that were paid, fees charged, and so forth, should also be prepared.

The executor of the estate is responsible for calculating and paying all taxes due on the estate. The various taxes that may be due were discussed in Chapter 9, and additional items for the executor's checklist will also be discussed. At this point, we will skip over the calculation and payment of taxes, and go to the finalization of the estate.

3. Distribute the Assets in Accordance with the Will—Obtain Releases

The executor makes final distribution of all estate assets at the end of the administration. In most cases, it will be necessary for each beneficiary to provide the executor with a release indicating that the beneficiary has received the distribution. Percy's family was located in another country. Some form of release would be sent to them for signature, indicating that they received what Percy intended them to receive and that the executor is released from any further liability. If any unknown debts of the estate are discovered after the distribution of the estate, state law may require payback of some or all of the distribution made. The releases from each beneficiary are also necessary to obtain release of any surety bond that has been obtained. If the executor is bonded, the releases from the beneficiaries might have to be filed with the probate court and an estate termination or final release from the court obtained before the surety company will release the bond.

4. File Petition to Be Discharged by the Court if Necessary

For most administrators, some form of petition or filing with the court is required indicating that the estate has been resolved and the duties of the administrator have been fulfilled. The state law of the state in which the decedent died may have specific requirements of the executor as to the forms or documents needed to close out the estate.

Summary

Estate administration is the process by which the personal representative of the estate liquidates and consolidates of all of the decedent's assets, pays the estate debts and expenses, and distributes the estate assets to the beneficiaries. The personal representative has a fiduciary responsibility to complete all of the estate administration tasks and may not delegate that responsibility. Upon completion of the administration, the personal representative must prepare and file any releases or closing documents required by state laws indicating the estate has been finalized.

Review Questions

1. Can an executor let someone else use the decedent's property rent-free while the estate is being administered?

2. Can an executor make partial distributions before the estate is fully finalized?

3. What are some examples of estate expenses that should be paid?

4. Is a mortgage an estate expense that should be paid?

5. What does it mean to "marshal estate assets"?

True or False

1. T F An executor can sign a listing agreement to sell real property that was owned by the decedent.

2. T F One of the executor's jobs is to avoid waste of estate assets.

3. T F An executor cannot pay any bills of the estate until he or she is certain that all of the assets have been marshaled.

4. T   F   An executor must obtain an EIN for the estate.

5. T   F   All mortgages must be paid off with estate assets.

Key Terms

Commission   Marshaling the assets
Dividend   Mortgage
Listing agreement   Waste

Figure 11-5 is an example of a checklist used in estate administration. It is to be used as guidance for an executor or administrator of an estate. Not all estates will require completing all of the jobs on the checklist. The checklist is also not an exclusive list of the things that need to be completed, as some estates that are very complex may require tasks that are not on the checklist.

Executor's Checklist

Decedent's Name: _____

Date of Death: _____

Date of Probate : _____

Birth date of Decedent: _____

Social Security Number: _____

EIN for Estate: _____

AFTER DEATH

    1.   Obtain the death certificate

    2.   Locate the decedent's will, if there is a will

    3.   Probate the decedent's will—if there is no will, apply for administration.

PROBATE

    4.   Arrange for bond if necessary.

    5.   Notify beneficiaries and creditors as required by state law.

    6.   Request post office forward decedent's mail to executor.

    7.   Secure the decedent's home and real property.

    8.   Give notice of appointment as representative to banks, investment brokers, and others.

    9.   Obtain an EIN and open an estate bank account.

Figure 11-5. Estate Administration Checklist

Figure 11-5. Continued

MARSHAL ASSETS

    10. Search for assets.

    11. List contents of all safe-deposit boxes.

    12. Have assets appraised by a qualified appraiser when advisable or required by law to establish value of assets in estate.

    13. File claims for any veteran's or Social Security benefits that are due.

    14. File claim for life insurance payable to the estate.

    15. Determine if the real property will be sold, and then hire a realtor.

    16. Review any lease or mortgages held by the decedent.

    17. Examine all insurance policies on real estate and personal property and have the insured's name changed to the estate's name.

    18. Collect all income due the decedent or the estate.

    19. Review each claim against the estate, and debt of the estate.

    20. Defend against any lawsuit against the decedent or the estate.

    21. Estimate cash needed for legacies, taxes, and other costs of administering the estate.

    22. Make partial distributions before the estate is finalized, if possible.

    23. Prepare data for final accounting; show all assets, income, and disbursements.

TAX OBLIGATIONS

    24. File the final income tax return for the decedent—Form 1040.

    25. File income tax returns for the estate during the period of administration if necessary—Form 1041.

    26. Obtain and organize all documents to be filed with Form 706 such as appraisals, trusts, etc.

    27. File a federal estate tax return (Form 706) within nine months of death. If unable to meet that deadline, apply for an extension before the expiration of nine months.

    28. Obtain a federal estate tax release.

    29. Determine if the state in which the decedent died imposes inheritance tax and/or estate tax.

    30. File state inheritance and estate tax returns as required.

    31. Obtain state tax releases as required.

    32. Review last will and testament to determine if the estate pays all taxes or if any taxes are to be apportioned among the beneficiaries.

DISTRIBUTE THE ESTATE

    33. Distribute the assets in accordance with the will

    34. File petition to be discharged by the court if necessary.

12

Estate Litigation

The basis of litigation against an estate falls into one of two general categories: an allegation that something is wrong with the will, or an allegation that something is wrong with the testator. This chapter will focus on allegations that something is wrong with the will. Allegations that there are problems with the will can include claims that the will is not drafted properly, that its provisions are not clear, or that there is doubt that the document actually is the decedent's will. The testator could have attempted to disinherit the surviving spouse, giving rise to litigation by the surviving spouse claiming the marital share or elective share. Allegations pertaining to the testator include claims that the testator was unduly influenced or lacked testamentary capacity. Undue influence and lack of testamentary capacity were examined in Chapter 3.

Estate litigation can be very costly and take years to resolve. It often involves members of the same family and may cause long-lasting rifts in their relationships. Unfortunately, some estate litigation is inevitable because of family dynamics. Other issues, such as errors or poor drafting on the attorney's part, can easily be avoided. In the first section of this chapter we will look at some examples of estate litigation that have occurred involving poorly drafted wills, and what can be done to avoid these issues. Next we will review the failure of the testator to provide for the marital share of the surviving spouse. Finally, we will address the litigation process focusing on the documents used in litigation.

A. Challenges to the Will

1. Drafting Errors

The first basis of a claim against an estate results from drafting errors or language that is unclear. The testator and the scrivener may have known what was intended at the time the will was written, but the will may have been written many, many years before. The testator has now passed away, and perhaps so has the scrivener. With no one left to explain the testator's intent, the beneficiaries can be left with a lot of unanswered questions. Add in the emotional issues and family dynamics, and you have a recipe for a long, contentious litigation. A poorly drafted will can lead to administration difficulties either because the testator's intent is not clear or the bequest does not contain enough information. Careful notes and careful preparation of the documents can avoid many estate litigation issues.

Practice Tip

Even if using a form or template, read all of the language for every will to avoid using "he" when "she" should be used or "children" when there is only one "child." Sometimes these small drafting errors or typos can lead to bigger interpretation issues.

The following are some examples of really bad language found in actual wills that the author had to administer or litigate. The will of an unmarried woman who was in her late 80s when she passed contained the following bequest:

I leave my estate to all of my nieces and nephews in equal shares, share and share alike.

This particular provision led to three years of litigation. The decedent did not specifically identify any of her nieces or nephews. After spending several months trying to get the names of all of the nieces and nephews, letters were sent out to the 17 individuals who had been identified. It was then discovered that there were more nieces and nephews who had not been identified because some of the other family members wanted to limit the pool of people who would be inheriting. Even after all of the potential heirs were notified, one additional individual was found who was a stepson of one nephew who had been adopted by that nephew prior to the nephew's death. The adopted son was eligible to take his father's share of the estate. Years of investigation and litigation could have been avoided if the testator was encouraged to name each beneficiary she wanted to include and to make alternerative dispositions if a beneficiary had predeceased her.

Practice Tip

Be careful about the spelling of a client's name and the names of children, grandchildren, and beneficiaries, especially if there is a junior, or same or similar names between a father and son.

Another example of a poorly drafted provision in a will that led to litigation and administration difficulties was the following:

I leave one-half of my estate to my three college roommates, and the remaining one-half to my alma mater, the College of St. Elizabeth.

The decedent was 96 years of age when she passed. She did not identify her college roommates in the will, and she did not leave contingent beneficiaries. Luckily, the decedent left a portion of her estate to her alma mater. Unlike the identity of her roommates, the name of the college was provided in the will. Discovering the names of the decedent's roommates took almost a year of investigation including reviewing the alumni records, old yearbooks, graduation photographs, and class records. After the names of the three roommates were discovered, additional research was needed to determine the married name of each of the women. The college roommates, had they survived, would have been as old as the decedent. However, none of the three roommates survived the decedent. For each of the three deceased beneficiaries, it was necessary to find children, grandchildren, and in some cases, great-grandchildren.

Several months of additional Internet research of online birth, marriage, and death records, obituaries, cemetery records, property ownership records, and social media sites resulted in the names of potential beneficiaries, most of whom doubted the veracity of the phone calls they were receiving. Imagine yourself getting a phone call from a complete stranger, telling you that you were the beneficiary of an estate of someone you did not know. Would you believe the caller, or would you hang up? For one beneficiary, convincing the person that the phone call was not a scam required hiring an attorney in the beneficiary's home state, then having the attorney contact the beneficiary and meet with the person directly. The attorney's fees to administer the estate ran into the tens of thousands of dollars. The difficulties with the will could have been avoided if more specific language describing the beneficiaries was used, and if contingent beneficiaries had been identified.

Practice Tip

If the client does not identify names, or contingent beneficiaries, or there are other gaps in vital information, a draft will can still be prepared and sent to the client with the missing information highlighted, or a line drawn so that the client knows to fill in the required information, such as the following:

If my sister Susan predeceases me, I leave her share of my estate to _____.

---

2. Testator's Intent

In order to properly administer an estate, it is necessary to interpret the testator's intent. The language of the will may not be clear, resulting in more than one way a provision could be interpreted. Some estates end up being litigated because the bequests made in the will are difficult to interpret and enforce. Take for example the will of Charles Vance Millar. Millar was a very successful lawyer and businessman from Canada. He was famous for enjoying practical jokes and pranks. Millar had no wife and no children. When he died it was discovered that his will contained his last practical joke. The tenth paragraph of Millar's will stated that his estate was to be maintained until ten years after his death, and then the entire estate was to be liquidated. The cash from the estate was to be given to the Toronto woman who gave birth to the most children in the ten-year time period following Millar's death. In the event of a tie, the bequest would be divided equally.

This provision in the will, and the media coverage and controversy surrounding it, became known as the "Great Stork Derby." In Canada, a made-for-television movie of the same name was produced in 2002. Millar died a very wealthy man after having made several very lucrative investments. His distant family members challenged the will because there was no bequest made to any family members. At the expiration of the ten-year period, the estate remained tied up in litigation for many years. Eventually, four families, each with nine children born during the ten-year period, split his estate. Two other mothers who had given birth to ten children, but each had one or more children that were stillborn, were given settlements. You can read more about Millar's will, and see photographs of the actual will at the following link: http://www.duhaime.org/LawFun/LawArticle-1281/The-Will-of-Charles-Vance-Millar-and-the-Stork-Derby.aspx.

It is unlikely that the average client will request such an unusual provision in his or her will. It is not unlikely that a client will want bequests to go to pets, or to charitable organizations that cease to exist by the time the testator dies, or to beneficiaries who do not outlive the testator. It is important to remind the client to name contingent beneficiaries and to provide for an alternate distribution of the estate if the charity no longer exists or the beneficiary already died.

3. Fraud

The two types of fraud that could give rise to a challenge to a will: fraud in the execution and fraud in the inducement. Fraud in the execution is when a testator is deceived as to what is in the will. A will is prepared for a testator, and the preparer of the will misrepresents what the will contains. This can happen in many circumstances but most often occurs when a relative or friend helps the testator prepare the will, instead of a lawyer. For example, Emilene Vance lives with her caregiver Josephine. Emilene asks her caregiver to type up a will for her. Emilene really likes Josephine and tells Josephine to divide up the estate equally among herself and Emilene's five grandchildren, so that each beneficiary receives one-sixth of the estate. Josephine types up the will and tells Emilene she has done what was asked, but the will actually leaves 100% of the estate to Josephine. Josephine presents the will to Emilene who signs the will as drafted. This will is fraudulent because it does not represent Emilene's testamentary intent.

Fraud in the inducement occurs when a person makes material misrepresentations of facts to the testator so that the testator makes a bequest that benefits that person. It is similar to undue influence except that the person making the statements is purposefully lying to the testator. For example, Emilene Vance has five grandchildren. One grandchild, Joseph, frequently comes to Emilene's house to visit. Joseph tells Emilene that his sisters Amelia and Amanda do not like Emilene. He says none of the other grandchildren really care for Emilene and will not come to visit her. Unfortunately, this is not true. The grandchildren care deeply for their grandmother but live on the other side of the country and cannot visit very often. After hearing Joseph's lies for many years, Emilene decides to cut Amelia and Amanda out of the will and significantly reduce the portion of her estate left to the other grandchildren. The majority of the estate is left to Joseph. Joseph did not unduly influence Emilene into leaving him the estate as much as he fraudulently induced her to do so by making material misrepresentations about how the other grandchildren felt.

Fraud in the inducement or fraud in the execution are usually not discovered until after the testator has died and the will is admitted to probate. It can be difficult to prove, unless prior drafts of the document, or the material mispresentations of fact, are discovered by the beneficiaries.

4.   Mistake

Another basis of estate litigation is an allegation that there was a mistake in how the will was drafted or if the testator actually signs the wrong will. This kind of mistake can occur when two married people go together to have their wills prepared and sign the wills at the same time. If the testator signs the wrong will, the document does not represent his testamentary intent. This type of mistake was reviewed by the New York Court of Appeal in the case of *In re Snide, 418 N.E.2d 656 (N.Y. 1981)*. A husband and wife went to a lawyer and had wills prepared in which they each left a portion of their estate to the other. They both executed wills at the same time. Because of the lawyer's error, each executed the will meant for the other. The error was not discovered until the husband died. The court then had to **reform**, or revise, the will that the husband had signed by correcting the names in the will so that the testator left his estate to his wife, and not to himself.

Reform: when a court revises or changes the contents of the will to better follow the testator's intent

---

Practice Tip

Estate litigation arising from a mistake in the will or in the signing of the will is preventable. In executing wills for a husband and wife, it is often helpful to have two paralegals so that one can assist the wife, and show her where to sign, and the other can assist the husband. Then each set of documents should be kept separated so that the right cover and envelope are used for each will.

---

5.   Is the Will Authentic?

It is not uncommon for a client to have prepared more than one will over his or her lifetime. Some clients change their will frequently in response to the birth of a new grandchild, niece, or nephew, or for more petty reasons, such as a relative who has annoyed them this week, so the offending relative is to be "written out" of the will. A client should always be reminded to physically destroy his or her old will to avoid confusion. If there is more than one will, there is a possibility that different heirs advocate for the validity of one will versus another will in which a bequest is eliminated or reduced. Which will is the most recent or which one is valid becomes a topic of litigation. One very famous example of such a will (or lack of a will) was that of Howard Hughes.

Hughes was a famous businessman, aviator, engineer, and filmmaker. He was also very eccentric, and later in life he became a recluse. His life has been the subject of books and movies, most recently, *The Aviator*, a film directed by Martin Scorsese, starring Leonardo DiCaprio. After Hughes' death, a story emerged that gas station owner Melvin Dummar gave a ride to a man he found along the road outside of Las Vegas. Dummar claimed that the man told him he was Howard Hughes. In the days following Hughes' death, Dummar claimed that someone came to his gas station and left an envelope on his desk. The envelope contained a handwritten will supposedly written by Howard Hughes. Dummar did not know what to do with the will, so he left it at the office of an official with the Church of Jesus Christ of Latter Day Saints (also known as the Mormons). This will became known as the "Mormon Will." The will divided Hughes' estate among various charities, including the Howard Hughes Medical Institute, several employees in various companies owned by Hughes, a first cousin, and both of his ex-wives, Ella Rice and Jean Peters. Not surprisingly, the Mormon will also left a sizable bequest, $156 million, to Dummar.

After almost a year of litigation, the Mormon will was found to be a forgery. Because the only will that was brought forward was deemed to be invalid, the Court in Nevada declared that Howard Hughes had died intestate. Having to distribute the estate by way of the laws of intestacy meant even more estate litigation from all of the potential intestate heirs. Many years after the last piece of Hughes' property was sold, there is still speculation about the actual size of the estate. More information about the estate can be found at: http://mormonmatters.org/2009/10/31/remembering-the-howard-hughes-mormon-will/.

6. Holographic Wills

Holographic wills, or wills written in the testator's own handwriting, are often controversial because of the circumstances under which the will was written. Perhaps the testator was very ill or injured, knew that death was imminent, but was unable to get to a lawyer. A will written under such stressful circumstances might be suspect. In many states, a holographic will cannot be admitted to probate without filing a complaint and submitting other evidence that the writing was intended to be the testator's will. As with all aspects of the law, each state has its own specific requirements for admission of a holographic will to probate. For example, in Virginia a holographic will is recognized even if it does not meet the requirements of a valid will under certain circumstances:

> Although a document, or a writing added upon a document, was not executed in compliance with 64.1-49 the document or writing shall be treated as if it had been executed in compliance with 64.1-49 if the proponent of the document or writing establishes by clear and convincing evidence that the decedent intended the document or writing to constitute (i) the decedent's will, (ii) a partial or complete revocation of the will, (iii) an addition to or an alteration of the will, or (iv) a partial or complete revival of his formerly revoked will or of a formerly revoked portion of the will. §64.1-49.1 Code of Virginia.

The statute requires that the person writing the holographic will include a statement such as "I intend this document to be my will" or that it was intended to revoke a prior will. Without some evidence that the testator intended the handwritten document to serve as a will, the court could find that a prior will still stands, or that the testator died intestate.

One famous holographic will is also one of the most unusual wills in the world. There is a fender on display in the law library of the University of Saskatchewan, Canada. It may seem like an odd item to display in a law library, but this fender is actually a will. Cecil George Harris was a Canadian farmer. On June 8, 1948, he was working on his tractor when it slipped into reverse, pinning him to another piece of farm equipment. Harris remained trapped between the two vehicles until his wife found him. He was rushed to the hospital but died of his wounds. Days later, his neighbor found the words "In case I die in this mess I leave all to the wife. Cecil Geo. Harris" etched into the fender of his tractor. The tractor fender will was admitted to probate as Harris' holographic will (http://news.usask.ca/archived_ocn/09-jan-23/see_what_we_found.php).

The Internet is great source of many different types of wills. The wills of famous people, actors, politicians, and musicians can all be found online. Once a testator dies, his or her will is admitted to probate and becomes a public document. Most public documents can be found online, either by accessing the direct source where the public records are kept, such as the county surrogate's office, or through a paid document search company.

7. Nuncupative Wills

A **nuncupative will** is an oral will. It is also referred to as a "deathbed will." The few states that allow for oral wills require that the testator be on his deathbed, or about to die, in order to give validity to the will. Most states in the United States do not recognize the validity of oral wills because of the possibility of fraud, or misinterpretation of the testator's intent. The few states that do recognize oral wills impose requirements such as limiting the dollar value of assets that pass under an oral will, or limiting the assets that can pass to personal property, not real property. An example of an oral will that might meet the requirements would be a statement made by someone whose death is imminent, in which the person states, "I leave my gold watch to my son John."

Nuncupative will: an oral will

If a state recognizes nuncupative wills, the state's statutes will list the requirements for admission of such a will. For example, the Ohio Revised Code at Section 2107.60 specifically allows for oral or nuncupative wills:

> An oral will, made in the last sickness, shall be valid in respect to personal property if reduced to writing and subscribed by two competent disinterested witnesses within ten days after the speaking of the testamentary words. The witnesses shall prove that the testator was of sound mind and memory, not under restraint, and that the testator called upon some person present at the time the testamentary words were spoken to bear testimony to the disposition as the testator's will.
>
> No oral will shall be admitted to record unless it is offered for probate within three months after the death of the testator.

Another state that recognizes oral wills is Vermont. The Vermont statutes limit the assets that can pass by way of an oral will to a maximum of $200:

> Vermont statutes, Title 14: Decedents' Estates and Fiduciary Relations Chapter 1: Wills, §6. Nuncupative will
>
>   A nuncupative will shall not pass personal estate when the estate thereby bequeathed exceeds the value of $200.00, nor shall such will be proved and allowed, unless a memorandum thereof is made in writing by a person present at the time of making such will, within six days from the making of it, nor unless it is presented for probate within six months from the death of the testator.

Most states do not permit nuncupative wills. In those states that do not recognize nuncupative wills, the state statute specifically requires that in order to be valid, the will must be in writing. For example, the Arizona Revised Statute §14-2502 requires that a valid will be in writing, signed by the testator, and witnessed.

8.   Soldier's and Sailor's Wills

Many years ago, states' laws used to allow for the requirements for what constitutes a valid will to be waived or relaxed if the will is prepared by a soldier or sailor who had been deployed. The laws were known as "soldiers and sailors wills" laws. These laws were necessary because a person in the miltary may prepare a will in one state at the base where he or she is stationed, only to be deployed overseas, be injured, and then eventually die in a military hospital located in a totally different country or state than where the will was prepared. Now, there is a federal law that pre-empts state laws and provides that a will prepared by someone in the military "is exempt from any requirement of form, formality, or recording before probate that is provided for testamentary instruments under the laws of a State." The full law can be found at http://www.law.cornell.edu/uscode/text/10/1044d

B.   Elective Share

1.   State Law

There is only one state in the United States in which a spouse can completely disinherit his or her spouse: Georgia. Every other state requires that the surviving spouse be able to get some minimum share of a deceased spouse's estate. The portion of a deceased spouse's estate to which the surviving spouse is entitled is known as the **elective share**, also referred to as the *widow's share*, *statutory share*, or *forced share*. For purposes of this text, the term *elective share* will be used to describe the minimum portion of the estate which the surviving spouse may elect to take instead of what he or she was left in the decedent's will. In Georgia, the law does not provide for an elective share. Instead, the surviving spouse is allowed to apply only for a maximum of one year of support from the estate of the deceased spouse.

Elective share: the minimum portion of the estate that the surviving spouse may elect to take instead of what he or she was left in the decedent's will; also referred to as widow's share, statutory share, or forced share

In every state except Georgia, the surviving spouse can file a claim against the estate for an elective share of the decedent's estate instead of the portion left to the surviving spouse in the will. Even if the decedent attempts to disinherit the spouse by making no provision for the spouse, the spouse can still claim a portion of the estate. In some jurisdictions, such as Florida, the elective share is set at a percentage of the value of the elective estate. Florida's elective share is 30 percent of the estate value. In New York, the elective share is $50,000 or one-third of the net estate. The elective share is calculated as a percentage or portion of the net estate value after the estate expenses and debts have been paid.

If a married person makes a will that does not provide for the surviving spouse, or leaves the surviving spouse less than the amount in the elective share, the surviving spouse can make a claim against the estate. In most states, if the spouse agrees to the share in the will or agrees to take no share at all, the spouse can sign a document that waives the elective share. The language found in the waiver is something that is unique to every state and probably every lawyer. The Uniform Probate Code (UPC) indicates that the waiver must be in writing, in the form of a contract or agreement, signed by the surviving spouse. See UPC 2-213.

2.   Uniform Probate Code

Elective share is defined in the UPC as the right to take elective-share amount equal to the value of the elective-share percentage of the **augmented estate**, determined by the length of time the spouse and the decedent were married to each other (UPC 2-202). The *augmented estate* adds back into the estate the value of anything the decedent gave away prior to death, even if the decedent made a gift or transferred the property to the surviving spouse. In addition, the augmented estate includes the decedent's nonprobate assets such as accounts that are held as joint accounts, payable on death (POD) or transferable on death (TOD), life insurance policies, and even joint assets owned with the surviving spouse. The UPC allows for an increase in the percentage to which a surviving spouse is entitled for every year the couple is married.

Augmented estate: the value of the estate plus the value of anything the decedent gave away prior to death, the decedent's nonprobate assets, and joint assets owned with the surviving spouse

If the decedent and the spouse were married to each other:	The percentage is:
Less than 1 year	3%
1 year but less than 2 years	6%
2 years but less than 3 years	12%
3 years but less than 4 years	18%
4 years but less than 5 years	24%
5 years but less than 6 years	30%
6 years but less than 7 years	36%
7 years but less than 8 years	42%
8 years but less than 9 years	48%
9 years but less than 10 years	54%
10 years but less than 11 years	60%

11 years but less than 12 years 68%
12 years but less than 13 years 76%
13 years but less than 14 years 84%
14 years but less than 15 years 92%
15 years or more 100%

Those states that have adopted the UPC follow this increasing percentage schedule.

3.   Elective Share Litigation

Litigation involving an elective share involves the valuation of the estate and calculation of the amount to which the surviving spouse is entitled. Elective share litigation can also focus on whether or not the suriviving spouse is entitled to claim the elective share. The claim for an elective share is filed against an estate by filing a complaint in the probate court.

The surviving spouse must file a complaint seeking an elective share within the time required by the law of the state in which the will was admitted to probate. The complaint will have to raise the claim that the surviving spouse is electing to take the share provided in the elective share statutes instead of the amount, if any, left in the will. After the complaint is filed, the parties will go through discovery, where each party will be able to get information to support his or her claim.

Calculation of the elective share will often involve valuation of estate assets using an appraiser to value property or an accountant to value a business interest. The personal representative of the estate will have to produce financial records so the parties can determine if assets were transferred by the decedent prior to death. An accounting of the estate expenses will have to be prepared.

The elective share is the portion to which a surviving "spouse" is entitled. So what happens if one spouse dies after an action for divorce is filed but before the final judgment of divorce is signed? This is a situation that arises more often than one would imagine. A careful examination of state law is necessary to determine what the result will be. In some states, such as South Carolina, the law provides that a divorce is not final until signed by the court and filed in the office of the clerk of court [S.C.Code Ann. §62-2-802(c)]. If a spouse dies after the divorce is filed but before the final judgment is signed and filed, the surviving spouse is still entitled to an elective share. In New Jersey, the opposite result occurs. New Jersey laws state that a surviving spouse is entitled to claim an elective share only if he or she had not been living separate and apart in different habitations under circumstances which would have given rise to a cause of action for divorce (N.J.S.A. 3B:8-1). In New Jersey if the parties were separated at the time of death, under circumstances that would have given rise to a cause of action for divorce, the surviving spouse is not entitled to claim an elective share if the spouse passes away.

C. Litigation Process

1. Complaint

Estate litigation is commenced with the filing of a complaint in the probate court of the county in which the decedent lived at the time of death and in which the will was admitted to probate. As we learned in Chapter 10, if there are questions about a will, prior to filing an estate litigation, it may be necessary or advisable to file a caveat to prevent the probate of a will. If the will has already been probated or if a caveat has been filed, the litigation begins with the filing of a complaint.

A claimant challenging a will must first establish the claimant's standing. **Standing** is a legal term that defines who is able to bring a lawsuit. In general terms, in order to have standing, a party must prove that he or she has a sufficient connection or interest in the litigation. The specific requirements for standing depend on the type of legal claim being made. In a probate matter challenging the validity of a will, the only people with standing are those who could potentially benefit from the estate. The parties with standing can include beneficiaries who have been disinherited in the will. A testator may have a prior will that included several additional family members but later changed that will to favor only one family member to the exclusion of the others. The excluded family members have standing to challenge the will. Another category of people with standing is those who would have been heirs at law but for the creation of the will. For example, if the testator excluded one of his or her children, and that child would have been entitled to a share of the estate if the testator died intestate, the excluded child may have standing to challenge the will. An example of the language used in a complaint to establish standing is the following:

> `Plaintiff is the daughter of the decedent and as such is the natural object of the decedent's affection.`

After plaintiff has established standing, additional allegations regarding the will are listed in the complaint.

If a will does not have the proper signatures, if it has been marked by the testator, or if some of the pages were damaged, then the will must be admitted by way of **solemn probate** or *probate in solemn form*. In Chapter 10 we learned that probate in solemn form is usually required when there is some defect or problem with the will. Clients should be reminded to never write on the will because that may invalidate the entire will. For example, if a testator wants a beneficiary out of the will, the testator cannot simply cross that person out. Probate in solemn form requires a complaint to be filed with the court seeking admission of the will. A sample of such a complaint can be found on the companion Web site.

A complaint for solemn probate may need to be a **verified complaint**. A *verified complaint* is one in which the complaint includes a verification which is a form of affidavit in which the plaintiff swears to the truth of the pleading. Verified complaints are only necessary if required by court rule. In the complaint the plaintiff

Standing: a legal term that defines who is able to bring a lawsuit

Solemn probate or probate in solemn form: required when there is some defect or problem with the will

Verified complaint: includes an affidavit in which the plaintiff swears to the truth of the pleading must establish his or her standing to bring the complaint and seek the admission of the will to probate on behalf of the beneficiaries.

A complaint alleging failure to provide for the elective share would have to allege the elements necessary to prove that claim: marriage to the decedent, failure to provide for the spouse in the will, and whether or not the surviving spouse has waived his or her right to the elective share. A sample complaint claiming an elective share can be found in the forms section of the companion Web site.

In New Jersey, a surviving spouse is entitled to an elective share if there were no facts and circumstances that would have given rise to a claim of divorce. In the first numbered paragraph, plaintiff establishes that he has standing to bring the complaint by setting forth that he is the surviving spouse of the decedent, and that the plaintiff and the decedent were not living in circumstances that would be the basis for a divorce complaint. Thereafter, each additional paragraph in the complaint sets forth the value of the estate, the value of the property transferred to the plaintiff, and the amount of assets held by the plaintiff. The conclusion is the calculation of the elective share, as well as the allegation that what was left to the plaintiff is less than the elective share to which he or she is entitled.

A probate complaint will typically be brought in the name of the estate, alleging facts that give rise to some relief to the plaintiff from the estate. The facts and allegation of each complaint will be unique. A paralegal should be familiar with the proof necessary to support a claim so that the complaint reflects how the facts of the case fit into the points that need to be proven.

Summary

Litigation challenging the will can arise because of drafting errors, difficulty in determining the testator's intent, fraud, mistake, or questions as to the authenticity of the will. Litigation is required for wills that are holographic or nuncupative, as those types of will are not self-proving. Another type of litigation is that involving a claim for an elective share. Estate litigation is started by the filing of a complaint.

Review Questions

1. What are some things a paralegal can do to help avoid estate litigation?
2. How is the elective share calculated?
3. Who has standing to challenge a will?
4. Can a testator cross out portions of his or her will that he or she no longer wants?
5. Research your state's laws. Does the state permit holographic wills? Nuncupative wills?

True or False

1. T   F   If a will is invalidated, the decedent's estate is distributed according to the laws of intestacy of the state in which the decedent lived at the time of death.

2. T   F   In valuing an elective share, certain pre-death transfers can be added back into the estate.

3. T   F   A testator can block challenges to his or her will by threatening to disinherit anyone who raises a challenge.

4. T   F   Mistakes in the will can be easily corrected after the testator's death.

5. T   F   Clients should always destroy their prior wills.

6. T   F   A husband and wife can do one joint will or sign each other's wills.

7. T   F   Every state in the United States allows for holographic wills.

8. T   F   The decedent's family usually has standing to challenge the decedent's will.

9. T   F   Most states that allow nuncupative wills restrict the dollar value of the assets that can be distributed.

10. T   F   A mistake in a will is a type of fraud that automatically invalidates the will.

Drafting Exercises

A new client, Elizabeth Bart, needs a will. Her four adult sons, Peter, Alex, Edward, and Miles are all married, and each has several children of their own. In each of the sample will provisions listed below, provide an explanation of the issues that could be caused by the wording of the provision, and suggest how the wording could be changed to eliminate problems.

1. I leave my entire estate to my grandchildren.

2. I leave my house at 224 Chelten Parkway, Boise, Idaho, to my son.

3. My son, Peter Bart, shall serve as the executor of my estate.

4. I leave my entire estate to my sons, Peter, Alex, and Edward.

5. If any of my sons challenges this will, he is to receive nothing.

Key Terms

Augmented estate
Elective share
Nuncupative will
Reform

Solemn probate or probate in solemn form
Standing
Verified complaint

13

Trust Administration

Trust administration is the management and distribution of assets held by a trust. The trustee appointed in the trust must follow the terms of the trust and complete the administration or risk being held personally responsible. The steps that the trustee must take in the administration of a trust, and the time required to complete those steps, are going to vary depending on the type of trust. This chapter will explore the steps that a trustee goes through to administer a trust by providing a set of facts that will be used to illustrate trust administration issues. A trust administration checklist is included at the end of the chapter.

Trust administration: the management and distribution of assets held in the name of a trust.

A. Review the Trust

The first step in advising a client about the administration of a trust is to review the trust document. Every trust is different. Some very simple trusts could hold a small amount of money and be in existence for only a short period of time. Other more complex trusts could govern the use of millions of dollars worth of real property and investments designed to provide income to a class of beneficiaries over the course of many years. Is it a trust agreement, or a declaration of trust? As we already discussed, some trusts, inter vivos trusts, are created in the grantor's lifetime, while others are testamentary trusts, created in a grantor's will. The first step in administering a trust is to fully review and understand the terms of the trust.

There are other issues that might impact the administration of a trust. The funding and administration of a testamentary trust may be impacted or delayed by problems with the estate administration. Perhaps the trust cannot be funded until the estate is resolved, or the amount of the funding is in question. The complexity of the trust, the beneficiaries, the amount and nature of the funds in the trust, and how the trust is created will all impact on the administration of the trust.

When meeting with a new client who is a trustee, or is about to become a trustee, it is helpful to start getting the information regarding the trust organized before the meeting. A trustee client who is coming into the office for an initial meeting should be given a checklist and be asked to fill it in to the best of his or her ability. The client should be instructed to bring any and all documentation pertaining to each item on the checklist, for example, deeds to properties, bank account or investment account statements, appraisals, the trust document, or the decedent's will if the trust is testamentary. A sample checklist is included at the end of the chapter.

The attorney should review the trust and all of the documents associated with the trust. The documents included in the review may include the will, the probate documents, and any documents associated with the trust assets, such as deeds, account statements, or any other ownership documents. The attorney should identify the beneficiaries or class of beneficiaries. The specific tasks involved in administering a trust will be unique to that trust; however, some of the tasks are common to all trusts. Let us look at how the trustee fulfills his or her duties while administering an example of a testamentary trust.

B. Fact Pattern

In order to illustrate the trust administration process, let us look at an example. Cynthia Nofuss is the trustee of a trust created in the last will and testament of her late brother, Edwin Nofuss, who passed away last month. The trust is for the benefit of Edwin's three daughters. The children are various ages: Mary, Edwin's daughter from his first marriage, is 35; Joan and Mae, his daughters from his second marriage, are 16 and 12, respectively. The trust is to be funded by two income-producing rental properties that Edwin and Cynthia owned jointly, a brokerage account, checking and savings accounts, and Edwin's home. Edwin has also appointed Cynthia as the guardian for the two younger children. We will assume that the will also contains a list of the trustee's powers. The administrative provisions of the trust include the following:

ARTICLE II — ADMINISTRATION

2.1   Income and Principal Distributions. The income and principal of this trust fund may be paid to or expended for the benefit of Joan and Mae at such times and in such amounts and manner as the Trustee in its sole and absolute discretion deems advisable to provide adequately and properly for the comfortable support, maintenance, welfare, education, medical care and comfort of Joan and Mae. The Trustee shall accumulate any undistributed income, and annually add the same to principal.

2.2   Preservation of Assets. The trustee should allow Joan and Mae to reside in my home until such time as they have each established a home of their own if it is feasible for them to do so. My trustee should make every effort to preserve a home for my children to the best of her ability.

2.4   Division into Separate Children's Shares. When my youngest child reaches age twenty-five, the balance of the funds in the trust should be divided into three equal shares, one share for each for my daughters Mary, Joan and Mae, and distributed to each child, free and clear of the trust.

Cynthia has brought the probated will to your office, and has asked for assistance in setting up and administering the trust.

C.   Attorney's Role

The steps necessary to administer the trust will vary based on the type of trust, the beneficiaries, the state in which the trust is located, what assets are in the trust, the authority given to the trustee, whether there is a co-trustee, and so forth. After reviewing the trust, the attorney and client must determine what the attorney's role is going to be. Is the attorney going to assist Cynthia as the trustee, establish the trust, and get started on the administration, but then is she going to administer the trust on her own, only calling the attorney when she needs help? Or is the attorney going to take a more active role, completing each task for Cynthia while communicating with her about the status? Or is the attorney's role going to be somewhere in between? In the first scenario, where the attorney is simply helping to establish the trust, the set up and organization of the trust are going to be simple. One large "pocket"-type file and as many subfiles as needed for different documents will be sufficient. The large pocket folders used by lawyers are called "red wells." The subfolders will be thinner manila folders with fasteners at the top.

The paralegal will be responsible for using the two-hole punch to punch holes in the tops of documents and attach them inside the file. Every office has its own system of organization, and every attorney has his or her quirks as to where things should be located. Most offices and attorneys keep correspondence in date order, with the most recent on top.

If the attorney is going to take a more active role, maintaining the trust file over a longer period of time will require much more organization. If the attorney is going to be actively working with the trust, monitoring the trust assets, collecting income, assisting with distributions, and so forth, then the trust administration file is going to require ongoing maintenance and organization. When the matter is first opened, the paralegal should set up individual files for each asset. In our example, we have been advised that the following assets will be placed into the trust: a number of income-producing rental properties, a brokerage account, checking and savings accounts, and Edwin's home. The main file should be opened under the name "Nofuss Family Trust" with Cynthia as the client. All of the subfiles should be labeled as follows:

"Nofuss Family Trust" — rental property 1
"Nofuss Family Trust" — rental property 2
"Nofuss Family Trust" — brokerage account
"Nofuss Family Trust" — checking account
"Nofuss Family Trust" — savings account
"Nofuss Family Trust" — Edwin's home

Each individual file should include information about the location of the asset and a checklist as to how that asset is going to be transferred into the trust. For example, the subfile for rental property 1 is going to contain the deed to the property and a checklist of the steps necessary to transfer title to that property into the name of the trust. In our example, Cynthia is also the executor of her brother's estate, so she will be responsible for signing a deed from the estate to the trust. The attorney may be assisting with both the estate and trust administration and would then prepare the deed from the estate to the trust for Cynthia's signature, and take responsibility for filing the new deed with the county registrar of deeds. Each of the rental property subfiles will have a number of additional subfiles for property taxes, expenses associated with the property, rental payments, and so forth.

The files for the brokerage accounts and checking and savings accounts should be set up in such a manner to allow for each new monthly statement to be added. Each of these accounts will have to be retitled in the name of the trust, with Cynthia identified as the trustee.

Practice Tip

Using three-ring binders labeled with the name of the client and the asset is a convenient way to keep the statements from various accounts organized.

D. Trustee's Role

Cynthia's first task is to accept her role as trustee and sign whatever documents are necessary to assume authority as the trustee. In a trust agreement, the trustee's role begins when she signs the trust agreement. In a testamentary trust, the trustee may not be aware that she was appointed as a trustee and does not begin to serve as the trustee until the will is admitted to probate. In many states, the trustee of a testamentary trust must sign documents accepting his or her role as trustee at the time the will is admitted to probate. If the trustee accepts his or her role as trustee, the trustee will get a letter of trusteeship, indicating appointment as a trustee.

Practice Tip

The letters of trusteeship should be kept in a separate file folder and not have holes punched into the documents. It will often be necessary to produce the original letter for banking or investments, so the additional originals should be easily accessible.

Figure 13-1 presents a sample letter of trusteeship used in the State of Vermont.

Figure 13-1. Sample Letter of Trusteeship

STATE OF VERMONT

DISTRICT OF _____

IN RE THE ESTATE OF _____

LATE OF _____

TO: _____ GREETINGS:

PROBATE COURT

DOCKET NO. _____

TRUSTEE'S LETTERS

WHEREAS, you have been appointed trustee of the above entitled trust under the Last Will and Testament of _____ as allowed by this court; and

WHEREAS, you have executed a bond to the Probate Court, to the satisfaction thereof, conditioned for the faithful discharge of the duties of a trustee, as required by the laws of this state:

BY THE AUTHORITY OF THE STATE OF VERMONT, you are appointed trustee of the above entitled estate and authorized and empowered to take charge of, manage and control all the trust estate, according to law and the will of the testator, a copy of which is attached. You will make a true inventory of all the real estate, and of all the goods, chattels, rights, or credits belonging to you as trustee, and which shall come to your possession or knowledge, and return the same to this court within 30 days from the date hereof. You will manage and dispose of all estate and effects, and faithfully discharge your trust in relation to the same, according to law and the will of the testator. You will render a full account of the trust property in your hands and the management and disposition of the same, and your receipts, disbursements, and charge therein, as often as once each year during your appointment, and other times when required by the court. At the expiration of your trust, you will settle your account with the court, and pay over and deliver all the estate and effects remaining in your hands or due from you on settlement, to the persons who shall be entitled to the same, according to law and the will of the testator.

(SEAL) Dated_____

Signed _____

Probate Court, District of _____

Most letters of trusteeship are drafted and issued by the probate court or surrogate's office. It is unlikely that a paralegal will have to draft a letter of trusteeship. The surrogate's office will issue several letters of trusteeship. There will be occasions in which a financial institution will want a recent letter of trusteeship, requiring the paralegal to contact the surrogate's office to obtain another letter with a more recent date. Because this trust is a testamentary trust, copies of the decedent's last will and testament as well as the death certificate should be maintained in separate subfiles.

E.   Notify Beneficiaries

After Cynthia has been issued the letters of trusteeship from the surrogate's office, she may have to provide notice to all beneficiaries in the form specified by the state's

---

NOTIFICATION BY TRUSTEE UNDER PROBATE CODE SECTION 16061.7

As required by law, you are hereby provided with notice of the following information regarding the

_____ Trust (hereafter "the Trust") now that the Trust is irrevocable following

the death of the Settlor, _____ on _____, 2014.

1.   The name of the Settlor of the Trust was: _____

2.   The Trust was executed on: _____

3.   The Trust was amended and restated in full on _____ and further amended on

_____.

4.   The name, address, and telephone number of the current Trustee is:

_____

The Trustee requests that correspondence relating to the Trust be directed to her at the following address:

_____

_____

_____

5.   The principal place of administration of the Trust shall be: _____

6.   You are entitled, as a possible beneficiary or heir at law of the decedent, to request from the trustee a true and complete copy of the "Terms of the Trust," as that term is defined in Probate Code §16060.5. However, in your case, the Trustee has elected to enclose with this Notification a true and complete copy of the _____ Trust dated _____.

WARNING: YOU MAY NOT BRING AN ACTION TO CONTEST THE TRUST MORE THAN 120 DAYS FROM THE DATE THIS NOTIFICATION BY THE TRUSTEE IS SERVED UPON YOU OR 60 DAYS FROM THE DAY ON WHICH A COPY OF THE TERMS OF THE TRUST IS MAILED OR PERSONALLY DELIVERED TO YOU DURING THAT 120-DAY PERIOD, WHICHEVER IS LATER.

Date: _____, 201__ _____

_____,
Trustee of the Trust

Figure 13-2. Notification by Trustee under Probate Code

laws. For example, California Probate Code Section 16061.7 requires that a specific notice that meets the requirements of the statute be sent within 60 days of the death of a grantor of a testamentary trust. The Code provides a form to be published, as shown in Figure 13-2.

Other states may have similar publication and notice requirements. The paralegal should be familiar with the notice requirements and mark the date on which notice must be provided in a prominent location on the file. The state statute or regulation may include a form that will provide the language necessary, or the attorney may have his or her own form that meets the requirements of the law. In this matter, two of the beneficiaries are minors, with Cynthia as their legal guardian. Cynthia can accept notice for Joan and Mary but should provide formal notice to Mary. Proof that the proper notice was given, such as a signed receipt or the green card from a certified mailing, must be kept in the file.

Practice Tip

Proof of service, or proof of notice, is often in the form of the green receipt card that comes from the U.S. Postal Service when a letter is sent by certified mail. The recipient of the letter signs the green card, and it is returned to the sender. The return address on the green card should include the initials of the paralegal sending the notice so that the green card comes back to the right person.

F. Obtain a Bond, Register the Trust, Request an EIN

Cynthia will have to obtain a surety bond, if required by the terms of the trust. The will may provide for the bond to be waived for the trustee or may require the trustee to obtain a bond. If a bond is required, proof that the bond has been secured has to be provided to the surrogate's office before the clerk will issue the letter of trusteeship. The amount of the bond would be based on the value of the assets placed into the trust. It protects the beneficiary from misappropriation of trust assets by the trustee. The bond can also protect the beneficiaries if the trustee fails to maintain the trust assets, or otherwise allows the trust's assets to diminish in value.

Practice Tip

Clients will need assistance in finding a bonding company and applying for a bond. The paralegal should be prepared to give the client several recommendations of bonding companies that offer competitive prices so that the client can compare prices.

The trustee may need to register the trust if required by state law. The registration requirement is primarily for charitable trusts, not personal trusts like the one in our

Employer identification number (EIN): serves as the taxpayer identification number for the trust

example. The trustee should obtain an **employer identification number (EIN)** if required by the type of trust. An EIN serves as the taxpayer identification number for the trust, much like a Social Security number is the taxpayer identification number for a person. In Chapter 5 we learned that a revocable trust could be owned and controlled by the grantor. Because the grantor maintains control of the trust assets, the grantor's Social Security number can be used for the trust. In an irrevocable trust, the grantor will no longer own the asset; it will be owned by the trust. An irrevocable trust requires an EIN.

The trust created in our example arose out of a last will and testament with the decedent as the grantor. Therefore, the terms of the trust cannot be altered or amended, making the trust an irrevocable trust. The trust is the true owner of the assets, requiring an EIN. The EIN is obtained by filing an SS-4 application with the IRS. The EIN can be obtained by downloading, completing, and mailing in a paper SS-4 form from the IRS. It is much more convenient to go to the online application Web site, fill in the information, and immediately receive the EIN [http://www.irs.gov/uac/Form-SS-4,-Application-for-Employer-Identification-Number-(EIN)].

Whether the application is completed through the mail or online, the IRS will issue a letter indicating the EIN that has been assigned. This number should be recorded in the file and a separate subfile created for the IRS document.

G.   Funding the Trust

In our example, we are going to assume that Cynthia is also the executor of Edwin's estate. She must ensure that all assets that are supposed to be transferred from the estate to the trust are properly titled in the name of the trust. If there are assets that are not in the name of the trust, she can authorize the attorney to take the necessary steps to get the assets in the name of the trust. As discussed above, this will involve preparing new deeds for the rental properties and for Edwin's residence so that the properties are owned in the name of the trust and retitling the brokerage and bank accounts.

Cynthia should prepare an inventory of estate assets, determining the value of all assets as of the date of trust formation, and keep assets secure. This is an administrative task that could be delegated to a paralegal without causing a breach of fiduciary duty. The inventory should include a list of the rental properties and the value of each property. Street address as well as block and lot should identify each property that will be in the trust. Cynthia should retain the services of a real property appraiser, if the executor did not, and establish the value of the properties at the time they were transferred to the trust. The chart in Figure 13-3 is an example of an inventory that can be used to record the value of assets in a trust.

Figure 13-3. Example of an Inventory

Asset	Location or Account Number	Value	Current Ownership
Rental property	11 Holiday Road, Ortles	$275,000	Estate
Rental property	15 Roosevelt Road, Brick	$200,000	Estate
Merrill Lynch account	Account #44565896	$385,000	Decedent
Checking account	Account #3349092438	$21,000	Executor
Savings account	Account #0022948457	$38,100	Decedent
Edwin's home	72 Old Tavern Road	$489,000	Decedent

The paralegal can customize the chart as needed. For example, it might be helpful to list the document or procedure necessary to change the title of an asset into the name of the trust, and when that document was filed or the procedure was completed. In our example, the rental properties are currently in the decedent's name. Those properties will have to be transferred into the name of the trust. Transfer will require the executor or personal representative to arrange for the preparation, signature, and filing of the proper deeds to transfer ownership. The paralegal in charge of the trust administration will want to monitor that process to ensure that all assets that belong in the trust actually get transferred to the trust. The attorney may also be representing Cynthia in her capacity as trustee and would therefore be required to prepare the deeds to transfer the properties to the trust.

Asset	Location or Account Number	Value	Current Ownership	Transfer
Rental property	11 Holiday Road, Ortles	$275,000	Estate	Deed by executor from estate to trust
Rental property	15 Roosevelt Road, Brick	$200,000	Estate	Deed by executor from estate to trust
Merrill Lynch account	Account #44565896	$385,000	Decedent	Work with financial representative to retitle account
Checking account	Account #3349092438	$21,000	Executor	Transfer account from executor (personally) to trust
Savings account	Account #0022948457	$38,100	Decedent	Transfer account from estate to trust
Edwin's home	72 Old Tavern Road	$489,000	Decedent	Deed by executor from estate to trust

Figure 13-4. Example of Tracking Transfer of Deeds

The rental properties currently have tenants. The rents that are paid by those tenants will be income to the trust. Cynthia should make arrangements to begin collecting monies owed to the trust. She should review the method by which her late brother managed the properties and determine if she wants to continue that method. Edwin may have used a property management company to oversee the properties because it was not convenient for him to be available to address tenant's problems. If there is a contract with a property management firm, that contract will have to be reviewed, and possibly re-signed by Cynthia as trustee in the name of the trust.

As soon as she has access to trust funds, Cynthia should begin to pay trust debts and expenses after determining that each of the debts and expenses is valid. She may begin using rental income to pay the mortgages on the rental properties or the property taxes, for example. She may need to retain the services of an accountant or bookkeepers to keep an accurate record of all trust income and expenditures. The cost associated with these services is an expense to the trust. It is also common for the paralegal to be responsible for simple bookkeeping tasks associated with trust (or estate) administration.

Practice Tip

Clients will often ask for the names of accountants, bookkeepers, or other professionals. The attorney should be prepared to offer the names of two or three trusted individuals who have a history with the attorney of providing good service.

One of the assets that will be placed into trust is Edwin's Merrill Lynch brokerage account. It will be necessary to speak to Edwin's financial advisor and complete the forms that Merrill Lynch requires in order to establish the trust. Placing this asset in the trust will require establishing a new account in the name of the trust, and then authorizing the transfer of the assets from the existing account into the trust account. The transfer of the asset into the newly formed trust account may require coordination with the executor or personal representative as he or she is the one with the authority to disburse assets from the decedent's estate.

After the trust account is established, Cynthia will be responsible for managing the investments following the prudent investor standard. She can consult with an investment advisor but will still be responsible for making investment decisions. She may not delegate decision-making authority to anyone else. The prudent investor standard is discussed at length in Chapter 5.

If Cynthia has retained an accountant, she should meet with the accountant to determine if a trust tax return will be required. The trust tax return is Form 1041, the Fiduciary Income Tax Return, and it must be filed annually. If taxes are due and Form 1041 is not filed annually and timely, penalties and interest may be assessed. Cynthia should also be prepared to provide an annual trust accounting to the trust beneficiaries if required by state law or the terms of the trust.

H.   Distributing the Trust

The terms of the trust allow Cynthia broad discretion in making distributions of trust income and/or principal. **Income** generally includes interest earned on bank accounts, CDs, bonds, or mortgages, and dividends on stocks and mutual funds. In the trust in our example, Cynthia will be collecting rents and adding the rents to the trust as income. **Undistributed income** is any income that the trustee uses his or her discretion to retain, which potentially goes back into the trust as principal and can accumulate. The **principal**, also known as the corpus or body of the trust, consists of the underlying assets, such as the rental properties. Cynthia is also the guardian of the two younger children who might now be living with her. It is possible that Cynthia moves into Edwin's home to care for the children, or Cynthia may move the children in with her and sell Edwin's home. If the home is sold, the proceeds from the sale can be invested in some type of managed investment for the beneficiaries.

Cynthia's discretion as to what would be a legitimate purpose for trust monies is described as "support, maintenance, welfare, education, medical care and comfort." Examples of appropriate distributions that can be made under this standard include the following:

- Regular mortgage payments
- Property taxes
- Suitable health insurance or care
- Property insurance
- Secondary education
- Purchase of a car
- Wedding expenses
- Down payment on a home

How and to whom Cynthia makes distribution of principal and income in our example is governed by the fact that Cynthia is also the guardian of the minor children. Cynthia might be using money from the trust to pay monthly expenses associated with their care, such as school tuition, clothing, food, or health insurance. Cynthia would be serving in the dual roles as guardian and trustee, which would make the distributions easier but would not relieve Cynthia of her reporting requirements for either role. State law may require that Cynthia file an annual guardianship accounting even if the terms of the trust do not require a trust accounting. Cynthia should be advised that she should be prepared to account for each expenditure she makes from the trust.

If Cynthia was not the guardian of the minor children, distributions from the trust could be made to the guardian. Depending on the size of the trust and the size of the distributions, it may be necessary to have the guardian sign a receipt for each distribution made. The payments to the guardian could be done in a set monthly amount that the guardian uses for all of the minor children's needs. If the trustee is making regular monthly payments, for example for school fees, or to the guardian, then a subfile should be set up with a schedule of the payments that are periodically updated with the cancelled checks and/or receipts.

Income: generally includes interest earned on bank accounts, CDs, bonds, or mortgages, and dividends on stocks and mutual funds; can also include rental income from real properties owned by the trust

Undistributed income: if the trust gives the trustee discretion in spending income, some of the income could remain undistributed; if that occurs, the trust will determine if undistributed income goes back into the trust as principal to accumulate

Principal: also called the corpus or body of the trust, consists of the underlying assets, such as the real properties, stocks, bonds, investment accounts, and so forth

Practice Tip

Make suggestions to the trustee how the receipts, cancelled checks, and so forth, for the expenditures should be organized in preparation of the annual accounting. If the attorney is providing ongoing trust administration services, the trustee should be providing all of the distribution checks to the attorney.

The trust in our example calls for distributions of shares of the trust after the youngest daughter turns age 25. Mary, Edwin's oldest child, is 35 years old. She is not entitled to any distribution of income and will not receive any distribution from the trust until Mae turns age 25. When Mae turns 25, the trust is to be divided into three shares, with one share distributed to each child. Cynthia should calculate the distribution to which each is entitled and make payment directly to each child. When the payment is made to each child, Cynthia should have each sign some kind of receipt acknowledging that she received the payment. The receipt should also include a release indicating that each beneficiary is releasing Cynthia from her obligations as trustee. This release would have to be submitted to the bonding company as proof that Cynthia fulfilled her duties as trustee. A sample of such a release is shown in Figure 13-5.

OCEAN COUNTY SURROGATE COURT
IN THE MATTER OF THE EDWIN NOFUSS IRREVOCABLE
FAMILY TRUST

Attorney(s): **CARLUCCIO, LEONE, DIMON, DOYLE & SACKS, L.L.C.**

Office Address & Tel. No.: **9 Robbins Street, Toms River, NJ 08753 (732) 797-1600**

KNOW ALL MEN BY THESE PRESENTS, That I, **Cynthia Nofuss** *the Trustee of the* **Edwin Nofuss Irrevocable Family Trust** *here in designated as the Obligors, Is here by held and firmly bound* **by the Edwin Nofuss Irrevocable Family Trust**

Mary Nofuss *here in designated as the Obligee, in the sum of lawful money of the United States of America, to be paid to the Obligee or to Obligee's certain Attorney, successors in office or assigns, for which payment well and truly to be made we bind ourselves, our heirs, executors, and administrators firmly by these presents. Sealed with my seal and dated the day of September, 2013.*

    And in Consideration Therefor, the Obligee has remised, released, and forever discharged and by these presents does remise, release, and forever discharge the Obligor from all claims and demands whatsoever, in law or in equity, on account of or in respect to the Edwin Nofuss Irrevocable Family Trust and of Obligee's interest therein.

    Now Therefore, *if any part or the whole of such payment to Obligee shall at any time hereafter appear to be needed to discharge any debt or debts, which the said co-trustees may not have other assets to pay, the Obligee will return said payments or such part thereof as may be necessary for the payment of the said debts.*

Figure 13-5. Sample Release Form

(continued)

Figure 13-5. Continued

The words "debt or debts" wherever used herein shall be deemed to include all taxes imposed upon or chargeable to the Edwin Nofuss Irrevocable Family Trust or owed by the deceased, including but not limited to Federal, New Jersey, or other State or Sovereignty transfer inheritance, estate, death, transfer, and income taxes, together with interest, penalties, costs, expenses, and counsel fees, if any.

Obligor is making the payments to the Obligee without consideration for the Obligee's tax obligations and Obligor is not responsible for the payment of any taxes owed by the Obligee as a result of these payments from the Edwin Nofuss Irrevocable Family Trust.

If more than one person executes the within instrument, then words used in the singular shall be considered to include the plural, and wherever herein any particular gender is used, it shall be inclusive of the masculine, feminine, and neuter gender, where the text so requires.

Signed, Sealed, and Delivered
in the presence of   _____ *L.S.*

_____   _____ *L.S.*

State of New Jersey, County of Ocean)ss.: Be it Remembered, *that on, 2013, before me, the subscriber, personally appeared Mary Nofuss who, I am satisfied, is the person named in and who executed the within Instrument, and thereupon she acknowledged that she signed, sealed, and delivered the same as act and deed, for the uses and purposes therein expressed.*

                                                                    _____

After significant amounts have been paid out of the trust, Cynthia might consider applying to the court to reduce the amount of the bond she is required to maintain.

The state law of the state in which the trust was established may require that the beneficiary provide other releases or that the language of the release include other terms. The paralegal should become familiar with the specific release language used when distributions from a trust are made. There may also be different language required when the distribution is made to a guardian on behalf of a minor child.

I. Beneficiaries

The trust created in Edwin's will benefits **income beneficiaries**, beneficiaries who get periodic distributions of income, and **remainderman**, beneficiaries who will receive a distribution of principal when the trust terminates. In our example, the trustee has discretion in paying out or accumulating income to Joan and Mae. Mary does not receive any distribution of principal until Mae, the youngest child, reaches age 25. The timing of the distributions may cause a conflict among the beneficiaries. Joan and Mae are income beneficiaries who will want the trustee to invest in things that will generate the highest possible rate of return and the most income. Mary is a remainderman and may be more concerned with preserving the value of all of the assets,

Income beneficiaries: beneficiaries who get periodic distributions of income

Remainderman: beneficiaries who will receive a distribution of principal when the trust terminates and providing for appreciation and growth. Moreover, the trust provides that any undistributed income becomes principal. Mary may not want Cynthia to be too generous in distributing income to Joan and Mae, or using income for their needs. Cynthia must balance her loyalty between the income beneficiaries and the remainder beneficiary.

Cynthia also has to be careful in allocating the payment of trust expenses and debts if there are both income beneficiaries and remaindermen. In our example, some of the investment properties may have mortgages. Cynthia must be careful to keep all of the beneficiaries' interests in mind when determining whether to use the principal of the trust to pay off the mortgage or to continue to pay off the debt with rental income generated by the property. The trustee may have to allocate a portion of the debt payment to each set of beneficiaries.

J. Trustee's Duties and Powers

The trustee is a fiduciary with certain specific duties and ethical standards. Many of the trustee's duties were discussed in Chapter 5. Cynthia can delegate some of the more administrative functions of the role of trustee to an agent; however, she remains responsible for the agent. The trustee cannot delegate any functions or tasks that involve decision making or use of the trustee's discretion. Cynthia can hire professionals, such as attorneys, accountants, or investment advisors, to advise or assist in the performance of her administrative duties. She may not, however, delegate decision-making authority to those professionals or blindly follow the professionals' advice. For example, Cynthia may decide to retain the services of an attorney and an investment advisor. She may rely on their professional advice, but she must always review the information and recommendations provided and make decisions. Cynthia can retain the services of an accountant to prepare a trust tax return, but it will be Cynthia who is required to sign the return.

1. Duty to Administer Trust

Cynthia has a duty to administer the trust. This means she must agree to carry out the terms of the trust agreement by maintaining the assets in the trust and making periodic distributions to the beneficiaries in keeping with the grantor's intent. The duties of the role of trustee are not to be taken lightly. Cynthia can be held personally responsible for failing to fulfill her duties.

2. Duty of Loyalty to the Beneficiaries

Cynthia has a duty of loyalty to the trust that has been created for her three nieces. The duty of loyalty is a general duty that includes several different obligations. She is obligated to administer the trust in a manner that is solely in the interests of the trust beneficiaries. She must not engage in self-dealing and must not engage in any act that puts his or her personal interests in conflict with those of any of the trust beneficiaries. The trustee cannot use trust property for her personal gain or for any manner that benefits her personally, even if there is no loss to the trust.

3.   Duty to Not Engage in Self-Dealing

The trustee has a general duty not to engage in self-dealing. This means the trustee cannot buy assets from the trust or sell assets to the trust. Cynthia cannot buy the trust's share of properties she owns jointly with the trust, and she cannot sell the trust her share of the jointly owned properties. The trustee must always remember that she is acting as a fiduciary and owes a duty of loyalty to the trust and all of the trust beneficiaries. In our example, if circumstances arise where jointly owned properties must be sold, it may be necessary for Cynthia to resign as trustee or to have an outside party handle the transaction to ensure that the sale occurs as an **arm's-length transaction**. An *arm's-length transaction* is one in which the parties hold themselves at "arm's length" and act independently with no relationship to each other to avoid a conflict of interest.

Arm's-length transaction: when the parties hold themselves at "arm's length" and act independently with no relationship to each other to avoid a conflict of interest

Self-dealing also includes commingling. Cynthia must not commingle any of her funds with trust funds. In our example, several of the rental properties Edwin owned were jointly owned with Cynthia. After Edwin's death, the trust becomes the co-owner with Cynthia. Even if Edwin and Cynthia previously used a joint account to deposit rents and pay expenses for the jointly owned properties, Cynthia must now open a separate account into which the trust portion of income must be deposited. The informal agreement may have worked fine between Cynthia and her brother, but for the purposes of the trust, the income must be kept separated and not comingled with Cynthia's income.

The duty to keep assets separate requires the trustee to keep separate bank accounts, brokerage accounts, and safe-deposit boxes for trust assets. Trust assets must always be kept separate from the trustee's personal assets, and the trustee must earmark the assets as specifically associated with the trust. The trustee may be liable if trust assets are lost, misplaced, or destroyed. For example, Cynthia might also have a brokerage account at the same firm as Edwin's account. When she meets with the financial advisor, she may find out that the trust will be subject to certain fees because there is not sufficient money in the trust brokerage account. She may not combine her account with her brother's account to raise the balance in the account to a level at which there will be no fees, even though this benefits the trust.

4.   Duty to Account

The trust agreement may require a trustee to prepare an annual **accounting** of the trust assets and expenditures from the trust. An *accounting*, as the term is used with regard to a trust, is the process of keeping financial records of the income and principal of the trust. Cynthia may have to keep accurate records and prepare annual accountings to fulfill her duty of administering the trust property. She will need to establish the value of each rental property, the income received from each property, and the expenses for each property, as well as all of the receipts and expenditures for all of the other assets in the trust. The trust, or state law, may also require the trustee to provide accountings to the court.

Accounting: the process of keeping financial records of the income and principal of the trust, as the term is used with regard to a trust

Preparing an accounting for the trust in our example can get complicated because the beneficial interests are split between two income beneficiaries and a remainder beneficiary. Therefore, expenses have to be split in a fair and reasonable manner between income and principal. The ordinary and current expenses, such as payment of taxes, repairs, and maintenance for the properties, will be paid out of trust income. Any expenses that are "extraordinary" or will only benefit the remainder beneficiary will be paid out of the principal. In our trust, an example of extraordinary expenses might include an improvement to one of the properties like an addition to the living space. In addition, any losses that are sustained from the rental properties owned by the trust will usually come from the principal. If, for example, one of the rental properties was destroyed by fire, the loss in value would reduce the principal of the trust. The trustee has a duty to properly classify all income and expenses so that they are credited or charged to the income or principal accounts.

5.   Duty to Avoid Waste

Waste: occurs when an asset that has value is diminished because of some action or inaction of the representative of the trust

Waste occurs when an asset that has value is diminished because of some action or inaction of the representative of the trust. Cynthia has a duty to protect and maintain the value of the trust assets. In our example, this means monitoring the properties and making sure that the insurances, repairs, and maintenance are all kept up. If a tenant in one of the properties is not paying rent, she will have to evict the tenant. The duty to avoid waste extends to the investment account. If Cynthia decides to liquidate that account and invest the proceeds in a risky investment, she may be liable to the beneficiaries if the investment becomes worthless.

6.   Additional Duties and Powers

In the trust in our example, we made an assumption that the trustee's powers were enumerated in the will, and by reference to state statute. As we learned in Chapter 4, the trustee's powers are included by reference to state statute and the Uniform Trust Code. The trustee can also look to the courts for further guidance if necessary. There are certain powers that a trustee does not normally have, unless specifically included in the trust document. For example, if the trust document allows for it, a trustee may have the power to modify or revoke the trust. If the trust does not specifically provide that power, then the trustee will typically have no power to alter the terms of the trust. The method of revoking or modifying the trust would also be specified in the trust instrument. For example, Edwin's will could stipulate that if, in Cynthia's discretion, any of his daughters is not able to handle a distribution of principal at age 25, Cynthia can continue to hold the funds in trust. This provision would essentially give Cynthia the power to modify the existing trust, which calls for a distribution at age 25.

There are some occasions when a trustee can undertake an activity that would otherwise be a prohibited conflict of interest. For example, in the trust that Edwin created, he provided that Mary would become the successor trustee if Cynthia were unable to complete her duties as trustee. This might create a conflict if Mary was also still a beneficiary of the trust, except that the grantor specifically gave Mary the right to become a trustee, presumably knowing that she might also be a beneficiary. The trust could contain a provision that would allow Mary to buy certain assets from the trust, such as Edwin's residence. A trustee would not be able to purchase trust assets without creating a conflict of interest without specific authority allowing the purchase.

Figure 13-6. Sample of a Petition for Termination of a Trust

STATE OF WISCONSIN - CIRCUIT COURT - BARRON COUNTY

In the Matter of the Trust of: **PETITION FOR TERMINATION OF**

TRUST

For the Benefit of:

File No.

_____, being first duly sworn on oath, petitions the Court as follows:

1. Petitioner is the Trustee, having been appointed by the Probate Court on _____.

2. The Trust should be terminated pursuant to the Last Will and Testament for the following reason(s):

    _____

    _____.

3. The terms of the Will have been complied with and the decedent's Will provides that the trust should now terminate.

4. The Closing Certificate for Fiduciaries is filed here with.

5. The Final Trust Account for the period _____ through _____ has been filed with the Court.

6. The names and addresses of all interested parties in this matter are:

    _____

    _____

    _____

7. The beneficiary(ies) has(have) filed a Waiver and Consent.

8. Petitioner respectfully requests that the Court approve all accountings of the Trustee, including the final trust account which is submitted herewith, authorize the termination of the Trust with the distribution of proceeds as shown in the final trust accounting, and discharge the trustee.

For Official Use

Dated: _____

_____
                                                    Petitioner/Trustee

Subscribed and sworn to before me

On _____.

_____

Notary Public, State of Wisconsin

My Commission expires: _____

_____ Petitioner/Trustee

K. Terminating the Trust

Cynthia will be responsible for continuing the administration of the trust for the next 13 years, until the youngest child turns 25. At that point, the trust purposes have been completed, and the trust can be terminated following the requirements of state law. In our example, trust termination comes after the trust purposes are completed. In other trusts, it may be necessary to terminate the trust because the trust purposes become illegal or impractical. Another reason a trust could be terminated is because it includes a provision that allows the trustee to terminate the trust if the trust assets go below a certain threshold amount. For example, if the trust assets go below $10,000 a trustee may be able to terminate the trust and distribute the remaining funds.

Termination of the trust may require Cynthia to provide a final accounting, obtain a release of any bond that was necessary, or file certain termination documents with the probate court. The state law of the state in which the trust was formed will have to be reviewed to ensure that the trustee complies with the state law requirements for termination of the trust. A sample of a petition for termination of a trust from Wisconsin is shown in Figure 13-6.

All of the documents that need to be filed with the Court in Wisconsin can be found on the county Web site (http://www.barroncountywi.gov/).

The steps outlined in this chapter are an example of the necessary steps that address the issues raised in our illustration, but are not an exclusive list of everything that a trustee could be expected to do. The administration of a trust can be complex, and there are many pitfalls into which a trustee can inadvertently fall. The trustee must keep careful records, fulfill his or her duties to the trust and the beneficiaries, and not engage in any form of self-dealing from the trust. Even the most careful trustees can find themselves facing litigation from the beneficiaries or outside parties.

Summary

Trust administration is the management and distribution of assets held by a trust. The trustee is responsible for knowing the terms of the trust and completing the administration in accordance with those terms. The trustee is responsible for getting all of the assets into the trust, managing those assets, and making payments to the beneficiaries. The trustee has many duties and responsibilities to the trust and the beneficiaries of the trust, such as a duty of loyalty, a duty not to engage in self-dealing, and a duty to avoid waste. When the terms of the trust have been completed, the trustee can usually terminate the trust.

Review Questions

1. A trust owns an extensive stamp collection. The trustee given responsibility for the trust is also a stamp collector and places the stamps in books and keeps the books on the same shelves where she stores her own collection. All of the books are carefully labeled, and the owners are identified as either the trustee or the trust. Has the trustee breached her duty?

2. Can a trustee can use his or her own Social Security number as the taxpayer identification number for the trust?

3. What are some of the trustee's duties?

4. What are some examples of tasks the trustee can delegate? What are some examples of things the trustee cannot delegate?

True or False

1. T   F   Co-trustees must work together.

2. T   F   In a trust agreement, the trustee's role begins when he or she signs the trust agreement.

3. T   F   A trustee has the authority to sign documents, such as a contract, on behalf of the trust.

4. T   F   A trustee is not responsible for transferring assets into the trust.

5. T   F   In a testamentary trust, the executor is responsible for filing the Form 1041, the Fiduciary Income Tax Return.

6. T   F   A trustee's primary duty of loyalty is to the youngest beneficiaries.

7. T   F   A trustee can retain the services of an accountant and/or an attorney and can delegate administrative duties.

8. T   F   A trustee is a fiduciary, with fiduciary duties.

9. T   F   Income generated by trust assets can be paid directly to the trustee and does not have to be deposited into the trust.

10. T   F   A trustee must always obtain a surety bond.

Trust Administration Exercise

You meet with a new client, Allan K. His aunt, Doris V., died last month. Allan is the executor of her estate and trustee of the trust created in the will. The trust is for the benefit of Allan's three children, Allan Jr., Adam, and Allayna, who are 15, 12, and 8 years old, respectively. Doris was always very fond of Allan and Allan's children. Allan has admitted the will to probate and has been issued letters of trusteeship. He has not finished the administration of the estate. He is still trying to determine the location of all of the assets and the amount that is in the estate. Allan believes he will be able to handle some of the administration of the estate on his own but is looking for assistance in creating the trust and guidance in administering the trust. Allan gives you the following documents:

- Last will and testament of Doris V.
- Trusteeship certificate
- Stock certificate for Prudential stock
- Deed for Doris' property—Allan transferred the property into his name
- Bank statement from Ocean Bank
- Investment statement from Morgan Stanley
- Bank account statements from Provident Bank

Questions

1. What kind of trust is the trust that will be established?

2. Does Allan have to get a bond in his capacity as trustee?

3. Who are the beneficiaries of the trust?

4. What part of the estate goes into the trust?

5. What law will govern the operation of the trust?

6. Was Allan correct in transferring the property into his name?

7. Would an EIN be required? Why?

8. What other professional should Allan consider retaining?

9. What are some examples of additional information needed from the trustee?

Organization of Trust

1. Describe how the file for this client would be organized.

2. What additional documentation will be necessary?

3. Describe what needs to be done regarding ownership of the following assets:

- Stock certificate for Prudential stock
- Deed for Doris' property in Allan's name
- Bank statement from Ocean Bank
- Investment statement from Morgan Stanley
- Bank account statements from Provident Bank

4. Prepare a form of inventory for the assets that have been identified.

Key Terms

Accounting	Principal
Arm's-length transaction	Remainderman
Employer identification number (EIN)	Trust administration
Income	Undistributed income
Income beneficiaries	Waste

TRUST ADMINISTRATION CHECKLIST

Complete this checklist to the best of your ability before meeting with the attorney. Bring the checklist and any documents you have pertaining to the trust with you to the meeting.

1. TRUSTEE

Name: _____

Address: _____ City: _____ Zip: _____

Phone: Home _____ Work _____ Cell _____

Fax _____ E-mail _____

Social Security Number (if individual): _____

Bond: _____ yes _____ no

Sucessor Trustee

Name: _____

Address: _____ City: _____ Zip: _____

Phone: Home _____ Work _____ Cell _____

Fax _____ E-mail _____

Social Security Number (if individual): _____

Bond: _____ yes _____ no

2. BENEFICIARIES

Name: _____ Birth date: _____ SSN: _____

Address: _____

City: _____ State: _____ Zip code: _____

Phone: (day) _____ (eve) _____ (fax) _____

Guardian required: _____ yes _____ no

Name: _____ Birth date: _____ SSN: _____

Address: _____

City: _____ State: _____ Zip code: _____

Phone: (day) _____ (eve) _____ (fax) _____

Guardian required: _____ yes _____ no

Name: _____ Birth date: _____ SSN: _____

Address: _____

City: _____ State: _____ Zip code: _____

Phone: (day) _____ (eve) _____ (fax) _____

Guardian required: _____ yes _____ no

Name: _____ Birth date: _____ SSN: _____

Address: _____

City: _____ State: _____ Zip code: _____

Phone: (day) _____ (eve) _____ (fax) _____

Guardian required: _____ yes _____ no

(continued)

3.   TRUST ASSETS

A.   Personal Property

1.   Vehicles

Item	VIN	Joint Owner(s)	Value
_____	_____	_____	$ _____
_____	_____	_____	$ _____
_____	_____	_____	$ _____

2.   Jewelry $ _____ Please attach any appraisals.

3.   Collectibles of any value over $5,000—art, coins, stamps, etc. (Y/N) _____ If yes, please attach any appraisals.

Describe Item/Collection	Approximate Value	Year Appraised
_____	_____	_____
_____	_____	_____
_____	_____	_____
_____	_____	_____

B.   Real Estate

1.   Personal residence:

Address: _____

Block and lot: _____

Value: _____ Mortgage balance, if any: _____ Equity: _____

Insurance policy: _____

2.   Other personal residences or vacation homes:

Address: _____

Block and lot: _____

Value: _____ Mortgage balance, if any: _____ Equity: _____

Insurance policy: _____

3.   Other investment real property:

Address: _____

Block and lot: _____

Value: _____ Mortgage balance, if any: _____ Equity: _____

Insurance policy: _____

C. Cash, Cash Deposits, and Cash Equivalents

1.   Checking accounts:

Name of financial institution:: _____

Account number: _____

Balance: _____

Name of financial institution: _____

Account number: _____

Balance: _____

Name of financial institution: _____

Account number: _____

Balance: _____

2.   <u>Savings accounts:</u>

Name of financial institution: _____

Account number: _____

Balance: _____

Name of financial institution: _____

Account number: _____

Balance: _____

Name of financial institution: _____

Account number: _____

Balance: _____

3.   <u>Money market accounts:</u>

Name of financial institution: _____

Account number: _____

Balance: _____

Name of financial institution: _____

Account number: _____

Balance: _____

Name of financial institution: _____

Account number: _____

Balance: _____

4.   <u>Certificates of deposit:</u>

Name of financial institution: _____

Certificate of deposit account number: _____

Balance: _____

(continued)

Name of financial institution: _____

Certificate of deposit account number: _____

Balance: _____

Name of financial institution: _____

Certificate of deposit account number: _____

Balance: _____

5.   Investment accounts:

Name of brokerage firm:_____

Broker's name: _____

Account number: _____ Balance: _____

Name of brokerage firm:_____

Broker's name: _____

Account number: _____ Balance: _____

Name of brokerage firm:_____

Broker's name: _____

Account number: _____ Balance: _____

D.   Investment Assets

1.   Publicly traded stocks and corporate bonds:

Entity: _____

Number of shares: _____ Value: _____

Name, address, and phone number of agent for transfer:

_____

_____

_____

Entity: _____

Number of shares: _____ Value: _____

Name, address, and phone number of agent for transfer:

_____

_____

_____

Entity: _____

Number of shares: _____ Value: _____

Name, address, and phone number of agent for transfer:

_____

_____

_____

2.   Municipal bonds:

Entity: _____

Number of shares: _____ Value: _____

Name, address, and phone number of agent for transfer:

_____

_____

_____

Entity: _____

Number of shares: _____ Value: _____

Name, address, and phone number of agent for transfer:

_____

_____

_____

3.   U.S. Treasury notes and bonds:

Denomination: _____ Number: _____

Expiration date: _____ Value: _____

Denomination: _____ Number: _____

Expiration date: _____ Value: _____

Denomination: _____ Number: _____

Expiration date: _____ Value: _____

4.   Other investments:

Investment: _____ Type: _____ Value: _____

_____

_____

(continued)

E. Pension and Profit-Sharing Plans, ESOPs, SEPs

1. Pension plans:

Name, address, and phone number of employer: _____

Employee: _____ Type of plan: _____ Value: _____

Name, address, and phone number of plan administrator:

_____

_____

2. Profit-sharing plans:

Name, address, and phone number of employer: _____

Employee: _____ Value: _____

Name, address, and phone number of plan administrator:

_____

_____

3. Individual Retirement Accounts (IRAs):

Name of financial institution: _____

Account number: _____ Balance: _____

_____

F. Annuities

Annuity company: _____

Contract number: _____ Current cash value: _____

Owner of policy: _____ Primary beneficiary(ies): _____

Contingent beneficiary(ies): _____

G. Life Insurance

Insurance company: _____ Policy number: _____ Face amount: _____

Owner of policy: _____

Primary beneficiary(ies): _____

Contingent beneficiary(ies): _____ Type of policy: Ordinary _____ Term/group _____

Current cash value: _____ Loans: _____

Accidental death benefits, if any: _____

Insurance company: _____ Policy number: _____ Face amount: _____

Owner of policy: _____

Primary beneficiary(ies): _____

Contingent beneficiary(ies): _____ Type of policy: Ordinary _____ Term/group _____

Current cash value: _____ Loans: _____

Accidental death benefits, if any: _____

Insurance company: _____ Policy number: _____ Face amount: _____

Owner of policy: _____

Primary beneficiary(ies): _____

Contingent beneficiary(ies): _____ Type of policy: Ordinary _____ Term/group _____

Current cash value: _____ Loans: _____

Accidental death benefits, if any: _____

H.   Life Insurance Owned by Trust

Insurance company: _____ Policy number: _____ Face amount: _____

Owner of policy: _____

Primary beneficiary(ies): _____

Contingent beneficiary(ies): _____ Type of policy: Ordinary _____ Term/group _____

Current cash value: _____ Loans: _____

Accidental death benefits, if any: _____

Trusts

Please list each trust and attach copies of each trust agreement and current financial statements.

_____

_____

4.   TRUST LIABILITIES

A.   Mortgages, Notes, Trust Deeds

Date of Note	Maker (Debtor)	Principal	Now Due	Int. %	Terms Secured?
_____	_____	$_____	_____	___%	_____
_____	_____	$_____	_____	___%	_____
_____	_____	$_____	_____	___%	_____

B.   Credit Cards, Utility Bills, Tax Bills, and Other Bills Due but Unpaid

Company Name and Address	Account Number	Balance	Payment Due
_____	_____	$_____	$_____
_____	_____	$_____	$_____
_____	_____	$_____	$_____
_____	_____	$_____	$_____

(continued)

ADDITIONAL INFORMATION

Trust Litigation

A trust, and the trustee, may become involved in litigation that arises from liability to the beneficiaries for breach of fiduciary duty, or breach of the trust, or liability to third parties. The beneficiaries may be seeking damages from the trustee, may want the trustee removed, or both. The trust may also be subject to litigation from an outside source, such as liability caused by an investment. This chapter will examine some of the aspects of trust litigation.

A. Standing

The first question to ask in any litigation, especially litigation involving a trust, is whether the party suing the trust has **standing**. In the legal realm, *standing* is defined as an ability to demonstrate to the court that the party has sufficient interest in the matter to proceed with the litigation. The person bringing the action must be able to demonstrate that he or she has a stake or interest in the outcome that is sufficient to entitle the person to bring the issue to court. In trust litigation, that would mean that the person bringing the issue to the court would have to a sufficient interest in the trust to have standing. Typically, the people who have standing in trust litigation are the people who are parties to the trust: the beneficiaries, the trustee, and the grantor. In our example there is only one trustee, but if there were co-trustees, any of the co-trustees would also have standing to sue.

Standing: an ability to demonstrate to the court that the party has sufficient interest in the matter to proceed with the litigation

The beneficiary or beneficiaries have standing to challenge the terms of the trust or the actions of the trustee. For example, in the Nofuss Family Trust we discussed in Chapter 13, Mary, as a beneficiary, would have standing to challenge the actions of the trustee if the trustee refused to distribute principal as required by the terms of the trust. Cynthia as the trustee also has standing. It may be necessary for Cynthia to apply to the court for an interpretation of a trust provision, or because she no longer wishes to be the trustee and the trust does not provide for a method to replace her. The grantor of a trust would have standing. In our example, the Nofuss Family Trust is a testamentary trust, so the grantor, Cynthia's brother Edwin, is no longer alive. If the trust were *inter vivos*, and established by Edwin during his lifetime, he would have standing as the grantor to challenge any action taken by the trustee.

A third party, or someone who is not a party to the trust, typically would not have standing. For example, the bank that holds the mortgage on Mary's house does not have standing to challenge the trust in order to force a distribution from the trust that would pay off the mortgage. A third party could have standing to challenge the trust if there was liability created by the trust. The Nofuss Family Trust owns several rental properties. A third party could have standing to raise a claim against the trust if, for example, a guest at one of the properties is injured. The trust could then be named as a defendant in an action brought by the injured person. Hopefully the trustee would have insurance on the property to cover the liability.

B. Breach of Duty

Trust litigation often involves allegations that the trustee breached his or her fiduciary duty. As we learned in Chapter 4, the trustee owes a fiduciary duty to all of the beneficiaries. A trustee, once he or she has accepted appointment, is in a fiduciary relation to the beneficiaries of the trust. [See *A. Scott & W. Fratcher*, The Law of Trusts §170, American Law Institute, *Restatement (Second) of Trusts*, §2 (1980).] A beneficiary or group of beneficiaries of a trust can challenge the trustee's actions, claiming that the trustee has breached his or her fiduciary duty. A fiduciary relationship involves discretionary authority and dependency: One person depends on another — the fiduciary — to serve his or her interests [*U.S. v. Chestman*, 947 F.2d 551, 567 (2d Cir. 1991)]. An agent owes a fiduciary duty to the principal and may not put itself in a position adverse to that of the principal [*Doyle v. Maruszczak*, 834 So. 2d 307, 309 (Fla. 5th D.C.A. 2003)]. The fiduciary obligation of loyalty flows not from the trust itself but from the relationship of trustee and beneficiary, and the essence of this relationship is that the trustee is charged with equitable duties toward the beneficiary [*Fuller Family Holdings, LLC, vs. The Northern Trust Company*, Ill. App. 3d, 863 N.E.2d 743, 309 Ill. Dec. 111 (Ill. App. 1st Dist. 2007)]. If the trustee fails to fulfill any of his or her duties, the trustee may be liable to the beneficiaries for breach of fiduciary duty.

To prevail on a breach of fiduciary duty, a plaintiff must show (1) the existence of a fiduciary duty, (2) a breach of that fiduciary duty, (3) causation, and (4) harm [*Koger v. Hartford Life Ins. Co.*, 28 S.W.3d 405, 411 (Mo. App. W.D. 2000)]. As we have learned in other chapters, the trustee's duties include, among other things, the duty to administer the trust according to its terms, the duty of loyalty to the beneficiaries, the duty to avoid commingling of funds, and a duty to preserve assets and prevent waste. A breach of any of these duties can give rise to a cause of action claiming breach of fiduciary duty.

A trustee can be found personally liable to the trust beneficiaries for negligent or intentional breach of fiduciary that causes the trust to suffer damages. One of the trustee's duties is a duty of loyalty to the beneficiaries. In Chapter 13 we learned that Cynthia's duty of loyalty to the trust includes a duty to administer the trust in a manner that is solely in the interests of the trust beneficiaries. She must not engage in self-dealing or any act that puts her personal interests in conflict with those of the beneficiaries. An example of breach of the duty of loyalty would be the following. Cynthia owns several other rental properties in addition to the ones in the Nofuss Family Trust. She decides to fire the property manager of the trust properties and take on those duties herself. She pays herself a salary equal to 5 percent of the annual rents collected from the properties. Unless the Nofuss Family Trust authorizes the payment of a salary to Cynthia, or Cynthia has obtained either a court order or the consent of all the beneficiaries, she has committed a violation of her duty of loyalty to the beneficiaries by engaging in self-dealing. Cynthia has personally engaged in a financial transaction involving properties owned by the trust.

A claim of breach of fiduciary duty may give rise to personal liability against the trustee. A trustee can be personally liable to the beneficiaries for any negligent or intentional breaches of any of the trustee's duties, which cause damages to the trust and/or the beneficiaries. If the trustee is found to be personally liable, the trustee will have to pay damages from his or her own assets if the trustee does not have a surety bond. A **surety bond** for a trustee is a type of insurance that protects against loss by guaranteeing the proper performance of the trustee and insuring against theft or misappropriation of trust assets.

Surety bond: A type of insurance that protects against loss by guaranteeing the proper performance of the trustee and insuring against theft or misappropriation of trust assets

C. Liability to Third Parties

Two ways in which liability to a third party could occur are as the result of a tort committed by the trust or by way of a contract between the trust and a third party. A **tort** is a wrongful act, whether intentional or accidental, that gives rise to damages. For example, consider the following: Cynthia fails to obtain a liability insurance policy for the rental properties owned by the Nofuss Family Trust. She feels it is too expensive and cancels the existing policy despite being warned by the insurance broker against doing so. A year after the policy is cancelled, a guest at one of the properties is injured. Cynthia may be found to be personally liable for the losses or damages incurred by the injured guest. If Cynthia had continued the appropriate insurance, the insurance company would have assumed liability for the injuries to the guest. The trustee has a right to **indemnification**, or protection against loss or damages from the trust estate, if she was not personally at fault. In this example, Cynthia may not be eligible for indemnification because she was negligent in not obtaining the proper insurance. If, however, Cynthia paid for insurance, but the insurance broker was stealing the premiums and not paying for the insurance, allowing it to lapse, Cynthia may claim indemnification from the trust because the lack of insurance was not personally her fault.

Tort: a wrongful act, whether intentional or accidental, that gives rise to damages

Indemnification: protection against loss or damages

The second way in which liability to a third party can occur is from a contract between the trust and a third party. A trustee is personally liable on all contracts that the trustee signs during the course of the trust administration. The trustee can limit personal liability by putting a **disclaimer** into the contract. A *disclaimer* is a limitation or denial of civil liability. For example, Cynthia signs a contract with the property manager who is responsible for managing the rental properties that are now owned by the Nofuss Family Trust. When Cynthia signs the contract, the attorney representing Cynthia includes the following language in the contract:

Disclaimer: a limitation or denial of civil liability

> This contract is signed by Cynthia Nofuss as the Trustee of the Nofuss Family Trust. This contract constitutes an agreement to pay for property management services as it pertains to the properties owned by the Nofuss Family Trust. Payment of the management fees will be made from the rents collected at the properties. To the extent said rents are insufficient to pay the agreed upon fee, the parties further agree that any deficiency will be satisfied from assets held by the Nofuss Family Trust, and not by Cynthia Nofuss individually.

Language similar to this in a contract will act as a disclaimer to limit the trustee's personal liability to a third party.

D. Liability for Third Parties

A trust can be responsible *to* a third party, as well as responsible *for* a third party. A trustee can be held liable for the actions of a third party if the trustee has delegated tasks to a third party. As we discussed in Chapter 13, a trustee can delegate certain administrative tasks without causing a breach of fiduciary duty. The trustee still remains personally liable for the administration of the trust. The trustee must be careful in choosing the tasks that are delegated, and the persons to whom the tasks are delegated. Tasks that can be delegated are those that are administrative in nature. Typically, an administrative task is one that does not involve any decision making or discretion. Examples of tasks that are administrative are paying the bills, reconciling the checkbook, or collecting rents. Tasks that involve decision making or discretion cannot be delegated. Examples of tasks that cannot be delegated include choosing stocks in a portfolio, purchasing additional rental properties, and liquidating a property.

> ### Practice Tip
>
> **A paralegal should be careful not to take any actions on behalf of a trust or a trustee that could be considered to involve decision making or discretion.**

A trustee is liabile for any malfeasance committed by anyone performing administrative tasks on behalf of the trust. For example, if the property manager who Cynthia hires steals some of the rent each month, Cynthia may still be personally liable for the loss of income to the trust if she did not choose the property manager carefully or did not monitor his or her activities. Cynthia remains responsible for the task of collecting the rents, even though she has delegated that task.

There are circumstances under which professionals can be retained to provide services to the trustee that do not give rise to trustee liability provided the trustee uses due diligence and care in choosing the professionals. For example, Cynthia decides she wants to retain the services of an accountant. She obtains the names of several accountants from recommendations from friends and other professionals. After conducting some of her own Internet research regarding each accountant, she narrows it down to three people with offices in the county in which she lives. She chooses an accountant after conducting interviews with each of them. Cynthia has shown the degree of care, skill, and caution that a reasonably prudent person would exercise in hiring an accountant to deal with her own financial issues. Cynthia has a right to rely on the accountant's advice. If the accountant makes a mistake in preparing the accountings or the tax return for the trust, it is unlikely that Cynthia would be held personally liable for the accountant's mistake. Cynthia cannot delegate the task of signing the tax return, but she would not be personally liable for mistakes in the return.

Cynthia is a layperson who is held to the standard of the reasonably prudent person. Cynthia may be held to a higher standard if she were a professional fiduciary such as an accountant, attorney, or a banking representative.

E. Remedies for Breach of Duty

When a beneficiary, or the grantor, challenges a trust, there are two types of remedies available: **equitable remedies** or money damages. *Equitable remedies* are those remedies that do not involve monetary damages but instead require specific performance in doing or not doing a specific task. In trust litigation, equitable remedies can include the following: removal of the trustee; an **injunction**, or temporary order of the court that stops a party from taking an action the party intends to take; or an order for specific performance requiring the trustee to take action. Very often, a legal challenge to a trust will include elements of all types of remedies included in the causes of action. Some trust agreements may contain an **exculpatory clause**, which is a provision in a trust or contract that relieves one party from liability. An example of an exculpatory clause is the following:

> The trustee, and any substitute or successor trustee, shall not be liable to any beneficiary for the trustee's acts or omissions, except in cases of willful misconduct, bad faith, or gross negligence.

An exculpatory clause that attempts to relieve a party from all liability is generally not enforceable as being against public policy. The clause cannot relieve a trustee of liability for acts that are done in bad faith or are intentionally wrong.

> **Equitable remedies:** those remedies that do not involve monetary damages but instead require specific performance in doing or not doing a specific task
>
> **Injunction:** a temporary order of the court that stops a party from taking an action the party intends to take
>
> **Exculpatory clause:** a provision in a trust or contract that relieves one party from liability

1. Monetary Damages

The most common remedy sought by beneficiaries is money damages. The amount of the damages claimed is calculated in different ways depending on the type of loss claimed. If the assets in the trust have lost value due to some breach of duty by the trustee, the party claiming the loss must be able to show that the trustee's breach caused the loss. Under the common law of trusts, "[t]he first duty of a trustee must be to preserve the trust property intact. To do this, he must not suffer the estate to waste or diminish, or fall out of repair" [George G. Bogert, *The Law of Trusts and Trustees*, §600, at 514. (2d ed.1980) cited in *White Mountain Apache Tribe v. US*, 249 F. 3d 1364 (Fed. Cir. 2001)].

The party claiming the breach must demonstrate what actions the trustee should have taken and the gain in value or profit the asset would have made had those actions been taken versus the current value of the asset. The party challenging the trust could also seek punitive damages against the trustee personally if there is any evidence that the trustee's breach was intentional or willful.

In our example, a breach of duty that might give rise to a monetary damage claim is the loss of value of several of the rental properties making up the trust. Let us assume that the properties are located in an area in which a large industry, employing thousands of people, closed two years prior. The properties have been slowly declining in value. The property manager has advised, several times, to sell the properties and stop the losses. The rental income has continued to decline, the value of the properties is declining, and eventually, the property manager cannot find a tenant for either of the properties. The trustee was advised that she should sell the properties, but she chose to ignore the advice. When she finally looks at the properties that the manager has mentioned, they have been abandoned by the tenants, have fallen into disrepair, and have lost significant value.

Mary, as a beneficiary, could claim that the trustee breached her fiduciary duties. Cynthia had a duty to preserve the value of the property. If the property manager put the recommendations regarding sale of the properties into writing, copies of those letters will need to be obtained. Obtaining appraisals indicating the value when the property manager first suggested selling the properties and the eventual sale price could prove that the loss in value was caused by the trustee's breach of fiduciary duty.

The measurement of monetary damages can also include liability for any profit made by the trustee personally, if the trustee is found to have engaged in self-dealing, or any missed profit.

2. Removal of a Trustee

The beneficiaries may seek to have the trustee removed, in addition to the money damages. If the trustee is found to have breached any of her duties, such as the duty of loyalty, avoiding self-dealing, or any of the duties of a trustee, she can be removed by the court.

The Uniform Trust Code (UTC) provides specific factors that could give rise to an action to remove a trustee, such as a serious breach of trust, lack of cooperation among co-trustees which substantially impairs the administration of the trust, a trustee who is unfit or unwilling to serve or persistently fails to administer the trust effectively; or a substantial change of circumstances or removal that is requested by all of the qualified beneficiaries (Uniform Trust Code, Section 706. Removal of Trustee). The UTC is a national codification of the law of trusts.

State laws also provide guidelines as to when a trustee can be removed. As of January 2013, 26 states and the District of Columbia have adopted the UTC. Two additional states, Kentucky and Mississippi, have introduced the UTC for adoption.

Other states that have not adopted the UTC still provide for the removal of a trustee. For example, the California Probate Code §15642 provides the following:

(a) A trustee may be removed in accordance with the trust instrument, by the court on its own motion, or on petition of a settlor, co-trustee, or beneficiary under Section 17200.

(b) The grounds for removal of a trustee by the court include the following:

   (1) Where the trustee has committed a breach of the trust

   (2) Where the trustee is insolvent or otherwise unfit to administer the trust

   (3) Where hostility or lack of cooperation among co-trustees impairs the administration of the trust

   (4) Where the trustee fails or declines to act

   (5) Where the trustee's compensation is excessive under the circumstances

As indicated in both the Uniform Trust Code and state codes, disagreement between two co-trustees can be the basis of removal of the trustees.

A conflict between the trustee and the beneficiaries could arise because the beneficiaries disagree about the management and administration of the trust. For example, Mary could challenge the trust seeking to have her portion of the principal of the trust distributed to her now, as opposed to many years in the future when the youngest child turns 25. Mary is not happy with the way that Cynthia is managing the trust and is impatient to receive her distribution. Mary questions every expenditure that Cynthia makes for either Joan or Mae. For example, Joan has recently been admitted to a very prestigious, but very expensive, university. Cynthia intends to sell one of the investment properties in order to fund the tuition payments. If Mary disagreed with the sale of the property, she could file a complaint seeking an injunction to stop the sale of the property.

The beneficiaries may also need to apply to the court to have the trustee removed if the trustee is unable to continue in her duties because of incapacitation. If the trust does not provide a method by which a substitute or successor trustee can be appointed, the beneficiaries may have to apply to the court to have a new trustee put in place. It may be necessary for the beneficiaries to produce some evidence of the trustee's incapacitation, such as a medical report or affidavit from a treating physician.

Figure 14-1 provides an example of a California petition to remove a trustee.

F.   Demand for Accounting

A separate cause of action that does not allege breach of duty is a demand for an accounting. The trust can include a provision that either requires the trustee to provide an accounting or waives that requirement. Because a trust is often used in lieu of a will so that the documents remain private, it is very common for a trust to waive the requirement that an annual accounting be filed. An annual filing requirement would defeat the grantor's goal of privacy. In some states, certain types of trusts, such as a trust for a minor, may impose a requirement of annual accounting to be submitted and approved by the probate court.

Figure 14-1. Petition to Remove a Trustee

ATTACHMENT PB-4034

ATTORNEY OR PARTY WITHOUT ATTORNEY *(Name, State Bar Number and Address):* TELEPHONE NUMBER: FAX NUMBER *(Optional):* EMAIL ADDRESS *(Optional):* ATTORNEY FOR *(Name):*	*FOR COURT USE ONLY*
SUPERIOR COURT OF CALIFORNIA, COUNTY OF SANTA CLARA STREET ADDRESS: 191 North First Street MAILING ADDRESS: 191 North First Street CITY AND ZIP CODE: San José, California 95113 BRANCH NAME: Downtown Courthouse - Probate Division	
IN RE *(Name of trust)*:	
PETITION TO REMOVE TRUSTEE	CASE NUMBER:

I, *(my name)*____________________________________, declare:

I am a: ☐ Beneficiary ☐ Settlor ☐ Other: ____________________

I am petitioning to remove *(name)* __________________________as trustee of the estate of the *(name of trust)* ________________________ for the following reasons:

____

____

____

____

____

____

____

____

____

☐ Check here if you need more space. Continue to explain on a separate piece of paper and attach it to this page.

I declare under penalty of perjury of the laws of the State of California that the foregoing is true and correct of my own knowledge.

______________	__________________	__________________
Today's date	Print your name here	Sign your name here

PB-4034 REV 01/01/13 **PETITION TO REMOVE TRUSTEE** (PROBATE) Page 1 of 1 www.courtinfo.ca.gov

Even if there is a provision in the trust that waives the requirement to provide an annual accounting, the common law may still allow the beneficiaries to demand an accounting. Common law has established that a trustee has a duty to keep the beneficiaries informed as to what is happening with the trust. The trustee must maintain accurate records of all receipts and expenditures made on behalf of the trust and if requested, provide an accounting to the beneficiaries.

If the trustee fails to fulfill this duty to account, the beneficiary can file a complaint or petition seeking to compel the trustee to provide the requested information. State law can provide guidance to a beneficiary seeking information about a trust. For example, Texas law allows a beneficiary to make a written demand that the trustee provide a written statement of accounts covering all transactions since the last accounting or since the creation of the trust. If the trustee fails or refuses to deliver the statement within 90 days, any beneficiary of the trust may file suit to compel the trustee to deliver the statement to all beneficiaries of the trust (TEX PR. CODE ANN. §113.151).

A sample of a verified complaint seeking a court order compelling an accounting is shown in Figure 14-2.

EIGHTH JUDICIAL DISTRICT COURT
COUNTY OF GRANT
STATE OF NEW MEXICO

MARY NOFUSS,

    Plaintiff,

v.   D-820-CV-2014

CYNTHIA NOFUSS, TRUSTEE

    Defendant.

COMPLAINT,
DEMAND FOR ACCOUNTING

Mary Nofuss appears through counsel and files this Complaint, Petition for Dissolution, and Demand for Accounting pursuant to New Mexico law. In support thereof, Plaintiff alleges as follows.

JURISDICTION AND VENUE

1. This Court has jurisdiction over the subject matter and the parties to the action, as Plaintiff's claims are brought under New Mexico law over which the State courts have jurisdiction.

Figure 14-2. Sample of a Verified Complaint Seeking a Court Order Compelling an Accounting

(continued)

Figure 14-2. Continued

2. Venue is proper because Plaintiff resides in Grant County, New Mexico. See NMSA 1978, §38-3-1. Plaintiff's causes of action also arose in Grant County.

PARTIES

3. Plaintiff is a resident of Grant County, New Mexico.

4. Defendant, upon information and belief, is a resident of Grant County, New Mexico.

5. Defendant is the Trustee of the Edwin Nofuss Family Trust.

FACTUAL ALLEGATIONS

6. In 2008, Defendant qualified as the Trustee of the Edwin Nofuss Family Trust (hereinafter referred to as the "Trust"). (See, Letter of Trusteeship Exhibit A.)

7. Defendant has maintained control of the assets in the Trust since the creation of the trust.

8. On December 16, 2009, Plaintiff made a written request for information pertaining to the disbursement, income, and principal of the Trust. (See Written demand for information Exhibit B.)

9. On December 29, 2009, Plaintiff, through counsel, suggested to Defendant that an accounting of all transaction from the inception of the trust to the end of 2009 be provided. (See Exhibit C.)

10. On January 7, 2010, Defendant responded through counsel that she was under no obligation to provide an accounting. (See Letter from Counsel Exhibit D.)

COUNT I: DEMAND FOR ACCOUNTING

11. Plaintiff incorporates by reference all preceding paragraphs.

12. Part and parcel to the previous requests, Plaintiff respectfully requests the Court order an accounting of the trust such that these matters can be resolved expeditiously and justly for all parties.

COUNT II: BREACH OF TRUSTEE'S DUTIES

13. Plaintiff incorporates by reference all preceding paragraphs.

14. Defendant breached the duties she owed to Plaintiff by virtue of the declaration of trust and the fiduciary relationship created when she agreed to serve as trustee.

15. This breach caused Plaintiff actual damage.

COUNT III: BAD FAITH/PUNITIVES

16. Plaintiff incorporates by reference all preceding paragraphs.

17. Defendant has acted in bad faith as described in this Complaint.

18. Plaintiff respectfully requests punitive damages to the extent permitted by law.

Figure 14-2. Continued

PRAYER FOR RELIEF

ACCORDINGLY, Plaintiffs seek relief from the Court as follows:

1. Order an accounting, and award an expeditious and just distribution of the assets and liabilities;

2. Award Plaintiff compensatory, punitive, and statutory damages to the extent permitted by law;

3. Award prejudgment and postjudgment interest to the extent permitted by law;

4. Award such other and further relief as is just and proper.

DEMAND FOR JURY TRIAL

Plaintiff hereby demands a jury trial for all issues triable by jury.

RESPECTFULLY SUBMITTED,

_____

ATTORNEY AT LAW

VERIFICATION

STATE OF NEW MEXICO   )

)SS.

COUNTY OF GRANT   )

I, MARY NOFUSS, being first duly sworn upon oath, depose and state that I am a Plaintiff in this case and that I read the above and foregoing COMPLAINT. I know the contents thereof, and the same is true and correct to the best of my knowledge and belief.

_____

MARY NOFUSS

SUBSCRIBED AND SWORN to before me this _____ day of _____, 2014, by MARY NOFUSS.

_____

MARY NOFUSS

My Commission Expires:_____

In this sample complaint, it is assumed that the trust was created in 2008 and that an accounting was requested in 2009 after the trust has only been in existence for one year. If a trust had been in existence for many years and none of the beneficiaries had ever requested an accounting, the beneficiaries' right to demand an accounting from the inception of the trust could be limited by a **statute of limitations**. A *statute of limitations* is a state law that restricts the time within which legal proceedings may be

Statute of limitations: a state law that restricts the time within which legal proceedings may be brought depending on whether the cause of action involves a contract, personal injury, libel, fraud, or other claim brought depending on whether the cause of action involves a contract, personal injury, libel, fraud, or other claim. The trust could be considered a contract under state law, which would limit the time in which a demand for an accounting could be brought to the time deadline for contract claims. The defendant can also assert that the plaintiff's claim is barred by the **doctrine of laches**. The *doctrine of laches* is an equitable defense asserting that the plaintiff slept on his or her rights, or that there was unreasonable delay in pursuing a right or claim in such a way as to prejudice the opposing party. Laches and the statute of limitations are example of affirmative defenses that are raised by the defendant in answering a complaint.

> **Doctrine of laches:** an equitable defense asserting that plaintiff slept on his or her rights, or that there was unreasonable delay in pursuing a right or claim in such a way as to prejudice the opposing party

In preparing the accounting, the trustee must ensure that expenses incurred must be properly allocated among trust assets. For example, in the Nofuss Family Trust, there are two rental properties. Ordinary and current expenses of those two properties, such as property taxes, insurance, repairs, maintenance, and management fees, should be paid from rental income generated by the properties. Any expenses that are extraordinary, such as expenses for improvements, could be paid from the principal. It would be unfair to Mary to pay the expenses associated with the properties from the funds held in the Merrill Lynch account, while distributing all of the rental income to Joan and Mae. If the trust owns several rental properties, and the trustee is unsure of the way in which costs should be allocated, the trustee can delegate the duty of preparing an accounting to a certified public accountant.

G.   Successor Trustee Liability

As we learned previously, a substitute trustee is one who assumes the role of trustee after the original trustee. A successor trustee takes over after the original trustee has qualified and served as trustee. A successor trustee is not liable for the misappropriation of funds or breach of duty of the prior trustee, unless the successor knew about the actions of the prior trustee and did nothing to stop them and did not inform the beneficiaries once the breach was discovered.

By way of example, let us assume that Cynthia had been redirecting some of the rental income received from the properties. She wants to retire and move to Port St. Lucie, Florida, to watch the New York Mets during spring training. She enlists the help of her cousin to take over as trustee with the agreement of the beneficiaries. As they are going over the books, the cousin finds out Cynthia has been keeping some of the money from the rents. The cousin never confronts Cynthia with this knowledge. The cousin qualifies as the successor trustee but does not take any action to get the money back from Cynthia. The cousin, as successor trustee, is now liable for the breach of duty committed by Cynthia during the time in which she served as trustee.

H.   Famous Trust: An Example

In Chapter 12 we discussed general estate litigation. Estate litigation is widely reported, and many examples of litigated cases can be found. The decedent's will, which governs the estate, becomes a public document when it is admitted to probate.

Trusts are not necessarily public documents unless the trust is a testamentary trust that is contained in a will that is admitted to probate. Many clients will choose to create a trust specifically for the reason that they want everything to remain private. In a will, the location of assets, names of beneficiaries, amount of distribution, and everything about the estate becomes public. In a trust, the grantor is able to be much more private.

One such very private trust is that established by William Randolph Hearst, founder of the Hearst publishing and communications empire. Hearst died in 1951 leaving a will that established a trust and a board of trustees to administer the Hearst Foundation, the William Randolph Hearst Foundation, and the family trust that now owns the Hearst Corporation. The trust created in his will does not terminate until the last of his grandchildren, who were alive at the time of his death, have died. Today, the Hearst Corporation is a multi-billion-dollar corporation that owns many newspapers, magazines, and television stations. The company has always been privately owned and continues to be controlled by the board of trustees, which consists of five family members and eight former executives.

In 1974, Hearst's granddaughter Patricia was kidnapped, and a huge ransom was demanded. The trustees claimed that members of the Hearst family, including minors and family members who have changed their surname by marriage, would be in grave danger of their lives and property if their identities were discovered through use of the probate files in Estate of Hearst. The trustees petitioned the Court in California to obtain an order cutting off public access to and sealing the probate files in Estate of Hearst. See *Estate of Hearst*, 67 Cal. App. 3d 777. The Hearst Family Trust has been involved in several different lawsuits, many from the beneficiaries.

Summary

A trust, and the trustee, is subject to litigation by any party that has standing. Trust litigation arises from liability to the beneficiaries for trustee's breach of fiduciary duty, or breach of the trust, or liability to third parties. The relief sought by the beneficiaries can include damages from the trustee, removal of the trustee, or both. Beneficiaries can also demand an accounting. A successor trustee may have continued liability if the successor knows about the previous trustee's breach of duty.

Review Questions

1. What are the two types of remedies a plaintiff can request in a challenge to a trust?

2. Research the state laws of the state in which you live. Has your state adopted the Uniform Trust Code?

3. What are two circumstances under which third party liability could be asserted against a trust?

4. Joan has been the beneficiary of a trust for 14 years. She wants to file a claim that the payment she was given in year two of the trust was insufficient. Her claim is subject to
   a. Indemnification
   b. Equitable remedies
   c. Doctrine of laches
   d. None of the above

5. Protection from liability can be found in an
   a. Indemnification
   b. Injunction
   c. Exculpatory clause
   d. Both *a* and *c*

6. For each of the following tasks, mark the task *A* for an administrative task that can be delegated, or *D* for a decision-making task that cannot be delegated:

Notifying beneficiaries of the filing of an accounting	A	D
Signing a tax return	A	D
Preparing an accounting of trust assets	A	D
Reviewing investment advice	A	D
Hiring an attorney or accountant	A	D
Paying trust expenses	A	D
Signing a contract for services to the trust	A	D

True or False

1. T F A beneficiary has standing to challenge a trust.

2. T F If a trustee qualifies and serves as trustee but then retires, the next trustee is the substitute trustee.

3. T F A trustee can be removed by the court if he or she is no longer able to fulfill the duties of a trustee.

4. T F The beneficiaries owe a duty of loyalty to the trustee and cannot challenge the trustee's actions.

5. T F A trustee can pay himself or herself a salary from the trust.

6. T F An exculpatory clause in a trust does not relieve a trustee of liability for intentional misconduct.

7. T F When the grantor of a trust dies, the trust must be filed like a will and becomes a public document.

8. T F An appraisal report may be necessary to prove a loss in value.

9. T   F   A co-trustee has standing to sue a trust or the other co-trustees.

10. T   F   Both administrative and decision-making tasks can be delegated by the trustee.

Drafting Exercise

Eleanor Branstone created a trust in her will for the benefit of her three adult children. Eleanor died in 2011. Alfred and Barry are both married and well established in their careers. Their sister Carol has had problems with drugs and alcohol, and her father was concerned that any money she received from an inheritance would be wasted. Alfred is the trustee. The trust allows for the trustee to make discretionary payments of income to Carol, but Alfred has not been making any payments, indicating to Carol that he is saving her money for her. Carol has been asking her brother for the last few months to provide her with information as to what monies are in the trust, how the money is invested, and what income is generated. Alfred has refused to provide the necessary information.

Using the sample complaint form included in this chapter, draft a complaint for Carol demanding an accounting.

Key Terms

Disclaimer
Doctrine of laches
Equitable remedies
Exculpatory clause
Indemnification

Injunction
Standing
Statute of limitations
Surety bond
Tort

Power of Attorney and Medical Directive

A complete estate plan consists of three documents: a last will and testament, a power of attorney, and some form of advance medical directive. In Chapter 4 we examined how to create a simple will. Now we will look at a power of attorney and medical directive. There will also be some general information about the need for a guardianship or conservatorship if those documents are not in place. This chapter will also include a brief discussion about medical documents that might be considered as part of an estate plan, that are prepared for someone with a terminal illness.

A.   Power of Attorney

A **power of attorney (POA)** is a legal document that is written authorization to act on someone else's behalf for financial purposes, such as for banking, business purposes, the purchase or sale of real estate, or any other legal purpose. The person signing the POA, the one authorizing the other person to act for him or her, is called the **principal.** The person authorized to act on behalf of the principal is called the **agent or attorney-in-fact.** Powers of attorney are common and are used in various areas of the law, not just estate planning.

The concept of the power of attorney was created in 1969 when the National Conference of Commissioners on Uniform State Laws promulgated the Uniform Probate Code (UPC). Ten years later the provisions of the code dealing with the durable power of attorney were modified and published as the Uniform Durable Power of Attorney Act (UDPA). All 50 states recognize some version of the durable power of attorney, having adopted either the UDPA or the UPC, or some variation of them. The Uniform Power of Attorney Act (UPOAA) was promulgated in 2006 to address issues that were not addressed by the UPC or the UPDA. The UPOAA supersedes UPDA and the sections of the UPC that addressed powers of attorney. The provisions contained in a durable power of attorney still vary

Power of attorney (POA): a written authorization to act on someone else's behalf for financial purposes, such as for banking, business purposes, the purchase or sale of real estate, or any other legal purpose

Principal: the person who signs the POA, authorizing the other person to act for him or her

Agent or attorney-in-fact: the person authorized to act on behalf of the principal from state to state despite repeated attempts to create a uniform law for all 50 states. Samples of powers of attorney from different states can be found at the American Bar Association Web site, or various other Web sites. Suggested links to possible sources of form powers of attorney are included on the companion Web site.

A power of attorney is most often used to take financial actions on behalf of the principal. Each state has specified what can, and cannot, be done using a power of attorney. There are certain powers that cannot be delegated using a power of attorney. For example, the principal cannot give the agent the power to make a will or even change an existing will. The testator of a will must be competent to make a will. If the testator is not competent, he or she cannot make a will, and the agent who was chosen cannot make the will for the testator. The agent also cannot change a life insurance beneficiary unless state law specifically allows that power to be granted, and the power of attorney document specifically grants that power. These restrictions on an agent's powers are designed to prevent **self-dealing.** *Self-dealing* is when the agent does something to benefit himself or herself instead of acting in the principal's best interest.

Self-dealing: when the agent does something to benefit himself or herself instead of acting in the principal's best interest

The requirements for being able to sign a power of attorney are similar to those of making a will. The principal must be competent in order to be able to sign a power of attorney. The level of competency is low and would be comparable to that required to execute a will. A power of attorney is automatically terminated when the principal dies, although most states make allowances for the actions taken by an attorney-in-fact after the principal died, if the attorney-in-fact was not aware of the principal's death. After the principal dies, the executor of the principal's estate takes over to deal with the assets of the deceased principal.

A power of attorney can state that the authority granted in the power of attorney will terminate on a specific date. The principal also has the right to revoke or terminate the power, as long as the principal is competent. The revocation of a power of attorney must be in writing, and notice of the revocation should be delivered to the attorney-in-fact. The revocation can be something simple, such as a written letter indicating that the power of attorney is revoked. Notice that the power of attorney was revoked should also be supplied to any third party that allowed the attorney-in-fact to act on behalf of the principal. If notice that the power of attorney is not provided, third parties, such as banks, could continue to rely on the power of attorney.

Durable power of attorney: one in which the grant of authority survives any period of disability of the principal

There are two basic types of power of attorney: durable and springing. A **durable power of attorney** is one in which the grant of authority survives any period of disability of the principal. This means that if a power of attorney is granted today, and many months or years from now the principal becomes incapacitated, the power of attorney remains valid and can still be used by the agent. An example of specific language that makes a power of attorney durable is the following:

> The powers you give your agent in this durable power of attorney are effective immediately and will continue to exist even if you can no longer make your own decisions. You can amend or change this durable power of attorney only by executing a new durable power of attorney. You have the right to revoke or terminate this durable power of attorney at any time, so long as you are competent.

A **springing power of attorney** is one in which the authority of the agent does not "spring" into being until the principal becomes incapacitated, or until some specific date. An example of language that identifies the power of attorney as being a springing power of attorney is the following:

> This document is a SPRINGING POWER OF ATTORNEY that will not come into effect until two persons who are doctors or psychologists declare that you are mentally incapacitated. At that point this document would come into effect and your attorney would have legal authority to manage your affairs.

General durable powers of attorney are usually included as part of an estate plan and are filed away with the other documents until needed. Each state uses its own state-specific format, and most lawyers customize the standard forms to fit the client's individual needs. The UPC provides a form power of attorney at Section 5B-301, as shown in Figure 15-1.

The form power of attorney from the UPC makes it clear that it cannot be used for healthcare decisions. An agent, a successor agent, and even a second successor agent should be named. Appointing three individuals ensures that someone will be available to assist the principal, if necessary. If the agent appointed is unable or unwilling to serve, the successor agent can take over. The form allows the principal to check off the powers that he or she wants the agent to have and those powers that the agent does not have.

Any type of form power of attorney, especially one with boxes that can be checked off, must be used with caution because the use of a power of attorney can have unintended consequences. For example, if checked, the agent could have the authority to change a beneficiary designation on a life insurance policy or delegate decision-making authority to another person. Many insurance and investment companies do not allow a power of attorney agent to change a beneficiary designation. If the power of attorney agent did change the beneficiary to himself or herself, this would be considered "self-dealing" in violation of the power of attorney statutes. The agent should also not take actions that benefit the agent's family such as changing a beneficiary to the agent's spouse or children. The agent will have full authority to buy and sell the principal's assets but must do so within the "prudent investor" standard discussed.

An agent appointed under a power of attorney is a fiduciary who is responsible for managing the funds of another person. The agent must adhere to the prudent investor standard that uses modern portfolio theory to guide investment decisions and requires risk versus return analyses. The fiduciary's performance is measured on the performance of the entire portfolio rather than individual investments. This means that an agent might make a single bad investment decision and still be compliant with the standard if the overall performance of the portfolio is good. The prudent investor standard and the Uniform Prudent Investor Act (UPIA) were discussed in more detail in Chapter 5. For purposes of this chapter it is sufficient to understand that the agent operating under a power of attorney is a fiduciary. The way in which the agent handles the funds of the principal will be evaluated in accordance with the UPIA.

Springing power of attorney: one in which the authority of the agent does not "spring" into being until the principal becomes incapacitated

Figure 15-1. UPC Form Power of Attorney

STATUTORY FORM POWER OF ATTORNEY
IMPORTANT INFORMATION

This power of attorney authorizes another person (your agent) to make decisions concerning your property for you (the principal). Your agent will be able to make decisions and act with respect to your property (including your money) whether or not you are able to act for yourself. The meaning of authority over subjects listed on this form is explained in the Uniform Power of Attorney Act.

This power of attorney does not authorize the agent to make healthcare decisions for you.

You should select someone you trust to serve as your agent. Unless you specify otherwise, generally the agent's authority will continue until you die or revoke the power of attorney or the agent resigns or is unable to act for you.

Your agent is entitled to reasonable compensation unless you state otherwise in the Special Instructions. This form provides for designation of one agent. If you wish to name more than one agent you may name a co-agent in the Special Instructions. Co-agents are not required to act together unless you include that requirement in the Special Instructions.

If your agent is unable or unwilling to act for you, your power of attorney will end unless you have named a successor agent. You may also name a second successor agent.

This power of attorney becomes effective immediately unless you state otherwise in the Special Instructions. If you have questions about the power of attorney or the authority you are granting to your agent, you should seek legal advice before signing this form.

DESIGNATION OF AGENT

I _____ name the following (Name of Principal)

person as my agent:

Name of Agent: _____

Agent's Address: _____

Agent's Telephone Number: _____

DESIGNATION OF SUCCESSOR AGENT(S) (OPTIONAL)

If my agent is unable or unwilling to act for me, I name as my successor agent:

Name of Successor Agent: _____

Successor Agent's Address: _____`_____

Successor Agent's Telephone Number: _____

If my successor agent is unable or unwilling to act for me, I name as my second successor agent:

Name of Second Successor Agent: _____

Second Successor Agent's Address: _____

Second Successor Agent's Telephone Number: _____ _____

Figure 15-1. Continued

GRANT OF GENERAL AUTHORITY

I grant my agent and any successor agent general authority to act for me with respect to the following subjects as defined in the Uniform Power of Attorney Act [insert citation].

(INITIAL each subject you want to include in the agent's general authority. If you wish to grant general authority over all of the subjects you may initial "All Preceding Subjects" instead of initialing each subject.)

(___) Real Property

(___) Tangible Personal Property

(___) Stocks and Bonds

(___) Commodities and Options

(___) Banks and Other Financial Institutions

(___) Operation of Entity or Business

(___) Insurance and Annuities

(___) Estates, Trusts, and Other Beneficial Interests

(___) Claims and Litigation

(___) Personal and Family Maintenance

(___) Benefits from Governmental Programs or Civil or Military Service

(___) Retirement Plans

(___) Taxes

(___) All Preceding Subjects

GRANT OF SPECIFIC AUTHORITY (OPTIONAL)

My agent MAY NOT do any of the following specific acts for me UNLESS I have INITIALED the specific authority listed below:

(CAUTION: Granting any of the following will give your agent the authority to take actions that could significantly reduce your property or change how your property is distributed at your death. INITIAL ONLY the specific authority you WANT to give your agent.)

(___) Create, amend, revoke, or terminate an inter vivos trust

(___) Make a gift, subject to the limitations of the Uniform Power of Attorney Act Section 217 of the act] and any special instructions in this power of attorney

(___) Create or change rights of survivorship

(___) Create or change a beneficiary designation

(___) Authorize another person to exercise the authority granted under this power of attorney

(___) Waive the principal's right to be a beneficiary of a joint and survivor annuity, including a survivor benefit under a retirement plan

---

(continued)

Figure 15-1. Continued

(____) Exercise fiduciary powers that the principal has authority to delegate

(____) Disclaim or refuse an interest in property, including a power of appointment

LIMITATION ON AGENT'S AUTHORITY

An agent that is not my ancestor, spouse, or descendant MAY NOT use my property to benefit the agent or a person to whom the agent owes an obligation of support unless I have included that authority in the Special Instructions.

SPECIAL INSTRUCTIONS (OPTIONAL)

You may give special instructions on the following lines:

_____

_____

_____

_____

_____

_____

_____

_____

EFFECTIVE DATE

This power of attorney is effective immediately unless I have stated otherwise in the Special Instructions.

NOMINATION OF [CONSERVATOR OR GUARDIAN] (OPTIONAL)

If it becomes necessary for a court to appoint a [conservator or guardian] of my estate or [guardian] of my person, I nominate the following person(s) for appointment:

Name of Nominee for [conservator or guardian] of my estate:

_____

Nominee's Address: _____

Nominee's Telephone Number:_____

Name of Nominee for [guardian] of my person: _____

Nominee's Address: _____

Nominee's Telephone Number: _____

Figure 15-1. Continued

RELIANCE ON THIS POWER OF ATTORNEY

Any person, including my agent, may rely upon the validity of this power of attorney or a copy of it unless that person knows it has terminated or is invalid.

SIGNATURE AND ACKNOWLEDGMENT

_____   _____

Your Signature   Date

_____

Your Name Printed

_____

Your Address

_____

Your Telephone Number

State of _____ [County] of _____

This document was acknowledged before me on _____, _____

by _____

(Name of Principal)

_____

Signature of Notary

(Seal, if any)

My commission expires: _____

This document prepared by:

_____

_____

Practice Tip

Advise the client to keep the fully executed power of attorney in a safe location that could be accessible by the person appointed as the agent. A safe-deposit box is not necessarily a good choice, unless the agent appointed has authority to enter the box.

An example of the use of a durable power of attorney is the following: A client, Bertha Jorgenson, asked the attorney to prepare a durable power of attorney many years ago. The power of attorney, dated July 2, 2005, names Bertha's niece Elizabeth as Bertha's attorney-in-fact. Bertha's health has declined significantly in the last few years, and Elizabeth has been using the power of attorney to access Bertha's bank accounts to pay bills and provide for care for Bertha. Bertha can continue to have input in the decisions Elizabeth makes for her, but ultimately, Elizabeth has the authority to make financial decisions. Elizabeth recently signed a contract with a care agency to provide a full-time home health aide to live with her aunt. When Elizabeth signs the contract, she should be advised to sign as follows:

Bertha Jorgenson

_____

Bertha Jorgenson, by her Power of
Attorney, Elizabeth Jorgenson

Practice Tip

It is often suggested that a client who is using a power of attorney to manage a principal's assets purchase a self-inking stamp at an office supply store that can be used to stamp this designation under the signature line. Having the stamp will avoid the attorney-in-fact forgetting the proper wording, or not using the proper wording because he or she gets tired of writing it if signing several documents at one time.

Because Bertha's power of attorney is durable, it remains valid when Bertha's health continues to decline and she later becomes incapacitated. Elizabeth will continue to be able to make financial decisions on Bertha's behalf, but must always make decisions that are in Bertha's best interest. If, while she is still competent, Bertha discovered that Elizabeth was misusing the power of attorney, Bertha could decide to revoke the power of attorney. Bertha would then write a letter to Elizabeth as follows:

> *Please be advised that the power of attorney of Bertha Jorgenson, dated July 2, 2005, naming you as the attorney-in-fact, is hereby revoked.*

_____

BERTHA JORGENSON

Subscribed, sworn to, and acknowledged before me by **BERTHA JORGENSON** *this_____ day of _____, 201_.*

_____

NOTARY PUBLIC (or Attorney)

The durable power of attorney can be general, granting full authority to the agent, or it can be limited to a specific task. Limited powers of attorney are very common in the purchase of real property. For example, a young couple is about to have their first baby, and they are also trying to buy a house. The wife grants her sister a power of attorney to sign any and all documents necessary to complete the purchase of their dream home in case she goes into labor before the closing. When the wife is out of the hospital, the power of attorney is terminated. There are situations in which a general durable power of attorney will not be accepted. Many financial institutions, investment companies, and banks have their own specific power of attorney document and will only recognize an agent's authority if that specific document is used. The IRS has its own particular form that must be used (http://www.irs.gov/pub/irs-pdf/f2848.pdf).

A general durable power of attorney must always be given cautiously. The completed document should be kept in a safe place that cannot be accessed by anyone other than the intended attorney-in-fact, such as a home safe or safe-deposit box. The attorney-in-fact is a fiduciary acting on behalf of the principal and owes the principal a duty to always act in the principal's best interest. If the attorney-in-fact engages in self-dealing or misappropriates the principal's money, the attorney-in-fact is said to have breached his or her fiduciary duty.

Practice Tip

Clients should be cautioned against making copies of the power of attorney. If the power of attorney must be used to access a bank account, for example, the attorney-in-fact will need to take the original power of attorney to the bank, meet with a bank manager, and present the original along with proper identification, and then the bank manager will make a photocopy of the power of attorney. It would not be sufficient to bring a copy to the bank.

The attorney-in-fact appointed in a springing power of attorney does not have the authority to act unless the principal become incapacitated. Each state defines the term *incapacitated* in its own way. Different requirements must be met for the springing power of attorney to become effective. For example, the springing power of attorney may require that two doctors find the principal to be incapacited before the authority in the POA is activated. In most instances, once the attorney-in-fact has the principal declared incapacitated and starts using the springing power of attorney, the principal cannot revoke the springing power of attorney.

The general durable power of attorney may be more appealing because it does not require the principal to be found incapacitated, and it can be revoked. In many circumstances the need for assistance comes gradually. Maybe a client needs assistance reviewing investment decisions but can still pay his or her own bills. With a general durable power of attorney, the client can direct which tasks require assistance and which do not. The client can also change who is designated as the attorney-in-fact. There is no need to be declared incapacitated. These factors may make the general durable power of attorney a better choice for the client.

For another client, there may be a fear that her autonomy or decision-making authority will be taken away prematurely. The client may not want or feel she needs someone to help her in any way until such time as she is completely incapacitated. The springing power of attorney may seem a better choice to address these concerns.

B. Advance Medical Directive

Advance healthcare directive: a document that appoints a health-care agent and records instructions for future healthcare decisions

An **advance healthcare directive** is a document that appoints a healthcare agent and records instructions for future healthcare decisions. Advance healthcare directives are recognized in all 50 states and the District of Columbia, but each state's law is different. There are surprising differences in how and when each state implements its version of the advance healthcare directive. The differences in the states' laws have arisen from various well-known state and federal cases such as *In re Quinlan*, 70 N.J. 10, 355 A.2d 647 (N.J. 1976); and *Cruzan v. Director, Missouri Dept. of Health*, 497 U.S. 261 (1990).

In *Quinlan*, the New Jersey Supreme Court was the first to address the issue of the "right to die." The Court held that under both the U.S. and New Jersey constitutions, Karen Quinlan had the right to decline medical treatment because such right was incorporated into an individual's right of privacy. In *Cruzan*, the U.S. Supreme Court recognized that every adult with capacity has the right to refuse treatment, even life-sustaining treatment, based on the Fourteenth Amendment. The U.S. Supreme Court also upheld a state's right to require that evidence of an incompetent's wishes as to the withdrawal of life-sustaining treatment be proved by clear and convincing evidence. After the U.S. Supreme Court ruling in *Cruzan*, the various states took a number of different paths in their right-to-die jurisprudence.

Since *Quinlan* and *Cruzan*, there have been many cases that have concerned the "right-to die" issue. In order to protect a person's future healthcare decision-making rights, many more states began authorizing advance healthcare directives so that healthcare decisions could be protected even if that person lost capacity. Due to many different influences, like religious, cultural, or bioethical issues, the states have come up with a plethora of different (and often contradictory) requirements in the execution and recognition of advance healthcare directives.

In 1990, the first federal statute dealing with the right to record future healthcare decisions, including what to do at the end of life, was passed. The law is called the Patient Self-Determination Act (PSDA). The PSDA requires Medicare-participating healthcare facilities to ask all patients if they have an advance healthcare directive and to provide information to patients about healthcare decision-making rights. Pursuant to the PSDA, an advance healthcare directive is defined as a "written instruction, such as a living will or durable power of attorney for health care, recognized under state law (whether statutory or as recognized by the courts of the state) relating to the provision of health care when the individual is incapacitated." Section 489.100. The PSDA did not create the right to record healthcare decisions; instead it required that the public be educated about the existence of that right and the need to record their wishes.

In 1993, the National Conference of Commissioners on Uniform State Laws approved the Uniform Health-Care Decisions Act (UHCD Act). The goal of the UHCD Act was to create greater uniformity. Despite the adoption of the UHCD Act by several states, there are still vast differences in the advance healthcare directive laws of the 50 states and the District of Columbia. In more recent years, the subject of living wills and advance directives was in the national news because of the Terri Schiavo case in Florida. The Schiavo case was a 15-year legal battle between Terri Schiavo's parents and her husband. Schiavo suffered a full cardiac arrest and as a result also suffered brain damage. After significant physical rehabilitation therapy was unsuccessful, she was determined to be in a persistent vegetative state. Her husband petitioned the court for permission to terminate life support while her parents opposed that application. After many years passed during which time the petition was granted, appealed, reversed, granted, and the appeal ran out, the feeding tube was removed, and Schiavo passed away.

Unlike the *Quinlan* and *Cruzan* cases, which were both ground-breaking legal decisions that led to the adoption of living will laws, the Schiavo matter involved well-established case law. The dispute in Schiavo was not about what the law should be, but instead was a dispute between family members over what Schiavo's wishes would have been.

A big difference among the states is what each state calls its advance healthcare directive document. The different types of documents that have been created by the states can be divided into three general categories. First, there are living wills, or advance directives. Second, there are durable powers of attorney for healthcare. Third, there are single documents that encompass both a living will and a power of attorney for healthcare.

A living will or advance healthcare directive can inform healthcare providers about the type of medical care that an individual wants provided or withheld. It will give instruction for medical treatment in the event of incapacity at the end of life, typically because of a terminal illness or a persistent vegetative state. Some states call the advance healthcare directive a "declaration." For example, Illinois law identifies the advance healthcare directive document as a "declaration." However, the document functions in the exact manner as an advance heathcare directive or a living will.

A durable power of attorney for healthcare is a document that identifies an agent to serve as a healthcare proxy or decision maker for the principal. Typically, the agent has broad decision-making authority when acting in this surrogate role and is not limited to decision making at the end of life, so no finding that the patient suffers from a terminal illness is necessary. States vary on whether or not the principal has to be found to be incapacitated in order for the agent to begin exercising his or her powers. Most states do not require such a finding, because if the principal is able to make healthcare decisions, healthcare providers are going to continue to look to the principal to make those decisions. It is only when the principal is unable to make those decisions that the healthcare proxy is asked to step in.

Certain states, for example, New Jersey, allow a single document to accomplish both tasks of appointing an agent, as in a healthcare power of attorney, and listing end-of-life healthcare instructions, as in a living will. Other states, like California, allow for different rights to be set forth in separate documents or combined into one document. Despite the statutory names for the advance medical directive, many clients still refer to the document as a "living will." It is important to learn the correct terminology for the state in which the paralegal is working. Forms for the advance directive used in each of the 50 states can be found at several Web sites (http://www .caringinfo.org/i4a/pages/index.cfm?pageid=3289; http://uslwr.com/formslist.shtm). The UHCD Act also includes the form shown in Figure 15-2 within the Act.

As indicated in the form, the principal has the right to choose to refuse any life-saving medical intervention. In addition, the principal can choose to be pain free, even if the administration of pain medications shortens life. The form also calls for the appointment of a healthcare representative and an alternate in case the first person chosen is not available or is unwilling to serve. The principal must sign the form in front of two witnesses who also must sign the form. In some states, having the form witnessed and signed by a notary public can be used in lieu of two witnesses.

It may be necessary for a client to sign a power of attorney and/or an advance medical directive with a "mark" instead of a full signature. In Chapter 4 we discussed the signature of a will using a mark. The same wording for the notary's signature can be used if a client is signing a power of attorney or advance medical directive using a mark.

STATE OF _____   )
                                                ss:
COUNTY OF _____)

   BE IT REMEMBERED *that on this* _____ *day of* _____, *201__, before me, the subscribed, a Notary Public of the State of* _____, *personally appeared FRANK BRYCE, who I am satisfied is the person mentioned in the within document, and I having first made known to him the contents thereof, he did place his mark upon this document, intending to give legal effect to same, and did acknowledge that he signed, sealed, and delivered the same as and for his voluntary act and deed for the uses and purposes therein expressed.*

                                                            _____
                                                            NOTARY PUBLIC

Practice Tip

An advance medical directive does not necessarily have to be prepared by an attorney. There are a variety of different forms available. A client entering the hospital will have an opportunity to provide a copy of his or her advance medical directive, or to complete a form available at the hospital. Even if a client has completed one of these forms, suggest that it be reviewed by an attorney to ensure that the form complies with the client's wishes.

Figure 15-2. Power of Attorney for Healthcare

POWER OF ATTORNEY FOR HEALTHCARE

PART 1. DESIGNATION OF AGENT

I designate the following individual as my agent to make healthcare decisions for me:

_____

(name of individual you choose as agent)

_____

(address) (city) (state) (zip code)

_____

(home phone) (work phone)

OPTIONAL: If I revoke my agent's authority or if my agent is not willing, able, or reasonably available to make a healthcare decision for me, I designate as my first alternate agent:

_____

(name of individual you choose as first alternate agent)

_____

(address) (city) (state) (zip code)

_____

(home phone) (work phone)

OPTIONAL: If I revoke the authority of my agent and first alternate agent or if neither is willing, able, or reasonably available to make a healthcare decision for me, I designate as my second alternate agent:

_____

(name of individual you choose as second alternate agent)

_____

(address) (city) (state) (zip code)

(2) AGENT'S AUTHORITY: My agent is authorized to make all healthcare decisions for me, including decisions to provide, withhold, or withdraw artificial nutrition and hydration and all other forms of healthcare to keep me alive, except as I state here:

_____

_____

_____

(Add additional sheets if needed.)

(3) WHEN AGENT'S AUTHORITY BECOMES EFFECTIVE: My agent's authority becomes effective when my primary physician determines that I am unable to make my own healthcare decisions unless I mark the following box. If I mark this box [ ], my agent's authority to make healthcare decisions for me takes effect immediately.

(continued)

Figure 15-2. Continued

(4) AGENT'S OBLIGATION: My agent shall make healthcare decisions for me in accordance with this power of attorney for healthcare, any instructions I give in Part 2 of this form, and my other wishes to the extent known to my agent. To the extent my wishes are unknown, my agent shall make healthcare decisions for me in accordance with what my agent determines to be in my best interest. In determining my best interest, my agent shall consider my personal values to the extent known to my agent.

(5) NOMINATION OF GUARDIAN: If a guardian of my person needs to be appointed for me by a court, I nominate the agent designated in this form. If that agent is not willing, able, or reasonably available to act as guardian, I nominate the alternate agents whom I have named, in the order designated.

PART 2. INSTRUCTIONS FOR HEALTHCARE

If you are satisfied to allow your agent to determine what is best for you in making end-of-life decisions, you need not fill out this part of the form. If you do fill out this part of the form, you may strike any wording you do not want.

(6) END-OF-LIFE DECISIONS: I direct that my healthcare providers and others involved in my care provide, withhold, or withdraw treatment in accordance with the choice I have marked below.

> [ ] (a) Choice Not To Prolong Life
>
> I do not want my life to be prolonged if (i) I have an incurable and irreversible condition that will result in my death within a relatively short time, (ii) I become unconscious and, to a reasonable degree of medical certainty, I will not regain consciousness, or (iii) the likely risks and burdens of treatment would outweigh the expected benefits, OR
>
> [ ] (b) Choice To Prolong Life
>
> I want my life to be prolonged as long as possible within the limits of generally accepted healthcare standards.

(7) ARTIFICIAL NUTRITION AND HYDRATION: Artificial nutrition and hydration must be provided, withheld, or withdrawn in accordance with the choice I have made in paragraph (6) unless I mark the following box. If I mark this box [ ], artificial nutrition and hydration must be provided regardless of my condition and regardless of the choice I have made in paragraph (6).

(8) RELIEF FROM PAIN: Except as I state in the following space, I direct that treatment for alleviation of pain or discomfort be provided at all times, even if it hastens my death:

_____

_____

Figure 15-2. Continued

(9) OTHER WISHES: (If you do not agree with any of the optional choices above and wish to write your own, or if you wish to add to the instructions you have given above, you may do so here.) I direct that:

_____

_____

(Add additional sheets if needed.)

PART 3. DONATION OF ORGANS AT DEATH (OPTIONAL)

(10) Upon my death (mark applicable box)

        [ ] (a) I give any needed organs, tissues, or parts, OR

        [ ] (b) I give the following organs, tissues, or parts only

        □ _____

(c) My gift is for the following purposes (strike any of the following you do not want)

        (i) Transplant

        (ii) Therapy

        (iii) Research

        (iv) Education

PART 4. PRIMARY PHYSICIAN (OPTIONAL)

(11) I designate the following physician as my primary physician:

_____

(name of physician)

_____

(address) (city) (state) (zip code)

_____

(phone)

OPTIONAL: If the physician I have designated above is not willing, able, or reasonably available to act as my primary physician, I designate the following physician as my primary physician:

_____

(name of physician)

_____

(address) (city) (state) (zip code)

_____

(phone)

(continued)

Figure 15-2. Continued

(12) EFFECT OF COPY: A copy of this form has the same effect as the original.

First witness

_____

(print name)

_____

(address)

_____

(city) (state)

_____

(signature of witness)

_____

(date)

Second witness

_____

(print name)

_____

(address)

_____

(city) (state)

_____

(signature of witness)

_____

(date)

An example of how an advance medical directive operates is the following: Bob Ogden is admitted to the hospital with symptoms of a stroke. He has a medical directive appointing his oldest daughter Meriope as his healthcare surrogate, and she is authorized to make medical decisions for him and to advocate the end-of-life decisions that he has made and recorded. Mr. Ogden is in critical condition, and after consultation with his doctors, his daughter advises his doctors that her father did not want to be kept alive on a respirator. Mr. Ogden survives the initial stroke but is completely debilitated. Doctors have advised that there is very little brain activity. It is unlikely he will recover any movement or regain consciousness. Meriope refuses to sign the consent to allow the hospital to insert the breathing tube.

Practice Tip

A client can make many copies of his or her advance medical directive. The client should be advised that the advance medical directive can be given to each physician seen on a regular basis, as well as copies made available if admission to a hospital is required.

If there is no advance healthcare directive in place, it may be necessary to appoint a surrogate decision maker. Section 5 of the UHCD Act provides a list of persons eligible to be appointed to serve as the surrogate decision maker in the absence of an advance directive:

(a) A surrogate may make a health-care decision for a patient who is an adult or emancipated minor if the patient has been determined by the primary physician to lack capacity and no agent or guardian has been appointed or the agent or guardian is not reasonably available.

(b) An adult or emancipated minor may designate any individual to act as surrogate by personally informing the supervising health-care provider. In the absence of a designation, or if the designee is not reasonably available, any member of the following classes of the patient's family who is reasonably available, in descending order of priority, may act as surrogate:

(1) the spouse, unless legally separated;

(2) an adult child;

(3) a parent; or

(4) an adult brother or sister.

(c) If none of the individuals eligible to act as surrogate under subsection (b) is reasonably available, an adult who has exhibited special care and concern for the patient, who is familiar with the patient's personal values, and who is reasonably available may act as surrogate.

Many states' laws include the same or similar provision as the UHCD Act allowing for the appointment of a surrogate decision maker if there is no valid advance healthcare directive in place. For example, Virginia law is similar to the UHCD Act and also provides a list of persons who are eligible to serve as the surrogate decision maker in order of priority as follows:

Whenever a patient is determined to be incapable of making an informed decision and (i) has not made an advance directive in accordance with this article or (ii) has made an advance directive in accordance with this article that does not indicate his wishes with respect to the health care at issue and does not appoint an agent, the attending physician may, upon compliance with the provisions of this section, provide, continue, withhold or withdraw health care upon the authorization of any of the following persons, in the specified order of priority, if the physician is not aware of any available, willing and capable person in a higher class:

1. A guardian for the patient. This subdivision shall not be construed to require such appointment in order that a health care decision can be made under this section; or
2. The patient's spouse except where a divorce action has been filed and the divorce is not final; or
3. An adult child of the patient; or
4. A parent of the patient; or
5. An adult brother or sister of the patient; or
6. Any other relative of the patient in the descending order of blood relationship. Va. §54.1-2986 (2006)

If an incapacitated individual lives in a state that has adopted the UHCD Act or has a similar law in place, a surrogate decision maker can be appointed for the individual in the absence of an advance medical directive.

There are many states that do not include a "default" provision but allow for the recognition of a surrogate decision maker. States that do not include such a default provision typically require some type of judicial intervention for the appointment of a guardian to make medical decisions for the incapacitated person. For example, New Jersey laws do not include a default provision similar to the UHCD Act, but instead provide for an emergency court proceeding to appoint a special medical guardian to make medical decisions for an incapacitated person. The special medical guardian can be a family member or an attorney appointed by the Court. The authority of the special medical guardian is usually temporary in nature and limited to making decisions about specific medical procedures. For long-term care needs, an incapacitated individual will still need a full guardian appointed.

C. POLST/MOLST

Many states are beginning to adopt regulations for documents known as Physician Order for Life-Sustaining Treatment (POLST) or Medical Order for Life-Sustaining Treatment (MOLST). These documents and the regulations giving rise to the documents are referred to as POLST or MOLST depending on the terminology used in the particular state. For purposes of this chapter, the term *POLST* will be used. The concept of the POLST is that once the decisions pertaining to the use of life-sustaining treatment are made, those decisions are incorporated into a medical order that becomes part of a patient's medical record to be reviewed and followed by every physician through the patient's medical treatment, regardless of the place in which that treatment is received. The POLST form is not intended to replace an advance medical directive. The only time a client can create a POLST document is if he or she has a serious, progressive, chronic illness. The POLST form, unlike an advance medical directive, is not prepared in advance to record the client's general wishes with regard to end-of-life decisions. Instead, the POLST is intended to address the specific care needed for treatment of the patient's specific illness. There is a national POLST organization (http://www.polst.org).

To finish with our example, let us examine what would happen with a MOLST or POLST document. Bob's daughter Meriope consults with the doctors and understands that Bob is critical and will not recover. It is very likely that he will have another stroke and will suffer cardiac arrest. Meriope requests that the doctor mark Bob's chart as "do not resuscitate" or DNR. The state in which Bob lives has adopted POLST legislation. Bob's physicians would then review his symptoms and prognosis, and if appropriate, make the DNR order part of Bob's permanent medical record. If Bob is later transferred to another facility for rehabilitation, that POLST order will go with him and be followed by the physicians at the rehabilitation facility.

Summary

A power of attorney (POA) allows a principal to designate someone to assist with financial decisions. A POA can be durable or springing. An advance medical directive (AMD) allows principal to designate a surrogate health care decision maker and to record-end-of life wishes. These two documents, along with a last will and testament, are part of a complete estate plan. Someone who is terminally ill may also consider having a POLST or MOLST document in the medical file.

Review Questions

1. What are the two types of financial powers of attorney?

2. What is the difference between a living will and a healthcare proxy or healthcare power of attorney?

3. What level of competency is required for execution of a power of attorney or medical directive?

True or False

1. T   F   A client does not need both a power of attorney and a medical directive.

2. T   F   A MOLST or POLST document can be used in lieu of an advance medical directive.

3. T   F   A principal does not need to be found incapacitated for an agent to use a general durable power of attorney.

4. T   F   An incapacitated person without a power of attorney and medical directive may need a guardian to assist with decisions.

5. T   F   A POA automatically terminates when the principal dies.

6. T   F   An agent on a POA can change the beneficiary designation on the principal's life insurance.

7. T   F   A POA is a record of the client's wishes regarding end-of-life care.

8. T   F   Only one person at a time can be named as a surrogate decision maker on a healthcare directive.

9. T   F   An attorney-in-fact appointed in a springing power of attorney does not have the authority to act unless the principal becomes incapacitated.

10. T   F   Clients should be instructed to keep their medical directive private and to not make any additional copies.

Drafting Exercise

Mr. and Mrs. Robert Ogden come into the office for some estate-planning information. In addition to preparing wills for the clients, they have asked for powers of attorney and medical directives. After discussing it with the attorney, they have decided that they want documents that are reciprocal, meaning that each will appoint the other first. They have indicated they would like their daughter, Rachel, to serve as the surrogate healthcare decision maker if they become disabled, and they would like their son Robert Jr. to serve as the power of attorney.

1. Review the state laws in the state in which you live. Do Mr. and Mrs. Ogden want a springing power of attorney or durable power of attorney? What additional questions should be asked or information given to the Ogdens to make that determination?

2. Draft a general durable power of attorney for Mr. and Mrs. Ogden.

3. Review the state laws and forms available for the state in which you live. Draft the appropriate document or documents to record Mr. and Mrs. Ogden's medical decisions, including end-of-life decisions, and appoint a healthcare agent. See, for example, http://www.caringinfo.org/i4a/pages/index.cfm?pageid=3289, http://www.livingwillid.com/state.html, and http://uslwr.com/formslist.shtm.

Key Terms

Advance healthcare directive	Principal
Agent or attorney-in-fact	Self-dealing
Durable power of attorney	Springing power of attorney
Power of attorney (POA)	

Jurisdictional Issues

The probate court is the state court in which issues pertaining to estates are addressed. Wills are registered, or probated in the probate court, and all litigation pertaining to the estate occurs there. The probate court also has **jurisdiction**, or the right to hear other types of cases such as guardianships, conservatorships, adoptions, or name changes. Some state probate courts also address involuntary mental commitments, while other states have special courts to address that issue. This chapter will provide a brief introduction to some of the different matters that are within the jurisdiction of the state probate court. In many states, the forms needed for probate, name changes, or adoption are found on the state judiciary Web site.

Jurisdiction: the right to hear a case

A. Guardianship

One of the other matters that a probate court has jurisdiction over is a **guardianship**. A *guardianship* is the process by which a person is appointed to make medical and/or financial decisions for someone who has become incapacitated. A guardianship requires the filing of a petition or complaint in the probate court requesting the appointment of a guardian for an alleged incapacitated person. When the guardian is appointed, the incapacitated person is referred to as the **ward**. The guardianship process is different in each state, but the common factor in all of the states' laws is the fact that the person is found by the court to be legally **incapacitated**. In general, the legal definition of *incapacitated* means unable to govern oneself and one's own affairs. A guardianship begins with some form of petition or complaint in the probate court identifying the alleged incapacitated person, family members, assets, and disabling condition, and seeking to have a guardian appointed. Figure 16-1 presents a sample petition.

As indicated in the form in Figure 16-1, in Vermont a petition for guardianship can be filed without any doctor's certification. The evaluation of the alleged incapacitated person is then ordered by the court. In other jurisdictions such as Massachusetts, New Jersey, Colorado, and others, the evaluations of the person's capacity have to be provided when the application is filed. The alleged incapacitated person must first be examined by a physician.

Guardianship: the process by which a person is appointed to make medical and/or financial decisions for someone who has become incapacitated

Ward: the incapacitated person for whom a guardian is appointed

Incapacitated: unable to govern oneself and one's own affairs

Figure 16-1. Sample Petition

STATE OF VERMONT   PROBATE COURT

DISTRICT OF _____   SS. DOCKET NO._____

GUARDIANSHIP OF: _____

OF: _____

PETITION FOR APPOINTMENT OF GUARDIAN FOR AN ADULT PERSON

The undersigned (petitioner) represents that it is necessary that a guardian be appointed for the following

individual (respondent):

Name: _____

Address: _____

DOB: _____

(Current location if different from above) _____

In support of this petition, the undersigned provides the following:

A. The name and address of anyone known to the petitioner who is:

Currently serving as a guardian (Attach a copy of appointment)

_____

Currently named as Agent in an Advance Directive document (Attach a copy)

_____

Currently acting as Agent under a Power of Attorney document (Attach a copy)

_____

B. The petitioner's relationship to the respondent is (check one):

☐ friend/neighbor ☐ public official ☐ relative_____

☐ social worker ☐ physician ☐ other (attach explanation)_____

C. The respondent is alleged to be a person in need of guardianship, is at least 18 years of age or will be within

four months of the filing of the petition, and is disabled from (check one):

☐ Mental Illness ☐ Developmental Disability ☐ Traumatic Brain Injury ☐ Other_____

D. List specific reasons with supporting facts as to why guardianship is sought:

E. The petitioner requests the following powers (check all that apply):

• To exercise general supervision over the person under guardianship, including care, habilitation, education, and employment.

• To give or withhold consent to medical or dental treatment, subject to the provisions of T14 VSA 3075, and any constitutional rights of the person under guardianship to refuse treatment;

• To exercise financial supervision over the income and resources of the person under guardianship;

• To approve or withhold approval of any contract, except for necessities, which the person under guardianship wishes to make;

• To approve or withhold approval of the sale or encumbrance of real property of the person under guardianship subject to the provisions of T. 14 VSA ☐ 2881, et seq.;

Figure 16-1. Continued

- To obtain legal advice and to commence or defend against court actions in the name of the person under guardianship.

F. Have other alternatives to guardianship been considered? If yes, please explain: _____

_____

G. Name and address of proposed guardian:

Telephone:

The undersigned understands that the Court must order an evaluation of the respondent to be performed by someone who has specific training and demonstrated competence to evaluate a person in need of guardianship. The evaluation shall be completed within 30 days of the filing of the petition with the court unless the time period is extended by the court for cause.

Name and address of evaluator:

The undersigned understands that the Court must appoint an attorney to represent the respondent in this proceeding.

Name and address of the respondent's attorney, if any:

Dated_____ Signed _____, Petitioner

Print name _____

Address _____

_____

_____

Telephone

I CONSENT TO BE APPOINTED GUARDIAN OF THE ABOVE RESPONDENT

Signature of proposed guardian: _____

Date: _____

Attachments as follows:

1. $ ☐ ☐ ☐.00 entry fee, payable to _____Probate Court

2. Statement of proposed respondent's assets and income (Form No. 73)

3. List of interested persons (Form No. 75)

4. Copy of advance directive and/or any power of attorney

5. You also may be required to submit consents necessary for a complete background check.

Guardianship shall be utilized only as necessary to promote the well-being of the individual and to protect the individual from violations of his or her human and civil rights. It shall be designed to encourage the development and maintenance of maximum self-reliance and independence in the individual and only the least restrictive form of guardianship shall be ordered to the extent required by the individual's actual mental and adaptive limitations. The state of Vermont recognizes the fundamental right of an adult with capacity to determine the extent of health care the individual will receive. 14 VSA 3060.

A sample of a complaint that would be used in the state of New Jersey is shown in Figure 16-2.

Figure 16-2. Sample Complaint

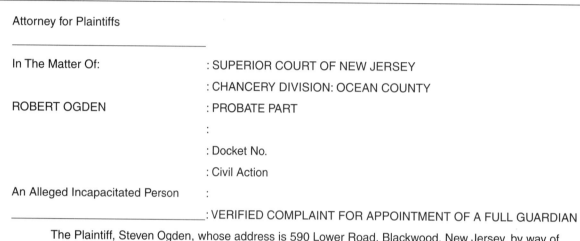

Attorney for Plaintiffs

_____

In The Matter Of: : SUPERIOR COURT OF NEW JERSEY

                                           : CHANCERY DIVISION: OCEAN COUNTY

ROBERT OGDEN   : PROBATE PART

                                           :

                                           : Docket No.

                                           : Civil Action

An Alleged Incapacitated Person   :

_____: VERIFIED COMPLAINT FOR APPOINTMENT OF A FULL GUARDIAN

The Plaintiff, Steven Ogden, whose address is 590 Lower Road, Blackwood, New Jersey, by way of complaint, says:

1.   Plaintiff, Steven Ogden, is the son of Robert Ogden.

2.   Robert Ogden is an Alleged Incapacitated Person. Robert Ogden is 89 years old. He currently lives at the Care Center Toms River, NJ 08721.

3.   The following are the known next of kin and interested parties of the alleged Incapacitated Person:

     Steven Ogden—son (age 54)
     590 Lower Rd.
     Blackwood, NJ 08012

     Ryan M. Ogden (age 52)
     address unknown

     Harriet Ogden (age 44)
     823 Summer Road
     Toms River, NJ 08012

4.   Plaintiff is not aware that Robert Ogden has a Last Will and Testament, Power of Attorney, or Living Will.

5.   Robert Ogden is unable to govern or manage his affairs as will appear from the certification and report of Dr. Jay and Dr. Frank (attached as Exhibit "A").

6.   The assets of Robert Ogden, the alleged incapacitated person, are more fully set forth in the Certification of Incapacitated Person's Estate filed herewith.

Figure 16-2. Continued

> 7.   Robert Ogden suffers from CVA with left-sided hemiparesis, depression, anxiety disorder a
>   condition from which he will not recover. He experiences auditory hallucinations, and paranoia. As
>   a result of the CVA, Mr. Ogden has limited insight and judgment, and it is the opinion of the
>   physicians that he is in need of a guardian.
>
>   WHEREFORE, Plaintiff demands judgment adjudging Robert Ogden incapacitated and appointing
> Plaintiff and dispensing with the requirement of a bond and for such other relief, as the Court may deem
> appropriate and necessary under the circumstances.
>
>
>
> CARLUCCIO, LEONE, DIMON,
>
> DOYLE AND SACKS, L.L.C.
>
> By: _____
>
> DIANA L. ANDERSON, ESQ.
>
>
>
> Dated:

The initial complaint or petition for guardianship usually also requires some preliminary accounting of the proposed ward's assets and income. This is presented to the court in the form of an affidavit or certification. The information used in the accounting of assets will be used to establish the amount of the **surety bond** the guardian may be required to obtain. A *surety bond* is a form of insurance that protects the ward if the guardian misappropriates or misuses the ward's funds. When a guardian is appointed, many courts require that a surety bond be posted in an amount equal to the assets of the ward that will be under the guardian's control. Reporting the assets is very basic, and no specific form is necessary as long as the pertinent information about assets and income is included. A sample of the document for reporting assets is shown in Figure 16-3.

The guardian appointed is given control over what is described as the "person and property" of the ward or incapacitated person. This means that the guardian controls all of the medical decisions, including where treatment is to be received and if inpatient treatment is necessary, and also controls all of the ward's assets. In many jurisdictions the guardian is required to report to the court on an annual basis as to how the ward's assets are being used. The guardian, like a trustee, personal representative, or executor, is a fiduciary. The guardian is responsible for using the ward's assets for the care of the ward and to invest the assets according to the prudent investor standard. If the ward owns any real property, special approval may have to be obtained before the real property can be sold by the guardian. These safeguards are put into place to avoid elder abuse or misappropriation of the ward's assets.

Surety bond: a form of insurance that protects the ward if the guardian misappropriates or misuses the ward's funds

Figure 16-3. Document for Reporting Assets

STATE OF VERMONT PROBATE COURT

DISTRICT OF _____

IN RE DOCKET NO. _____

_____

STATEMENT OF PROPOSED WARD'S ASSETS AND INCOME

ASSETS—Description and approximate value:

_____

_____

_____

_____

_____

INCOME—Description and approximate amount (include public benefits and pensions):

_____

_____

_____

_____

_____

_____

Signed _____

Print Name_____

Dated _____

Address _____

_____

Telephone ( ) _____

Interested party: all family members and relatives who are entitled to serve as guardian

It is also generally required that the petition, along with medical evidence of incapacitation, be filed with the appropriate court and given to all interested parties. An **interested party** for a guardianship would include all other family members and relatives who also are entitled to serve as the guardian. An example of a document identifying the interested parties is shown in Figure 16-4.

Figure 16-4. Sample Document Identifying the Interested Parties

STATE OF VERMONT   PROBATE COURT

DISTRICT OF _____

IN RE   DOCKET NO. _____

_____

LIST OF INTERESTED PERSONS FOR A GUARDIANSHIP

List here all persons interested in the guardianship proceeding. For a minor, the list must include the proposed ward, the parent(s) of the proposed ward, the proposed guardian, and any person who has had principal care and custody of the proposed ward during the last 30 days. For an adult, the list must include the proposed ward, the proposed guardian, the spouse of the proposed ward, or if none, the parents of the proposed ward, the adult children of the proposed ward if the spouse is proposed guardian, the nearest adult relative of the proposed ward if the proposed ward has no living parent, spouse, or adult child, and anyone else directed by the court. List the attorney for the proposed ward, if known. Each listing must include the name, mailing address, including zip code, and the relationship of the person to the proposed ward. Use additional forms if necessary.

Name (Print)	Mailing Address	Relationship

The Court can appoint a single guardian or co-guardians. In some jurisdictions the court can appoint one guardian to be the guardian of the person, with responsibility for all personal and medical decisions, and another to be guardian of the property, with the responsibility for all financial decisions. The court will try, if possible, to appoint a limited guardian to preserve as many of the rights of the incapacitated person as possible.

Practice Tip

If the paralegal works in an office that files a number of guardianships every year, a complete set of blank pleadings or forms needed for the guardianship should be created and kept in a computer file.

The guardianship process takes a number of weeks if not months to move through the courts. It requires physicians to provide reports about the mental status of the person who is alleged to lack capacity. The guardianship proceeding can be time consuming and costly, not to mention potentially embarrassing for the person who is found to be incapacitated and not capable of managing his or her own affairs. With a durable power of attorney and medical directive, the principal can appoint the necessary advocates in advance and avoid a guardianship.

Examples of various states' guardianship forms available online are the following:

Alaska: http://courts.alaska.gov/guardianship.htm#forms
New York State: http://www.nycourts.gov/forms/surrogates/guardianship.shtml
Ohio: https://www.franklincountyohio.gov/probate/forms/guardianship/
Vermont: https://www.vermontjudiciary.org/GTC/Probate/adultguardianship.aspx

B. Conservatorship

Conservator: a person appointed by the court to make financial decisions for an incapacitated person

A **conservator** is a person appointed by the court to make financial decisions for the incapacitated person. The conservator typically has the power to enter into contracts, pay bills, invest assets, and perform other financial functions for the protected person but does not make personal decisions such as where to live, or medical decisions. It is similar to a guardianship in that it requires some form of petition or complaint to be filed with the probate or surrogate's court as well as a finding that the person is incapacitated. Some states make a distinction between a guardianship and conservatorship based on the capacity of the person in question. Other states distinguish between a guardian and a conservator on based on the duties performed. A conservator can be appointed on a voluntary basis for a person who is not incapacitated but recognizes that he or she needs help. A conservator can also be appointed to care for another person who cannot care for himself or herself.

In some states, the term *conservator* can also mean someone who serves in the role that other states refer to as a *guardian*. For example, in California, the description of the duties of the conservator and the reason for appointment of a conservator are similar to the role of a court-appointed guardian in other states. Go to the Web site http://www.courts.ca.gov/selfhelp-conservatorship.htm which describes the role of the conservator in California. Compare the description and forms used in California to those used in Michigan where a guardian can be appointed to provide for personal care and custody, and a conservator appointed to administer a person's property and finances (http://courts.mi.gov/Administration/SCAO/Forms/Pages/Guardian-and-Conservator.aspx). Other states allow for a guardian of the person or property to be appointed, or allow for the voluntary appointment of a conservator.

Practice Tip

Research your state's laws and familiarize yourself with the correct terms to use.

C. Return to Capacity

A person who is subject to a guardianship has been found by the court to be legally incapacitated. The definition of legally incapacitated can vary from state to state, but common in all of the states' definition is the concept that the ward lacks the ability to care for himself or herself. The condition in which the ward finds himself or herself may be something that is either temporary or resolved through medical treatment. If the ward regains capacity, an application can be made to the court to dissolve the guardianship. The return to capacity application would include medical evidence, in the form of an affidavit from a physician, that the ward has regained capacity and is able to resume control of his or her own life.

An example of such a situation would be a person who lived alone, with no family, and had some emergent medical event, such as a fall, a car accident, or a stroke. The medical condition left the person temporarily unable to provide care and in need of an advocate to assist with medical decisions. If the person recovered sufficiently, a return to capacity application can be submitted to the court to allow the person to resume control of his or her own affairs. The guardianship can be dissolved, and the person can regain his or her legal rights.

D. Involuntary Mental Commitments

An **involuntary commitment** is a state law procedure by which a person is found to be a danger to one's self or to others, is unwilling to accept treatment or be voluntarily admitted to a treatment facility, and is in need of evaluation, short-term treatment, or hospitalization. Involuntary commitments are under the jurisdiction of the probate court. However, the actual hearings are sometimes conducted within the treatment facility. An involuntary commitment is short term, usually only 72 hours, and can be initiated by the police, a doctor, nurse, or mental health professional such

Involuntary commitment: a state law procedure by which a person is found to be a danger to self and to others, is unwilling to accept treatment or be voluntarily admitted to a treatment facility, and is in need of evaluation, short-term treatment, or hospitalization

Figure 16-5. Sample Petition Form for an Involuntary Commitment or Hospitalization

---

STATE OF MAINE

APPLICATION FOR EMERGENCY INVOLUNTARY ADMISSION TO A MENTAL HOSPITAL

1. Application

I hereby apply under 34-B M.R.S.A. § 3863 for emergency admission of _____

Proposed patient

To_____. I believe that the proposed patient has a mental illness and therefore

Mental Hospital

poses a likelihood of serious harm because_____

_____

Grounds for belief, including nature of illness and harm

_____	_____	_____	_____
Date	Applicant's printed name	Applicant's signature	Applicant's capacity

Name and address of proposed patient's guardian, spouse, parent, adult child, next of kin, or friend:

_____

2. Certifying Examination. I hereby certify that:

(a) I am a licensed _____ and that I examined _____ today.

MD/DO/PhD/PA/NP/RN,CS   Proposed patient

(b) My opinion is that the proposed patient has a mental illness and that

[suicide, self-injury] the illness causes a substantial risk of physical harm to the proposed patient because

_____

Symptoms and grounds, including recent actions or behaviors (**threats of or attempts at suicide or serious bodily harm**) caused by illness

[harm to others] the illness causes a substantial risk of harm to others because_____

_____

Symptoms and grounds, including recent actions or behaviors caused by illness that placed others in **reasonable fear of violent behavior** or serious harm

[self-protection] the illness creates a reasonable certainty that the proposed patient will suffer severe physical

or mental injury or impairment because_____.

_____.

Symptoms and grounds, including recent actions or behaviors caused by illness showing proposed patient's **inability to protect self from harm**

(c) I have confirmed that adequate community resources are unavailable for care and treatment of this person's mental illness.

(d) I believe that _____ is the least restrictive form of transportation for the patient's clinical needs.
Ambulance or other (please specify)

_____	_____	_____	_____
Date	Time	Examiner's printed name	Examiner's signature

Figure 16-5. Continued

---

3. Judicial Review and Endorsement.

Upon review pursuant to 34-B M.R.S.A. § 3863(3), I find this application and certificate to be regular and in accordance with the law, and I hereby authorize _____ _____to take

Person authorized to take proposed patient into custody

_____ into custody and transport him or her to _____.

Proposed patient		Mental hospital

_____ _____		_____	_____	_____
Date	Time	Judicial officer's printed name	Judicial officer's signature	Judicial officer's capacity (District, Probate or Superior Court Judge or Justice; Justice of the Peace)

---

as a psychologist or psychiatrist. The person subject to the commitment has the use of a public defender to advocate that commitment is not necessary.

The standard of proof for an involuntary commitment varies from state to state. In many states the finding of a mental illness is a prerequisite to an involuntary commitment. In other states the person has to be "gravely disabled." A state-by-state listing of the standards used for involuntary commitment can be found at http://mentalillnesspolicy.org/studies/state-standards-involuntary-treatment.html

In many cases, short-term involuntary commitments are used in emergency situations that are later followed by the filing of a guardianship application. The application for an involuntary commitment can be brought by a mental health treatment or screening facility. Figure 16-5 is a sample petition form for an involuntary commitment or hospitalization that is used in Maine.

A paralegal should be familiar with the involuntary commitment procedure as it may lead to an attempt to have a guardian appointed for the person at the end of the involuntary commitment. Caution should be used as a mental illness diagnosis is not proof that the person is incapacitated. For example, an adult may be diagnosed with bipolar disorder or schizophrenia, but with medication and treatment may be competent to sign legal documents.

E. Adoption

Adoptions are also under the jurisdiction of the probate court. An **adoption** is a legal proceeding by which a person, or persons, assumes the rights and obligations of parenting another person. It is the legal creation of a parent-child relationship between persons who are otherwise not related by blood. Adoption can occur for infants, children, and adults. For most attorneys, doing an adoption is the happiest

Adoption: a legal proceeding by which a person, or persons, assumes the rights and obligations of parenting another person day in court they will ever have. At the end of the adoption, everyone is happy, even the judge and the court staff. The adoption is usually a joyous occasion for all parties.

The state's law may differentiate the form of pleadings needed between a private adoption and an agency adoption. There may also be a need for an agency, such as a child welfare or protection agency, to remove the child from his or her home, sever the parental rights of the birth parents, and then place that child up for adoption. There may be significant legal proceedings that occur before the adoption can be completed. All of the issues that can arise in an adoption are beyond the scope of this text. For purposes of this text it is sufficient to be familiar with a petition for adoption and to understand the circumstances under which an adoption can occur under the jurisdiction of the probate court.

Figure 16-6 is a petition for adoption form used for a private adoption in New Jersey.

As indicated in the pleadings, it is necessary to submit affidavits confirming the consent of the birth mother and birth father. It is also necessary to determine if either biological parent is a member, or is eligible to be a member, of a federally recognized Indian tribe. If either parent meets this qualification, an investigation pursuant to the Indian Child Welfare Act (ICWA) must be conducted.

The majority of adoptions that occur are adoptions of infants and children. Adoptions can occur when the birth parents surrender the infant for adoption by voluntarily giving up their parental rights or when a child welfare agency involuntarily severs parental rights, after removing the child from the home. Adoptions can also occur when a stepparent adopts a spouse's children or when other family members are raising a child after the death of a parent.

Every state in the United States also provides for the ability of an adult to be adopted. The adoption of a child occurs because of the need of the child for a parent and the willingness of a person to assume the role of the parent. So why would an adult need or even want to be adopted? Adult adoptions can occur for many reasons. For example, an adult adoption can be done because of the change in healthcare laws, allowing adult children to stay on a parent's health plan. Adult adoptions can formalize a long-standing relationship between parties. Adult adoption can also be done for purposes of avoiding or lessening inheritance taxes that would be imposed if an estate is left to a party who is not related by blood. Adult adoptions also occur between people who do not want to get married, but adopt for purposes of financial or estate issues.

Every state allows for the adoption of adults. See, for example, Alaska Code 25.23.010, Texas Family Code §162.501, Nevada Code §127.190, Louisiana Civil Code 213, Georgia Code §19-8-21, South Carolina Code §63-9-1120, Kentucky Revised Statutes §405.390, and Vermont Statutes Annotated Title 15A §5-101. Each state requires that the adult being adopted give his or her consent to the adoption. There are conditions placed on the ability to adopt an adult, such as the New Jersey requirements that the adopting parent or parents are at least ten years older than the person to be adopted (N.J.S.A. 2A:22-2). In Alabama an adult may only be adopted if he or she is disabled (State Code of Alabama, Section 26-10A-6). Illinois requires that the adult who is going to be adopted has resided in the home of the person intending to adopt him or her for more than two years before the adoption proceedings are filed (Illinois Compiled Statutes, Chapter 750, Act 50 "Adoption Act").

Figure 16-6. Petition for Adoption Form

In the Matter of:

:

THE ADOPTION OF A CHILD BY

_____ and _____,

husband and wife.

: SUPERIOR COURT OF NEW JERSEY

CHANCERY DIVISION:

: OCEAN COUNTY:

: PROBATE PART

:

: DOCKET NO.

: CIVIL ACTION

COMPLAINT FOR ADOPTION

The petitioners, _____ and _____, husband and wife, say:

1.   The petitioner, _____, is ___ years of age. The petitioner, _____, is ___ years of age. The petitioners are husband and wife residing at _____, New Jersey. Both of the petitioners are citizens of the United States and are not related to the child to be adopted.

2.   The name of the child to be adopted is: _____, born _____, at _____.

3.   The petitioners received the child to be adopted from the birth mother on or about _____, as explained in the Affidavit of Circumstances Surrounding Placement of Child submitted herewith, and the child has been under the continuous care of the petitioners from that date until the filing of this Complaint.

4.   The name of the birth mother of the child is _____, who resides at _____. The name of the birth father is _____, who resides at _____.

5.   The birth parents have never been married.

6.   The child to be adopted has no property other than his or her clothing, personal items, and other necessities furnished to him or her by the petitioners.

7.   The name by which the child to be adopted shall be known is:_____.

8.   The petitioner, _____, is a _____. The petitioner, _____, is a homemaker. The petitioners are well-able to support the child to be adopted.

9.   The petitioners have no other children.

10. The Consent of Birth Mother is annexed hereto as Exhibit "A".

(continued)

Figure 16-6. Continued

---

11. The Affidavit of Birth Mother is annexed hereto as Exhibit "B".

12. The birth mother's Notice Regarding Reimbursement of Expenses is annexed hereto as Exhibit "C".

13. The birth mother's Affidavit Regarding Waiver of Right to Counseling is annexed hereto as Exhibit "D".

14. The Consent of Birth Father is annexed hereto as Exhibit "E".

15. The Affidavit of Birth Father is annexed hereto as Exhibit "F".

16. The Acknowledgment of Paternity is annexed hereto as Exhibit "G".

WHEREFORE, the petitioners demand judgment of this court granting the adoption of the child by the Petitioners.

_____

Attorney for Petitioners

Dated:

F. Name Change

Name change: the legal proceeding by which a person adopts a name that is different from the name given to the person at the time of birth or adoption

A **name change** is the legal proceeding by which a person adopts a name that is different from the name given to the person at the time of birth or adoption. Name changes can also occur as part of a divorce, typically at the same time as the finalization of the divorce. The laws of each state govern the procedures for a name change. Generally a person can adopt any name he or she wants, for any reason. There are usually some state law restrictions on the choice of name. For example, the name chosen cannot be intentionally misleading, like a celebrity name; it cannot be any kind of threat or racial slur; and it cannot be intended to incite violence. The court also usually requires that the person seeking the name change recite in the pleadings that the name change is not being done for fraudulent reasons such as trying to avoid a debt. The applicant may be required to give a reasonable explanation for wanting to change his or her name. A fee is generally payable, and the applicant may be required to post legal notices in newspapers to announce the name change.

A petition requesting a name change is filed with the court along with a proposed form of order for the judge to use. If the order is acceptable to the judge, the judge will sign the order and send it back. A self-addressed stamped envelope will also be required. In New York, there is also a requirement that the proposed name change be published. Figure 16-7 is an example of a name change publication notice:

Figure 16-7. Petition for a Name Change

_____ **COURT OF THE STATE OF NEW YORK**

COUNTY OF _____

IN THE MATTER OF THE APPLICATION OF

_____ ,

Petitioner,

PETITION FOR A

NAME CHANGE

FOR LEAVE TO CHANGE _____ **NAME TO:**

(His/Her)

Index #_____

_____ ,

(Proposed New Name)

TO THE _____**COURT OF THE STATE OF NEW YORK:**

The Petition of _____ respectfully shows this

court:

1. The petitioner resides at No._____ , in

(Street Address)

the_____of_____ , County of _____ , and

has so resided for a period of _____years and_____months prior to the making of this application.

2. The petitioner_____was born at_____

on the _____day of_____ , _____and is now_____years

of age. (Attached hereto and made a part hereof is a copy of the petitioner's birth certificate.)

3. The petitioner proposes to change said His/Her name to_____ .

4. The petitioner is a natural born citizen of the United States.

5. The petitioner is/is not married and has/has not been married previously.

6. The petitioner: (check one):

_____ has never been convicted of a crime.

_____ has been convicted of a crime, the details of which are attached in a separate state-

ment, annexed hereto and made a part hereof.

7. The petitioner has never been adjudicated a bankrupt.

8. There are no judgments or liens of record and no actions pending against your petitioner in any

court of this state or of the United States, or of any governmental subdivision thereof, or elsewhere whether the

court be of record or not. There are no bankruptcy or insolvency proceedings, voluntary or involuntary, pending

against your petitioner in any court whatsoever or before any officer, person, body or board having jurisdiction

thereof and your petitioner has not, at any time, made any assignments for the benefit of creditor. (If there have

been, enter details instead of previous statement.)

(continued)

Figure 16-7. Continued

9. There are no claims, demands, liabilities, or obligations of any kind whatsoever on a written instrument or otherwise against your infants under the only names by which they have been known which are the names sought herein to be abandoned, and your infants have no creditors who may be adversely affected or prejudiced in any way by the proposed change of name. (If there have been, enter details instead of previous statement.)

10. The petitioner is/is not responsible for child support obligations. (If there are child support obligations, details are attached in a separate statement.)

11. The petitioner is/is not responsible for spousal support obligations. (If there are spousal support obligations, details are attached in a separate statement.)

12. The grounds of this application to change the petitioner's name are as follows:

_____

_____

_____

13. No previous application has been made for the relief sought herein.

WHEREFORE, petitioner respectfully prays for an order permitting the petitioner_____

to assume the name _____

in place of that of

_____.

(Current Name)

DATED:_____, 20_____.

_____
(Signature of petitioner)

STATE OF NEW YORK)

ss.:   **INDIVIDUAL VERIFICATION**

COUNTY OF_____)

THIS IS TO CERTIFY that I, _____being

duly sworn deposes and says: your deponent is the Petitioner in the within action; your deponent has read the foregoing Petition and knows the contents thereof. The same is true to deponent's own knowledge, except as to the matters therein stated to be alleged on information and belief, and as to those matters deponent believes it to be true.

Sworn to before me this _____

Petitioner

_____day of _____, 20_____

_____
Notary Public

Sample Name Change Publication Notice

Notice is hereby given that an order entered by the Supreme Court of Rockland County on May _____, 1997, Index # _____/97, copy of which may be examined at the County Clerk, located in Rockland County, 11 New Pine Rd., New City, grants me the right affected on June _____, 1997, to assume the name of Jane Doe _____. My address is _____ Anonymous Dr., Rockland City, New York, on May _____, 1997.

Most states allow a person to change names simply by using a different name. However, some type of court order is usually required if the person changing his or her name wants that name to be accepted by banks, motor vehicle services, or the government. Some states make specific allowances for transgender persons to change names either before or after gender reassignment surgery. Other states do not make a special distinction for persons undergoing gender reassignment, but instead generally make name changes available to all persons regardless of reason.

A sample of the documents needed to complete a name change can be found on the New York Courts Web site (http://www.nycourts.gov/forms/namechange.shtml).

Summary

The probate court serves many functions. It has jurisdiction over guardianships, conservatorships, adoptions, and name changes. Some state probate courts also address involuntary mental commitments. A guardianship or conservatorship often deals with an elderly person who has lost the capacity to make decisions. An adoption can include the adoption of a child or an adult.

Review Questions

1. What are three other types of matters that are heard in the probate court?

2. What are some of the differences between a guardianship and a conservatorship?

3. Can an adult be adopted? What are some of the restrictions/requirements?

4. What are some reasons why a name change petition is necessary?

True or False

1. T   F   Two people can serve together as co-guardians.

2. T   F   A guardian is a fiduciary.

3. T F   An involuntary mental commitment is permanent.

4. T F   In some states, a person can change his or her name simply by using another name.

5. T F   If you owe a lot of debt, you can apply to the court for a name change and walk away from the debt.

6. T F   The probate court has jurisdiction over divorces and can enter an order allowing a wife to return to using her maiden name as part of a divorce.

7. T F   A guardian can sell the ward's property at any time if necessary to raise funds to provide for care.

8. T F   A guardian can be given control over both the person and the person's property.

9. T F   The probate court has jurisdiction to appoint a conservator.

10. T F   Only children under the age of 18 can be adopted.

Drafting Exercise

A new client, Elizabeth Jorgenson, brings in her 90-year-old aunt, Bertha Jorgenson, to get a power of attorney. Bertha has just temporarily moved in with Elizabeth and will be moving to an assisted living facility. She receives Social Security and a nice pension form Exxon Mobil, where she used to work. After meeting with Bertha, the attorney advises that Bertha does not have capacity to sign a POA and discusses a guardianship. Elizabeth agrees to the guardianship, and you are asked to begin drafting a guardianship complaint. Using the sample complaint included in the text from the state of New Jersey, start a draft of a complaint, and prepare a list of information that Elizabeth will be required to provide.

Key Terms

Adoption	Involuntary commitment
Conservator	Jurisdiction
Guardianship	Name change
Incapacitated	Surety bond
Interested party	Ward

17

Long-Term Care Planning and Elder Abuse

The area of elder law includes more than just wills, trusts, and estates. An elder law attorney may specialize in those areas but will often be asked to provide advice on other nonlegal issues that are relevant to older clients and their families. An important component of an elder law or estate law practice is assisting with long-term care planning, including funding that care and where the care will be provided. The discussion about long-term care planning can arise out of a client's need for advice for himself or herself or in order to assist an elderly parent or relative.

When the need for care arises, there are a myriad of issues with which a client will need assistance. Paying for long-term care can be expensive; assets may have to be liquidated to pay the cost. Coordinating the care for a married couple can be difficult if they have different care needs. Familiarity with various options for senior living and available care settings will be invaluable in providing a full-service approach to elder law and estate law.

Older clients who suffer from dementia or who are in a weakened physical or mental condition may be vulnerable to elder abuse. It is important to learn the signs of elder abuse and how to protect the client from such abuse. This chapter will provide an overview of the housing options available, the different levels of care provided in facilities, and various methods of paying for the care that is needed. It will also address the issue of elder abuse.

A. Housing and Care Options

1. Need for Care

As we age, each of us will most likely require some form of assistance. Most of us can think of examples in our own lives of elderly relatives who died at home or in a nursing home or care facility. Grandma might have moved in after Grandpa died, living in the spare bedroom until she passed away. Perhaps a grandparent had Parkinson's or Alzheimer's disease, which required long-term nursing home care. Maybe an elderly parent lives independently, requiring only limited assistance with shopping, medical appointments, or housekeeping. Whatever the specifics of the care needed by our elderly relatives, most of us can relate to the need for care. The need for care will increase as one grows old.

The need for care also may arise from a sudden medical event that makes a current living situation inappropriate. A person who has a stroke may not be able to continue living in a home with a lot of stairs or a home that does not have a bathroom and bedroom available on the first floor. Someone who has developed memory issues may be able to cope for a long while with a part-time caregiver but then suddenly deteriorate and need to move to a facility to receive more comprehensive care. One can plan for eventual care needs, but one must also be able to respond to care needs that were unanticipated. The optimal situation is to live in an appropriate environment in which the increase in care needs can be met and to have assets available to pay for that care.

There are certain afflictions, such as Alzheimer's or dementia, in which there is a fairly predictable decline in the person's abilities combined with a fairly predictable increase in the person's care needs. Individuals do not recover from certain diseases like Alzheimer's, and the need for continued care for the rest of the individual's life is certain. The level of care needed is described by reference to the assistance needed with an individual's **activities of daily living (ADLs)** The term *activity of daily living* is self-explanatory — the activities of daily living are those things that a competent adult does for himself or herself on a daily basis, including getting up from bed or transferring from the bed to a wheelchair or commode chair, using the toilet, bathing, getting dressed, making breakfast, eating breakfast, and communicating with loved ones. An individual with a disease like Alzheimer's will need assistance with completing some or all of the ADLs. The amount of assistance needed is measured by the number of ADLs with which the individual needs assistance.

Activities of daily living (ADLs): the activities of daily living are those things that a competent adult does for himself or herself on a daily basis

2. Housing Options

The baby boomer generation is aging. This fact has been the topic of news reports for many years. The housing market has responded to the demands of the aging population. There are now many housing options available to seniors which can accommodate various levels of care.

One such type of housing specifically marketed to seniors is an **independent-living community**. This type of community provides age-restricted housing to active, independent adults. At least one occupant of the house must meet a minimum age requirement, and there are rules prohibiting young children or children of a certain age from living within the community. The communities typically have single-family homes, a central clubhouse, and recreational facilities, but they do not provide any type of care for the residents. The housing style in an adult community usually allows for aging in place by providing such features as a master bedroom with en suite bathroom on the ground floor, no front steps, and an attached garage.

Independent-living community: a community that provides age-restricted housing to active, independent adults

If someone cannot live completely independently or anticipates needing some help in the foreseeable future, assisted living can be a good option. An **assisted-living facility** is a living environment in which some care or assistance is provided. The level of care provided can vary from place to place. Primarily, it is for a person who is still ambulatory, and who can take care of most, if not all, of his or her own ADLs but needs some assistance. An assisted-living facility frequently provides one or two meals a day. The individual units may or may not also have full cooking facilities that would also allow residents to prepare meals for themselves.

Assisted-living facility: a living environment in which some care or assistance is provided

Assisted-living facilities can also be part of a larger **congregate-care facility** in which varying levels of care are provided. A *congregate-care facility* will typically have units or sections of housing for seniors that are more independent, and sections for those requiring more care. This combination of care-type facility can be a good solution for a married couple in which one spouse requires more care than the other spouse can provide.

Congregate-care facility: a living environment with units or sections for more independent living and sections for those requiring more care

3. Care Facilities

There are various types of care facilities that are available. The choice of facility is going to be based on the length of time care will be needed and the level of care required.

1. An **intermediate-care facility** is one that provides care at a level between an assisted-living facility and a skilled nursing facility. An assisted-living facility and a skilled nursing care facility can be within the same building, as in the congregate-care facility, or within a campus or collection of buildings. If different levels of care are not available, the choice may be made to go directly to an intermediate-care facility, even if that level of care is not yet needed, as long as it is anticipated that such care would be needed in the foreseeable future. Choosing intermediate care can prevent a second difficult transition when the care need does increase.

Intermediate-care facility: a living environment that provides care at a level between an assisted-living facility and a skilled nursing facility

2. A **skilled nursing facility** is a long-term care facility that has the staff and equipment to give **skilled nursing care.** Medicare defines *skilled nursing care* as care given or supervised by registered nurses (RNs). Nurses provide direct care; manage, observe, and evaluate a patient's care; and teach the patient and his or her family caregiver. Their responsibilities include giving IV drugs, administering injections, providing tube feedings, changing dressings, doing wound care, and teaching about diabetes care. Terms such as rest home, nursing home, old-age home, retirement home, or convalescent home are often used to describe long-term residential skilled nursing care facilities. Each state provides specific regulations as to the types of care received at each type of facility.

Skilled nursing facility: a living environment that has the nursing facility, staff, and equipment to give skilled nursing care

Skilled nursing care: care given or supervised by registered nurses (RNs)

In addition to skilled nursing care, skilled nursing facilities provide assistance with all ADLs including bathing, toileting, and eating.

Any service that can be done safely by a nonmedical person without the supervision of a nurse is not skilled nursing care. Nonskilled care, such as the care needed

Custodial care: nonskilled, non-medical care such as the care needed for assistance with ADLs

for assistance with ADLs, is **custodial care** or nonmedical care. Custodial care is not covered by medical insurance or Medicare. Payment for this type of care is provided only by long-term-care insurance policies.

Many in-patient long-term-care facilities offer specialized programs for "memory care" or Alzheimer's care. Skilled nursing facilities may provide special programs for the residents designed to both help maintain memory and to address the behavioral issues associated with memory loss. It is often necessary for residents with Alzheimer's and other senile dementia issues to be housed in a more secure area to prevent wandering.

Rehabilitative-care facility: a facility that provides short-term care following an accident, operation, or injury

3. A **rehabilitative-care facility** provides short-term rehabilitative care following an accident, operation, or injury. Occupational therapy, physical therapy, speech therapy, or many other types of rehabilitation are provided in a residential, hospital-like setting. It is designed to return a patient to his or her previous level of health, or to relearn or reacquire physical skills such as walking, speaking, or eating. For example, in-patient rehabilitative care may be required following knee replacement surgery to develop strength in the leg and to heal from the surgery. The rehabilitative care is short term, with a goal of returning to a level of being able to function independently. Another example of rehabilitative care is the care needed after a stroke when a patient may require speech therapy, occupational therapy, and physical therapy.

Practice Tip

Gather some brochures or marketing materials from local facilities to provide clients with housing options or prepare a list of such facilities from an Internet search.

---

4. Providing Care at Home

A home health aide can provide long-term care in an individual's home. Care providers can have different qualifications such as certified nursing assistant (CNA) or home health aide (HHA) certification. The training requirements for a HHA certification vary from state to state. A home health aide can be a part-time care provider or can reside in the home with the care recipient, providing 24-hour care.

A question from clients often arises about using a home health care agency or privately hiring an individual caregiver. A home health aide provided through an agency is likely to be more expensive per hour than someone hired independently. Hiring a caregiver through an agency is somewhat easier and safer because the agency does a background check, ensures that the certification or licensing requirements have been met, and handles all payroll issues including payment of worker's compensation, social security, and taxes. Hiring an individual caregiver and paying the caregiver in cash may give rise to questions if the person later needs Medicaid because Medicaid will require all of the cash payments to be accounted for.

Many in-home caregivers are unpaid family members such as the spouse or children who provide day-to-day care. When family caregivers need a break, they turn to **respite care.** *Respite care* is short-term temporary care that provides a break for someone who is caring for a family member. Respite care can provide a much-needed break for an unpaid caregiver. Using respite care has been shown to reduce the likelihood of neglect or abuse. It can also help protect against caregiver "burnout." Respite care can be provided by an agency in the home or by temporary placement in a facility outside of the home.

Respite care: short-term temporary care that provides a break for someone who is caring for a family member

Many seniors receiving care at home also attend adult day care. **Adult day care** provides meals, socialization, and hygiene-related services. The programs are run during specific daytime hours with the participants returning to their homes each evening. Adult day care is often used when the full-time caregiver is a family member who still works. The services provided by an adult day care facility can help keep an elderly relative out of long-term care by providing assistance for the caregiver. The activities provided by an adult day care center will ensure that the participant is not home alone while allowing a family member who is providing care to continue working outside of the home. Many centers provide on-site nurses, transportation, and many other services.

Adult day care: a program run outside the home during specific daytime hours, which provides meals, socialization, and hygiene-related services

5.   End-of-Life Care

The care provided at the end of life is **hospice care.** When mentioning "hospice" there is frequently a misconception that the patient or the patient's family is giving up. The response to the question of "have you considered hospice" is often "we're not ready for that" or something similar. Hospice care is not "giving up"; it is simply a change in the care philosophy.

Hospice care: palliative care provided at the end of life focusing on keeping the patient comfortable and addressing disease-related symptoms, but not providing treatment for the disease

Hospice care is palliative, not curative. That means that the care focuses on keeping the patient comfortable, addressing disease-related symptoms but not providing treatment for the disease. It allows a patient to remain in control of his or her own care, while managing any pain or discomfort caused by the disease affecting the patient. In order to qualify for hospice, the patient usually must have a prognosis of less than six months to live. Medicare will cover hospice care for two periods of 90 days each with an unlimited number of additional 60-day periods of care. Medicare will also pay for a consultation to help a patient decide if hospice is the right option. Hospice will provide supportive care for the patient's family. The cost of hospice care is covered by Medicare, Medicaid, and many private insurance companies. The care can be provided in the patient's home or in a nursing home or in-patient facility such as a hospital or nursing home.

B.   Paying for Long-Term Care

1.   Long-Term Care Insurance

Long-term care insurance (LTC) is an insurance policy sold to help fund the cost of providing long-term care, whether that care is provided at home or in a facility. The benefit is paid to help cover the cost of a home health aide, assisted living, adult

Long-term care insurance: an insurance policy sold to help fund the cost of providing long-term care day care, nursing home, memory care, or any other type of long-term care that is provided. If someone requires long-term care, the majority of the care that is provided is not medical in nature, but custodial. The cost of custodial care is not covered by medical insurance and can be exorbitant. According to Genworth's 2013 Cost of Care Survey, the median annual cost of nursing home care is $83,950. Across the country, the annual cost of nursing home care ranges from a high of $133,225 in Massachusetts and $125,732 in New York, to a low of $58,035 in Missouri, and $61,320 in Texas. The Web site listing the average cost of care for each state can be found at https://www.genworth.com/corporate/about-genworth/industry-expertise/cost-of-care.html.

There are many companies that sell long-term care insurance, and there are many different benefits offered. The monthly cost, or premiums, for a policy can vary greatly depending on which benefits are included in the policy. For example, if certain inflation protection factors are built into the policy, the cost may be increased. An inflation protection factor will insure against the loss in value in a daily premium.

Example

Policy A — No Inflation Protection

Policy benefits will pay $50 per day for every day that an individual is in a skilled nursing facility or requires home care. At the time the policy was written, the average daily cost of a skilled nursing facility was $50 per day. Twenty years after taking out the policy and paying the premiums, the individual has a medical issue and begins receiving care in a skilled nursing facility. At the time the insured files a claim, the cost of care in the facility has now skyrocketed to $150 per day. The policy will only pay the $50 per day premium written in the policy.

Policy B — Inflation Protection

Policy benefits provide for inflation protection of 3 percent per year, so that every year the policy remains in effect, the daily benefit increases by a 3 percent inflation rate. Over the course of 20 years, the daily benefit keeps up with inflation and now offers $150 per day in benefits paid which covers the daily cost of care.

Trigger: the conditions that cause a long-term care policy to begin paying benefits

Another thing that greatly affects the cost is when the policy benefits are paid. The point at which a claim is paid is often referred to as a **trigger.** The factors that trigger the payment of benefits under a long-term care policy are the individual's ability to complete his or her ADLs. As described above, the ADLs are those things that a competent adult does for himself or herself on a daily basis, such as getting up from bed or transferring from the bed, toileting, bathing, dressing, eating, and communicating. When someone begins to lose the ability to complete ADLs, assistance or care is needed. Policies are written with a requirement of the loss of a certain number of ADLs to trigger the payment of benefits. For example, a policy could be written that would require the loss of three or four ADLs in order to keep the premiums lower. The individual's need for care would have to be great before the policy would pay benefits. Policies that require only the loss of two ADLs are more costly because the individual's care need does not have to be as great before payment of the benefit is triggered.

Losing an ADL can be as simple as being very unsteady in gait, not able to stand in a shower, or not able to get into and out of a bathtub. If the individual develops a gait or balance issue, it could also affect the ability to transfer from a bed to a wheelchair or commode chair. With a gait and transfer issue, the individual could be eligible for benefits under a policy that requires only the loss of two ADLs.

Practice Tip

It is helpful to find two or three reputable long-term care insurance brokers and keep their business cards in the office to offer to clients without specifically endorsing any one particular individual.

---

2. Combination Policies

There are combination policies available that combine elements of traditional life insurance and long-term care insurance. For example, a combination policy may provide life insurance benefits of $250,000. If the policy owner dies without needing long-term care, his or her beneficiaries receive the full proceeds of the policy. If the policy owner requires long-term care, the life insurance proceeds are reduced by the amount of long-term care benefits paid. Any portion of death benefit not used for long-term care will go to the beneficiaries as a death benefit. If the policy was worth $250,000 and $100,000 of long-term care benefits are used, $150,000 of death benefit is still available.

3. Using Life Insurance to Pay for Long-Term Care

If an individual cannot afford long-term care insurance or has not obtained such insurance before the onset of a disease or illness requiring long-term care, there are other means of paying for care. There are three ways by which an individual can tap into the value accumulated in a life insurance policy to help pay for the cost of long-term care.

1. Life settlement: A life settlement is the sale of an existing life insurance policy for the current value of the policy. The policy is sold, and there is little or no death benefit available to the beneficiaries of the policy. It is not the same as surrendering the policy back to the issuing insurer for the cash surrender value. The option of doing a life settlement is available only to women aged 74 years or older and men aged 70 years or older.

> **Life settlement:** sale of an existing life insurance policy for the current value of the policy

2. Viatical settlement: The second way that the value of an existing life insurance policy can be tapped to pay for long-term care is through a viatical settlement. A *viatical settlement* is a process by which an existing life insurance policy is sold to a third party. It is possible to sell the policy only if the individual is terminally ill and has a life expectancy of two years or less. The viatical company to whom the policy is sold pays the individual a portion of the death benefit proceeds, with no death benefits being paid to any of the previous beneficiaries of the policy.

> **Viatical settlement:** a process by which an existing life insurance policy is sold to a third party

3. Accelerated death benefits: Accelerated death benefits allow an individual to get an advance on the life insurance death benefit. Life insurance policies can be written to allow for such advances in the event of a terminal illness, when funds are need for long-term care, such as permanent residence in a skilled nursing facility. The maximum benefit available is 50 percent of the death benefit. The monies paid are not taxed, but the amount paid is deducted from the death benefit paid to the beneficiaries.

4.   Reverse Mortgage

In a **conventional mortgage**, the borrower receives a sum of money to purchase a house and then makes a monthly payment to the lender. Each payment consists of a certain amount of principal and interest. Each payment of principal decreases the loan and thereby increases the equity in the home. A **reverse mortgage** is a different type of home mortgage that converts a portion of the equity in a home into cash, which is then paid to the homeowner.

In order to qualify for a reverse mortgage, the homeowners have to be a minimum of 62 years old and either own the home outright or have a small enough mortgage that it can be paid off with the proceeds of the reverse mortgage. The homeowners must have the resources available to continue to pay the property taxes and homeowner's insurance. The home must be a single-family home or a home with up to four units in which the person borrowing the money occupies one unit. A condominium or manufactured home may also be able to meet the requirements.

The funds obtained from a reverse mortgage can be paid to the homeowners in a lump sum, monthly payments, a line of credit, or some combination of these payment methods. A monthly income stream from a reverse mortgage can be used to fund long-term care in the home, allowing the homeowner to stay in his or her home. When the homeowners die, sell the house, or no longer live in the home for 12 consecutive months, the loan comes due. A reverse mortgage is a **nonrecourse loan**. This means that the lender has recourse, or the ability to collect from the property, not from the homeowners or the homeowners' heirs. When the homeowner no longer lives in the house, the family or heirs have the option of paying off the reverse mortgage or selling the property. If the proceeds of the sale of the property are insufficient to pay off the mortgage, the lender cannot require that the family pay the outstanding amount.

Reverse mortgages are not appropriate for every senior. The financing costs and interest can make the loan very expensive. In addition, the interest compounds over the life of the loan which can cause the loan to grow dramatically over time. The longer a homeowner has a reverse mortgage, the more likely it is that most or all of the home equity is depleted when the homeowner passes away or no longer lives in the home. Despite these negatives, the reverse mortgage can be a good option for seniors who would otherwise not be able to afford to pay for home care.

5.   Social Security

Social security is a federal benefit program for retirees, disabled persons, and the families of retired, disabled, or deceased workers, which provides monthly income. It

Conventional mortgage: one in which the borrower receives a sum of money to purchase a house and then makes a monthly payment to the lender

Reverse mortgage: a nonrecourse loan on the equity value of a home that provides either monthly payments or a lump sum payment that can be used for care

Nonrecourse loan: a loan where the lender cannot collect from the homeowners or the homeowner's heirs but only from the property itself; when the property is sold, if the proceeds do not satisfy the outstanding amount of the loan, the lender cannot collect from the owner

Social security: a federal benefit program for retirees, disabled persons, and the families of retired, disabled, or deceased workers was developed in 1935 as part of President Franklin D. Roosevelt's New Deal plan to help keep Americans out of poverty and lift the United States out of the Great Depression. Social security is funded through payroll taxes. Social security benefits include Medicare and Medicaid. The ability to receive retirement benefits is based on the year someone was born. Some retirees can begin collecting as early as 62, others not until age 67. The amount of social security that is received is based on the average wages the person earned over his or her lifetime. In January 2013, the average monthly benefit for a retired worker was $1,264 a month. Spouses may also be eligible for social security benefits even if the spouse has very little or no work history. Widows/widowers, disabled workers, spouses, and children of disabled or deceased workers can all be eligible to receive benefits. The maximum social security benefit for a worker retiring at the 2013 full retirement age (66) is $2,533 a month. Social security can supplement a pension or other retirement benefits, but it is inadequate to pay the monthly costs of long-term care either in a facility or at home.

6.   Pensions—Employee Benefits

A **pension** is a retirement plan in which a specific amount is paid every month to a retiree based on the number of years of service with the company. Some pension plans also provide the employee with monthly income if the employee becomes disabled. A pension can be either a **defined benefit plan** or a **defined contribution plan**. In a *defined benefit plan*, the amount paid upon retirement is determined by a set formula and remains the same, independent of investment returns. In a *defined contribution plan*, the employee and employer contribute funds into an individual retirement account for each employee. The funds in the account are invested, and the amount of the benefit can go up, or down, with fluctuations in the market. An example of a defined contribution pension benefit plan is an IRA (individual retirement account) or 401(k).

Pension benefits are income that can also be used to help pay for long-term care needs. The majority of seniors do not have adequate monthly income to pay for long-term care needs even when combining social security and pension benefits. Without long-term care insurance, the person needing care is forced to use up savings accounts and retirement accounts and then turn to alternative means of paying for the care as set forth above.

Pension: a retirement plan in which a specific amount is paid every month to a retiree based on the number of years of service with the company

Defined benefit plan: a pension plan in which the amount paid upon retirement is determined by a set formula and remains the same, independent of investment returns

Defined contribution plan: a pension plan in which the employee and employer contribute funds into an individual retirement account for each employee, and the funds in the account are invested, allowing the amount of benefit to go up or down with fluctuations in the market

7.   Veteran's Benefits

There are many benefits available to veterans and their families. The benefits include disability compensation, education, healthcare, home loans, insurance, pension, vocational rehabilitation and employment, aid and attendance and homebound benefits, and burial and memorial benefits. People who are eligible for Veterans Administration (VA) benefits include uniformed service members who are currently serving, and veterans, or the spouse, child, or parent of a deceased or disabled service member or veteran.

Veterans who have a service-connected disability are entitled to disability compensation. In order to be eligible for disability compensation, the veteran's disability had to have arisen during service, or was worsened or aggravated by service, and is related to the veteran's service. To receive disability compensation, the veteran must have been discharged under other than dishonorable conditions. This means a conditional discharge, an honorable discharge, or any other form of discharge from service that is not a dishonorable discharge. A veteran may require the assistance of an attorney if the veteran needs to change the condition of his or her discharge in order to become eligible for benefits.

Veterans who have limited income (or no income) and are either aged 65 or older or are permanently and totally disabled may be entitled to a veteran's pension. In order for a veteran to be eligible for a veteran's pension, the veteran has to have annual income that is below the maximum amount set by law. If the veteran has more annual income than the maximum allowable amount, the veteran is not entitled to a veteran's pension.

Veterans who are eligible for a VA pension and require the aid and attendance of another person or are housebound may be eligible for additional monetary payment called Aid and Attendance. In order to be eligible, the veteran must require assistance with ADLs. Aid and Attendance benefits are paid to the veteran only as an additional benefit to the veteran's monthly pension. In order to be eligible for Aid and Attendance, a veteran must first be eligible for a pension. The income eligibility requirements to receive Aid and Attendance are higher than the basis pension.

A veteran's dependents and survivors may also be eligible for certain VA benefits. Dependency and Indemnity Compensation (DIC) is a monthly benefit paid to a surviving spouse of a veteran. The monthly benefit may also include payments for dependent children. The DIC benefit is available to an eligible spouse of a service member who died during active military service or from a service-connected disability, or of a veteran who was rated totally disabled at the time of death. The parents of a veteran may also be eligible for DIC based on financial need.

Most veterans applying for veterans benefits do not need an attorney. The assistance of an attorney may be necessary if the veteran is denied benefits for which the veteran believes he or she is eligible or, as discussed above, the veteran wants to appeal the discharge classification. The veteran may retain an attorney to file an appeal of the benefits denial or discharge. Most attorneys who do VA benefit work are accredited by the VA. The National Organization of Veterans Advocates (NOVA) Website has a list of attorneys who have been accredited by the VA. The Web site also lists non-attorney advocates who can assist with claims: https://vetadvocates.org.

An in-depth discussion of all of the veteran's benefits available and the way in which a veteran becomes eligible for benefits is beyond the scope of this text. The paralegal should be aware that veteran's benefits may provide an additional source of income to the veteran and/or the veteran's spouse and children, and may also provide long-term care benefits in the form of Aid and Attendance.

8.   Responsible Party

Every resident entering a care facility is required to sign an admissions agreement. The agreement will list the facility's policies on things such as roommates and private rooms, payment of fees, use of different doctors, laundry, holding a bed open if the resident is temporarily in the hospital, and so forth. The agreement must be signed by the resident. If the resident is unable to sign the agreement, or the facility feels the resident does not understand the agreement, the facility may look to another family member to sign on behalf of the resident.

Family members must be careful that they do not inadvertently become responsible for paying for the care their loved one is receiving by signing the admissions agreement as the responsible party. The person signing the agreement on behalf of the resident should be the resident's power of attorney. The person then signs the admission agreement only as power of attorney and not individually. If the agreement is signed by a power of attorney, the agent appointed under the power of attorney is agreeing to use the resident's funds to provide for the resident's care. If a family member signs the admissions agreement as the responsible party, the family member is agreeing to be responsible for paying for the resident's care. Admission agreements are often long, formal contracts, and must be read with care. Clients who are assisting a loved one with transitioning to a care facility will often ask the attorney to review the agreement. A sample of an admissions agreement that is fairly typical in New Jersey can be found on the companion Web site.

C. **Elder Abuse**

Elder abuse is defined in the Federal Elder Justice Act as the knowing infliction of physical or psychological harm or the knowing deprivation of goods or services that are necessary to meet essential needs or to avoid physical or psychological harm (Subtitle H in Title VI of Public Act 111–148 PPACA). Elder abuse can be physical, mental/emotional, sexual, or financial. Elder abuse can also be in the form of neglect or abandonment of the senior. It can occur in a facility or in the home. The abuser can be a care provider, family member, or anyone who is in a position to exploit an elderly person.

> **Elder abuse:** the knowing infliction of physical or psychological harm or the knowing deprivation of goods or services that are necessary to meet essential needs or to avoid physical or psychological harm

Elder abuse can be unintentional. As mentioned above, many caregivers are untrained, unpaid family members squeezed into what is called the "sandwich generation": families that have young children at home that need care and an elderly parent who needs care. The situation can lead to a lot of frustration, which can lead to verbally abusive behavior. Even if abuse is unintentional, it is still unacceptable. There are many support groups available for family caregivers such as the Alzheimer's Association (http://www.alz.org) and the Care Giver Action Group (http://caregiveraction.org).

If you suspect elder abuse, it should be reported immediately. There are laws in all 50 states aimed at preventing elder abuse. Many states have specific task forces assigned to investigating allegations of elder abuse. States have enacted laws making financial abuse of anyone considered a "vulnerable adult" a crime. In California, Missouri, Massachusetts, and other states, certain professionals are **mandated reporters**—persons who have assumed responsibility for an elder or dependent adult. For example, there are mandatory reporting laws in place requiring a caretaker, social worker, physician, or other professional who has reasonable cause to suspect or believe that an elderly person is being abused to make a report.

> **Mandated reporters:** persons who have assumed responsibility for an elder or dependent adult or other professional who has reasonable cause to suspect or believe that an elderly person is being abused to make a report

The office of Adult Protective Services (APS) is the typical name for the governmental agency responsible for investigating reports of elder abuse and providing victims of elder abuse with treatment and protective services. The agency could be known as Adult Protective Services, Agency on Aging, or County Department of Social Services. For purposes of this text, the agency will be referred to as APS. The APS office is often called upon to initiate a guardianship action in order to protect an elderly person from an abusive situation. Most county APS offices have 24-hour emergency contact numbers where reports of abuse can be made anonymously.

An example of how an issue of elder abuse can arise is the following. A power of attorney had previously been prepared for a client Charles Barbar. A bank teller from the local bank calls the office reporting that Mr. Barbar's nephew, Nathan, has brought him in three times in the last few weeks, each time withdrawing large sums of money using the power of attorney. The teller knows the attorney who prepared the power of attorney because the attorney's office is next door to the bank. After several phone calls to Mr. Barbar, the attorney begins to suspect that Nathan is financially abusing Mr. Barbar. These suspicions were reported to the Adult Protective Services office and county prosecutor. An investigation was conducted revealing that his nephew was financially abusing Mr. Barbar. Nathan was withdrawing large sums of money from Mr. Barbar but was not using the money for Mr. Barbar's care. The money was being spent by Nathan to pay off gambling debts. Nathan was not providing care for Mr. Barbar. His living conditions were unhygienic, he was not receiving his medications properly, and he did not have adequate food in the house. Mr. Barbar was clearly being neglected. It appeared that Nathan was financially abusing Mr. Barbar as well as neglecting his care. APS initiated a guardianship to protect Mr. Barbar from financial abuse and neglect.

Practice Tip

The paralegal should have the contact numbers for the county office responsible for investigating reports of elder abuse.

The elder law attorney is often asked for information on many different topics beyond just wills, trusts, and estates. Knowing at least some basic information about other issues facing seniors will enhance the attorney's practice.

Summary

Estate planning can include planning for long term care, sources of funding for care, including government and veteran's benefits, and where the care will be provided. Clients may seek advice for themselves, an elderly parent, or relative. The estate planning and elder law attorney should always be on the lookout for sign of elder abuse, whether physical, emotional, or financial. The attorney and paralegal should know the steps to be taken if abuse is suspected.

Review Questions

1. Name three types of care facilities and briefly describe the levels of care available.

2. How can life insurance be used to pay for long-term care?

3. What are some of the requirements to be eligible for a reverse mortgage?

4. What is the difference between a conventional mortgage and a reverse mortgage?

True or False

1. T   F   Respite care is a type of long-term care.

2. T   F   Medicare pays for long-term care.

3. T   F   Eating, bathing, and walking are examples of activities of daily living.

4. T   F   Adult day care can be used in conjunction with a family caregiver or home health aide.

5. T   F   Long-term care insurance pays only for care in a facility.

6. T   F   Any amount still on a reverse mortgage after the property is sold has to be paid from the decedent's estate.

7. T   F   Elder abuse is not a crime.

8. T   F   Social security pays benefits to retired workers, disabled workers, and the spouses and children of deceased or disabled workers.

9. T   F   Every veteran that was ever in the service will receive a veteran's pension.

Key Terms

Activities of daily living
Adult day care
Assisted-living facility
Congregate-care facility
Conventional mortgage
Custodial care
Defined benefit plan
Defined contribution plan
Elder abuse
Hospice care
Independent-living
 community
Intermediate-care facility

Life settlement
Long-term care insurance
Mandated reporters
Nonrecourse loan
Pension
Rehabilitative-care facility
Respite care
Reverse mortgage
Skilled nursing care
Skilled nursing facility
Social security
Trigger
Viatical settlement

Administrative Issues

This chapter will cover some of the miscellaneous administrative duties that a paralegal will be required to address. Some of these duties are not unique to wills, estates, and trusts but are necessary in every area of a law practice. This chapter will focus on the day-to-day administrative requirements that a paralegal could encounter with a focus on the wills, estates, and trusts aspects of administrative duties.

A. Retainer Agreements

A **retainer agreement** is a form of contract between an attorney and a client that establishes the fee that will be paid for the services provided, and the scope of the services. Many attorneys do not ask clients to sign retainer agreements when doing estate-planning documents. There is a perception that there is no need for an agreement since the attorney is "only" preparing a will. This is a mistake. Attorney fee agreements should be prepared for every client, no matter how routine the legal services provided. In some jurisdictions, for some types of matters, a retainer agreement is required by law.

The fees can be hourly or transactional. **Hourly fees** are charged per hour, or any portion of an hour that an attorney works on a file. If the attorney is charging by the hour, the attorney must prepare an itemized statement of all time spent, and costs for the client. **Transactional fees or flat fees** are set fees that are established for each document or transaction, for example, $500 for preparation of a simple will, or $250 for preparation of a power of attorney. Whether the attorney has agreed to prepare the documents for a flat fee or to charge by the hour, the terms of the arrangement should be recorded in a retainer agreement.

There are some ethical considerations of which the paralegal should be aware in preparing and signing a retainer agreement. The Model Rules suggest that the terms of the representation between the attorney and the client be communicated to the client, preferably in writing [MRPC 1.5 (b)]. A retainer agreement defines who the client is and what the lawyer agrees to do and the fee the client agrees to pay. It avoids

Retainer agreement: a form of contract between an attorney and a client that establishes the fee that will be paid for the services provided, and the scope of the services

Hourly fees: charged per hour, or any portion of an hour that an attorney works on a file

Transactional fees or flat fees: set fees that are established for each document or transaction miscommunication between the lawyer and the client. The retainer agreement lists the attorney's responsibilities to the client.

> ## Practice Tip
>
> The ABA Model Rules of Professional Conduct can be accessed at the following link: http://www.americanbar.org/groups/professional_responsibility/publications/model_rules_of_professional_conduct/model_rules_of_professional_conduct_table_of_contents.html

Let us look at a sample set of facts. In Chapter 2, we reviewed some facts for Mary Cattermole and her elderly mother Ann. Mary Cattermole had called the office and asked to make an appointment for her 88-year-old mother, Ann Norbert. Ann needs some estate-planning documents. Mary and her husband Reg bring Ann to the attorney's office. The attorney meets with Ann, without Mary present. Ann has another child, an adult son named Jeffrey, who is not present at the meeting. The attorney determines that Ann has the necessary capacity to enter into an attorney-client relationship and to execute estate-planning documents. An estate-planning retainer agreement should be prepared for Ann and then signed by Ann and the attorney. A sample estate retainer agreement is shown in Figure 18-1.

ESTATE PLANNING RETAINER AGREEMENT

THIS AGREEMENT, dated January 19, 20_____, is made BETWEEN the Client, **ANN NORBERT**, whose address is 4 Magnolia Terrace, Anytown, referred to individually and collectively as "You," AND **DIANA L. ANDERSON, ESQUIRE,** whose office address is 9 Robbins Street, Mytown, referred to as "Attorney."

   1. **Legal Services To Be Provided**. You agree that Attorney will represent you in the following matter(s):

Consultation regarding potential estate taxes and preparation of estate-planning documents. The legal work includes all necessary conferences, asset gathering, correspondence, preparation and drafting of Last Will and Testament, Codicils, and related work to properly represent you in this matter.

   2. **Additional Legal Services**. If you need any other services which may or may not be related to the above matter, you and Attorney may make a new agreement to provide the other services.

   3. **Legal Fees**. Attorney cannot predict or guarantee what your final bill will be. This will depend on the amount of time spent on your case and the amount of other expenses.

Figure 18-1. Sample Estate Retainer Agreement

Figure 18-1. Continued

Hourly Rate. You agree to pay Attorney for legal services at the following rates:

Rate Per Hour	**Services Of**
$400.00	Diana L. Anderson, Esq., in connection with the above Services.
$100.00	Legal Assistant
OR	

Fee. You agree to pay Attorney the sum of $500 for the preparation of a Last Will and Testament.

4.   **Costs and Expenses**. In addition to legal fees, you must pay the following costs and expenses:

Filing Fees for filing of documents, if necessary, photocopying charges, and any other necessary expenses in this matter.

Signatures. You and Attorney have read and agree to this Agreement. Attorney has answered all of your questions and fully explained this Agreement to your complete satisfaction. You have been given a copy of this Agreement.

Attorney: Client:

_____   _____

DIANA L. ANDERSON   **ANN NORBERT**

Most attorneys use form retainer agreements that are modified to fit each specific client. The length and complexity of the retainer is going to depend on the legal issues being addressed. The paralegal should keep a form bank of retainer agreements used for various types of cases, and refer back to the previously used forms when creating a new retainer for a client.

A copy of the signed retainer should be kept in Ann's file along with all of Ann's contact information, the intake sheet if one was used, and the attorney's notes. A copy of the retainer should be given to Ann. The retainer agreement will list the fees charged for the services provided. Both the attorney's fees and the paralegal's fees are included.

B.   Establishing Attorney's Fees

The Model Rules require that an attorney's fee be reasonable. Rule 1.5 describes how to determine if the fee is reasonable. The paralegal will not be responsible for establishing the fees but will often be responsible for communicating the fees to the client. Potential clients will often call the office shopping around, and ask the cost of preparing a will, or power of attorney. Caution should be used in quoting a price before meeting with the client, even if transactional or flat fees are used. A client may claim he or she needs a "simple will" and ask for the estimated fee, only to reveal later that he or she has a large estate, and the client actually needs complex estate tax planning documents.

C. Payment of Attorney Fees

Other family members of an elderly client often offer to pay for an elderly relative to have a will prepared. An elderly client may have previously relied on a spouse to do all of the finances and paperwork, and now relies on an adult child to write checks or pay bills. Let us continue with the example from above but add in some more facts. The paralegal prepares the retainer, the retainer is reviewed by the attorney, and then given to Ann for signature. As Ann is signing the retainer, Mary pulls out her wallet, asks what the retainer fee will be, and whether or not the attorney accepts credit cards.

Is it acceptable to allow someone else to pay for attorney's fees? Can Mary pay Ann's retainer fee or legal fee? To answer that question, you can reference MRPC 1.8 (2)(f). What should a paralegal do when presented with this situation? Discuss the payment arrangements with the attorney. It will be necessary to get Ann's consent before you accept payment from Mary. Find out if Mary is paying using her own money, or if Mary is just offering to assist Ann with completing the payment arrangements but the funds used for payment belong to Ann. Even if Mary is paying for Ann, using Mary's money, Ann is still the client.

D. Recording Client Information and Attorney Time

Most law firms are going to use some type of time-recording software that allows for time entries and file numbers to be entered and invoices generated. This software may also be able to record the client name and contact information. For wills, estates, and trusts, additional information may need to be included in the client contact information such as the following:

1. Date of death
2. EIN of estate or trust
3. Date of birth
4. Timeline of due dates for tax returns
5. Names and addresses of beneficiaries

The organization and recording of the information needed to complete estate administration, trust administration, or will clients will be unique to each law firm, attorney, or client.

> ## *Practice Tip*
>
> Information used on a day-to-day basis should be available with the client contact information, and on the front of the client's file. Anticipating what information will be needed is a matter of experience, as well as the needs and habits of the attorney.

E. Maintaining Confidentiality

An attorney has a duty to maintain confidentiality of all of the client's information. For the paralegal this means not discussing the client's information with the client's other family members, as well as not discussing the client's information with anyone other than the client. What the client shares with the attorney or the paralegal should never be repeated to anyone, even the client's other family members. The nature of a client's assets or how the client wants his or her estate distributed is confidential information and should never be shared with anyone unless authorized by the client.

Additional Facts: Earlier in this chapter and in Chapter 2, we looked at an example of some ethical issues that could potentially arise with a new client by using the example of Mary Cattermole, Mary's husband Reg, and her elderly mother Ann Norbert. Ann's adult son Jeffrey, who was not present at the meeting, calls the office after the meeting and wants to get a copy of the draft documents that were prepared for his mother. He says he wants to be sure his children's names are spelled correctly.

What Are the Ethical Considerations?

- Ann's documents are confidential. Even though the documents are still in a draft form and have not been executed, the documents still contain confidential information that Ann may not want Jeffrey to know.
- Jeffrey is not the client and has no right to review his mother's documents for content or for accuracy.
- MRPC 1.6 requires that the discussions between the attorney and the client remain confidential, and that the result of those conversations (for example, the decision to create estate-planning documents) also remains confidential.
- Attorney-client privilege extends to the paralegal and to the client's documents.

What Should You Do?

If Ann is with Jeffrey and she is available to come to the phone, speak to her and ask her permission to send a copy of the documents to Jeffrey. If Ann is not available, tell Jeffrey to have his mother contact the office and give her consent to have the documents released. In some states, it is necessary to get consent in writing. Explain to Jeffrey that you are requesting this for the client's protection, and to maintain confidentiality.

> ### Practice Tip
>
> It is a good habit to get consent to disclose documents in writing even if not required by the state in which you live. Consent to disclose documents to other family members can be part of the initial interview when first meeting the client with a statement such as, "Are there any family members you would like to have copies of your draft documents?" or "Are there any family members who should not receive copies of your draft documents?"

The duty to maintain confidentiality continues even after the attorney-client relationship has ended. This means that after the documents are completed and the file is closed, the attorney still has a duty to treat those documents as privileged, and to not release the documents without proper authority. Let us examine another example of when it would be acceptable to release documents.

Additional Facts: One of the documents prepared for Ann was an advance medical directive. Ann named her daughter Mary as her surrogate decision maker. Ann is having a medical issue, and her daughter Mary is out of town. Ann's son Jeffrey is named as the secondary, or backup, surrogate decision maker, but he does not have access to the documents. He needs a copy of the advance medical decision to take to the hospital so the doctors will discuss his mother's medical condition with him.

What Are the Ethical Considerations?

- Is it a breach of confidentiality or the attorney-client privilege to release a copy of Ann's advance medical directive to her son Jeffrey, who is her surrogate decision maker?

What Should You Do?

In this situation, a copy of the advance directive can be released to Jeffrey. In most states, a copy of an advance directive is acceptable. It is not necessary to have the original. Many clients keep a copy with them, or provide copies to each doctor they see on a regular basis. The paralegal should confirm with the attorney that it is acceptable to give Jeffrey a copy and then make the copy available to him.

F.   Conflicts of Interest

A conflict of interest occurs when representing one client will be directly adverse to another client. In estate planning, conflicts of interest can also arise when representing several family members if a disagreement arises among them (MRPC 1.7).

In an elder law and estate-planning context, a conflict of interest can also arise if an attorney represents a client for estate-planning purposes and then at some later date, the client loses capacity, and the family wishes to file a guardianship.

The guardianship action is actually adverse to the client. An attorney who prepared the estate-planning documents for a client cannot then file a guardianship action against that same client. To illustrate this point, let us continue with our client Ann.

Additional Facts: A will, power of attorney, and medical directive are prepared for Ann. The legal bill is paid, and the attorney-client relationship is completed. Several years later, Reg and Mary call the office again. Ann had become estranged from her daughter and destroyed the power of attorney and advance medical directive. Unfortunately, Ann has had a stroke and is in the hospital. A neighbor of Ann's called Mary, but no one at the hospital will speak to Mary about Ann's condition. Mary has been told she will need to file a petition with the court to become her mother's guardian, and she wants to hire the attorney who prepared her estate-planning documents.

When preparing the estate-planning documents, Ann was the client. Now Ann is incapacitated, and the documents are no longer valid because she destroyed them. Even if the attorney has copies, Ann destroying the documents shows her intent to revoke the powers given to Mary. Because Ann no longer has valid documents, she needs a guardian to advocate for her medical needs. Ann is no longer the client. Mary, and possibly Mary's brother Jeffrey, would be the clients in the guardianship petition.

What Are the Ethical Considerations?

■ Filing a guardianship petition with Mary as the client is adverse to Ann, a former client.

■ Ann has lost capacity and cannot consent to or waive the potential conflict.

What Should You Do?

This call should be given to the attorney, who will most likely have to refer Mary to another elder law attorney to file the guardianship petition. An appointment should not be made for Mary without discussing the potential conflict with the attorney.

Let us look at a completely different situation in which a conflict of interest could arise and how to resolve that conflict.

Additional Facts: After Ann's estate-planning documents are complete, Reg and Mary call the attorney back and ask for an appointment to discuss their own estate-planning issues. Reg and Mary make an appointment, go through the client intake process, and meet with the attorney. The attorney agrees to prepare some estate-planning documents, and Reg and Mary sign a retainer. The wills that the attorney intends to prepare for Reg and Mary are reciprocal wills, meaning Reg will leave everything to Mary, and Mary will leave everything to Reg. If they both pass, they will leave the estate to their children. The day after the appointment, Reg calls the office asking to speak to the attorney by himself. He indicates that he wants to discuss something privately with the attorney and does not want his wife to know about the conversation.

What Are the Ethical Considerations?

■ Reg and Mary are both clients. Agreeing to keep information that Reg provides a secret from Mary is a conflict of the duty owed to Mary.

What Should You Do?

It is good practice to discuss potential conflict of interest at the first meeting with the client. If the clients are husband and wife, they should be told that the information each of them provides could not be kept confidential if the information impacts the other party. It is common to require a husband and wife to sign a consent agreement indicating that they understand this potential conflict of interest and agree to disclose everything to each other. A sample of such a consent agreement is in Figure 18-2.

If the parties cannot agree and do not want to sign the agreement, then each will need to obtain separate counsel. A conflict of interest between a husband and wife does not often occur when preparing estate-planning documents. Discussing the potential for a conflict at the first meeting, and getting the clients to sign the consent form ensure that the clients are aware of the attorney's position and ethical obligations.

Conflicts of interest can arise in other situations. Let us add to our fact pattern to see how a conflict of interest might arise in an estate challenge situation.

Additional Facts: Many years after the attorney prepared documents for Ann, she passes away. Mary probates the will herself, but Ann's son Jeffrey raises a challenge to the will. Jeffrey calls the office and wants to get copies of the notes and any prior wills and wants to meet with the attorney to discuss the will.

CONSENT TO JOINT REPRESENTATION

We, REGINALD CATERMOLE and MARY CATERMOLE, understand that the Model Rules of Professional Conduct, Rule 1.7, says in part that a lawyer shall not represent a client if the representation of that client will be directly adverse to another client unless: (1) the lawyer reasonably believes that representation will not adversely affect the relationship with the other client; and (2) each client consents after a full disclosure of the circumstances and consultation with the client.

We have been advised by Diana L. Anderson, Esquire, that she believes that representing both of us in the preparation of estate-planning document will not adversely affect the relationship with either of us. We hereby acknowledge that full disclosure of the circumstances has been made to us and that we have been consulted regarding the conflict of interest or the appearance of such conflict of interest.

We consent to the joint representation by Diana L. Anderson, Esquire in accordance with Rule of Professional Conduct 1.7. We understand that information either of us provides to the attorney will not be kept confidential from either of us. We agree that should this circumstance change, and our interests become adverse, that one party will obtain separate counsel.

REGINALD CATERMOLE   Date: _____

MARY CATERMOLE   Date: _____

Figure 18-2. Consent to Joint Representation

What Are the Ethical Considerations?

■ The conversations the attorney had with Ann, the notes that were taken, and any previous drafts of the will are all attorney-client privileged.

■ The attorney also represented Mary and Reg in preparing estate-planning documents.

What Should You Do?

After discussing with the attorney, Jeffrey's call should be returned, and he should be told that the attorney could not share any of the documents with him because Ann's file is attorney-client privileged. In addition, the attorney cannot discuss the matter with Jeffrey because the attorney has also represented Mary, and Jeffrey's interests in Ann's estate are adversarial to Mary.

It is absolutely essential for the paralegal to be familiar with the ethical rules that attorneys must follow. The paralegal will not be expected to make decisions regarding the ethical issues that come up, but instead will be expected to recognize his or her role in preventing inadvertent ethical violations. If there are any potential ethical problems, the problems should be brought to the immediate attention of the attorney for whom the paralegal works. Any ethical violations by a paralegal can result in a disciplinary action against the attorney. Research your state's laws, and be familiar with them.

Summary

A retainer agreement should be prepared for every client, even if the work provided is very limited, such as the preparation of a single document. The paralegal should become familiar with the ethics rules, including client confidentiality, and the various ways in which a conflict of interest could arise.

Review Questions

1. Can an attorney represent a husband and wife in preparing an estate plan, or does each party need to get a separate lawyer?

2. Can an attorney represent a client for estate-planning purposes and then years later represent the client's adult daughter in a guardianship against the client?

3. Is it permissible to give copies of a client's documents:
   a. To the client
   b. To the client's spouse
   c. To the client's children
   d. To a financial representative

4. You recommend to your next-door neighbor Louise that she comes to the office for a consultation about estate planning with the attorney for whom you are

working. She does and decides to have some documents prepared that the attorney gives to you to complete. Later that evening, you see some of your other neighbors outside, and you casually mention that Louise was in your office today. Is that a breach of confidentiality? Why or why not?

5. You observe an adult child instructing her mother how to answer questions while they are waiting in the lobby for a meeting with an attorney. What is your obligation to discuss this with the attorney?

True or False

1. T   F   If a client needs only a simple will, a retainer agreement is not necessary.

2. T   F   An attorney can represent an elderly person in preparing estate-planning documents and later represent the person's daughter in a guardianship action seeking to have the person found to be incapacitated.

3. T   F   Legal fees for estate-planning documents can be charged by the hour or by the document.

4. T   F   A conflict of interest can arise when representing several family members in the administration of an estate.

5. T   F   The client is the only person who can obtain copies of the client's documents.

6. T   F   Clients can consent to joint representation.

7. T   F   A paralegal can discuss the contents of a client's will with anyone because the paralegal is not bound by the attorney-client privilege.

8. T   F   Some states require consent for release of documents to be in writing.

9. T   F   An adult child can tell the attorney his mother's wishes for the distribution of her estate, and the attorney does not have to speak to Mom.

10. T   F   An adult child can pay for his mother's will without raising any ethical issues.

Key Terms

Hourly fees
Retainer agreement

Transactional fees or
   flat fees

Glossary

A/B will: type of will that addresses estate tax issues, that contains two trusts: The first trust, or the "A" trust, is a marital trust, and the second trust is the "B" trust, which is known the *credit shelter*, or *by-pass marital trust*.

Account of convenience: a joint account designation done for an elderly person's convenience.

Accounting: a report of income and expenditures in which the total balance remaining is determined for a certain period of time.

Activities of daily living: those things that a competent adult does for himself or herself on a daily basis.

Ademption by extinction: occurs when property is sold by the testator prior to death, and is therefore not owned by the testator as of the date of death.

Ademption by satisfaction: occurs when the testator has already given the beneficiary the asset prior to death.

Administrator: the person appointed as the representative of the estate when there is no will, or if the executor appointed in the will cannot serve or if there is some problem with the will.

Administrator ad litem: an administrator "during the litigation." An administrator ad litem is appointed by the court when there is any court proceeding in which the estate of a deceased person must be represented and there is no executor or administrator for the estate.

Administrator ad prosequendum: an administrator appointed for the purposes of prosecuting a wrongful death.

Adoption: a legal proceeding by which a person, or persons, assumes the rights and obligations of parenting another person.

Adult: someone who has reached the age of majority, usually age 18 or older, or someone who is married or emancipated, even if younger than the age of majority.

Adult day care: a program run outside the home during specific daytime hours, which provides meals, socialization and hygiene-related services.

Advance health care directive: see *advance medical directive.*

Advance medical directive: a legal document that records a person's choices with regard to medical treatment and appoints a representative to help with medical decisions if the person is unable to make those decisions; also known as an *advance health care directive.*

Agent: the person authorized to act on behalf of the principal; also known as *attorney-in-fact.*

Ancestors: the relatives in the generation above the decedent; also known as *ascendants.*

Ancillary administration: see *ancillary probate.*

Ancillary probate: to prove, validate and register a will in another jurisdiction where real property is owned; also known as *ancillary administration.*

Annuity: a form of insurance or investment product that is designed to pay out a stream of payments to the owner at a later point in time.

Anti-lapse statutes: state laws that will save a bequest if it has been made to a person who has predeceased the testator, and that person is included in the list of beneficiaries protected by the statute.

Arm's-length transaction: transaction in which there is no relationship between the parties.

Ascendants: see *ancestors.*

Ascertainable standard: a standard that governs the use of trust assets and prevents the assets from being considered part of the trustee's assets for estate tax purposes.

Assisted-living facility: a living environment in which some care or assistance is provided.

Attestation clause: a statement indicating that the notary swears or affirms an oath that the signatures are of the people identified in the document.

Attorney-in-fact: see *agent.*

Augmented estate: the value of the estate plus the value of anything the decedent gave away prior to death, the decedent's non-probate assets, and joint assets owned with the surviving spouse.

Basis: the purchase price paid for an asset.

Beneficiary: the person who is receiving the benefits (or proceeds) of an estate, retirement plan, annuity, trust or life insurance policy.

Bequest: a provision in the will that directs the distribution of assets to a beneficiary.

Beyond a reasonable doubt: the highest level of proof requiring the trier of fact has no doubt as to the guilt of the party.

Body of the trust: see *corpus.*

Bounty: the assets that one owns, either real or personal property.

Burden of proof: the set of requirements that a party must meet to prove the case.

By-pass trust: type of trust where the trust property is not subject to federal estate tax in the surviving spouse's estate. The assets placed into the trust "by-pass" the surviving spouse and "by-pass" the tax; also known as a *credit shelter trust.*

Capacity: ability to govern yourself and your own affairs.

Capital gains taxes: taxes that are imposed on the gain in an investment.

Case law: law that is developed in the courts through the application of statutory law to specific facts.

Caveat: a warning against allowing probate of a will.

Charitable remainder annuity trust: a trust that annually pays the donor a fixed percentage of the value of the donated assets at the time those assets were placed in the trust.

Charitable remainder unitrust: trust with a fixed annual percentage payout, but a variable dollar amount as the assets are revalued each year.

Clear and convincing evidence: a mid-level standard requiring the party to prove that the allegations are more probable to be true than not.

Clifford trust: a type of *irrevocable inter vivos trust* that was previously used to shelter income producing assets.

Codicil: an amendment to a will.

Codified: collected and organized into a code.

Co-fiduciary: two people to serve together as a fiduciary.

Collateral descendants: those that descended from an ancestor that is common to the decedent, but who are not direct descendants of the decedent.

Collateral relatives: those who have a common ancestor to the decedent.

Commission: payment to the personal representative for all of the work that is required, calculated as a percentage of the principal and income of the estate.

Common form: the process by which a will is admitted to probate when the will conforms to all of the state's requirements, also known as informal probate.

Common law: the law that is developed in the courts through the decisions of judges.

Community property: property owned by married couples with each spouse owning a fifty-percent (50%) interest in the property.

Competent: capacity to write a will.

Congregate-care facility: a facility with units or sections for more independent living and sections for those requiring more care.

Conservator: a person appointed by the court to make financial decisions for an incapacitated person.

Constructive trust: a trust created by a court regardless of the parties' intentions and is an equitable remedy imposed by a court.

Contestant: person raising the allegations in the complaint, also known as the plaintiff or petitioner.

Contingent beneficiaries: beneficiaries who are eligible to receive a distribution if the first (primary) beneficiary has predeceased.

Conventional mortgage: mortgage where the borrower receives a sum of money to purchase a house and then makes a monthly payment to the lender.

Corpus: the money or assets in the trust; also called *principal* or *body of the trust.*

Credit shelter trust: see *by-pass trust.*

Credit shelter will: a will containing a credit shelter trust that shelters assets from estate tax.

Curtesy: a husband's entitlement to a life estate property that his wife possessed at her death.

Custodial care: non-skilled, non-medical care such as the care needed for assistance with *activities of daily living.*

Cy-près doctrine: an abbreviated form of the French term *cy-près comme possible,* which means "as near as possible" which requires that when a trust or a bequest in a will cannot be completed, the funds in the trust or bequest should be used to the nearest possible purpose.

Decedent: the person who has died.

Declaration of trust: a trust that is revocable and where the grantor serves as the trustee.

Deductions: amounts taken out of the gross estate that reduce its value.

Defined benefit plan: a pension plan in which the amount paid upon retirement is determined by a set formula and remains the same, independent of investment returns.

Defined contribution plan: a pension plan in which the employee and employer contribute funds into an individual retirement account for each employee, and the funds in the account are invested, allowing the amount of benefit to go up, or down, with fluctuations in the market.

Degree of consanguinity: the blood relationship of the heirs; also called *degree of kinship.*

Degree of kinship: see *degree of consanguinity.*

Demonstrative bequest: a gift of a certain amount of property from a specific source.

Descendants: relatives in the generation below the decedent, such as the decedent's children.

Devise: a distribution of real property in a will.

Devisee: the person who receives the *devise*.

Disclaimer: a limitation or denial of civil liability.

Discretionary trust: see *sprinkling trust*.

Disinherit: to exclude someone from the will.

Distributees: see *heirs*.

Diversify the investments: invest in a number of different types of things.

Dividend: a distribution of money made to a shareholder of stock of a company.

Doctrine of laches: an equitable defense asserting that plaintiff neglected to act, or that there was unreasonable delay in pursuing a right or claim in such a way as to prejudice the opposing party.

Domicile: see *legal residence*.

Domiciliary probate: occurs when a decedent's will is probated in the state in which the decedent was domiciled.

Dower: a wife's interest in her husband's property upon his death.

Durable power of attorney: a grant of authority that survives any period of disability of the principal.

Elder abuse: the knowing infliction of physical or psychological harm or the knowing deprivation of goods or services that are necessary to meet essential needs or to avoid physical or psychological harm.

Elective share: the minimum portion of the estate which the surviving spouse may elect to take instead of what he or she was left in the decedent's will; also referred to as *widow's share*, *statutory share*, or *forced share*.

Employer Identification Number (EIN):   serves as the taxpayer identification number for the trust.

Equitable remedies: those remedies that do not involve monetary damages but instead require specific performance in doing, or not doing a specific task.

Escheat: occurs when a person dies intestate without any other person capable of taking the property as an heir; the assets in the estate are transferred to the state in which the decedent lived at the time of death.

Estate: all of the assets and possessions of the person who died.

Estate plan: the documents that comprise the plan that is put together to manage a person's assets and care, if the person becomes incapacitated or dies.

Estate planning: a general term to describe the plan to distribute possessions after death.

Exculpatory clause: a provision in a trust or contract that relieves one party from liability.

Executed: signed by the testator, trustee, or grantor and the witnesses, in the specific way required by the state in which the testator lives.

Executing the will: the testator signing the will by the testator with the witnesses present, in the specific way required by the state in which the testator lives.

Executor: the fiduciary appointed in a will who is responsible for marshaling, or gathering, the decedent's assets, paying all of the decedent's debts and then distributing the assets to the beneficiaries named in the will; also called *personal representative.*

Express trust: trust specifically created by the expressed intentions of the grantor or settlor, and is evidenced by a written document setting forth the grantor's goal for use of the trust monies, the terms and conditions of distribution and identification of the beneficiaries.

Fair market value: the price at which the property would sell in an *arm's-length transaction* between a willing buyer and a willing seller.

Family trust: trust that is generally funded by the assets left in the decedent's estate that are not included in the marital trust. The grantor decides the terms of the trust, the beneficiaries, and appoints a trustee to administer the trust.

Fee simple: a term used to describe when a property owner owns all of the rights associated with a piece of property; also called *fee simple absolute.*

Fee simple absolute: see *fee simple.*

Fiduciary: someone who is responsible for the property or assets of another person.

Fiduciary duty: a legal and moral obligation to manage the trust property in a responsible and productive manner.

First party special needs trust: a *special needs trust* where the source of the funds is the disabled person's own money.

Flat fees: see *transactional fee*s.

Forced share: see *elective share.*

Foreign executor: an executor from another state.

Formal probate: see *solemn form probate.*

Four unities: the four elements — time, title, interest and possession — required to create a joint tenancy.

Fractional share formula: formulat that funds both the marital trust and the credit shelter trust proportionally, allocating a portion of each asset to the marital trust in the proportion that each trust bears to the total value.

General bequest: a gift of property payable from any asset in the testator's estate.

General power of appointment: occurs when the surviving spouse has the ablity to name the beneficiaries of the marital trust assets that remain at his or her death.

Generation-skipping trust: trust where the contributed assets are passed down to the grantor's grandchildren, not the grantor's children.

Grantor: the person who typically directs the creation of the trust and provides the assets that are placed into the trust; also called a *settlor*, *trustor*, or *trust maker.*

Gross estate: all of a decedent's real and personal property that will be transferred from the decedent to a beneficiary.

Gross value: the fair market value of a property, not reduced by any mortgages or liabilities.

Guardian: someone who is legally responsible for the person and property of a minor or an incapacitated adult.

Guardianship: the process by which a person is appointed to make medical and/or financial decisions for someone who has become incapacitated.

Heirs: persons who, by application of the laws of intestacy, inherit the property of a person who died intestate; also called *next of kin* and *distributes.*

Holographic will: a will that is written in the testator's own handwriting.

Hospice care: palliative care provided at the end of life, focusing on keeping the patient comfortable, addressing disease-related symptoms, but not providing treatment for the disease.

Hourly fees: amount charged per hour, or any portion of an hour that an attorney works on a file.

Implied trust: trust that comes about by operation of law, and the terms and conditions of the trust are developed from the intent of the parties.

In terrorem clause: a clause in a will threatening to disinherit anyone who challenges the will.

Incapacitated: unable to govern oneself and one's own affairs.

Incidents of ownership: proof that a person owns an asset if the person exercises any of the ownership rights such as the right to modify or sell the asset, the right to gift or otherwise transfer the asset, or the right to obtain income from the asset.

Income: interest, dividends, or rent earned on the principal, coming into the trust.

Income beneficiaries: beneficiaries who receive periodic distributions of income.

Indemnification: protection against loss or damages.

Independent-living community: a community that provides age-restricted housing to active, independent adults.

Informal probate: see *small estate probate.*

Injunction: a temporary order of the court that stops a party from taking an action.

Interested party: one who stands to benefit from the will.

Intermediate care facility: a facility that provides care at a level between an assisted living facility and a skilled nursing facility.

Inter vivos trust: a trust created during the client's lifetime; also called a *living trust.*

Intestate: when a person dies without having written a will.

Intestate statutes: the laws of each of the 50 states provide for the distribution of an intestate estate.

Involuntary commitment: a state law procedure by which a person is found to be a danger to self and to others, is unwilling to accept treatment or be voluntarily admitted to a treatment facility, and is in need of evaluation, short term treatment or hospitalization.

Irrevocable: may not be revoked, modified, or amended.

Irrevocable life insurance trust: a trust that owns a life insurance policy.

Issue: children, grandchildren or great grandchildren; lineal decsendants.

Joint tenancy: a form of ownership of real property in which two or more people own property together.

Jurisdiction: the right to hear a case.

Lapse of a bequest: occurs when the beneficiary dies, or predeceases the testator.

Last will and testament: a legal document that provides for the distribution of the property of someone who has died.

Laws of intestacy: see *laws of intestate succession.*

Laws of intestate succession: govern how an estate is distributed if the decedent fails to make a will, or dies intestate; also known as *laws of intestacy.*

Legal residence: the state in which the individual votes, has a driver's license, and pays state taxes; also known as *domicile.*

Legatee: a person who receives real property through a will; the term can also be used to describe a beneficiary who receives personal property.

Life settlement: is the sale of an existing life insurance policy for the current value of the policy. The policy is sold, and there is little or no death benefit available to the beneficiaries of the policy.

Lifetime exemption: the amount of the combined total of taxable gifts, and the taxable estate that is exempt from taxation.

Lineal descendants: those descended one from the other or all from a common ancestor.

Liquid asset: cash or cash equivalent.

Listing agreement: a contract between the realtor and the estate setting forth the terms of the sale.

Living trust: see *Inter vivos trust.*

Long-term care insurance: an insurance policy sold to help fund the cost of providing long-term care.

Mandated reporters: persons who have assumed responsibility for an elder or dependent adult or other professional who has reasonable cause to suspect or believe that an elderly person is being abused to make a report.

Marital share: see *elective share.*

Marital trust: trust that allows for assets to pass from the decedent spouse to the surviving spouse without being taxed.

Marshaling the assets: the consolidation of the estate assets.

Mortgage: a debt secured by real property.

Mutual fund: a company that brings together money from many people and invests it in stocks, bonds or other assets.

Name change: the legal proceeding by which a person adopts a name that is different from the name given to the person at the time of birth or adoption.

Net estate: *gross estate less* all allowable deductions.

Next of kin: see *heirs.*

Non-probate estate: all of the decedent's assets that pass either by operation of state law, by form of ownership, or by the provisions of the will.

Nonrecourse loan: a loan where the lender cannot collect from the homeowners or the homeowner's heirs, but only from the property itself, when the property is sold, if the proceeds do not satisfy the outstanding amount of the load, the lender cannot collect from the owner.

Nuncupative will: a will that is dictated to another person in the presence of a witness.

One pot trust: a trust that keeps all of the assets together in one pool, and directs the trustee to make distributions as needed.

Operation of law: assets pass by the application of an ownership law, such as joint ownership, designation as *POD* or *TOD*, or a *beneficiary* designation.

Pecuniary share: the smallest amount that, if allowed as a marital deduction, would result in the least possible federal estate tax.

Pension: a retirement plan in which a specific amount is paid every month to a retiree based on the number of years of service with the company.

Per capita: a distribution of an estate to each of the individual residuary beneficiaries and heirs of a deceased beneficiary.

Per stirpes: by representation; distribution of a beneficary's share to the heirs of a beneficiary, if the beneficiary has predeceased the testator.

Personal memorandum: a memorandum written by the testator that makes distributions of personal property.

Personal property: movable items such as personal possessions, bank accounts, cars or other items.

Personal representative: the person appointed by a last will and testament to be in charge of the estate; also called *executor.*

POD: payable on death; a designation on an account that a specific beneficiary is to receive that account. The POD designation is used for checking accounts and savings accounts held at a bank.

Portablity: the concept that any unused portion of the exemption (or exclusion) can be transported to the surviving spouse.

Portfolio: the stocks, bonds or other assets in a mutual fund. See also *Trust's portfolio.*

Power of appointment: surviving spouse can direct, either during her lifetime or in her will, that trust assets should go to her children or grandchildren.

Power of attorney: a legal document that appoints a representative to help with financial decisions if the person is unable to make those decisions.

Preamble: the first section of the will that identifies the testator, and states that the testator intends the document to be his last will and testament.

Prenuptial agreement: the agreement to keep property separate after marriage.

Preponderance of evidence: the party has to prove that the allegation is more likely to be true than not.

Pretermitted child: a child born after the execution of the will.

Pretermitted heir: a person who would have been a beneficiary under a will, but the testator did not know about that person.

Primary beneficiary: the first person to receive the benefits of the policy.

Principal: the money or assets in the trust is known as the *corpus* or *principal* of the trust. See also *corpus*.

Probate: the process by which the validity and legality of a will is proven in court.

Probate estate: all of the decedent's assets that are in the decedent's name alone.

Qualified personal residence trust: a trust that places a residence in a trust either for the benefit of one's spouse and children or for a charity.

Qualified terminable interest property (QTIP): a type of trust created in a will that allows income to the spouse for life, but restricts the spouse's ability to redirect the assets in the trust after his or her death, typically used in second marriages.

Real property: real estate, such as vacant land, a home, or a commercial building, it includes anything that is growing on the land, such as crops, or timber.

Reform: when a court revises or changes the contents of the will to better follow the testator's intent.

Rehabilitative-care facility: a facility that provides short-term care following an accident, operation or injury.

Remainder interest: the interest that goes to the beneficiaries.

Remaindermen: beneficiaries who will receive a distribution of principal when the trust terminates.

Renounce: to give up or disclaim the right to receive from the estate, or to serve as the personal representative.

Renunciation: a form by which a potential beneficiary of an estate either gives up the right to serve as a fiduciary, or gives up the right to take from the estate, also known as a waiver.

Residuary bequest: the distribution of the money and assets remaining in the *residuary estate*, which is the amount remaining after payment of estate expenses, taxes, and the specific, demonstrative and general bequests, if any.

Residuary estate: the amount remaining after payment of estate expenses, taxes, and the specific, demonstrative and general bequests, if any.

Respite care: short-term temporary care that provides a break for someone who is caring for a family member.

Resulting trust: a trust created by a court based on what the law presumes to be the intent of the parties, but does not take into consideration the expressed intent of the parties.

Retained interest: the interest that the grantor retains.

Retainer agreement: a form of contract between an attorney and a client that establishes the fee that will be paid for the services provided, and the scope of the services.

Reverse marital formula: a funding formula by which the credit shelter trust is funded first and the remaining assets go into the marital trust.

Reverse mortgage: a non-recourse loan on the equity value of a home that provides either monthly payments or a lump sum payment that can be used for care.

Revocable: able to be revoked, modified, or amended.

Revocable trust: a trust in which the grantors have reserved for themselves the right to make changes to the trust, or to revoke the trust in its entirety.

Right of survivorship: occurs if one of the joint tenants dies, that owner's interest in the property will pass to the surviving owner or owners by operation of law.

Scrivener: the person that writes the will (usually an attorney) for the testator.

Second-to-die policy: an insurance policy in which both the husband and wife are insured, and the policy only pays out after the second of them passes away.

Self-dealing: occurs when the agent does something to benefit himself or herself instead of acting in the principal's best interest.

Self-proving affidavit: a section of the will that is signed by a notary, attesting to the fact that the witnesses were present when the will was signed by the testator.

Self-settled spendthrift trust: a *spendthrift trust* created by the grantor to protect the grantor's assets from the grantor's creditors.

Settlor: see *grantor*.

Skilled nursing care: care given or supervised by registered nurses (RN).

Skilled nursing facility: facility with staff and equipment to give skilled nursing care.

Skip person: a transferee who is a member of a generation that is two or more generations below the generation of the decedent.

Sliding scale: a tax rate that starts at one level and then increases as the value of the estate increases.

Small estate probate: a simplified probate process by which a personal representative is appointed to administer an estate in an abbreviated procedure; also known as *informal probate*.

Social security: a federal benefit program for retirees, disabled persons, and the families of retired, disabled or deceased workers.

Solemn form probate: the probate process that is required when there is some defect of problem with the will, also known as *formal probate*.

Special needs trust (SNT): a trust formed for the benefit of a disabled person, that will allow the disabled person to hold assets while continuing to qualify for income- or asset-based governmental benefits.

Spendthrift trust: a trust in which no beneficiary has the right or power to receive any income or principal from the trust.

Springing power of attorney: authority of the agent that does not "spring" into being until the principal becomes incapacitated.

Sprinkling trust: a trust that gives the trustee discretion to pay out or accumulate income; also known as a *spray trust* or a *discretionary trust*.

Spray trust: see *sprinkling trust*.

Standing: a legal term that defines who is able to bring a lawsuit.

Statute of limitations: state law requiring that an action be brought within a certain time.

Statutory law: law that is found in statutes that has been adopted by the legislature and codified, or arranged in a code.

Statutory share: see *elective share.*

Substitute trustee: new trustee who is chosen if the named trustee does not qualify and never acts as trustee and a new trustee is chosen.

Successor trustee: the trustee that takes over if the initial trustee can no longer fulfill the duties of serving as trustee.

Surety bond: a type of insurance that will protect an asset if a fiduciary fails to fufill their fiduciary duty.

Survival presumption clause: a clause used in a reciprocal will that establishes a presumption that one spouse died first, and the other survived even if it is not possible to determine which spouse died first.

Suspicious circumstances: factors that switch which party bears the burden of proof in a case alleging lack of testamentary capacity.

Taxable estate: all of the decedent's real and personal property that is transferred from the decedent to a beneficiary by way of the decedent's will, by intestate succession, through a trust, or by the distribution of investment accounts directly to beneficiaries.

Tax-wise will: will that is appropriate for estates that will be subject to federal and/ or state estate or inheritance taxes because of the size, or value, of the estate.

Tenants-by-the-entirety: a special form of joint tenancy for married couples.

Tenants-in-common: describes an ownership interest of two or more people who own separate but undivided interests in property.

Testamentary capacity: ability of the testator to understand the objects of his or her affection and the nature of his or her bounty.

Testamentary trust: a trust created in a last will and testament.

Testate: occurs when a person dies having written a will.

Testator: a male that has written a will.

Testatrix: a female that has written a will.

Third party special needs trust: a *special needs trust* where the source of the funds can be gifts or bequests from various friends and family members or the trust can be set up in the last will and testament of the disabled person, under a parent or other family member.

TOD: transferable on death; a way to designate a specific beneficiary that is to receive that account, the TOD designation is used for stocks, bonds, mutual funds or other similar investments.

Tort: a wrongful act, whether intentional or accidental, that gives rise to damages.

Totten trust: an informal trust that is created when the grantor puts money into a bank account and designates that upon the death of the grantor, the monies in the account passes to a named beneficiary by way of a POD designation.

Transactional fees: set fees that are established for each document or transaction; also known as *flat fees.*

Trigger: the conditions that cause a long term care policy to begin paying benefits.

Trust: a legal document that establishes the rules for the use of funds that are held for another person or group of people.

Trust administration: the management and distribution of assets held in the name of a trust.

Trust agreement: a trust that requires that the trustee agree to abide by the terms of the trust.

Trust assets: see *trust property.*

Trust formation date: the date the trust was signed.

Trust fund: the income and principal added together.

Trust maker: see *grantor.*

Trust property: any type of real property or personal property, whether a tangible asset or an intangible asset; also called *trust assets.*

Trustee: an individual or institution named that is given control of assets to be used for the benefit of another person.

Trustee's commission: a statutory fee to which the trustee is entitled that is a percentage of the corpus and the income of the trust.

Trustor: see *grantor*.

Trust's portfolio: the different investments held by a trust.

Undistributed income: if the trust gives the trustee discretion in spending income, some of the income could remain undistributed. If that occurs, the trust will determine if undistributed income goes back into the trust as principal to accumulate.

Undue Influence: a legal claim challenging the validity of a last will and testament, alleging that the will is not the testator's own decisions, but is instead the product of influence exerted by another person.

Unified credit: a credit for gift and estate taxes due.

Unified Gift and Estate Tax: Title 26 of the United States Code, a combination of gift tax and estate tax.

Unjust enrichment: occurs when a person unfairly benefits from another person's mistake or at another person's expense. In common terms it is when something unfair occurs, and the court tries to correct the unfairness.

Unlimited marital deduction: no federal estate taxes are imposed between spouses; the surviving spouse does not pay federal estate taxes.

Up-front marital formula: a funding formula by which the marital trust is funded first and the remaining assets are used to fund the credit shelter trust.

Valid trust purpose: any legal purpose.

Verified complaint: complaint that includes an affidavit in which the plaintiff swears to the truth of the pleading.

Viatical settlement: a process by which an existing life insurance policy is sold to a third party.

Ward: the incapacitated person for whom a guardian is appointed.

Waste: occurs when an asset that has value is diminished because of some action or inaction of the representative of the estate.

Widow's share: see *elective share*.

Index